ON-LINE COMPUTING

ON-LINE COMPUTING

Time-Shared Man-Computer Systems

Edited by WALTER J. KARPLUS
University of California, Los Angeles, California

McGRAW-HILL BOOK COMPANY
New York *San Francisco* *Toronto* *London* *Sydney*

ON-LINE COMPUTING

33355

34567890MP721069

CONTRIBUTORS

BAUER, WALTER F., *President, Informatics, Inc., Sherman Oaks, California*

CULLER, GLEN J., *Associate Professor of Mathematics, University of California, Santa Barbara, California*

DAVID, EDWARD E., JR., *Executive Director, Communications Systems Research Division, Bell Telephone Laboratories, Murray Hill, New Jersey*

FAGEN, ROBERT E., *President, Computer Communications, Inc., Inglewood, California*

FEIN, LOUIS, *Consultant, Synnoetic Systems, Palo Alto, California*

FERNBACH, SIDNEY, *Head, Computer and Theoretical Physics Divisions, Lawrence Radiation Laboratory, University of California, Livermore, California*

FRIED, BURTON E., *Professor of Physics, University of California, Los Angeles, California*

HARDWAY, C. L.*, *Systems Manager—Graphic Data Processing Systems, International Business Machines Corporation, Harrison, New York*

HAYES, ROBERT M., *Professor of Library Science, University of California, Los Angeles, California*

HUSKEY, HARRY D., *Professor of Electrical Engineering and Mathematics, University of California, Berkeley, California*

PARKER, DONN B., *Staff Specialist, Advanced Systems, Control Data Corporation, Palo Alto, California*

WILKINSON, W. L., *Member, Scientific Staff, Logistics Research Project, George Washington University, Washington, D. C.*

* Deceased

v

PREFACE

A fundamental and far reaching metamorphosis is in progress in the digital computer field. Computer centers which have heretofore adhered exclusively to rigidly-scheduled batch operations in which only a few professional computer operators are permitted direct access to the digital computer, are being thrown open to simultaneous and direct use by tens, hundreds, even thousands of widely-dispersed users. This changing approach has had profound effects upon computer hardware organization, software programming systems, as well as upon user philosophy. The key concepts in this evolution are "on-line," "man-computer," and "time-sharing."

A computer is considered to be *on-line* if a device external to the computer system and the computer itself alternately take action, such that the external device affects the data-processing operation within the computer and such that the computer affects the external device in a significant manner. If the external device requires human intervention, a *man-computer* system exists. If each of a number of devices in a man-computer system can be serviced either sequentially or simultaneously, so that each remote operator can function as if he alone were in communication with the computer, the system is termed a *time-shared* on-line system.

It is the objective of the present text to provide the application-oriented reader with a perspective of the time-shared computer field with special emphasis on applications requiring man-computer interaction. To this end the methodology and basic concepts underlying the design and specification of on-line computers are first introduced. Detailed discussions of electronics and circuit design are avoided in favor of considerations of more general systems concepts. This is followed by descriptions of the application of on-line techniques in five major scientific and technical areas.

Each of the eleven parts of the text was prepared by a recognized expert in his field, and the approach in each chapter is one of "in-depth analysis," rather than the providing of a general survey. It should therefore be recognized by the reader, that the space devoted to various specific topics does not necessarily reflect their relative importance in the computer field today. For example, in discussing the organization of on-line systems, a detailed description of one important commercial system, the Control Data 6060, is provided. Other important on-line systems such as General Electric's Datanet, IBM's QUICKTRAN, and MIT's Project MAC receive only incidental mention. Similarly, in discussing the utilization of on-line computers in engineering design, only one design area is covered in detail, although a wide variety of other design applications could have been described. Yet to do all of the diverse on-line systems and applications complete justice would have required either a text of impractical length or excessive superficiality in each specific description. An effort has been been made in every instance, however, to provide adequate references to publications discussing alternate realizations or techniques.

In editing every attempt has been made to assure continuity and to make the various chapters "hang together," but a certain amount of redundancy has been deliberately introduced so as to enhance the value of the text as a reference work. For example, fundamental questions of economics occur and recur in virtually every chapter, even though this topic is summarized and discussed in considerable detail in a separate chapter devoted exclusively to economics. Thus, it is hoped that each chapter can stand by itself as a separate contribution to the on-line field, and that by studying all of the chapters, a comprehensive insight into the problems and potentialities of time-shared computing will be attained.

Chapter I, which serves as a general introduction to the subject, includes definitions of the major concepts involved in on-line computing as well as a description of a relatively small time-shared system developed at the University of California at Berkeley.

The fundamental considerations and methodologies involved in the organization of large commercial time-shared systems are described in Chapter II, followed by a more detailed description of one specific on-line system.

Chapter III is devoted to a discussion of graphic display consoles, design alternatives, and a comparison of various practical realizations.

The economics of on-line systems and particularly the all-important subject of the profitability of on-line operations as compared to batch operations are discussed in Chapter IV.

Chapter V deals with the psychological and physiological aspects of on-line system design. The limitation and potentialities of human senses, which must necessarily come into play in man-computer systems, are considered in a quantitative fashion.

Chapter VI includes a detailed description of the use of on-line techniques, including graphical display, for the solution of mathematical problems. The methods described in this chapter have already had an important impact on teaching and on the use of computers at several major universities.

In Chapter VII the utilization of graphical display consoles and time-sharing techniques for mechanical design is treated in considerable detail. Hardware as well as software considerations are treated.

Chapter VIII is devoted to a discussion of the use of time-shared computing techniques in a military environment. In particular, a specific strategic command system is described in detail, together with conclusions and recommendations resulting from extensive operating experience.

Chapter IX includes a relatively theoretical presentation of the fundamental concepts underlying file organization. This topic forms the basis for the now emerging science of information retrieval.

Chapter X includes a brief discussion of some of the sociological aspects of on-line computing and more generally automatic computing and automation. It is not the purpose of that chapter to prescribe remedies to the social dislocations arising from automation, but rather to increase the reader's awareness of some of the broader implications of on-line computing.

A complete user's manual of a presently operating on-line is presented in the appendix.

The present text evolved from notes for a lecture series presented at four locations in California during the fall semester of 1965. This series was sponsored by the Engineering Extension and Physical Sciences Extension of the University of California at Los Angeles, and by the Engineering Extension of the University of California at Berkeley. Professor Charles B. Tompkins served as statewide coordinator. In that capacity he was the prime moving force in organizing the series and in selecting the lecturers, and was of invaluable assistance to the editor. Professor

Harry D. Huskey and Mr. Harold C. Tallman also made significant contributions in the administration and coordination of the lecture series. The editor would also like to acknowledge the contributions offered by Dr. Merrill M. Flood, Dr. Bruce H. McCormick, and Mr. Thomas B. Steel, Jr., lecturers in the statewide series whose busy schedules prevented them from completing their manuscripts in time for inclusion in the present text but who made available much valuable and helpful material.

Walter J. Karplus

CONTENTS

xi

  W. L. Wilkinson 220
 IX. A Theory for File Organization   *R. M. Hayes* 264
  X. Sociological Considerations   *L. Fein* 290

     APPENDIX: User's Manual for an On-line System   *G. J. Culler* .. 303

     Index 325

INTRODUCTION

I

Sidney Fernbach

Lawrence Radiation Laboratory
University of California
Livermore, California

Harry D. Huskey

University of California
Berkeley, California

1.1   The Advent of Time-sharing

The modern computer field is only approximately twenty years old. Nonetheless, significant evolutionary changes have taken place during this period, as ever new applications areas and classes of computer users have made ever-changing demands of a rapidly advancing technology. It is useful to reflect briefly upon the origin of today's "OK concepts" such as *on-line, time-sharing,* and *man-computer*.

The earliest electronic digital computers[1,2,3] to arrive on the scene were used primarily for scientific work, that is, the solution of mathematical models representing physical phenomena.   These computer systems rep-

Years	Average speed in instructions per second	Size of "standard" core memories
1953–1958	20,000	1K to 4K
1958–1963	100,000	32K
1963–1965	500,000	65K
1965–1967	3,000,000	131K
1967–	12,000,000	131K + 2 million "mass core"

Fig. 1.1 Large machine growth trend. (*Courtesy Robert E. Fagen.*)

resented such a tremendous advance over the commonly used desk calculators or slide rules that it seemed inconceivable that many such systems would be needed to satisfy the computing requirements of the scientific community. How wrong predictions can be!

Fortunately, these early machines were slow enough, compared with today's common speeds, that a man sitting at the console of the computer could keep up with the various steps of the calculation. Knowing what he had programmed the computer to do, he knew at each instant of time whether the computer was proceeding properly. He could stop the calculator, request some intermediate results on the console typewriter, as well as add, delete, or modify data. Very often the computer stood idle while some changes were being made on punched cards or paper tape, or even magnetic tape. Thus the man had a very close relationship with the machine; in a sense he was on-line with it. It is true that his reaction time and that of the computer were not ideally suited to each other, but they were by far more closely matched than they now are, considering today's computer speeds. Figure 1.1 shows the increase in speed and size of standard computer memory since 1953.

As the users of the equipment learned to fill up all available time and newer, faster systems became available, this mismatch of the human interface with that of the computer system became less tolerable. Monitor or batch-processing systems were designed so that problems were grouped to utilize every possible unit of available time. The user was thrown off-line. He had to prepare cards, which, when they left his hands, concluded his interaction with the machine. He finally did get the cards back along with some output results on paper. This again became intolerable, especially when the system became so loaded that the user could not get back on the computer for a considerable length of time, perhaps eight hours or even longer. His so-called "turnaround time" became unsatisfactorily long and forced great delays in his ability to get his job done.

In searching for solutions to provide the user with better schedules, an interesting discovery was made. Each section of the entire computer system consisting of input-output equipment as well as memory and control was busy only part of the time. By overlapping input-output problems with central processor problems, greater utilization of the various parts of the system could be achieved. The "throughput" or quantity of work done per unit of time could be substantially increased in many cases. This was the beginning of time-sharing. With more elaborate control codes than had existed prior to this time (which naturally took up more memory space), it was possible to run several jobs simultaneously, without delaying the completion of any one appreciably over what it would be if run separately. From these beginnings, time-sharing has become much more elaborate and has succeeded in helping the user into a more natural relationship with the computer. Finally, the development of small terminals and large data files, for what might be termed "inventory" applications, has recently generated significant interest in placing the user back "on-line" with the computer.

1.2 Terminology

Before continuing the discussion of man-computer systems, the terms used in this subject area will be defined more precisely.

This presentation limits its attention to stored program digital computers. Thus, wherever it appears, the word "computer" will have this meaning. A similar discussion of man-computer systems using analog and hybrid computers could be made.

A *man-computer system* as considered here must have the following characteristic: The system cannot function without at least one man and at least one stored program digital computer. The *digital computer* is a device capable of storing information consisting of data and instructions, and which, by means of the instructions, can perform some form of logical operations upon the stored information. Typically, of course, these operations will include the basic arithmetic processes of addition, subtraction, multiplication, and division. Thus, applications of computers in process control where the man is present only for reasons of safety, or applications where man takes action only in case of malfunction, will not be considered as a man-computer system.

In a man-computer system the man will be said to be *on-line* if he and the computer alternately take action, each action depending in some way upon the preceding actions. The most interesting situation also involves *sustained attention* on the part of the man. Sustained attention can occur if the computer responds to manual actions without too much delay. The actual maximum delay depends upon the kind of problem, the disposition of the user, and perhaps the quality of the response when it comes.

Times of a few seconds with absolute upper limits in the tens of seconds seem to be reasonable. In credit-reference checking, the delay should only occasionally be noticed by the customer.

A system is said to be *conversational* if it responds in a "cooperative and considerate" way to the user. The more similar the language is to English (or some "natural" language), and the more free the format, the more frequently the system is said to be "conversational."

Multiprogramming refers to two or more independent programs residing in a computer system which may be running concurrently or may share hardware facilities under the control of a monitor or executive program; or the programs may be more or less independent parts of a major program which may be executed concurrently or in an interleaved manner. For example, in the time-sharing system described later in this chapter a user may start up two independent programs, and each program will be run in an interleaved manner.

Multiprocessing refers to hardware capable of carrying out two or more independent processes concurrently. The term usually refers to hardware subsystems with some kind of "general-purpose" capability. The interesting case involves two or more arithmetic units capable of executing two independent programs residing in the same memory system. An input-output channel is not sophisticated (general-purpose) enough to be considered to be one in a set of multiprocessors.

A computer system is said to be running in *real time* if there is a computer program and some other process running "in-step" in such a way that the associated process is not caused to run slower by the computer program. Typically, part of the system consists of actual physical devices, and the whole system is said to run in real time if the physical subsystems run at their natural rate.

1.3   Classification of Man-computer Systems

Process Control. In many process control situations the man acts only in case of failure. However, in some cases the decisions are sufficiently complex that a man may be kept in the control loop. Some early payroll programs failed because they attempted to account for every possible combination of events. More recently, system developers have learned to divide the tasks, giving the frequently occurring "standard" cases to the computer and referring "difficult" cases to a person for decision. For example, in a university environment most decisions in scheduling of classrooms, students to classes, or instructors to classes, are straightforward and easily done on the computer.

There may be examples not meeting all the conditions of the scheduling algorithm which can be better handled manually. Also, when scheduling is nearly complete, and assuming the facilities are expected to be nearly completely used, the decisions become more and more difficult.

Monitoring. Man-computer systems have been used for monitoring applications. A well-publicized military example is SAGE.[4] In the last year the use of computers to monitor the condition of a medical patient (for example, while in the operating room, or while under postoperative surveillance) is receiving substantial attention.

Inquiry. Recent reports say that 45 per cent of the American public have flown on a commercial airliner. Most of these people have had (perhaps indirect) contact with a reservation system. Such a system keeps an inventory of available space and has terminals permitting agents to query and to modify (in limited ways) the inventory record.

Police departments are interested in such systems in order to run a quick check on a suspect, such as one stopped for running a red light. At the University of California similar equipment is being proposed to permit a student to obtain quickly a degree check (graduation requirements yet to be satisfied).

Design Automation. On-line systems which will aid the design engineer have been discussed in the literature.[5] Chapter VII describes such a system. These may convert essentially freehand drawings into precision drawings; permit quick updating of information files; and, in some cases, using such techniques as animation, permit easy checking of dynamic behavior of devices.

General Problem Solving. Whereas the above systems are designed to solve specific problems, accept limited (usually, strictly formatted) languages, and typically, give one of a fixed set of responses, a general problem system accepts a variety of languages, with a range of format restrictions, and it responds in ways which may be controlled by the user. A good general problem-solving system places the full capability of the computer in the hands of the user and, as will be seen, creates a number of problems in system design.

1.4 A Small Time-sharing System

The on-line systems described in subsequent chapters of this text are generally designated as "large" time-sharing systems.[4,5,6,7,8,9] They are designed to utilize the largest available digital computers as the central processor and to provide service to hundreds of consoles at widely dispersed locations. While projects of this type continue to exert the most significant influence upon system and application developments, more modest systems have also played an important role in providing the experience necessary for successful on-line computation. It appears appropriate therefore that a brief description of such a small on-line system be included in the present chapter. At the same time, this dis-

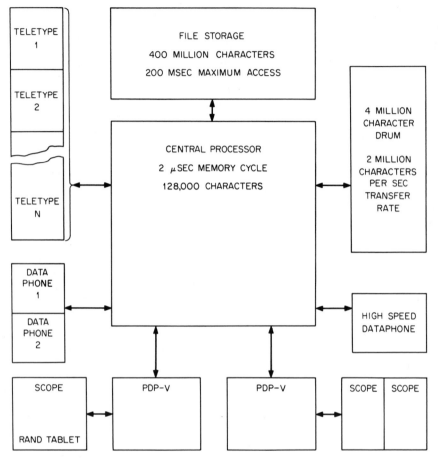

Fig. 1.2   The time-sharing computer of Project Genie.

cussion will focus the reader's attention on the variety of significant aspects of on-line system design and specification which recur repeatedly in other chapters of this text.

Hardware.   The significant components of the time-sharing computer of Project Genie at the University of California, Berkeley, are shown in Fig. 1.2.   This system is designed for experimentation in man-machine systems.   Consequently, it is not optimized for servicing a large collection of users as are more ambitious on-line systems.   For example, this system does not have hardware means of doing floating-point arithmetic. This almost makes it possible to shut the system down quickly and incorporate new ideas without protest from a body of users.

The central computer is a modified Scientific Data Systems 930.   The memory was separated into odd and even addresses in order to permit drum transfers at full core rate, and simultaneous operation of the central processor. Actually, during a drum transfer the central processor runs at about 60 per cent of full speed. Extra memory ports and a subroutine transfer command, permitting reentrant programs, were added. The system is designed to service fifteen users without undue delays. Besides teletypes and data phones, the system communicates with two PDP-Vs which in turn support display units. One of the displays has a Rand tablet associated with it.

The purpose of the project is to improve the computer as a "research tool." Improvements might possibly be made in the system, in languages provided to the user, and in hardware aspects of the man-machine interface.

The User Software Interface. When the user "logs in," he is communicating with the *Executive* (EXEC) (see Fig. 1.3). He may now call any of several subsystems into action. In any such subsystem he would again have several choices of action. This is true even at the level of writing a statement in FORTRAN; that is, he has to decide what character is to be placed in the next position of the FORTRAN statement.

Thus, the user moves himself through a tree structure from node to node. In Fig. 1.3 he starts in the EXEC and moves to FORTRAN by making an appropriate input. At any point in the system two successive "Rub-outs" (a teletype key) return him to EXEC.

The file service routines allow him to create and destroy files, such files remaining in the data file when he "logs out." He can also "edit" or "append" to existing files. The Assembler permits the user to write computer programs in "machine language." The input to the Assembler can be directly from one of the teletypes, from the display-Rand tablet, or from some file which was established at some previous time. The out-

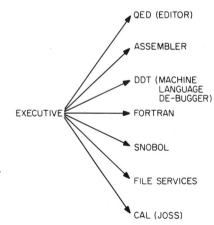

Fig. 1.3 Time-sharing software system.

put of the Assembler is another file, which can be stored, executed, printed, edited, etc. Except for a very few Executive functions, this Assembler gives the user the full capability of the computer.

When working with machine language programs at an on-line station, such systems as DDT[10] are extremely useful. The system available at Project Genie permits the user to run segments of his program, type out values of variables, change commands and constants, and type out parts of the program. In all this the symbol table, or namelist of the Assembler, is retained so that the user refers to all items by the terminology used in the source language.

Whereas the Assembly language is a "programmer's" tool, a user's tool is the language CAL which is Berkeley's version of JOSS.[11] The Assembly language permits the user to program the full capability of the computer; CAL is an interpretive system which is "fail-safe" and "forgiving." With the Assembler and the other systems like CAL, the user can do nothing to disturb other users. However, in the case of CAL (the same is true of JOSS) it is even difficult for the user to harm himself.

Statements may be typed in and executed one by one, or a program may be established to be executed at some later time. Syntactic errors evoke a "?" from the system. Execution of statements with undefined variables causes a suitable error message to be typed. Numbered statements are stored in order with respect to their number. The statement "DO STEP 3.42" causes that particular statement and only that statement to be executed, regardless of what statements precede or follow it.

With such a capability one may start in the middle of a program—writing, modifying, and checking as one goes. Using the numbering scheme, statements may be deleted, new statements may be inserted at any position, and existing statements may be easily corrected or modified. In other words, one does not have to plan the whole computation; one does not even have to plan how to get started.

In order for any general problem-solving time-sharing system to be successful, software tools such as those described above must be available.

1.5   Essential Hardware Characteristics

Three characteristics that a time-sharing computer should have in order to perform well in the general problem-solving area are the following: (1) protection (of users from each other), (2) ability to run common programs, and (3) efficient handling of interruptions.

Protection. Protection can be obtained by a hardware paging system. This is illustrated in Fig. 1.4. The address of an instruction consists of two parts. The first (most significant) part refers to a page. The second part of the address refers to the word location on that page. When a command is executed, the first part of the address specifies a page. If

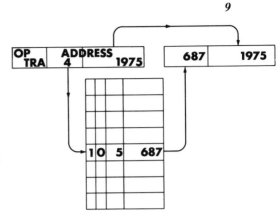

Fig. 1.4 Addressing with page registers.

reference to that page is legal for that program, the specified page register is accessed for an address component. This component and the other part of the address are catenated to form the final hardware address. With flip-flop page registers, the paging happens very fast. In the Berkeley computer, time was available in the command cycle so that the computer runs no slower with paging than without.

The important characteristics of such a paging system are the following:

1. The user's memory is numbered from zero to the maximum permitted. (In the Berkeley system this maximum is 16384. Larger programs may be run by establishing "forks.")

2. Only the pages in which references occur need be resident in core.

3. Store instructions can set bits in the page register which, when users are changed, determines whether that page needs to be rewritten on the drum.

A new user is started by marking all current pages illegal, then restoring the contents of the arithmetic, index, and command counting registers to that which existed at the time the user was last dismissed. Accessing his next command will produce an interrupt (since his page is not present), and the Executive begins to load the referenced page. Information can be kept either in portions of the hardware page registers (as illustrated in Fig. 1.4) or more economically in software tables which tell the system to whom the various existing pages belong. In this way, on occasion, it may be possible to start the new user without a drum transfer.

The above scheme does not solve any problems of relocation arising from a user trying to assemble several previously written subprograms into one major program. Conceptually, paging type hardware with variable block size and associative memory look-up features could be used to solve this problem, but the economics of so doing does not appear favorable at the present time.[12]

Reentrant or Common Programs. When several users are doing a

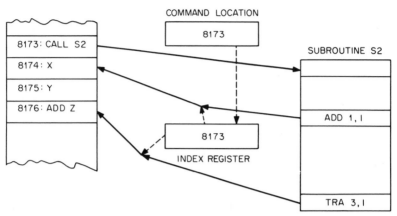

Fig. 1.5 Reentrant or common programs.

FORTRAN compilation at the same time it is more efficient if they are able to use the same copy of the compiler. This requires that none of the compiler be modified during a compilation, and that all data (source strings, object program, and tables developed during the compilation) be kept in user's memory. With the paging system described above, special means are required to access user's data and to return to the proper place in the proper user's program. A method of accomplishing this is described in Fig. 1.5.

The upper part of the diagram illustrates the user's memory. Assume that in location 8173 of his memory, he calls subroutine $S2$. Suppose the subroutine requires two parameters X and Y, whose locations (names, not values) are placed in locations 8174 and 8175. When the subroutine is completed, control must return to 8176.

When the subroutine is called, the contents of the command counter is transferred to the index register. The subroutine can address the parameter X with the indexed address "1" (the index register contains 8173 and one more is 8174 or the location of X). If this user is dismissed, his index register is saved. Before starting up again, the index register and the paging will be restored and the user's program will continue as if no interruption occurred. Thus, several users may have entered the same subroutine before any one of them is finished with it.

Efficient Interruption. Most interruptions do not cause dismissal of a user. Rather, interruptions usually transfer into the monitor which, using absolute (not paged) addressing, or via user's paging, can process buffers in a few commands and return control to the user.

1.6   A Summary of Characteristics

The most essential characteristics of a general problem-solving on-line system are the following:

1. Sufficient system storage to handle a problem during its creation, debugging, and running. Typically, this involves storage time on the order of a week.

2. The system should have live response. Delays of a few seconds are probably all right; perhaps twenty seconds is too long. The essential point is that the user's attention stays entirely on the problem.

3. Shelf storage should be available to take care of problems which are not expected to be active over periods of weeks or months.

4. Efficient editing capability should be available. It is particularly important to be able to reorganize data structures easily.

1.7 Man Interface Design

Most of the previous discussion has been relative to teletypelike terminals. However, display scopes have exciting possibilities. Although display scopes are at present expensive, the expectation is for their price to be reduced. The real flexibility of the display scope is perhaps yet to be exploited. To illustrate some possibilities consider the following:

Others have talked in terms of "leading the user down the path." Display scopes may make it possible to do just that. More specifically, it is proposed here that the names of the keys of a small keyboard be displayed on the scope (Fig. 1.6). The flexibility of the scope permits changing the meaning of the keyboard from moment to moment. Thus, at any instant only syntactically correct choices may be offered the user. This is illustrated in the sequence of Figs. 1.6, 1.7, and 1.8.

In these authors' opinion some keyboards are far too complicated. That

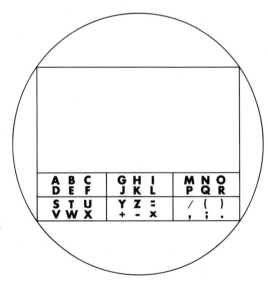

Fig. 1.6 Scope-displayed keyboard.

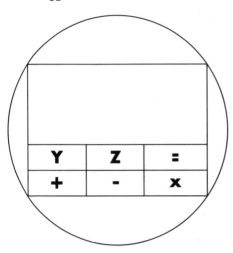

Fig. 1.7   Second keyboard.

is not to say that complication is undesirable if more can be really accomplished.   If the results would justify it, a complicated "piano" keyboard could be used and to utilize it fully the user could be given years of intensive training.   However, it is doubtful if more could be accomplished this way than by exploiting fully the flexibility of the scope-keyboard combination.

The keyboards of Figs. 1.6, 1.7, and 1.8 are designed from the point of view that the user should have the choice of relatively few options at any step in the solution process.   The suggestion has been made that such simple keyboards would be useful to those who are physically handicapped.

In the development of systems, two kinds of users should be considered. One is the novice (or intermittent) user, and the other is the well-trained

PAY = HOURS × RATE

NET = PAY - DED

TAX =

PAY	HOURS	RATE
NET	DED	letters

Fig. 1.8   Identifiers as key labels.

expert. For one, a "fail-safe" system is essential; for the other, an increase in efficiency with overhead reduction by removal of checking features might be worthwhile.

1.8 Economics of On-line Computing

In the time-sharing system of Project Genie, 15 users can be served on a not more than three-second cycle, giving each one 200 milliseconds. Overhead is approximately 15 per cent. In other words, if used in batch processing the total computing done would only increase by 20 per cent. If 30 users were served, the maximum cycle would go up to six seconds with the same overhead.

In general, not all users respond fast enough to keep the system busy, so the foregoing are worst-case figures. On the other hand, users complain about worst-case performance rather than average performance.

In order to compare batch processing with on-line problem solving, assume the following:

1. FORTRAN is used in each case.

2. An average of four passes in the batch processing is required to debug the program.

3. The program can be debugged in 30 minutes on-line.

4. Four minutes of central computer time will support one hour's use of a teletype.

The direct cost is of the same order of magnitude under these assumptions. The real value of the on-line technique is that the answer is available in 30 minutes, whereas it may take several days under batch processing.

1.9 Hardware Requirements and Trends

The succeeding chapters of this text are devoted to descriptions of the design and the application of on-line computers employing currently available hardware. This section contains a brief look-ahead to the future to enumerate some of the hardware requirements and developments expected in the next decade.

First, it must be recognized that computers have grown in the last 20 years from devices that could rapidly access several hundred words of information to devices that could even more rapidly address millions of words of information. The unit of time has changed from a thousandth of a second to a billionth of a second (10^{-3} to 10^{-9}). Supplementary memory devices such as magnetic disks and drums have grown larger in capacity and are more densely packed with bits of information than ever before. Magnetic tapes are used quite heavily, but are not significantly faster than they have been, although they are more reliable. Cards and paper tape are still used, still slow, but to a great extent used with minimum interference in running programs.   The keyboard is even slower than cards for input, but when used properly with the memory devices mentioned above in a time-sharing mode, it is finding a useful place in the scheme of things.

If one is to have an efficient man-machine relationship, the machine must be kept occupied with useful work while the man is thinking or manipulating his keyboard.   Hence time-sharing is almost essential in such an operation.   To carry out this time-sharing operation, the system must have rapid and random access to information or problems other than those being worked on at the moment.   These may be stored in the fast memory or in the peripheral memories.   Since computer central processors normally operate on data out of fast memory, information stored on peripheral devices must be transferred to fast memory to be operated upon.   The ideal solution to keep from excessive juggling of information to satisfy multiusers simultaneously is to provide unlimited fast memory so that all information needed can be stored therein.   Unfortunately memory of such size could cost billions of dollars.

One of the most useful peripheral memory devices is the magnetic disk.   It provides large capacity, small volume, and costs considerably less than magnetic core memories.   Disk files built today provide storage capabilities of up to a billion bits (an order of magnitude greater than the largest magnetic core memory proposed for an order of magnitude fewer dollars).   Because of the economic considerations, disk files are showing up as essential ingredients for most time-sharing systems.   Magnetic drums are very similar to disks.   Their chief defects are that they are more expensive and occupy more space per bit.   Their chief virtues at present are that generally they are faster than disks and allow for more accesses per unit time.   Although these magnetic storage devices have been in use for just about as long as the computer has existed, even in sophisticated laboratories their use is rather primitive.   Perhaps the time-sharing systems now being built will help bring out better schemes for using these devices and perhaps better design.   It is quite interesting that even though it is evident that many accesses per unit time to disk will be essential, there is little pressure on the manufacturer to build many-headed disk files.

Another area that should be of some concern to builders of time-sharing systems is that of total memory requirements.   From the applications that one might cite, it becomes evident that even a billion bits of memory are not sufficient to store information that might be needed.   Magnetic tapes, of course, provide unlimited storage capabilities.   Unfortunately, hundreds of tape drives would be necessary to store billions of bits if one were to try to eliminate the operator in getting access.   Even without the operator, tapes are not designed for random access but rather for sequential access. Thus there could be considerable time delay in accessing information on large numbers of tapes. There should be devices capable of storing trillions of bits of information, even if the access time is not so fast as that on disk files. These are only now coming into being. For the most part, they consist of small strips of magnetic tape or photographic materials which can be stored in bins and randomly addressed and accessed. Access times seem to be in the millisecond to second range. In the cases where photographic material is used, one cannot immediately reaccess information because of a required photographic development process. This could delay accesses even to minutes.

The central processor also has to be considered from the point of view of multiuse or multiaccess. It is clear that the central processing unit (CPU) has to be protected from too many disruptions from the outside world. This can be done by providing special hardware registers, a small peripheral processor to deal with communications, or even a separate computer which can be directly coupled to the main CPU through a common memory. Even a simple processor, if it has the hardware capabilities of handling many interruptions, can do the job. Many types of systems have been proposed, and at this moment it is not clear what the ultimate solution will be. The direct coupled systems have gained considerable support, so much so that they are the systems one hears most about these days. Even though hardware is more reliable than ever before, there are still more errors occurring in processing data than one would like. Because of this and also because of the symmetry possible, direct coupled systems being ordered today consist of two identical processors sharing common memory hierarchies. If one is down, the other can take over; if one is too heavily loaded, the other can help out; diagnostics can be run more routinely because of the symmetry. Furthermore, users seem to be more willing to sacrifice some capability by operating two such systems rather than an equivalently priced single system of greater capability.

Special hardware is also being installed into these processors such as to provide protection for certain areas of memory, to provide the capability of recovering from an interruption, to provide greater addressing capability, and to provide for greater freedom in extensive communication with the outside world. Concerning memory protection, there is great concern. As pointed out in Sec. 1.4, one must guarantee that one user will not wipe out another user's data or instructions. Much of this can be done by programming if not by hardware, but will it be foolproof? Even more serious is the problem of protecting classified or otherwise confidential data from getting into the wrong user's hands. Every user's files must be as adequately protected as if the data were in a locked file or even a file safe. Some of the data could be payroll or banking information, defense secrets, or otherwise classified codes. The simplest solution to the problem is, of course, to provide different facilities for the various degrees of sensitivity and for specialized users.

Another area of renewed activity in the light of the improving man-machine relationship is that of less expensive input-output stations such as those described in Chap. III. There is a variety of requirements for these devices, depending on the application. Some users have high-input, low-output requirements. The other combinations are also possible. Some users want hard copy records, some films; some do not concern themselves with records. For some, typewriter output is sufficient; for others, higher speeds are desirable. Hence one sees varieties of cathode-ray tube, typewriter, plotter, and printer combinations being put together. Relatively high-speed printers are becoming available for $5,000. Good quality plotters are in the same range. Teletypewriters are available for under $500. Cathode-ray-tube prices have greater ranges, depending on size, speed, photographic capabilities, character generation capability, light pen attachments, etc. For those who could do with a very inexpensive one-way display, the possibility of adding production model TV sets into the system is now being explored. There is little doubt that they will be put into operation relatively soon.

Much information in existing files, libraries, etc., is in the form of documents, drawings, graphical data, etc. It is conceivable that much or most of this could be put into digital form for storage and retrieval, being converted to analog form upon being read. It may turn out much more desirable to store the information for the user in the original form but put into a file designed for relatively fast and efficient retrieval in whole or part. These image files are not now in great use but conceivably will in the future serve as important additions to the man-digital computer system.

REFERENCES

1. Wilkes, M. V.: The EDSAC Computer, *EJCC*, 1951, pp. 79–83.
2. Huskey, H. D., R. Thorensen, B. F. Ambrosio, and E. C. Yowell: The SWAC, Design Features and Operating Experience, *Proc. IRE*, pp. 1294–1299, October, 1963.
3. Greenwald, S., R. C. Haueter, and S. N. Alexander: SEAC, *Proc. IRE*, pp. 1300–1312, October, 1963.
4. Everett, R. R., C. A. Zraket, and H. D. Benington: SAGE: A Data Processing System for Air Defense, *EJCC*, pp. 148–155, 1957.
5. Jacks, E. L.: A Laboratory for the Study of Graphical Man-machine Communication, *FJCC*, pp. 343–350, 1964.
6. Schwartz, J.: A General Purpose Time-sharing System, *SJCC*, pp. 397–411, 1964.
7. Corbato, F. J., M. M. Daggett, and R. C. Daley: An Experimental Time-sharing System, *SJCC*, pp. 335–344, 1962.

8. Glaser, E. L., J. F. Couleur, and G. A. Oliver: System Design of a Computer for Time Sharing Applications, *FJCC*, pp. 197–202, 1965.
9. University of Michigan Orders IBM Sharing System, *EDP Weekly*, vol. 6, no. 5, p. 9, May 24, 1965.
10. McCarthy, J., S. Boilen, E. Fredkin, and J. C. R. Licklider: A Time Sharing Debugging System for a Small Computer, *SJCC*, pp. 51–57, 1963.
11. Shaw, J. C.: JOSS: A Designer's View of an Experimental On-line Computing System, *FJCC*, pp. 455–464, 1964.
12. Arden, B. W., B. A. Galler, T. C. O'Brien, and F. H. Westervelt: Programming and Addressing Structure in a Time-sharing Environment, *Jour. ACM*, pp. 1–16, January, 1966.

Part 1

ON-LINE
SYSTEMS

SYSTEM ANALYSIS AND DESIGN*

II

Robert E. Fagen

Computer Communications Inc.
Inglewood, California

2.1 Introductory Remarks

The purpose of this chapter is to discuss and describe the general considerations that govern the design of time-shared on-line computer networks.
Unfortunately the techniques involved in time-shared operations are as
yet too new for any systematic and comprehensive design philosophy to
have emerged.   Necessarily therefore any discussion of system analysis
and design must be based on detailed experience with a specific system for
a specific application.   Nonetheless a certain amount of generalization
is desirable to permit extensions of current design approaches to new
classes of users and to new problem areas.   This chapter contains two
major parts.   The first part is devoted to an analysis of time-shared
systems in general, the classification of users, and the organization of
such systems.   The second part includes a description of a specific time-
shared computer system.   This system is but one of a number of highly

---

* This paper and some of the systems described were produced while the author
was employed by Control Data Corporation.

developed and successful commercial systems available at the present time. It is presented here primarily as an example of the concepts and techniques discussed.

GENERAL TIME-SHARING ANALYSIS

2.2   Classes of Time-sharing Users

The process of analyzing and designing a remote time-sharing system depends heavily upon the point of view taken, and the point of view usually depends on the most critical problem to be solved. In this connection it is helpful to define some very general categories of uses and users, for then it becomes easier to discuss in more detail the time-sharing variables that affect a system design.

To categorize the types of remote uses, it is necessary to analyze the user himself. This analysis starts with the type of application or usage he is to be provided, follows the specification of the hardware console or terminal to be provided at his desk or remote location, includes the types of operations he is to be allowed and the exact rules and the language he uses in operating his console. Once this is done for an individual user, it becomes possible to specify the communications and transmission media, to determine the number of independent locations that can be serviced, to establish the rules for service, and finally to determine and design the operating system and other operating programs that must reside within the main frame of the central computer to regulate and service the entire complex.

In categorizing the types of remote users, one can identify three main classes of applications. At times these have been referred to as Class A, Class B, and Class C remote time-sharing systems. Although these classes are not necessarily exhaustive or mutually exclusive, they do serve to describe some very typical uses and help to isolate and identify further details that must be considered. These three classes are described briefly below.

Class A: Specialized Remote User Consoles.   In a Class A system, the users have a special console tailored to their one specific application. Each application or specialty gives rise to another member of the Class A family. For a specific application or member of the family there is a frozen "user language," usually expressed in simple terms through the design of the console keyboard itself. For example, the set of control keys and the labels on the keyboard keys themselves will usually contain terms and operations that are specifically chosen to have meaning to the user in the light of his own application, and these keys together with their rules of usage would constitute the user language. Some examples of

Fig. 2.1

members of the Class A family include airline or motel reservation terminals, industrial data collectors, and the remote calculator shown in Fig. 2.1. The remote calculator is referred to extensively in subsequent sections to furnish an example of the methods used in the design of one specific system. Since each member of the Class A family has a unique terminal or console with a specific frozen language and rules for operation, and serves a specific type of user, it is possible to specify all of the conditions of operation that are necessary to provide the desired sort of service to the user. The rules of access and the type of turnaround response that the user must get to satisfy his requirements can then also be determined. Finally, since the service involved is specific, it is usually possible to measure in economic terms the value of the service and thus to determine whether the provision of the service by the central time-sharing approach (as opposed to providing each user with a local self-contained private computer or other physically separate hardware) is economically justified. Class A users typically are concerned only with their application and terminal devices, and have no direct concern for or knowledge of what happens at the central computer site. In other words, a user is concerned only with getting his work done; whether his data are processed at a remote location or at his immediate location makes no difference whatsoever to the user. For example, in the case of the remote calculator, a user is better off thinking of all of the operations as though they took place in the calculator itself, and viewing the calculator as a completely local, private, self-contained device.

Class B: Generalized Remote Conversation Consoles. In contrast to the specialized applications of Class A, another broad category of usage is described by what is frequently called "remote conversation" consoles. As the name implies, the user is aware of and in direct communication with programs or data files existing at the central computer site, and is provided the means for calling these into service within a rather short response time. This type of service is in reality an extension of the sort of capability provided to programmers for console debugging, but is more generally intended to make these facilities available to a larger number of users at remote locations, and also make the facilities much more general than traditionally available for the narrower task of program debugging. In fact, one may as well conceive of remote conversation usage as comprising a family, called Class B, of usage with rather general rules of operation, general languages that can be employed, and flexible rules of service and access to be supplied the user. Examples of use include on-line debugging through a "reentrant" compiler implementing some compiler language such as FORTRAN, general operation on files and library programs stored in "private" or "public" file locations at the central computer site, and systems for information entry and retrieval typical of many business applications or library abstract searches, etc. Thus, Class B users are typically programmers, high-level computer operators, or research workers with special need for access to files at the computer site. They are concerned with—and converse with—programs or data files in certain locations (physical or symbolic) at the central computer site.

This description shows that a completely different approach than that taken in Class A is necessary. First, the type of physical input-output media and the names of the control keys themselves are obviously much more general, since no one language or input-output data form is specified. It is natural then to design consoles that are fairly general and flexible. Two such typical consoles in prevalent use are the teletypewriter and the keyboard–cathode-ray-tube display console. The advantage of the former is that the teletypewriter keyboard provides a typical and completely general input medium, and the teletypewriter hard copy for output provides a general output medium. Both are suitable for most "conversational" applications, regardless of the input language or output format. A somewhat more flexible but also more expensive approach is through the cathode-ray-tube devices such as shown in Fig. 2.2. While in these devices the typical keyboards for data entry are quite similar to those of the teletypewriter, the use of the cathode-ray-tube display as an output device has many advantages. The contents of the display itself can be used, manipulated, and edited, as part of the input-output process; also, the output responses are much faster and more flexible. Since the sorts of input and output are general and may in some cases involve significant quantities of data, it is in some cases advantageous to add optional input-output equipment to the display console itself. Examples of this include the addition of a low-speed desk-size

Fig. 2.2

card reader* as illustrated in Fig. 2.3 and/or the addition of typewriter
or line printer for hard copy output.   Since the consoles, regardless of
the choice of physical embodiment, allow very general input and output,
the specification of a Class B system is complete only when one defines
the service to be provided.   In Class B an open-ended list of services is

* The card reader shown in Fig. 2.3 is produced by the National Cash Register
Company and was slightly modified for use with the remote conversation console
shown in Fig. 2.2.

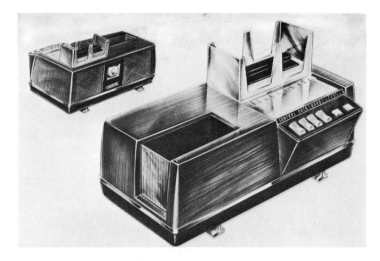

Fig. 2.3   Desk-size auxiliary card reader.

possible through any given terminal. For each of these services, a completely different arrangement of operating system and programming system philosophy must be employed, since the service will itself dictate the sort of control and usage of the central facility in terms of computer capacity, filing capacity, and programming system reaction that is required. Some of the earliest applications of the Class B type, all using teletypewriterlike terminals, include the developments at M.I.T. connected with Project MAC, the JOSS system developed at the Rand Corporation, and the QUICKTRAN* service developed by the IBM Corporation.

Class C: Remote Computer Centers. In contrast to the classes above which are designed to give a network of single individuals highly specialized access and service, the Class C system and user are actually a remote computer center. This kind of service is also referred to as a "remote batch processor." In a Class C system, the operator of the remote computer center loads programs for execution exactly as if he were at the main computer site. Runs are scheduled and executed automatically at the main computer site (and treated as if they were originated in a common batch-processing load) and the output is automatically returned to the originating remote site as shown in artist's concept in Fig. 2.4. A number of remote computer centers can share a single "main frame" at one central site in this way, each in effect having the same capability as if the main frame were physically present. This type of time-sharing allows for many sources of jobs through a common entry point (typically called a "job stack") at the main computer center, and has the effect of supplying an effectively balanced load to the main computer. As discussed in Ref. 1, this provides a means for distributing the

* Trademark of the IBM Corporation.

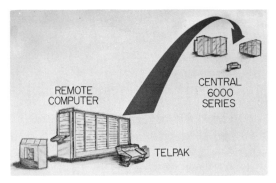

Fig. 2.4 Remote computer center.

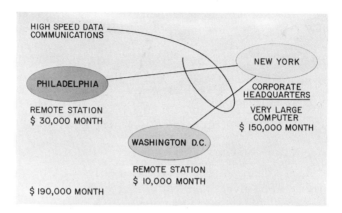

Fig. 2.5 Centralized system.

cost of the main computer to the remote sites and relieves each of the
remote sites of the necessity of owning and maintaining an expensive
computer facility, since the only equipment needed at the remote site is
a small- or medium-size computer and a minimum complement of peripheral equipment.

While in a way the Class C system could be thought of as an extension
of Class B (or rather, Class B terminals could be used to submit remote
batch-processing jobs), the main difference is that a typical Class C center
is actually a computer center as opposed to an individual, and the inten-
tion is to allow batch processing of any jobs that could be run at the main
computer site to be originated from and returned to the remote computer
center.   Since most batch-processing work loads involve large volumes
of punched card entry and large volumes of printed output and possibly
also punched card output, the type of peripheral equipment used at the
remote site would tend to be more nearly that associated with a computer
center rather than the smaller, cheaper, and lower data-rate equipment
typical in the Class A and Class B systems.   Also, the communications
bandwidth employed would differ, the typical bandwidths for Class A
and Class B being from 200 bits per second to 2,400 bits per second (and
generally using data sets that can transmit over a single-voice-grade telephone channel), with the Class C system using bandwidths that start
at the TELPAK A* range of 40,800 bits per second.

As Fig. 2.5 indicates, typical applications of Class C systems are found
in multidivisional geographically dispersed institutions; in these cases,

* Registered trademark of American Telephone and Telegraph Company and
Bell System.

the Class C time-sharing approach allows a single organization to share
one large computing facility and distribute the capacity among many
branches in different cities, yet simultaneously giving each remote location essentially the same degree of use and control of the batch-processing
facility at the central site.   One of the early applications of Class C first
became operational at the U.S. Weather Bureau, using a Control Data®
3100 computer as a remote computer to a Control Data® 6600 located 12
miles away; a description of this system is contained in Ref. 2.

2.3   Time-sharing Variables

Once a definition of the type of user network (in terms of the type of
service to be given in one of the three classes above) is determined, the
next step is to isolate and define the most important of those variables or
questions that must be considered.   These variables or questions relate
to the entire network and separate into considerations of the central
computer organization, the communications network and the grade of
service to be given to the users, and the amount of traffic or information
flow which passes through the system and poses demands upon the hardware facilities.   The key to economic time-sharing of a central computing
facility by a network of remote users involves the solution of several
important problems.   First, the submission of information from the network of remote users must be regulated and arranged in a manner that
prevents unwanted mutual interaction or interference.   Second, the problems from all the remote users, treated as a single part of the work load,
must be processed concurrently but not interfere with what might be
termed normal or traditional jobs that are entered at the computer center
itself.   Finally, the burden of achieving this concurrency and noninter-
ference must be placed entirely on the hardware and software complex,
and not on the users or originators of programs.   The main computer
center must treat the traditional submission of batch-processing programs
from programmers and the submission of problems from the remote user
network as two sources of work that can be processed simultaneously and
without restriction.   In order to do this, a thorough description of the
hardware arrangement at the central facility itself is obviously necessary;
superimposed on this is the actual mechanism for regulating the entry
of and output for the problems that are submitted, and this regulation is
the task of the operating system and other software packages that must
be provided with the hardware.   The interplay between the hardware
system and the operating system software is heavily dependent on the
original design of the hardware system itself; however, once a remote time-
sharing network is described in terms of the remote users, one may as
well regard the hardware system and the operating software system as a
single entity, regardless of which happened to have been specified first.

Central Computer Organization. As indicated, discussion of the organization of the central computer and of the organization of the operating system is really one and the same topic. Although a central computer can be time-shared regardless of its organization so long as certain minimal features are present, the type of computer organization that started to emerge in the early 1960s tends to lend itself much more readily to time-sharing of the ideal sort described above. In particular, the tendency toward isolation of the central processor or processors, the isolation of and possibility of multiple access to main memory, and the provision of isolated input-output channels with programmable buffering capability have made possible the separation of input-output and control-processing functions from the performance of the computation-processing functions. The organization of main memory has also made strides, starting with this period of time, that allow a number of individual programs to reside in memory at one time without mutual interference. Residence in main memory for an individual program implies that that program may, under suitable conditions, have control and have the central processor assigned to its execution; having a number of programs in residence simultaneously means that control can be instantaneously switched between them on an interrupt basis; this feature is the key to having a number of operations or programs proceed apparently at the same time. If a central computer is organized into four main portions, namely, the central processor or processors (CP), the main memory (CM), the peripheral or I/O processors (PP), and the I/O or data channels, the definition of the central computer organization then involves the logical rules of organization and interplay between the four items mentioned. On an individual basis, some of the hardware variables then to be considered are:

1. *The speed of the central processor or processors (CP) and the number of CPs available (which may be one in many instances but might be two or even more in some computer organizations).*

2. *The size and organization of main memory (CM) and the ability of different programs to reside in CM at once without conflict. Also the rules of access from CM to some form of slower but larger auxiliary memory storage (e.g., drums, disks, magnetic-tape units, or extended mass-core memory).* While from a logical standpoint, time-sharing can be achieved regardless of the size of CM and the precise extensions to auxiliary memory, the degree to which time-sharing can be made economical changes drastically with the size of CM, and even more so with the rules of access to auxiliary memories. The advent in the late 1960s of cheap auxiliary mass-core memories will effect a great improvement in the economics of time-sharing; as stressed previously, time-sharing is certainly possible and has been achieved in many instances without convenient auxiliary memories, but

each improvement in this area represents an increase in capability and capacity, and this rate of change is much more important than that achieved by comparable improvements in the speed of the central processor itself. The advent of disk storage as opposed to magnetic-tape storage for auxiliary memory extension already created many new avenues in time-sharing in the early and mid-1960s, but the improvement to be felt with the use of extended mass core as the primary auxiliary memory will, for many applications—particularly of the Class B type—represent an even more dramatic improvement.

3. *The arrangement of I/O processors (PPs), the number of PPs available, and the rules for parallelism for operation between individual PPs and between the PPs and the CPs. Also the data rates possible between the PPs and the various I/O devices (e.g., magnetic tapes, card readers, remote consoles, or multiplexers for networks of remote consoles, etc.).* Divorcing the operation of the PPs from the operation of the CP allows for parallelism and simultaneous input-output processing of data from a number of sources without affecting the action of the CP or CPs as they perform work on the computational load as represented by the programs resident in central memory. It is this possibility that allows for simultaneous communication with inputs from a number of sources and the apparent time-sharing of the central computer facility among a number of independent users.

The hardware organization itself mainly affects the considerations in 1, 2, and 3. For any particular application or service, the actual program that supplies this service, and its relationship to the operating system software that regulates the hardware complex, must be analyzed in terms of the amount of attention in time or memory space required. These considerations involve the operating system software and its relationship to the special programs or software necessary to handle and service the remote user network. Included in these considerations for a given service are:

a. The amount of central memory space occupied by the main program that services the remote user network.

b. The CP real time that is required for the execution of this main program to supply the remote users with the desired grade of service, expressed as a percentage of CP real time that is available.

c. The number of PPs required to provide for processing of input-output for the remote user network.

d. The use of auxiliary storage for temporary working space, provision for memory overflow, temporary and permanent storage and handling of data files, etc.

Items *a*, *b*, *c*, and *d* are parameters of the operating software and significantly affect the interaction between the operating system and the set of programs that occupy the system at any one time.

Grade of Service to Users.   Turning attention to the individual users in the remote network, there are two main considerations.   The first relates to the rules for the exchange of housekeeping or control information between the user and the central computer facility.   The second relates to the rules for turnaround time on user requests that demand computation service.   In the first instance the exchange of control information raises two questions:

1. *The specification of rules of access for submission of input data and receipt of output data.*   For example, a user may be given unlimited access and be allowed to transmit input data and control information at any time, or he may, at certain times, be provided with a complete rejection in the form of a "busy signal"; as a compromise between these two extremes, he may be given a delay indication or set of delay rules under which he must wait for a specified period of time before his communication of data or control information can commence.

2. *For any individual rule of access the collective rules of service for the network of users.*   For example, a number of users may be offered access on any basis (unlimited, delay, or busy signal); alternatively the entire set of users may be offered simultaneous unlimited access; and as a compromise alternative, certain subsets of users may be allowed simultaneous unlimited access, with all other users being provided delays or busy signal indications in periods of overload.

The second consideration involves the grade of service to users measured not in terms of the rules for exchange of control or housekeeping data, but rather in terms of the turnaround time provided on problems or requests for actual computation.   In the present discussion this is divorced from the service given in terms of data entry and output, so that one rule may apply for the former, and yet a completely different rule may apply for the actual receipt of results resulting in computation or action requests.   Specification of the type of service for problems submitted has two ingredients:

1. *The turnaround time on jobs (sometimes referred to as total job time).* This turnaround time measures the total elapsed time from the completion of a request for service made in terms of the input data submitted to the beginning of the receipt of output data answering the request.   Since this total elapsed time may vary, depending both on the nature of the problem submitted and on the loading of the system from other sources at the same time, the measurement of total job time is usually expressed in terms of a statistical distribution conditional on the intrinsic time

(sometimes referred to as problem solution time) required by the request, and also conditional on the traffic loading conditions of the total system.

2. *Rules for service on computation requests that occur in periods of traffic overload or that overextend physical capacity.* These are related to the queuing philosophy employed, and may include delay or rejection or combinations of both.

Measurements of User Traffic. Once a tentative description of the central computing facility and of the remote user network is obtained—in terms of the variables mentioned in the last two paragraphs—it is possible to describe and to measure the flow of traffic that will impose demands on the hardware facilities. This measurement is the key to a determination of the economics of the system, both to the owner of the central computing facility and to the remote user. To the latter especially, the feasibility and attractiveness of the service he receives depend on the rules of access and turnaround time and on the cost of obtaining this service; if comparable service and results can be obtained by a self-contained local unit, the remote time-sharing approach cannot be justified.

Measurement of the traffic intensity and description of the various blockage or congestion points in the system provide a "second look" at the other variables; that is, the result of the first analysis may show that changes—in order to achieve economic goals or adequate service—are necessary either in the central computing facility or in the access rules for the remote user network. This really means that the three main considerations discussed here (central facility, remote user network, and traffic load) cannot be considered independently. However, since a starting point is necessary, the order of consideration suggested here seems the most practical, particularly since the traffic cannot be described or measured until the other two sets of variables are defined at least in preliminary form.

The ideas and concepts involved in the description of user traffic bear a very close resemblance to the traditional topics of congestion or queuing theory that had origins in the analysis of telephone traffic. As mentioned in the introduction, provision of a time-sharing facility involving a central computer brings the computer industry closer to some of the methods common to public utilities, particularly the communications industry. In the latter, the practice and analysis of sharing facilities (transmission paths and switching centers) among a community of users is commonplace; these same techniques (and even to some extent, the same facilities) come into play upon the addition of a shared digital computer at some point in the network, the computer adding just one more kind of physical hardware to the overall shared complex. It is no accident, then, that the analysis and design—and methods of economic justification—involved in time-sharing computer systems do not differ in some respects from the counterparts in communications systems.

While striking similarities do exist between the "data-processing" and "communications" portions of a system (when considering problems of time-sharing and traffic loading), there are also fundamental differences. In most analyses of congestion, a single element must be identified upon which simultaneous demands are imposed. For example, in the telephone system, there are a limited number of trunks between any two points or cities, and when these trunks are busy, no further traffic is possible; the element of congestion, then, is simply the limitation on physical transmission paths. When a digital computer comprises the congestion element (e.g., is time-shared among a number of users), the situation is more complex and has facets that have no counterpart in the telephone model in particular or in the communications industry in general. The list of considerations given in the previous paragraph on central computer organization suggests some of these. Although well beyond the scope of this chapter, the following mentions a few examples to illustrate some of the most important features that are unique to analysis of congestion in a computer facility.

When a computer facility is regarded as the congestion point, several areas arise that require definition. First, the physical quantity that is being shared may be any one of the below, or in fact complex combinations of any one of these:

1. Real time on the central processor or central processors
2. Space in central memory
3. Availability of and real time on the peripheral processors
4. Availability of and real time on the input-output channels
5. Attention from the operating system (software) as it directs the activities of the entire hardware complex

The interplay between the items above can be quite complex, and the precise point of congestion may be difficult to isolate, since the demands on the items above may impose time limitations or physical limitations in diverse parts of the computer system, and at different rates. In order to circumvent this for a first approximation in any analysis, it is usually necessary to view the entire computer as a single entity, and treat the congestion point as one ideal element; it is most convenient to think of this element as the central processor (or central processors) and then to regard the commodity being shared as real time on the central processor. It is then left to a "subsidiary" data-flow analysis to reduce all the other interdependent blockages—due to memory space, input-output restrictions, and software housekeeping—to a single effect which is lumped into the real time requirements on the central processor. Once this is done, the queuing analysis can proceed in a fairly standard fashion; however, it must be emphasized that the design and analysis of the subsidiary data flow is a procedure unique to the computer industry and entails many questions of computer organization and operating system software design.

In any congestion model where incoming problems or requests are allowed to form queues for attention of the one facility being time-shared, it is common to suppose that the facility can, upon completing a problem, be made available instantaneously to the problems waiting on the queue; conversely, it is usually supposed that a problem waiting on the queue is in position to be serviced immediately as soon as it is the next eligible and as soon as the shared facility is available.   This is not usually the case in a shared computer facility, however; problems that are queued generally involve sequences of program coding and possibly other elements of data such as programs, data files, etc.; the queue itself and the other elements of data may well be scattered through different physical parts of central memory and the auxiliary memories.   Retrieving these, as well as assembling them into appropriate order once a problem becomes eligible for attention, is an operating system software problem, which may itself introduce blockages or delays.   While these can sometimes be described or measured, this facet alone does introduce a unique feature into the classical queuing model and also serves as one of the more difficult software design questions.   In fact, it is this one question alone that serves to distinguish, from a software point of view, the most dramatic differences between the Class A, Class B, and Class C systems.   Although not possible to describe in detail here, there are striking differences between these three systems in the scope and types of data-handling techniques involved in handling queues of problems, and also in the sort of physical information these queues tend to contain.   It is also in this area that the most radical design changes and improvements are felt upon each improvement in the size and speed of auxiliary memories and upon each improvement in the way these auxiliary memories are logically organized with respect to the main memory and to the processing units in the computer facility.   Since physical space and real time for shuttling data between the memory units is the fundamental consideration, it is clear that this one aspect of computer hardware organization has a profound effect on software design and on the timing of a queuing situation.

Once the hardware-software complex is viewed (in the light of the remarks above) as presenting one lumped "bottleneck" to the traffic flow, it is possible to proceed to identify the next elements of traffic congestion. In the following, it will be assumed that real time on the central processor presents the single congestion point as far as the shared computer facility is concerned; it will further be assumed that some fraction of each time unit of available central processor time is devoted to servicing the remote user network, and that the remainder of each time unit is available to normal jobs originating at the computer center and is unavailable to the remote user network.

With a fixed allocation of computer real time, it is possible to measure the traffic intensity imposed upon the computer by problems originating from the remote users. Before isolating those variables that must be described to measure this traffic intensity, one further distinction must be borne in mind. For convenience, it is assumed here that the problems that arrive represent demands for attention of the central processor, and in this respect require a finite period of time on the processor. The exchange of input data, control information, and output data between the computer and the user network is treated separately, and for simplicity it is assumed that none of this requires any central processor time, and in fact proceeds completely independently of and concurrently with central processor action. It is further assumed that the system hardware and communications paths themselves are adequate to cope with this load of control or housekeeping information, and therefore that this type of information interchange is not part of the traffic load, and in fact involves instantaneous and delay-free service to the user network. Whether this assumption is realistic depends, of course, on the actual hardware configuration present in any given system; if it is not true, any delay or physical limitations can be analyzed and lumped with the elements which do bear on the traffic load. For simplicity, however, it is best to separate these two types of information interchange and regard the actual problem solutions as the only element creating a time-sharing situation.

With this distinction, it is now possible to define several quantities related to the problems submitted by the remote users.

1. *Problem Solution Time (PST)*. For an individual request for computation service, this is defined as the total real time on the CP required to complete the request if the CP is devoted full time to the request. In other words, it is simply the total running time that would be required for this problem if no other problem were present and if the computer were devoted full time to its solution.

2. *Problem Arrival Rate*. For an individual user or terminal, this is defined as the rate at which problems are submitted. The time between successive problem originations is measured from the actual instant at which a button is pressed that indicates an end to control or input data and an initiation of a request to perform computations or data processing upon these data.

3. *Traffic Intensity*. This is the quantity equivalent to the variable ρ of classical queuing theory and is the single most descriptive variable in the determination of system loading. In qualitative terms, traffic inten-

sity is a measurement of the demand for computation time that arrives
per time unit as compared with the amount of computation time being
made available per time unit and thus is a measurement of the system's
ability to cope with the computation load that is arriving.

To express the quantity ρ analytically, we give several formulas below:

Let

n be the number of remote users that are active and have
       simultaneous access.

a be the average number of problems submitted by a single
       user per unit time (the average problem arrival rate).

$A = na$ be the average number of problems submitted by the entire
       remote user network per unit time.   (In some models, it is
       convenient to regard the user network as having an unlimited
       number of users, with an overall problem arrival rate A, as
       opposed to assuming a finite user population of n users, each
       with an individual contribution to the total problem stream.)

d be the fractional portion of real time on the CP that is
       devoted to the remote user network.   The quantity d ranges
       between 0 and 1; for a 100 per cent duty cycle (full-time CP
       usage), $d = 1$; for half-time usage, $d = .50$, etc.

T be the random variable representing problem solution time
       and

$\langle T \rangle$ be the statistical average of the problem solution time
       distribution.

Then the traffic intensity ρ is given by:

$$\rho = \frac{na\langle T \rangle}{d} \quad \text{for a finite user network, or}$$

$$\rho = \frac{A\langle T \rangle}{d} \quad \text{for an idealized ``infinite'' model user network}$$

The quantity ρ is itself an average; when less than unity it implies that
the system is underloaded and can cope with a steady-state traffic load at
this level without formation of infinitely expanding queues, and when
greater than unity implies an overloaded condition and hence the necessity of rejection or expanding queues.   The traffic intensity itself might
fluctuate during any time period.   Also, a precise study of elapsed time
or delay on problems submitted depends both on the fluctuation in traffic
intensity and on the actual distribution of PSTs along with the queuing
rules employed.   Thus, while ρ is a simple descriptive measure that
quickly determines overall system loading, it is not in itself adequate for
a precise determination of conditional total job time distributions.

SPECIFIC DESIGN DETAIL

2.4   User's View of the 6060 Remote Calculator

In the following sections, all of the general considerations described above will be illustrated by one specific example.   The example chosen is a network of Control Data 6060 remote calculators time-sharing a central Control Data 6600 computer as described in Ref. 3.   Once the selection of the user network (which in this case is one of the members of the Class A family of specialized remote applications) and a specific central computer such as the 6600 is made, all of the pertinent design requirements are fixed, and the determination of all the time-sharing variables and an economic analysis is possible.   In the following a brief description of the user's view of the 6060 remote calculator will be given, followed in Secs. 2.5 and 2.6 by design considerations and solutions to all parts of the specific time-sharing system.   This will illustrate the points that are encountered in any time-sharing system; however, it is emphasized that the calculator is a member of the Class A family and thus details of using language, service, and requirements for operating software are determined implicitly.   While the types of considerations are identical for the design of a Class B time-sharing network, the operating software requirements (as indicated previously) may differ radically depending on the specific language and service to be provided.

The remote calculator is a small portable device intended for desktop scientific computation and numerical analysis.   A picture of the keyboard is shown in Fig. 2.6, and a photograph of the actual physical device as it would appear on a user's desk is given in Fig. 2.7.   The device itself, from a hardware point of view, is merely an input-output terminal and serves to transmit and receive coded binary streams of information over phone lines to a central computer.   All of the burden of interpretation and computation is left to the central computer, and the remote calculator itself has no internal buffering memory or computation logic.

From the user's point of view, the keyboard itself suggests a very simple "language" of use, and the device as a whole appears to the user as a self-contained means for entering complex numerical problems and receiving the answers immediately in numerical form on the read-out display.   As far as the user is concerned, the computation appears to take place within the device itself, and the fact that a remote computer is involved is of no concern to the user, except that initial contact is made with the computer center by his telephone which is then used as a transmitting and receiving device.

The term "language" is a more formidable one than necessary to describe the rules of operation of the calculator.   The conventions of use

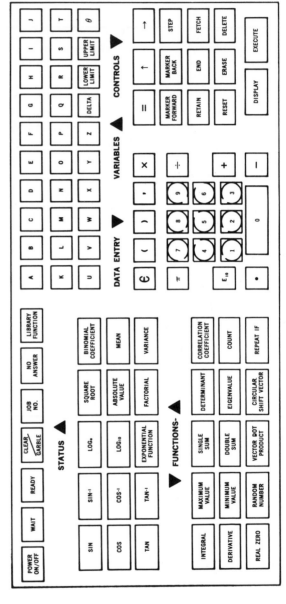

Fig. 2.6

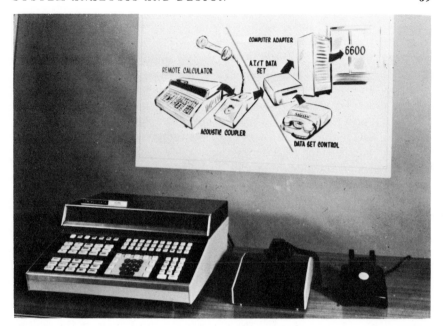

Fig. 2.7

of the calculator are well defined and for the most part exceedingly simple. In fact, the key labels themselves—together with the natural way in which mathematical notation is used—provide the user with just about all he needs by way of instruction. Use is very simple to master and many of the features (such as functional and algebraic notation, statements, iterations, etc.) available in a standard programming language are available to the user in a vastly simplified form. References 4 and 5 provide a complete user's guide to operation and examples of use.

The calculator is intended as a powerful desk "scratch pad" tool for computation. Any arithmetic expression or formula can be explicitly and directly entered through the keys, and a single key calls for computation and display of results. Display is immediate, in decimal notation—either fixed or floating depending on the range of the answer—and appears directly on the decimal read-out.

While using the 6060, the user actually behaves exactly as though he were operating a traditional self-contained desk calculator. His "feedback" from the computer is split into two kinds—and this distinction is important to the later discussion of the central 6600 operation. The first kind of feedback is the key-by-key ackowledgment—by lamps within the keys—of the receipt of the key codes by the computer. This applies either to the process of data entry, or to the examination of data already entered. In either case, the process is immediate, and no delays in response are experienced. As will be seen later, only the peripheral processors of the central 6600 are involved, and no action is required of the central processor. The second type of feedback is the display of the results of an evaluation or computation. In this case, the user calls for central processor action on his data by hitting one of two keys—either DISPLAY or EXECUTE. (For purposes here, these can be regarded as identical, the distinction being clear only through a detailed discussion of keyboard conventions.) After a request for computation, the WAIT light appears on the calculator and further data entry is locked out until the computation is complete and displayed. The user can, however, abort a computation before completion and thereby free his calculator for further use.

The delay that a user experiences upon requesting a computation depends on three factors. The first is the problem solution time (PST) of the problem submitted. It is clear that the PST varies from problem to problem; in fact, there is almost no upper time limit, since operations and iterations are permitted, and simple statements could call for almost endless computation.

The second factor affecting the delay is the duty cycle of the central processor, as it is time-shared with normal jobs in the central 6600. The third factor causing delay is the sharing of this allocated time-slice among a number of calculator users, the worst case arising when all calculators in the network are connected and fully utilized simultaneously.

It is clear from the above that the total job time (TJT), defined to be the elapsed time from the instant the EXECUTE key is hit to the time the answer appears on the read-out, is dependent on:

1. The PST of the problem.

2. The number of calculators busy and the statistical distribution of the PSTs of jobs they are submitting.

3. The duty cycle of the central processor as assigned to the calculators. (Note that items 2 and 3 actually determine the traffic intensity; thus the TJT distribution is simply conditional on the PST and on the traffic intensity.)

While the delay encountered is dependent on these three factors in a complex manner, one design goal partially removes this dependency. This goal is to return an answer as quickly as a user can react (i.e., within a second) for all short problems where an answer can reasonably be expected immediately—and to allow delays for longer problems where considerable computation is involved and where, therefore, the user is psychologically set to endure delays. In this way, the turnaround for "short" problems is (as far as the user can tell) a constant—and therefore independent of congestion from other busy users—while the statistical variations in turnaround are all forced toward the "long-problem" end of the spectrum. Psychologically, this makes the device appear more private and self-contained, and irritation encountered upon delays is lessened, since delays are noticed only when most expected (i.e., when the problem submitted is "long" in the first place). Furthermore, variations in the TJT for long problems, caused by fluctuation in prevailing traffic intensity, are not easily observable by the user, who would tend to be much more sensitive to delays on those short problems for which he expects "instantaneous" answers.

2.5 Organization of the 6600 Hardware Operating System

Although a network of remote calculators can be made to operate in a time-sharing mode with any computer that is appropriately organized, the illustration chosen here discusses the time-sharing aspects when the central computer is a Control Data 6600. Historically, the 6600 was chosen as the first machine on which to implement this particular time-sharing system. The organization of the 6600 itself represents a drastic departure from previous machines, in directions that enhance the capability to time-share in many complex modes, and will provide an illustration of many facets of time-sharing that would be impossible in earlier "traditional" large-scale computer systems. A complete description of the 6600 can be found in Refs. 6 and 7.

Figure 2.8 gives a very broad outline of the organization of a 6600.

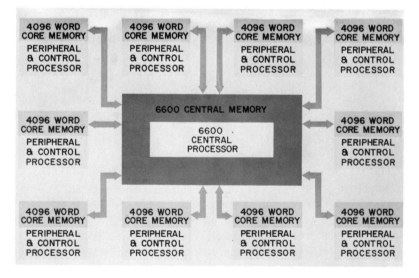

Fig. 2.8 Control Data 6600 block diagram.

The 6600 has a single main frame containing four main functional sections characterized briefly below:

Single CP	Max. instruction rate = 3,000,000 instructions/sec.
Single CM	131,000 60-bit words. Programs in CM protected by hardware EXCHANGE JUMP feature. CP operates on programs out of CM as directed by PPs.
10 PPs	Operate independently and concurrently with CP, acting as control processors and as programmable I/O buffers. Each has access to any of 12 I/O channels. All PPs can read in and out of CM, and direct CP to any program in CM through EXCHANGE JUMP.
12 I/O channels	Operating at max. one megacycle word (12-bit) rate, communicate with external peripheral equipment (card readers, printers, mag tapes, disk, card punches, multiplexers, etc.)

Figure 2.8 shows only the central processor, central memory, and the ten peripheral processors, each with its own memory. Also part of the main frame, but not shown, are the twelve I/O channels, through which the peripheral processors receive and transmit data from external sources such as peripheral equipment, multiplexers for remote devices, or other on-line devices.

Since the rules by which the peripheral processors operate in sharing the access to the I/O channels, in reading in and out of central memory, and in directing the operation of the central processor are very simple and flexible, the actual operation of a machine can be specified and understood only in the context of an operating software system. One of the operating systems that has been developed for the 6600 has been named SIPROS, and its rules of operation will be described briefly. More detail on the organization of this system can be found in Refs. 8 and 9.

SIPROS controls all of the hardware in the system and regulates the loading of jobs that are eligible for execution into central memory. It also regulates and controls the assignment of peripheral processors and peripheral equipment to perform system functions and input-output functions for the jobs as required on a dynamic basis. SIPROS itself resides in two of the peripheral processors which play executive and monitor roles; the other peripheral processors are all available in a pool under system control for specific task assignments. However, any of these peripheral processors can be removed from the pool and assigned to any job which is loaded in central memory and eligible for execution. In this way one of the jobs in central memory, should it have one or more peripheral processors assigned to it, could (while still being regarded by SIPROS as an ordinary job under its control) actually look logically like a "subordinate" operating system controlled by its own peripheral processors. Figure 2.9 illustrates this and shows SIPROS resident in peripheral processors and a portion of central memory and in control of those

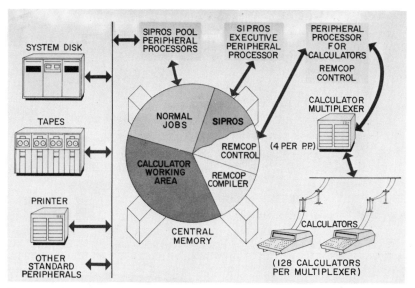

Fig. 2.9 Class A (remote calculator).

jobs in central memory labeled "normal jobs." These normal jobs can be thought of as traditional batch-processing jobs that are flowing through the system. One other job in the system is labeled REMCOP, and this is the name chosen for the "remote calculator operating program." This program itself resides in central memory, but also has assigned to it several peripheral processors on a permanent basis, with a portion of the REMCOP program residing in those peripheral processors. Within the time scale and conditions allotted to it by SIPROS, REMCOP acts as a separate operating system in control of the inputs from, outputs to, and scheduling and execution of problems submitted from the remote calculator network. The presence of REMCOP in no way interferes with the normal jobs that are flowing through the system, since it is itself treated by SIPROS as any other normal job would be treated. Thus REMCOP can operate independently of and without conflict with a normal batch-processing load, and programmers submitting normal programs do not ever "know" that these will be time-shared in any way with other batch programs or with the remote calculator network. Similarly, remote calculator users are in no way restricted by the presence of other remote calculators or of the normal jobs in the central computer.

2.6 Estimates of Time-sharing Variables

In this section, a description of each of the variables of a general time-sharing system will be given in terms of a fixed network of calculators sharing a central 6600.

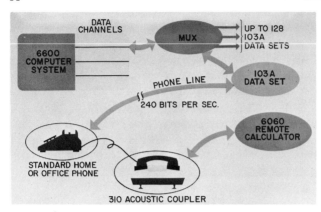

Fig. 2.10 Typical calculator connection.

The Calculator to 6600 Network. A complete system, as illustrated in Fig. 2.9, consists of a number of remote calculators, multiplexers to connect the incoming phone line terminals to a 6600 I/O channel, a central 6600 under control of SIPROS, and an operating software package called REMCOP running as a job under SIPROS and controlling the calculator network. Figure 2.10 illustrates the connections involved from a single remote calculator to the 6600 computer center. While the upper limit of the number of calculators that can be allowed is quite flexible, for purposes of this discussion attention will be confined to the simplest case of a single multiplexer. (Larger networks could be serviced by adding multiplexers, and thereby devoting a larger portion of the 6600 hardware and time to the calculators.)

A multiplexer communicates with a 6600 peripheral processor through a single 6600 I/O channel. One peripheral processor (PP) and I/O channel could accommodate up to four multiplexers, and each multiplexer can handle up to 128 separate remote calculators. Each calculator is connected by any standard telephone line (local or long distance) by an ATT 103A data set to the multiplexer. Location of the calculators then is completely arbitrary and requires only a telephone and standard power outlet. No installation is required, the device is portable, and no environmental restrictions are imposed.

Any user is free at any time to dial the center, and is guaranteed an immediate automatic response. As soon as he gets this, he is "on the air" in seconds and gets a READY signal from the computer. From then on he is on-line and can hit keys—and obtain immediate feedback verification—with no delay and no restriction.

Figure 2.11 shows the portions of the 6600 hardware that are actually devoted to servicing the calculator network. One of the twelve I/O channels is assigned to the multiplexer servicing the 128 calculators. Two of the 10 PPs are assigned permanently to the REMCOP program. A maximum of 32K of central memory is assigned to REMCOP for working space and for the compiler and other resident CM portions of REM-COP. Finally, a time-slice representing a maximum 5 per cent of CP time is allocated by SIPROS to the REMCOP job by devoting up to 50 consecutive milliseconds out of each second of real time for REMCOP, and by reserving the remaining 950 milliseconds for execution of other jobs in central memory.

SIPROS controls all peripheral equipment, I/O channels, and central memory. It allocates (i.e., releases from system control) two peripheral processors, one I/O channel, 32K of central memory to REMCOP.

REMCOP is treated as a normal SIPROS job. It will receive periodic—or on demand—attention from the central processor and will remain in control of its allocated 32K of central memory space and its two peripheral processors so long as the job is loaded (i.e., so long as the calculator network is "live" within the system).

The maximum 32K of CM space allotted to REMCOP is utilized as follows:

Approximately 10K of space is used for the REMCOP control resident and communications flags for SIPROS and for the REMCOP compiler and associated copies of subroutines. Space for data storage for active calculators is also reserved on a per calculator basis; this amounts to approximately 100 CM words per calculator. The remainder of the space is allocated to retention of the most active portions of the queues of partially executed problems. All other central memory space is used or controlled by SIPROS for other jobs.

The two peripheral processors that are separated from the SIPROS pool form part of the REMCOP system. Each contains resident portions

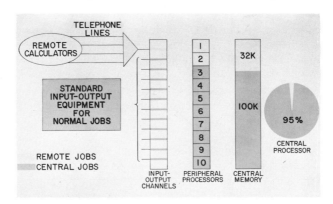

Fig. 2.11 6600 series time-sharing block diagram.

of the REMCOP program, and communications links with each other and with the 32K of central memory.

One of the PPs is permanently assigned to monitoring the multiplexer over the assigned I/O channel. One multiplexer presents data at a worst-case rate of approximately 125KC, which is far below the maximum one megacycle peripheral processor word-transfer rate. This peripheral processor then performs the following functions:

1. Returns verifying code through multiplexer to originating calculator
2. Sorts all received strings of characters, by originating calculator, for intermediate storage or immediate storage or immediate action
3. Communicates with the other peripheral processor when storage or execution activity is required, and writes strings into central memory

The second peripheral processor serves as executive and monitor. It maintains status lists of all calculators, the location and disposition of their data, status of queues of problems waiting for service or partially executed, and monitors and sets flags regulating the demand or release of the central processor from SIPROS. It also performs the EXCHANGE JUMP to assign the central processor to the appropriate job within the REMCOP 32K of central memory, and to remove central processor on time limit, completion, or other exit conditions. It also handles all return of results through the multiplexer to the originating calculator.

The monitoring, housekeeping, data manipulation, and input-output functions of these two peripheral processors proceed independently of any central processor action, and do not interfere with its processing. For this reason—even though the central processor devotes a low percentage of its time to REMCOP—the REMCOP peripheral processors are always in action and service all data I/O to the calculator network with no delay.

Dynamically, the data associated with any calculator's activity may be scattered throughout the system. Data that must be kept for each calculator by REMCOP include:

1. The current working sequence of characters
2. Variable values
3. Sequences that have been defined by the user for storage
4. Partially executed programs acting on the current working sequence, held in queues for central processor attention

The actual physical location of these four items may also change dynamically. For example, items 1 and 2 are kept in central memory, but may be transferred to auxiliary memory should the originator remain connected but call for no action for appreciable time periods. Item 3 similarly may be in central memory or auxiliary memory; in items 1 and

3, these are initially received by the peripheral processor monitoring the multiplexer, which then acts as a temporary storage buffer.

The treatment of item 4 depends on the queuing arrangements, which will be described in the next section. To an extent, these queues are kept in central memory, but as priority drops, they may be backed off to auxiliary memory.

SIPROS has full use of the remaining eight peripheral processors and 100K of central memory for processing any other jobs in normal manner. No restriction whatsoever is imposed on this normal work load of programs, and their processing proceeds automatically under SIPROS with no interference from REMCOP.

Since a maximum of 5 per cent of the time of the central processor is occupied with REMCOP (and then time-shared among the 128 calculator users), the remaining 95 per cent is devoted, through SIPROS, to processing of normal jobs in the ordinary manner.

Thus, if we were to compare two situations—one where a normal job load is being processed without the presence of REMCOP or busy calculators, and the other where a network of 128 calculators is on-line and busy full-time—the only noticeable effect on throughput of normal jobs would be an observable slowdown of about 5 per cent.

Grade of Service to Users and Queuing System. In the calculator system, three problems must be solved by the queuing system:

1. A calculator submitting a "short" problem must get his answer in a second (i.e., his TJT time must be a second or less).

2. No calculator submitting a "long" problem can be allowed to "hog" the central processor or introduce congestion for other calculators, and no calculator can be permitted to "hog" central memory space.

3. No calculator should be "denied the right" to submit a "long" problem, so long as he is willing to wait (and have his set tied up for the duration of the wait).

To achieve this objective, the following (oversimplified) queuing system is employed. Recall that this queuing system applies only to central processor time and therefore to response for DISPLAY or EXECUTE commands and not to the data-entry and verification process which is essentially delay-free. Also, this model applies to our assumption of 128 calculators all on-line (and all active in the worst case).

1. Out of each second, a consecutive 50-millisecond slice of central processor time is allocated to REMCOP. The remaining 950 msec is assigned by SIPROS to eligible "normal" jobs.

2. A queue (Queue 1) is formed of all problems requesting action (e.g., DISPLAY or EXECUTE key code received). This queue is served in

order of arrival (first come, first served) by the central processor during the 50-msec period.

3. The central processor compiles a problem once submitted from Queue 1 and either works to completion—or spends a maximum of 5 msec (compilation and execution) should completion not occur—on the problem.

4. Those problems not completed in 5 msec are interrupted (with intermediate results and object code saved) and placed in another queue (Queue 2). Queue 2 is serviced (approximately) in inverse order of arrival (last come, first served). More precisely, an index indicating the number of central processor "turns" a problem has had serves to determine, along with absolute order of arrival, the seniority in the queue.

5. Queue 2 is served only if Queue 1 is empty. Each trip from Queue 2 to the CP provides another 5 msec of execution time, and a subsequent return to Queue 2 unless completion has been effected.

6. The data (incomplete results, program, etc.) for Queue 2 are retained in central memory, with the "low end of the totem pole" backed off to auxiliary memory.

7. Calculators with problems on either queue are locked out of further communication. However, a CLEAR key in effect aborts the computation or, in present terms, removes the problem from the queue.

From the queuing system employed, it is clear that those problems with a PST of 5 msec or less have the best chance, depending on the traffic intensity, of resulting in a turnaround of one second or less. To get a feeling of the type of problem that might have a PST of under 5 msec on the 6600, one can observe that between 10,000 and 15,000 CP instructions can be completed in this time interval. So long as fewer instructions than this are sufficient to compile the problem and then to execute the compiled code, the problem will have a PST of under 5 msec (and will then be regarded as "short"). Clearly, most numerical computations fall in this category; the only exceptions are those involving a large number of iterations, and these also—by breaking up the computation into a sequence of pieces or by sacrificing accuracy in results—can be made into "short" problems. For example, the remote calculator problem requesting the numerical computation (by trapezoidal rule) of

$$\int_0^{\pi/3} (\sin \theta + \sin 2\theta + \cdots + \sin 10\theta) \, d\theta$$

in increments of .0001 requires (by actual measurement, using REMCOP on the 6600) 7 seconds for completion, and thus has a PST of 7000 msec. However, the numerical computation of

$$\int_0^{\pi/6} \sin k\theta \, d\theta$$

in increments of 0.01 has a PST of slightly under 4 msec; this example illustrates both sacrifice of precision and the use of additivity in reducing "long" problems to sequences of "short" ones.

Measurement of Traffic Intensity. Reference to the formulas for traffic intensity given earlier shows that the CP duty cycle, the problem average arrival rate, and the PST distribution must all be specified or known before the traffic intensity—and hence conditions of system loading—can be determined.

Experiments with actual calculator users indicate that a normal active user originates an average of 6 computation requests per minute. With 128 independent users all active simultaneously, this would lead to a complete arrival rate given by

$$A = na = (128)(0.1) = 12.8/\text{sec}$$

For simplicity in the following, it will be assumed that $A = 10/\text{sec}$ in a typically busy period, and that this arrival rate is submitted by a theoretically infinite community of users.

The duty cycle, when the CP is allocated to REMCOP for 5 per cent of the total time in the manner indicated above, is $d = 0.05$.

The actual distribution of PST (problem solution time) for the 6060 remote calculator is unknown. It will not be known until much active live using experience by many typical users has been logged and studied; in fact, the distribution itself may change gradually as using habits and experience build up. For design purposes, a number of "approximate" distributions have been hypothesized and studied; several have been used as inputs to a simulation model to determine turnaround distributions and queue behavior in steady-state busy periods, as well as to observe behavior under conditions of fluctuating traffic intensity.

As an illustration, consider the following hypothetical distribution of problem solution time (PST):

PST, msec	Probability
2	0.8
5	0.1
10	0.05
20	0.05

For this distribution, $\langle T \rangle = 3.6$ msec; with $A = 10/\text{sec}$, and $d = 0.05$, the previous formula for traffic intensity ρ gives

$$\rho = \frac{A\langle T \rangle}{d} = \frac{10(3.6) \times 10^{-3}}{0.05} = 0.72$$

and for this distribution the system would be underloaded.

A simple alternative hypothetical distribution given below shows several interesting things:

PST, msec	Probability
4	0.90
100	0.10

For this distribution, $\langle T \rangle = 13.6$, and with $d = 0.05$ and $A = 10/\text{sec}$ as before, the traffic intensity becomes

$$\rho = \frac{10(13.6) \times 10^{-3}}{0.05} = 2.72$$

and the system is badly overloaded. This means that under steady-state traffic conditions with this intensity, the queue of delayed problems would tend to increase indefinitely.

Consideration of this overloaded case—bearing in mind how the two queues operate—shows that 9 out of 10 of the arrivals per second coming to Queue 1 require only 4 msec and thus complete in their 5-msec turn— Queue 1 is in general emptied at the end of a 50-msec duty cycle, since on the average only $9(4 \text{ msec}) + 1(5 \text{ msec}) = 41$ msec is required. Thus the 4-msec jobs—90 per cent of the population—are turned around in one second even though the system is overloaded. A little more thought shows that the 100-msec jobs all find their way to Queue 2 and will require at least 20 shots of 5 msec each to complete, but since Queue 2 expands indefinitely (getting an average of one new entry each second), there will be no chance for any 100-msec job to get the required 20 trips (since there will almost always be a later arrival with fewer trips and hence higher priority on the queue). In this particular example, the 4-msec jobs are unaffected by the large traffic overload, and would with very high probability be completed and results returned to the user with less than one second delay. The 100-msec jobs, however, pay the penalty, and would queue up indefinitely on Queue 2 with essentially no chance of completion.

This illustrates the independence from traffic of turnaround for short jobs—and also indicates the existence of a "critical PST"—dependent on traffic intensity, with the property that problems with PST greater than "critical" have no hope of completion. In the example above, this critical limit must be less than 100 msec, and in general, this critical limit will decrease as the traffic intensity increases.

It can easily be seen that increasing the duty cycle to $d = 0.20$ in the example above (i.e., devoting 20 per cent of CP time) would lead to an underloaded system with $\rho = 0.68$, and would produce a 1-second turnaround on the 4-msec jobs and on the 100-msec jobs as well.

Use of Simulation to Predict Operating Results. Known analytical models for queuing systems do not always adequately describe an actual physical system and conversely, the details of an actual system may lead to models that are intractable analytically. Thus, the prediction of behavior of a specific system such as the calculator network might well involve simulation experiments to augment mathematical analysis. For one of the most up-to-date treatises on the mathematics of queuing systems, see Ref. 10.

To facilitate the calculator system design, a 1604A program was written to measure all the operating characteristics described here. Results of typical experiments are described here for illustration and are discussed more completely in Ref. 11. These experimental runs have accelerated the process—impossible otherwise without live users and much data gathering—of measuring what will actually happen under varying traffic loads, queuing systems, CP duty cycles, etc., to a system of remote calculators as described here.

The program allows as parameters:

1. Input arrival rate and fluctuations in arrival rate
2. Problem solution time distribution
3. CP duty cycle
4. Allocation of time slices to the two queues during the duty cycle
5. Choice of arbitrary queue truncation on overflow, and other variations in queuing rules

There are a number of alternatives for experimentation. Once conditions are set, the experimenter can simulate arbitrary periods of live use and measure conditions that would apply. Output of the runs provide measurements such as conditional job turnaround time, distribution of the size of Queue 1 and Queue 2, etc. These runs have also demonstrated the existence of a "critical time limit" under overloaded conditions of traffic intensity. Many of these observations have since been predicted analytically; these results and many experimental runs are contained in Ref. 11, which includes a self-contained description of some of this material.

ASSUMPTIONS: (Case 1)
Infinite independent random sources, $A = 10/\text{sec}$
Distribution of problem solution times:

PST, msec	Probability
1	0.25
2	0.25
3	0.15
4	0.08
5–10	0.25
10–140	0.02

(This distribution has $\rho = 0.979$)

Two-queue system with allotment in 2-msec shots
CP duty cycle d = 0.05 (50 msec out of each 1 second)

RESULTS:

Average size of Queue 1 at beginning of 50-msec duty cycle = 9.5
Average size of Queue 1 at end of 50-msec duty cycle   = 0
Average size of Queue 2 (steady state)   = 8.28
Conditional distribution of job turnaround is given in Table 2.1.

ASSUMPTIONS: (Case 2)

Same as Case 1, except for distribution of problem solution times.

PST, msec	Probability
1–2	0.8500
2–4	0.0238
4–6	0.0190
6–8	0.0152
8–10	0.0120
10–50	0.0400
50–200	0.0400

(For this case, it can be shown that $\rho = 1.57$)

RESULTS:

Average size of Queue 1 at beginning of duty cycle = 9.5
Average size of Queue 1 at end of duty cycle   = 0
Size of Queue 2: Indefinitely expanding (system overloaded, no steady state)
Critical time limit = 54 msec (jobs with problem solution time longer than 54 msec have no chance of completion)
Turnaround for short jobs: All jobs with problem solution times less than 4-msec turnaround in 2 seconds or less.

TABLE 2.1 *Conditional Total Job Time Distribution*

Total job time (in seconds)	Problem solution time (PST), msec						
	1–2	3–4	5–6	7–8	9–10	10–50	51–140
0–1	100	99.64	93.66	79.93	68.96	18.32	
1–2		0.36	4.98	13.92	17.78	24.26	0.83
2–3			0.91	3.75	8.69	14.85	3.02
3–6			0.45	2.33	4.31	24.75	11.54
6–10				0.07	0.27	10.89	12.09
10–20						5.94	22.25
20–100						0.99	31.59
100–600							18.68

2.7 Economic Analyses and Projections

Three items of expense in any time-sharing system are the costs of the terminal hardware, the costs associated with communications (including data-set terminals and transmission line costs), and the costs associated with time on the central computer installation. When these costs to the user are totaled, the sum must be in balance with the economic utility of the service provided the user and must be competitive with alternative ways of doing the same job, primarily in this instance by a self-contained computer or other special devices. To illustrate economic considerations, some estimates of price will be given in terms of the remote calculator example; this will also indicate the trends in the economics of time-sharing.

The hardware cost to the user, on a monthly rental basis, for a terminal such as the remote calculator will vary between $75 and $150 per month. This figure is based on current production techniques and on the costs of all the components that must enter into the fabrication of such a terminal. Significant reduction in this price can be achieved only through mass production of the constituent components and of the terminal itself, and it is hard to foresee even a factor of two in expense improvement. Thus there is essentially a "floor" associated with this element of cost. The costs associated with communications arise from two sources. The first is the cost of the data sets necessary both at the user's location and at the computer center. At present these total approximately $50 per month in rental, and no significant drop in these rates can be foreseen. The second element is the cost of the voice-grade telephone line itself; in this case, for local distances (i.e., where the user is located in the same city as the computer center) the monthly rate even for private line service would probably not exceed $30 and may in some cases be less. Thus, for a local dialing situation the total monthly communications costs might be on the order of $75. However, for long-distance situations the monthly transmission line costs would be much higher and in fact, except for unusual circumstances, would probably throw the economics completely out of balance, since the transmission costs themselves would far outweigh the computer and terminal hardware portions of the cost.

As seen from the above, the two factors related to the terminal hardware and the communications together represent a floor of approximately $150 to $200 per month, and it is unlikely that any dramatic improvements in these prices will be effected in the near future. Thus, the final controlling element of cost is that associated with the central computer itself. In the case of a single module of 128 remote calculators' time-sharing a 6600, and using the 5 per cent duty cycle for the prime shift on a monthly basis, it is clear that at least 5 per cent of the prime shift monthly expenses of operation of the computer center must be borne by the network of calculator users. The costs of running the center include the lease or depreciation of the computer hardware itself, and also all of the overhead expenses and labor incurred in operating and maintaining the center and the calculator network. For purposes of this discussion, it will be assumed that this operating cost is on the order of $200,000 monthly for a typical 6600 center (roughly $100,000 of this represents a typical lease price). If 5 per cent of this figure is to be spread over 128 users, it is clear that each user could be required to contribute as little as $100 per month; this amount represents a floor, based on the capability and price of 6600 class machines, for the costs associated with the computer center. It is interesting to note that this cost is almost equal to each of the other two costs, and thus terminal hardware, communications, and computer costs all contribute roughly equal amounts. The calculator user could then be billed as little as $300 per month on a flat rental basis for prime shift usage of his calculator. Note that in order to obtain this ideal, it must be possible to utilize fully the remainder of the 95 per cent of the computer center's capacity during the prime shift without interference or restriction; otherwise the calculator network would have to return more revenue to defray the computer center's operation. However, as described in the previous section, it is possible to operate a calculator network using only 5 per cent of the capacity and still operate in the remaining 95 per cent of the time without interference (and hence to produce the required revenue from other sources in that time).

It is interesting to look backward to earlier generation machines. For example, when the Control Data 1604 first went into service in the early 1960s, a typical figure for operating expense might have been from $60,000 to $70,000 monthly ($30,000 to $40,000 of which would have been the monthly lease for the computer hardware). A 1604 (which has 32K of memory and a central processing speed roughly 20 times slower than that of the 6600) could accommodate a network of 64 calculator users and still provide essentially the same type and grade of service as that given by the 6600 network that has been described in detail. However, the entire memory and the full time on the arithmetic unit would be required; thus, since the entire installation would be fully devoted to the prime shift and unavailable for any other work, during this period, the full expense of the computer center would have to be borne by the calculator network; this would amount to about $1,000 per month for each user, and would be clearly out of balance with the other two elements of cost. Looking to future machines, it is easy to foresee a significant drop in the expense represented by the computer center; as a matter of fact by 1970, mass-core memories and greater central processor speeds could reduce the required revenue per calculator to $25 per month or even less. Thus, the computer costs will actually become much less significant than the relatively fixed remote terminal and communications costs.

Returning to the example of the 6600 network, which will be a feasible economic yardstick for the years 1966 to 1970, the remote calculator service could be offered for as little as $300 monthly. To compare this with comparable service that could be obtained by a self-contained desk-size computer, one would have to design such a device that provided all the same features with equivalent turnaround on problems submitted. To do this would require a memory capable of holding a compiler (since the calculator language must be implemented by a compiler of equal capacity to the REMCOP compiler); the machine would also need sufficient stored program logic to execute the instructions generated by the compiler. With the components available in the mid-1960s, it is unlikely that such a computer could be portable and be built to market for under $30,000, which is roughly equivalent to $750 monthly. Thus, with the technology provided by the 6600 generation machines, the remote calculator application is justifiable economically as a time-sharing device and service; the same would not have been true with earlier machines, as the illustration with the 1604 indicates.

The economies and advances yet to be realized in large computers, together with new techniques in communications between central computers and networks of remote users provide an almost unlimited variety of new possibilities in "man to machine" communications. These will undoubtedly constitute the major direction of computer application and exploitation for the foreseeable future.

REFERENCES

1. Clayton, B. B., E. K. Dorff, R. E. Fagen, and J. D. Johnson: *Remote Time Sharing of a Centralized 6600*, Proc. FJCC, 1964, Spartan Books, Inc., AFIPS, vol. 26, part II, pp. 59–67.
2. Control Data Corporation: *SIPROS Import 31/Export Reference Manual*, Publication 38701600.
3. Control Data Corporation: *Time Sharing the Control Data 6600 with a Network of Control Data 6060 Remote Calculators*, Publication 100167.
4. Control Data Corporation: *6060 Remote Calculator Reference Manual*, Publication 60147900.
5. Control Data Corporation: *The Control Data 6060 Remote Calculator for Anyone with a Computational Problem*, Publication 550134.
6. Control Data Corporation: *6600 Reference Manual*, Publication 6004500B.
7. Thornton, James E.: *Parallel Operation in the Control Data 6600*, Proc. FJCC, 1964, Spartan Books, Inc., AFIPS, vol. 26, part II, pp. 33–40.
8. Control Data Corporation, *Operating System/Reference Manual, SIPROS 66*, Publication 60101800B.
9. Clayton, B. B., E. K. Dorff, and R. E. Fagen: *An Operating System and Programming System for the 6600*, Proc. FJCC, 1964, Spartan Books, Inc., AFIPS, vol. 26, part II, pp. 41–57.
10. Riordan, John: *Stochastic Service Systems*, Wiley, 1961.
11. Control Data Corporation: *Analysis and Simulation of Some Queuing Problems Arising in a Subscriber Network of Remote Calculators*, Publication 100172.

GRAPHIC DATA INPUT-OUTPUT EQUIPMENT *

C. L. Hardway

International Business Machines Corporation
Harrison, New York

3.1 Introductory Remarks

Of key importance in the design and utilization of an on-line computing system is the method by which the human operator communicates with the computer. At present there are two major approaches to the design of input-output equipment for this purpose. One widely used approach is to adapt input-output equipment used in conjunction with conventional digital computers. This involves the utilization of special typewriters and printers to facilitate written communication between man and machine. A second approach to input and output involves the utilization of graphic display devices, usually employing cathode-ray tubes. These tubes, in conjunction with sophisticated electronic devices which permit "writing" on the face of the tube, make possible a mode of man-computer communication based on pictures as well as on words and numbers.

* C. L. Hardway died in a tragic accident on September 30, 1965. The preparation of this chapter was completed by his colleagues at IBM.

The introduction of such graphic data processing—the computer-handling of geometrical figures and related data—has given computer users a powerful new tool. Display terminals and light pencils are used for almost-real-time, "conversational" communication of graphic concepts between man and computer. The capability for immediate viewing of results decreases the time and increases the soundness of decisions.

The first large-scale application of display equipment was the SAGE (Semiautomatic Ground Environment) air-defense computer system, initiated in the fifties. In this system, operators used light guns and function keys to instruct the computer, and monitored the results on display screens. Another significant development during this same period was the research undertaken by M.I.T. in Project APT (Automatically Programmed Tools). The purpose of the project was to study the use of numerical techniques to control the cutting path of a machine-driven tool. Further developments in numerical control have taken place under a cooperative program sponsored by aerospace companies. From these efforts emerged a geometry-oriented language and concepts applicable to the manipulation of graphic data. Another contribution was I. E. Sutherland's work at M.I.T. on Sketchpad, a system for man-machine communication using graphics. In Sketchpad, a man can convey data in graphic form to the computer through the cathode-ray-tube display, and receive computed results in the same manner. Of major significance is the shift from disciplined machine routines to system control by the user. Reinforcing the growing body of knowledge, Project MAC (Machine-aided Cognition or Multiaccess Computing), at M.I.T., has made significant contributions in these related fields. One of the chief objectives of the program is the development of a large, time-shared computer system. System organization concepts have been developed in both hardware and programming. More recently, the General Motors Research Laboratory announced its study on the potential use of computers in the graphic requirements of design. In all of these examples, new techniques have been developed.

Similarly, the growing sophistication in programming is significant for graphic data processing. Initially, extensive use was made of symbolic languages using tedious and time-consuming methods, all machine-oriented and used only by skilled programming personnel. Advances made in COBOL developed a business-oriented language, while FORTRAN and ALGOL were scientifically-oriented languages. APT and Sketchpad contributed geometry- and graphics-oriented languages. All of these milestones in technology and methodology play a significant role in providing a base from which graphic data processing can expand.

EQUIPMENT

3.2 Cathode-ray Tube

Cathode-ray tubes are used extensively in the design of computer display systems because of their fast response times, flexibility in the display of information, reliability, display quality, and ease of replacement.

Three commonly used methods for the formation of characters are raster scanning, character tracing, and beam forming. In raster scanning, a series of evenly spaced horizontal lines is drawn across the space to be occupied by the character. Recording of the individual lines is then achieved by unblanking or turning the beam on for the period of time required. Employing the raster scan, characters can also be created from a dot pattern. The mode of operation is similar, in that the beam is swept across the character position, with unblanking taking place at the specific point where it is desired to display the dot.

In the character-tracing technique, a somewhat different approach is taken, the character being formed by a series of continuous lines or strokes. Some character-generation systems use programmed dots in place of lines. In these systems, a fixed number of dots is used to form the character. The third class of character generation in common use today employs an etched stencil mounted in the glass-tube envelope. In this tube, the beam from the electron gun is directed through the aperture of the desired character and projected onto the tube face.

In order to assess the relative merits of the various character-generation systems, they must be related to a specific set of design parameters. One approach cannot be said to be superior to another without the inclusion of such factors as cost, maintainability, character rates and sizes, and quality.

Since the electron beam can be directed to desired positions on the tube face to form characters, it can also be used for graphic display of lines or vectors. For example, the tube face can be considered to contain a grid coordinate of 1,024 vertical by 1,024 horizontal points, or approximately one million addressable positions. To draw a vector, the beam is directed in a blanked or turned-off status to the desired beginning point of the line. There the beam is turned on and instructed to proceed in the direction desired to the end point of the line, and then turned off. Vectors can be drawn in either an absolute or relative mode.

3.3 Displays

Displays can be divided into two groups, tabletop and console. The two groups differ not only in size but also in function. Tabletop units usually have tubes of 7 to 12 inches, display 100 to 1,000 characters, and are used primarily for alphameric applications. Console displays can be larger (tubes of 16 to 21 inches), display up to 4,000 characters, and have varying degrees of graphic capability.

Both the tabletop and console displays use the same building blocks: a cathode-ray tube, some method of regenerating the data display to overcome phosphor decay, some device for drawing graphic or character data on the face of the tube, a computer interface, and various interaction devices such as keyboards and a light pen. These elements are carefully integrated to provide the desired performance. The image on the cathode-ray tube must be regenerated at a rate usually in excess of 30 cycles per second. The regeneration speed necessary is dependent upon many factors, including the persistence of the phosphor, ambient light level in the viewing room, and intensity level of the electron beam.

Most display equipment regenerates in the range between 30 and 40 cycles per second, using some type of memory device to provide the repetitive data for this regeneration cycle. These memories fall into two general groups: random access and cyclic. Core memory is used wherever random access is required. Some display devices regenerate directly from processor storage over a data channel, while others have a separate, local magnetic-core buffer provided expressly for this purpose.

When central processing unit (CPU) storage is used to regenerate the display, the computer program and the display have direct access to the same data stored in CPU memory. There is, however, memory-cycle interference between the display unit and the CPU. Since the display may be considered to be running continuously, there can be a constant drain on the CPU memory which becomes very acute when multiple consoles are attached. Separate core-storage buffers relieve the CPU of this regeneration load and provide independent, random-access storage to the display devices.

When cyclic devices are used for regeneration, they are independent from CPU storage; devices used include magnetic drums, disk drives, and delay lines. The choice of a cyclic buffer usually implies synchronous display operation. Each data element coming from the buffer is available in a fixed-time interval and must be displayed in a fixed-time interval.

Capacity, speed, and cost are the important criteria used in the selection of a buffer. Once the selection is made, it affects other operating characteristics of the display. For console displays, core buffers using 4, 8, and 16K characters are available, as well as drums with a capacity of more than 60K words. For the smaller tabletop displays, small core arrays of 100 to 200 characters, or delay lines are sometimes used to maintain the 30- to 40-cycle regeneration rates required. Character generation is available in rates ranging from 20,000 to 110,000 characters per second. The interfacing element provides attachment to the CPU and its design is dependent upon CPU channel configuration and device-buffering configuration to provide adequate data rates between the two.

The final components required for the console are the interaction elements. They include various keyboards, light pens, and shaft position encoders, to name a few. Keyboards are available in various forms, including alphameric, numeric, standard typewriter and function key configurations. They all function basically the same. A single-key depression is translated into some form of data. However, they differ in how the data are handled once a key is depressed.

An alphameric keyboard signal may be fed directly into the CPU across the computer interface, a single character at a time, the instant it is depressed; or these key data may be stored, displayed, assembled into complete messages, and then transmitted to the CPU upon operator command. The application for which the console is intended determines the type of keyboard attached. Function keyboards give display consoles great flexibility. Program-defined operations are tied directly to a single-key depression.

Most tabletop display devices have keyboards available for data entry. In addition to various keyboard configurations, the larger consoles have light pens. The light pen allows the operator to point to any part of the display for identification by the CPU and to draw lines and other figures on the tube face. The light pen consists of a penlike tube which houses a photosensitive device that senses the light displayed on the face of the cathode-ray tube. This light signal is usually converted to a time reference in order to identify some specific display element or location on the tube face. With this information, the program can determine the spot where the light pen is pointed. Light pens are available in various degrees of functional complexity. The simpler forms allow the operator to point to some existing data on the face of the tube to be identified by the program. More elaborate light-pen configurations allow a complete drawing and tracking capability. Tracking can be performed by the hardware or program, or some combination of the two. When hardware is used to perform the tracking function of the light pen, updating is executed at 50 to 100 times a second, which allows pen motion at a rate of 10 to 20 inches per second across the face of the tube. This auxiliary equipment relieves the CPU of the time-consuming task of track updating.

Shaft-position encoder is another common console input device. Many functions to be performed cn the display, such as scale change and rotation of the image, are conveniently controlled by use of a control knob. This control provides a read-out of the angular position of the shaft, which can be read by the computer. The shaft rotations are thus translated into some digital value that provides a basis of control for this scaling and rotation of the displays. In addition, there are a great many devices such as joy sticks and spheres to allow random positioning of a

Fig. 3.1 Display station (design model).

spot or cross hair on the face of the tube.   All of these elements—cathode-ray tube, regeneration-buffer, drawing and character-writing capability, computer interface, and man-machine interaction devices—are carefully integrated to provide the desired performance.   The operator seated in front of his display has direct access to a powerful computer and a central filing system.   Figure 3.1 depicts a tabletop display; Fig. 3.2 illustrates a console model.

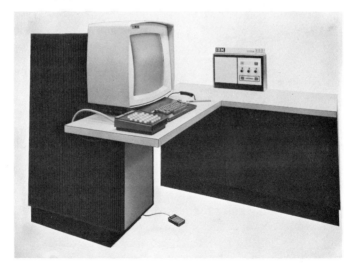

Fig. 3.2 Console display.

3.4 Recorders

A recorder provides a method for permanently recording, in graphic and alphameric form, the output of a computer. It does this by exposing photosensitive films or papers to light. The basic elements of a recorder are a control unit, a cathode-ray tube, and a cameralike device for recording the image. The control unit acts as interface to the data source and converts the incoming digital pulses to analog signals for control of cathode-ray-tube beam motion. Through this controlled movement of the electron beam over the tube face, and the capability to expose light-sensitive materials at specified locations, recorders approach the versatility of manual methods in the presentation of alphameric and graphic data. Moreover, recorders are able to accomplish these tasks at computer-compatible speeds.

To achieve this flexibility, a number of factors have to be considered by the design engineer and trade-offs made to suit the recorder to customer requirements. Thus, a particular recorder will contain those features necessary for its intended applications. Precision cathode-ray tubes in the 5- to 7-inch size are used to provide the best combination of a small spot, uniform spot diameter, and even light output as the beam traverses the tube face. By this cathode-ray-tube selection, it is possible to record data in detailed form and to maintain the uniformity in appearance essential for acceptance of output by the user.

To overcome beam distortion in the outer portion of the tube, a reduced area providing a higher-quality image is selected. For example, on 5-inch tubes, a 3-inch square is considered usable for purposes of quality production. The usable area is divided into a coordinate grid system of 1024 or 4096 horizontal and vertical addressable positions, providing considerable versatility in locating the beam on the tube face. Whether a 1024 or 4096 matrix is selected is dependent upon the degree of precision required in recording a spot in a specific location on the tube face, and other factors such as compatibility with scanning systems.

Versatility in the presentation of the data is achieved by a variety of methods. For example, it is possible to expand or reduce the spot size, providing selectable line widths for emphasis of certain portions of the recorded data. In a similar manner, the light-beam intensity can be increased or reduced to provide different line densities. In selecting the spot size, the user must allow for ultimate spot or line width where there is an intent to magnify the recorded data. Similar care must be taken in choosing a recording medium which will faithfully reproduce the desired spot or line densities. In the recording of characters, selection is usually made from a character set of 64 symbols. These include alphabetic characters, numerals, and grammatical and special symbols. In those

Fig. 3.3 Film recorder (design model).

applications where this is a limitation, particularly in the use of special symbols, the equipment designer will provide for a 128-character set.   As an alternative, the user can choose the line-drawing mode of operation and create characters and symbols as needed.   Additional features usually available to increase versatility in the presentation of textural material are selectable character heights, densities, and orientations.   From these choices, the user has wide latitude in the presentation of his data and can produce aesthetically acceptable results.

The generation rates are a function of the symbol generator used in a particular recorder, and the speed of the circuitry associated with the cathode-ray tube.   Here again, decisions must be made to balance quality of output and speed with the particular character-generation method selected or available.   Character-generation rates can vary from 10,000 to 110,000 characters per second and vector or line-drawing speeds range from 5 to 140 kc.   Figure 3.3 represents a film-type recorder.

3.5   Scanners

The function of the scanner is just the reverse of that of the recorder. The input to the scanner is the graphic image on film or paper, and the output is a string of bits, a digital representation of the image which can be operated on by a digital computer.

A film scanner can use much of the same hardware as a film recorder. The same cathode-ray tube and optics can be used to focus a spot of light onto the film.   The density of the emulsion at that point on the film determines how much of the light is transmitted through film. This transmitted light can be sensed by a photomultiplier tube. In the case of a paper scanner, the photomultiplier will sense reflected instead of transmitted light.

In either case, the information at one point on the image is converted into an electrical signal. The digitization of this signal is a function of the types of inputs the scanner is meant to handle. If photographs are to be scanned and it is important to retain the gray tones, then the electrical signals are converted into as many as 64 or more levels. If engineering drawings are to be scanned where the information is contained in black lines on a white background, it is only necessary to decide whether or not the light transmitted through or reflected from a particular spot exceeds a given threshold. Because the density of the lines and background varies from drawing to drawing, the threshold should be variable. If the threshold is variable under computer control, the feedback loop is complete and the threshold can be adjusted by the program according to the results of the scanning.

If a continuous line is to be followed, it is possible to predict from the previously accumulated data where the next scans should be performed in order to minimize the total number of scans per graphic record. This is equivalent to closing another feedback loop, since positioning is now a function of the scanning results.

The cathode-ray-tube scanners which are commercially available are

Fig. 3.4 Film scanner (design model).

two-level scanners. The number of addressable points varies from 1,000 to 16,000 in each dimension. The ratio of spot width to record size is roughly one in 2,000. Reading speeds vary from 20,000 to 160,000 bits per second. A typical model of a scanner is shown in Fig. 3.4.

SYSTEM CONSIDERATIONS

3.6 Configurations

A broad spectrum of system configurations can be formed with graphic data processing equipment currently available. Typical configurations are:

1. The system under control of a single application program, utilizing one console. The console is used primarily as a monitor but is occasionally used to stop the program and make changes in the data, or to allow the user to inject his own judgment at a decision point.

2. The system under control of a single application program, utilizing multiple consoles. Each console user is concerned with a unique set of data, but all require the services of the same program. An example is parts programming for numerical control. Each console user is describing a different part, but all have the need to perform the same calculations.

3. The system control switched between a foreground program and a background program. The foreground program services one or more consoles but does not utilize the full processing capacity of the system. When it becomes necessary for the foreground program to wait for the user at the console, control is transferred to the background program. When the foreground program is ready to be serviced, control is switched back.

4. System control switched between multiple application programs. Higher-priority applications are given control over lower-priority applications. The number of consoles used by a program is dependent on the application requirements.

5. A special program called a "systems supervisor" switches control from a program waiting for the user at the console to a program ready to be serviced. Supervisors have been designed which give each user the appearance of receiving continuous service.

3.7 Methodologies

A number of basic programming methodologies have been developed to facilitate processing graphic information in computer systems designed to handle numbers. One of the most fundamental steps in developing a graphics application is to define how the information, like that shown in

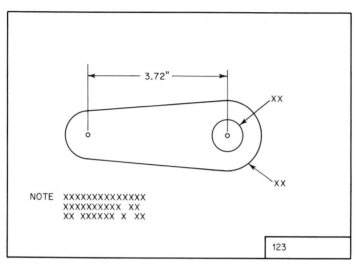

Fig. 3.5 Engineering drawing.

Fig. 3.5, will be represented inside the system. This definition depends upon the information essential to the application and the operations to be performed on it. Any methodology for representing graphic information rests on:

1. The method used to represent graphic elements
2. The method used to represent relationships between graphic elements

Basic graphic elements easily identified are points, lines, circles, and arcs. Some applications do not use all of these elements; other applications require additional elements, such as conics and cubic splines. Some applications require that elements be viewed as residing in a three-dimensional space, that is, points defined with x, y, and z coordinates.

The relationships between graphic elements can be divided into four classes. These classes, with typical examples, are:

1. Topological relationships.
   - *a.* Connectivity. Two elements are connected when they have one or more defining points in common.
   - *b.* Closure. A figure is closed when it is formed from a connected chain of elements which terminate at the starting point.
   - *c.* Inside-Outside. An element is inside or outside of a closed figure.
2. Geometric relationships.
   - *a.* A line can be horizontal.
   - *b.* Two lines can be parallel.

    c. Two lines can be perpendicular.

    d. Three points can be colinear.

3. Numeric relationships.

    a. The distance between two points is a specified value.

    b. The radius of a circle is a specified value.

    c. The angle between two lines is a specified value.

4. Set-Subset relationships.

    a. A set of elements share a common property; e.g., outline.

    b. A set of elements is a subset of a larger collection.

A variety of data-representation methodologies has been successfully adapted to handling graphic information. These methodologies are of two general types. The first type gives an implicit representation to the relationships between the elements. For example, the fact that two lines are parallel is carried implicitly in the coordinate values of the end points of the two lines. This technique of representing graphic information either discards the original definition of the graphic element or saves it in a secondary storage area. The second type of methodology gives an explicit representation to the relationships between the graphic elements.

The methodology used depends upon the application requirements, since the two types reflect a trade-off between memory requirements and processing requirements. For example, the second type is used when the application requires significant analysis and manipulation of graphic relationships. Suppose we have reached the point in the development of an application depicted in Fig. 3.6. The graphic information to be handled by the system has been defined, and the way it will be represented in the system has been specified. The internal representation of the information is referred to as the model or the data base.

The next major step is to define how the information in the source document will be entered into the system. Several methodologies for this purpose have been developed. One uses language statements patterned after numerical control languages such as APT. The statements can be written on a data sheet, key-punched, and then read into the system, or they can be keyed-in through an on-line keyboard associated with the display console. This last approach provides for immediate visual feedback which greatly reduces the job time.

The use of some graphic languages tends to focus the user's thinking on the mechanics of drawing graphic data with a numerically controlled pen. The graphic information is implicit in the statement. It is quite analogous to a person being forced to concentrate on *how* to write, i.e., on the mechanics of moving the pencil rather than on the message that he wants to convey.

Another method for entering graphic information uses console pro-

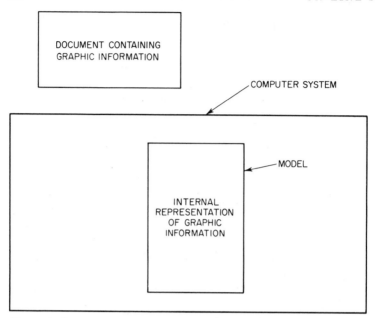

Fig. 3.6 Document representation.

cedures instead of language statements. These procedures are composed of actions, executed by the user at the console. Because of the flexibility of the light pen, programmed function keys, and alphameric keyboard, console procedures are easily designed to meet the requirements of different applications.

Procedures have been designed which allow the user to express himself with actions closely resembling sketching or working at a drafting board. Once the console procedures have been defined, the computer is programmed to monitor the actions of the console user, interpret them, and arrange the information in the model. Although writing this program requires detailed knowledge of computer instructions and data formats, the user does not have to be concerned with these details. He works with the application-oriented procedures designed for his use.

Furthermore, properly designed programs will display information on the console which guides the user in how to use the facilities which have been programmed. This communication back and forth between the system and the user is referred to as "conversational" mode. The program should be written to display in a meaningful way the information being entered by the user. Then, if an error is made, corrective action can be taken immediately.

An input methodology, not so well developed as language statements and console procedures, utilizes optical scanning of the source document.

The information required by the application is extracted from the scan data and then stored in the model.

The various input methodologies allow us to add to the diagram as illustrated in Fig. 3.7.

Another essential methodology is concerned with generating graphic output. This is accomplished by a set of routines which are designed to extract the necessary information from the data base and generate the orders required by the graphic device. The graphic orders are transmitted to the graphic control unit buffer for execution. In the case of cathode-ray-tube displays, the orders are executed 30 to 40 times per second. The display routines are initiated from statements in the language or console procedures. This is shown in Fig. 3.8. There is a display subroutine for each type of graphic element in the data base. The display routines include the facility to change scale, translate, and/or rotate the data on the display. A combination of scaling and translating gives the user a detailed look into the data base.

Two points should be noted. The graphic information is represented in two different places in two different formats: in the data base and

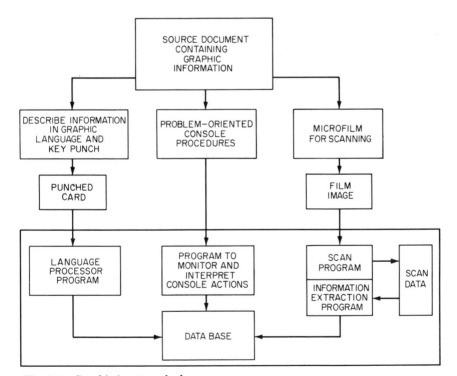

Fig. 3.7 Graphic input methods.

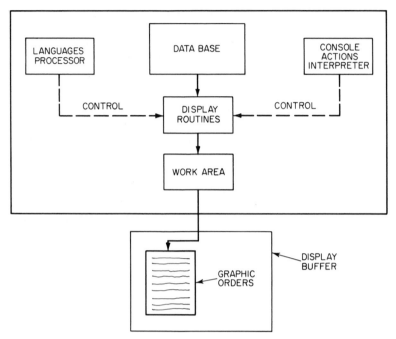

Fig. 3.8   Graphic output methods.

in the display buffer in the form of graphic orders.   Although the precision and range with which points are defined is limited in the display buffer, this limitation does not apply to the data base.   There numerical values are expressed in floating-point form and, if necessary, double-precision floating point.   The precision for critical dimensions is obtained by entering these values through the numeric keyboard.

The data base is formatted and organized to facilitate processing by a digital computer.   Data in the data base are all but incomprehensible to human beings.   The most effective way for man to see and understand the data base is to display it on a graphic console.

Console procedures depend heavily on the use of the light pen for indicating, to the program, elements which are to be processed, changed, or used in some way.   The element detected by the light pen is on the display; the data to be used by the program are in the data base.   Therefore effective use of light pens depends upon a methodology for backtracking from the displayed element to the associated information in the data base.   This methodology can be described by reference to Fig. 3.9.

In order to provide a backtracking capability, it is necessary to add to the display routines the function of building a cross-reference table.   This table contains the base address of the element in the data base, and

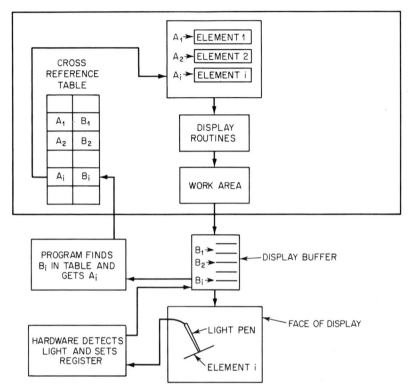

Fig. 3.9   Computer interpretation of operator action.

the base address of the graphic orders in the buffer which generates the display of the element on the face of the screen.

When the light pen is active and senses the light generated by the cathode-ray tube as it draws the element, the buffer-address register is set with the address, B_i, of the order which is being executed. This address is made available to a program which finds the address, B_i, in the cross-reference table and, with it, the address, A_i, of the master data in the data base. The value, A_i, is given to the program which will operate on the data in the data base indicated by the light pen.

3.8   Application Programs

So far, we have discussed methodologies for getting graphic information into a system and back out again. The purpose of entering information into the system depends on the application. Figure 3.10 shows how the application routines are related to the other program routines already described.

The application program operates on data in the data base. It can be

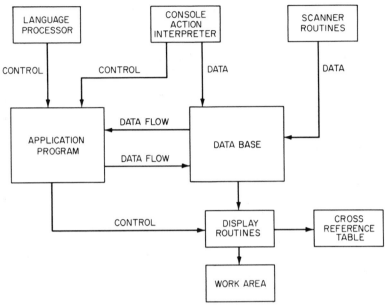

Fig. 3.10   Application program relationships.

controlled from language statements or console procedures. The results of the calculations may be stored back in the data base, or they may be printed out or stored in some other way. The application program also can produce graphic output by passing the necessary control information to the display routines. The arrangement of program modules in the system allows for more than one application from the same data base.

It is important, when designing multiple-console application programs, to have the consoles share the same copy of the program. The alternative is to make copies of the program for each console and treat them as independent applications. This places an unnecessary demand on memory requirements or the system supervisor.

Programs and routines can be shared by independent users if they are so written that they are either serially reusable or can be reentered. Serially reusable routines are self-initializing. Therefore, a second user cannot begin to use such a routine until the first user is finished. Routines which can be reentered do not modify themselves. Therefore, two users can use the routine without affecting each other.

3.9 Summary

An extensive background in hardware and programming technology has been gained in the use of console equipment. Direct man-machine communications through the use of graphic techniques has been amply demonstrated. Geometry-oriented languages are available and procedures have been developed for manipulation of graphic data.

System organization concepts have evolved, making possible a variety of system configurations using currently available hardware. Selection can be from a single display device to a fully integrated multiconsole installation.

Programming methodologies are being designed for representing, entering, displaying, and recording graphic information in computer systems. The specific equipment and methodologies to be used depend upon the application.

REFERENCES

1. Coons, S. A.: An Outline of the Requirements for a Computer-aided Design System, AFIPS, 1963, *Spring Joint Computer Conference Proceedings*, pp. 299–304.
2. Stotz, R.: Man-machine Console Facilities for Computer-aided Design, AFIPS, 1963, *Spring Joint Computer Conference Proceedings*, pp. 323–328.
3. Sutherland, I. E.: Sketchpad, a Man-machine Graphical Communication System, AFIPS, 1963, *Spring Joint Computer Conference Proceedings*, pp. 329–346.
4. Johnson, T. E.: Sketchpad III: A Computer Program for Drawing in Three Dimensions, AFIPS, 1963, *Spring Joint Computer Conference Proceedings*, pp. 347–353.
5. Howard, J. H. (ed.): *Electronic Information Display Systems*, Spartan Books, Inc., 1963.
6. Gomolak, L. S.: Better and Faster Design by Machine, *Electronics Magazine*, June 1, 1964.
7. Start Planning for the New Output Techniques, *EDP Analyzer*, Canning Publications, June, 1964.
8. Hargreaves, B., J. D. Joyce, and G. L. Cole: Image Processing Hardware for a Man-machine Graphical Communication System, AFIPS, 1964, *Fall Joint Computer Conference Proceedings*, pp. 363–386.
9. Jacks, E. L.: A Laboratory for the Study of Graphical Man-machine Communication, AFIPS, 1964, *Fall Joint Computer Conference Proceedings*, pp. 343–350.
10. *On-line Computing Systems*, Proceedings of the Symposium sponsored by the University of California at Los Angeles and Informatics Inc., Feb. 2–4, 1965.
11. Corbin, H. S.: A Survey of CRT Display Consoles, *Control Engineering*, vol. 12, pp. 77–83, December, 1965.

THE
ECONOMICS
OF
ON-LINE
SYSTEMS*

Walter F. Bauer
Informatics, Inc.
Sherman Oaks, California

4.1 Introductory Remarks

The subject of economics pervades all aspects of on-line computer operation. In fact the entire philosophy of time-shared computations is based upon the recognition that one or a small number of users cannot efficiently utilize a large central processor and would thus be motivated by economic concerns. It is not surprising, therefore, that virtually every chapter in this text contains at least a brief section dealing with the economic aspects of the specific topic under discussion. At the same time, it is important and useful to take a broader look at the economic question, to formulate certain general and comprehensive approaches, and to attempt to profit from past experience. This chapter begins with a brief review of the motivations and objectives of cost-effectiveness analy-

* The writer is indebted to William B. Moore, Rome Air Development Center; Jules Schwartz, System Development Corporation, and Robert L. Patrick, private consultant, for giving freely of their time to discuss the subject. The facts and opinions they provided were useful and stimulating.

ses. This is followed by a detailed discussion of the relative economic advantages and disadvantages of batch processing and of on-line processing. Economic factors entering into system design and scheduling are next considered. The chapter closes with five sections devoted to cost analyses of on-line hardware and software.

Most writings, both formal and informal, on the subject of economics of on-line systems have originated from System Development Corporation and from the Massachusetts Institute of Technology. These discussions, however, are not specifically oriented toward cost and effectiveness, but touch upon these matters in the description of the design of specific systems. There are two papers[1,2] which deal explicitly with the problem of economics. These papers, as well as the various articles and reports listed at the end of the chapter, form a background to the present discussion.

4.2 Motivations and Objectives

Some observers might present the interesting argument that cost-effectiveness analyses are useless because the *convenience* of the user is the important factor. They would point out that our culture is oriented toward convenience and that, as an example, the automobile automatic transmission would never have come into use if there had been a prior requirement for a cost-effectiveness justification.

An investigation of the development of these "convenience" items in our culture would probably disclose something along the following lines. The capability or feature is first a luxury item—no more than a convenience factor for which some are willing to pay a substantial price. Later the costs of manufacture and of application begin to approach the costs of the "conventional" approach. This will undoubtedly happen in on-line computing. In the near future, it will not be significantly more expensive to obtain a computer which has the special hardware features for efficient on-line systems work than to obtain one without these features. Also, the on-line system software will be produced almost as inexpensively as batch-processing software. Indeed, the future may see little difference between the costs and complexity of the batch-processing and on-line systems.

One cannot "prove" once and for all the economic advantages of on-line systems. In general, the parameters and factors involved in the application environment are so many and varied that one cannot arrive at a quantitative overall proof. However, for a given environment and a given set of application parameters, one can provide a set of powerful arguments which build a strong case for or against the on-line system. The principles involved can be examined carefully. The parameters and factors can be isolated and their implications understood. In many cases, all factors can be reduced to dollars and comparisons made in terms of two or three quantities representing two or three basic approaches.

In many cases, the user objectives and requirements for the system are such that the on-line character of the system is, for all practical purposes, mandatory. There is no other way of meeting the requirements. Examples of such systems are travel reservation systems, command and control systems, and stock quotation systems. These systems have the common requirement that the user have ready access to the data in the machine; the answers would be of little use if he had to wait the minutes or hours required of batch processing. Therefore, in these cases, the question is not whether batch processing or on-line processing is better. Rather, the question immediately becomes one of the best design of the on-line system.

However, there are many systems where a choice exists. Many of the early systems were designed to solve sophisticated equations of mathematics and physics. If a system were designed, for example, to be of specific use in the solution of nonlinear integro-differential equations, the question immediately arises as to what percentage of the time the computer is to be used for the solution of such equations. Another question which arises is the importance of the timeliness of such solutions in view of the fact that batch systems can—given enough time—provide the answers.

The economics of on-line systems can be examined from four main points of view. These four viewpoints make up the four major sections of this chapter. One of these is to examine the comparative costs of batch processing and on-line processing, assuming that the applications lend themselves to a choice. This would be of primary interest to those planning equipment, software or systems which may involve either type of approach or combinations of both. Still another point of view is the examination of the relationship between technical design and economics. Of course, all technical design, in the final analysis, is oriented toward optimizing cost-effectiveness, but frequently designs are made with evaluation parameters remaining removed from costs. A third viewpoint is hardware and software costs—the examination of the various cost factors in implementing and running systems. A fourth is cost and pricing—the business side of on-line systems—which deals with accounting methods and how customers should be, or might be, charged for their service.

The systems which are mostly considered are of a general-purpose nature. In fact, some authors have used the phrase "generalized time-sharing systems" to describe them.

BATCH VERSUS ON - LINE PROCESSING

4.3 Fundamental Consideration

Batch processing is the conventional way of using the computer. Nearly all computer processing today is performed by batch processing. Batch processing consists of collecting input data, information queries, and production-run requests, including compilations, and performing them as a collection. On-line processing is, in a sense, the opposite. As one writer[1] put it, on-line processing is like doing batch processing where the batch size is one. In view of these facts, it is appropriate to compare batch processing and on-line processing, focusing on all of the similarities and differences, the arguments for and the arguments against.

A point of departure in a discussion such as this is to review some of the fundamentals of on-line systems as compared with batch-processing systems. In a recent nonprofessional magazine which reported on the new revolution in on-line systems, some ridiculous statements were made. In referring to the sharply reduced data-processing costs attributed to on-line systems, it was stated that on-line operation would cost "$325 for 25 hours per month on a 7040 computer that would normally rent for $14,000 per month." The writer, with apparently no background in computers, was confusing *console* time with main processor time. He apparently did not realize that in the on-line system, the user shares the computer with many, many others during his 25 hours per month. For the lay public, such a mistake is understandable; for the professional, it is inexcusable.

The fundamental fact, therefore, that one must keep in mind about time-sharing systems is that the computer is being *shared* with many others who are essentially using the computer simultaneously. With 100 users using the computer in the same general way, each user has, over any given period of time, essentially a computer of $1/100$ the speed of the time-shared computer. In fact, the capability is $1/100$, less that percentage of computer time which is devoted to overhead and to supporting or nonproductive operations such as scheduling. In the above case of the 7040 computer, instead of paying $14,000 per month rental, the user is actually paying $2,222 times the number of people with whom he is sharing the computer. That is, if he shares the computer with 10 others, he would pay the equivalent of $22,220 per month, for this is how much he would have to pay to get the amount of computer time equal to one shift's worth of computing, or 172 hours of computer time. The figures become even worse for the user being charged $325 for 25 hours per month, when one considers the losses in efficiency due to overhead.

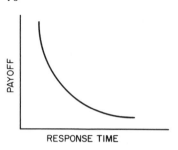
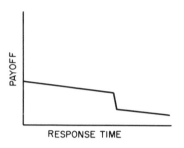

Fig. 4.1   Payoff functions comparison.

Another point frequently missed in comparing batch with on-line is that the casual user or the user who needs only a fraction of a shift is not required to pay for the idle time. One of the advantages of on-line systems is that the user pays only according to how much time he uses, and the system owners or operators pay for the idle time; the latter must speculate on the amount of use of the system. In the event of a cooperative cost-shared system, the users pay for all idle time probably through usage experience schedules which will correct or modify nominal usage rates. However, in a commercial system, the owners will pay for the unused time in terms of a reduction in profits. The user who is not sure his computing needs will take up a shift or more of the computer he needs, benefits by using or being a customer of an on-line system. There is, therefore, advantage to the casual or small user.

R. L. Patrick[1] has suggested an approach to the question of on-line versus batch systems. He suggests that the entire question revolves around the characteristic of the payoff function. He cites two types of payoff functions as shown in Fig. 4.1. In the first case, a short-response time produces a very great payoff. If the stockbroker can answer a question about stock prices quickly, he has impressed his customer and his chances of making a sale are enhanced. If the payoff function looks like the second diagram of Fig. 4.1, there is no advantage in a quick response, and one might just as well batch the data requests. An application with this type of payoff function is a payroll computation or a set of such computations.

4.4   Arguments Pro and Con

In making the choice between on-line and batch processing, there are a number of factors in favor of the on-line approach and a number in favor of the batch approach. It is instructive to enumerate the factors on each side of the fulcrum and examine each briefly.

Figure 4.2 shows the factors favoring and inveighing against on-line systems. To decide in favor of on-line versus batch implies that efficiency and flexibility factors on the part of the user and with respect to the machine outweigh the increased costs for the computer software, for consoles, and for the communication system. The increases in the systems costs for on-line are discussed in Secs. 4.11 and 4.12. The following paragraphs discuss some of the factors noted in favor of on-line operation.

First and foremost, there is the factor of "user efficiency." One of the best understood processes which accrues increased efficiency is the on-line programming or the debugging of programs on-line. Although there seem to be few carefully documented studies of this, one writer[3] claims efficiency increases for on-line debugging of 3:1 to 5:1.* The advantages of approaching the computer at any time are easy to appreciate, especially in the case of requests which involve only a small amount of computer time. Imagine the inefficiency of a busy executive who had to compress all of his telephone calls into 2 one-half hour periods—one in the morning and one in the afternoon!

In addition to the efficiency of the user, there is an efficiency referred to as "large-computer efficiency." This refers to the fact that one hour of computing on a high-speed computer costs less than 10 hours of computing on a much smaller computer which runs 10 times slower. The cost per computation, in other words, is less on the larger machine than it is on the smaller. In time-sharing, the user gets the advantage of this cost-capability relationship. Even if no other factors were present, it is likely that he would find the sharing of the large computer more advantageous than having his own smaller computer.

Application flexibility refers to the ability to have a "small" machine or a "large" machine, depending upon the problem requirements. The time-sharing user can use the machine along with 100 other users and,

* Mr. W. Moore of the USAF Rome Air Development Center has informed the writer of a military system in a classified application where user efficiency increased by the ratio 7:1.

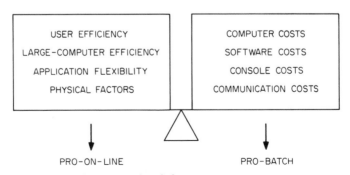

Fig. 4.2 On-line versus batch factors.

therefore, use only $\frac{1}{100}$ of the capacity. However, if he has a production problem which can be run during the off hours, he can have the equivalent of 100 users or, in other words, the entire machine. The systems programming remains the same, and he need not take his problem to a new location to realize the benefits. In other words, the time-shared computer can reconfigure itself to be a small machine to many or a large machine to only a few.

The physical factors representing an advantage for on-line systems should not be overlooked. The user of the time-shared system need not worry about air conditioning, space, and the like. He need only have a room in his office area for an operating console. In addition, he saves the cost of traveling to and from the computer in the event the computer must be located remotely from him.

4.5 Input and Interrogation

One of the advantages which is so often overlooked in comparing on-line and batch systems is the process of preparing input to the computer. Whether that input is to be prepared for the files of the computer or whether that input constitutes a command to the computer system or a request, there are significant advantages in inputting the information directly as in an on-line system as compared with batch processing which nominally consists of punching and verifying cards.

Figure 4.3 shows the conventional procedure in inputting data to a computer and having that request fulfilled. As shown on the figure, there are many people and many processes which are involved. Forms must be completed, cards must be punched and verified, the information must be dispatched correctly, and there are administrative processes to be done such as logging and recording. In an on-line system, the computer does almost all of these tasks. In other words, the man at the console can effectively be the "consumer" of the figure, and he need be the only one in the chain. The request can be made in an application-oriented language and the computer can output the requests for user consumption. Key-punching is accomplished effectively through the user-operator keying-in the data by means of the application-oriented language. Data verification is done by the computer's reflecting back to the user on the cathode-ray-tube scope exactly what has been inputted, or a restatement of the input information. The computer, of course, can perform all of the logging and recording operations. The communications system and the remote console take care of routing the information to the user. Furthermore, a properly designed system will result in fewer input errors than a conventional system since, for one thing, there are fewer steps necessary.

In order to fix the ideas, the reader is invited to consider, as an example,

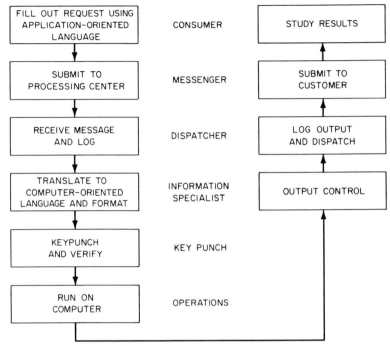

Fig. 4.3   Conventional procedure in request fulfillment.

the process of making modifications to an insurance policy or recording
the data pertinent to that policy, such as premium payments, rates, and
the like.   One of the people responsible for keeping the information
correctly filed in the computer can receive the information from source
documents (perhaps a letter from the insured) or information which he
has received verbally over the telephone.   He inputs the data directly
into the console by electronically filling out a form which the computer
provides on the cathode-ray tube.   The details of the remaining operations which the computer can perform on behalf of the input process are
straightforward, and are left as an exercise for the reader.

4.6   Operating and Implementing Experience

Comparing quantitative values such as costs and efficiency factors for
batch systems and on-line systems under comparable conditions is a
difficult, almost impossible matter.   One simply does not design and
fully implement an on-line system for a given set of requirements and
then design and implement a batch system for the same set of requirements.   Such controlled experiments and comparative systems are
almost out of the question since they are so prohibitive in cost, and are
not likely to prove anything for a wide spectrum of computer applica-

tions in any event. The best that one can hope for in comparing a batch system with an on-line system is detailed studies and analyses enhanced by simulation to ensure practical handling of all factors.

Experience with the time-sharing system at System Development Corporation (SDC) indicates the following percentages of use of the machine: 60 to 70 per cent computation; 20 per cent swap time; 5 per cent overhead; the remainder un-overlapped I/O. It is pointed out that the 70 per cent computation figure is comparable to the percentage of "green-light" time or run time in a batch system. However, defenders of the batch system are quick to point out that one only pays for green-light time, and of course, in an on-line system, the computer is actively working during the remaining 30 per cent of the time, performing overhead and indirect support of the basic computation. Therefore, these figures are, unfortunately, inconclusive. The 60 to 70 per cent production time, however, is remarkably high in consideration of the newness of the system design and the fact that the computer at SDC was in no way designed for time-sharing. In fact, one improvement will soon be made: the 20 per cent swap time will be reduced to 5 per cent with dynamic relocatability hardware to be soon added. This will result in a production level of 75 to 85 per cent which, in view of the potential benefits, would seem to cast a heavy vote in favor of the on-line system.

Hardware and software costs for on-line systems are discussed in more detail in sections 4.11 and 4.12. However, a few remarks are appropriate here. One of these is that all knowledgeable and experienced software-system designers agree that a sophisticated batch system is as expensive as an on-line system. Unfortunately, most people in examining costs compare the on-line system with its large amount of sophistication, as they are planning it, with a batch system which was planned and implemented years ago, and which is obsolete even compared with today's batch-processing technology.

Still another comment is that the costs of implementing on-line systems software will be greatly reduced over the next two to three years. The increase in efficiency in implementing systems of this type is remarkable. Consider, for example, that in 1956 it took 20 man-years to develop the first FORTRAN compiler. A FORTRAN compiler now can be assembled in 2 man-years.

DESIGN CONSIDERATIONS

4.7   Design Factors and Economics

One cannot proceed very far in exploring the economics of on-line systems without turning attention to the design of the system and the relation of that design to system economics. If on-line operation is deemed essential in the application, then the attention immediately turns to design factors. Also, if preliminary studies show that on-line systems have advantages, either economic or noneconomic, over batch systems, then again, the subject turns to one of the system design. There is little doubt that design and system economics are inextricably related; indeed, system design is performed in terms of the system economics.

The following is a reasonable statement of the overall system design problem: to design the system so as to obtain the maximum usage and efficiency of people and computing equipment in view of the total money spent.

Some of the factors involved in this design are cost of labor, cost of response delay, machine costs, and software-system costs. However, the study of system design quickly gravitates to considerations of efficiency of machine-usage and system-configuration factors. The various costs mentioned earlier do, of course, figure heavily in examining machine usage and system configuration. Before discussing the problem of system design, it is necessary to fix a number of definitions which will be used in the discussion.

User refers to a person actively using the system at a console. He may be, at any given instant of time, not actively giving to or receiving from the machine information; however, he is in attendance at the console and has registered "in" with the system. *Number of users* refers to the number of such active participants. *User stations* refers to the number of consoles at which users can sit and make use of the system. The number of stations, obviously, is equal to or greater than the number of users. *Response time* refers to the time from actuation of a key at a console to the time that a meaningful result occurs as a result of that key actuation. The results can be a cathode-ray-tube display or an output of another type. The type of response may vary from simply repeating an alphanumeric character in typewriter fashion or, at the other end of the spectrum, it may refer to the time from program initiation during checkout to the time when meaningful results of that checkout have been obtained and have been displayed or otherwise produced for the user. It is important to understand that response time does not normally refer to the time of completion of production runs. It is normally the time associated with attendance by a user or operator at the console as he awaits meaningful results. *Computer efficiency* refers to that fraction of the computer time (usually main frame or main processor time) that is used directly in behalf of producing usable results for the user or console operator. *Computer time* can be split into two general types: "direct" and "overhead." Direct computer time refers to the activities in direct support of the user or console operator. Overhead refers to all others. Therefore, determining the contents of a register is a direct usage of the system, whereas the system processing required to allow the system to decide which user to turn its attention to next is of the "overhead" type. Other examples of "direct" are any computations performed in program debugging and, of course, any production run.

Utilizing the preceding definitions, a statement of on-line system design is as follows: To maximize the number of users within the constraints of staying within a certain maximum response time for all users and maintaining a machine efficiency greater than some minimum. This definition warrants some examination.

In the above statement of the problem, the "number of users" can refer either to the average number of active users being currently served by the computer, or it can refer to the number of console stations (users) which are being serviced with sufficient rapidity not to incur any loss of efficiency of the user. The result would be the same for the two quantities. The number of active users (n) and the number of service console stations (N) are related; they depend on the programming staff procedures, the problem mix, and the amount and quality of the debugging aids made available on the system. The ratio N/n will be large if the users must do a great deal of cogitation to determine the next steps to be taken. In the case where a very large percentage of the problems being encountered by the time-shared system are on-line debugging, then a large ratio N/n could imply that the programmers are not efficient or that the debugging aids are not efficient.

The phrase "response time" bears some scrutiny in the foregoing definition of the problem. For users at console stations, response time is exactly as defined above; that is, it refers to the time period elapsed between actuation of a key at a console and the computer system's response to that actuation. Although response time usually does not include the time delay in the case of production problems, the above statement of the problem and the use of response time could be extended to that as well. However, in general, the statement of the problem refers to maximizing the number of users who are directly engaged in the system, for that is when time is at a premium because the assumption is made that the user can do no other work or work no other problems when he is at the console awaiting the results of his inputs and commands to the system.

The number of users, either N or n, in the above discussion, is a measure of the system throughput. If one ignores for the moment the production problems not requiring on-line operation or presence at the console, then this number of users is exactly the measure of throughput and maximizing this number maximizes throughput. Handling of production runs and the system design with respect to optimizing waiting time is discussed below when the topic of schedulers and executive systems is presented.

An alternative statement of the problem of optimizing cost effectiveness of a time-sharing system is as follows: Given a minimum number of users and a maximum response time for those users, maximize the efficiency of the computing system.

The above statement of the problem assumes that there is a given computer system for which the efficiency is to be maximized by procedures and programming. However, one could broaden this to include hardware costs as well as efficiency of usage of the system.

A qualitative examination of this statement of the problem shows that as the basic quantum of time (as in a round robin scheduling system) decreases, the number of users increases. However, decreasing the time quantum incurs a loss of machine efficiency, for a greater portion of the computer time is devoted to operations of the executive and the swapping of computer programs in and out of working core storage. As the time quantum is made smaller, the number of users increases, for the ones requiring short processing time are not delayed; and as long as machine efficiency does not reduce too far, those requiring larger amounts of computation do not suffer intolerably. However, machine inefficiencies do take over as the quantum size is reduced and the number of users does not continue to increase with decreasing queue.

An examination of the two statements of the problem shows that there are three main design parameters involved: number of users, response time, and machine efficiency. The three quantities are not independent; however, their relationship is very complex and subtle. In order to have a single function which is being optimized, the system designer could establish relationships between these quantities. However, this might result in arbitrary or subjective decisions on those relationships. Possibly a better approach is simply to hold one or two quantities constant and vary the others to determine the system's cost-effectiveness variations within the framework of fewer variables.

4.8   System Design Studies

Most of the system design studies have been accomplished at System Development Corporation. These studies have been accomplished largely through a system simulator. Although the results of the system simulation are limited because they apply to the system configuration utilizing the Q32V computer, it is instructive to examine them here.

G. H. Fine and P. V. McIsaac[4] have written a paper on the techniques and results of the simulation of a time-sharing system. The simulation program was written for the SDC time-sharing system. It ran under the time-sharing system and emphasized the investigation of many of the design parameters of that particular system. Some of the inputs to the simulation were job characteristics, job arrival rate, job mixes, number of input-output channels, core and drum size, access and word-transfer rates, and computer-malfunction statistics.

Unfortunately, many of the results of the simulation are obscured by the fact that the Q32V computer could not overlap input-output and processing, and therefore swap times tended to be very high, overshadowing much of the other types of computer utilization. However, the results are interesting. One of the sets of simulator findings involves the use of round robin scheduling and modifying quantum of service in steps from 100 milliseconds to 1600 milliseconds. The result showed that swap time for this particular system was reduced from 50 per cent down to 10 per cent while the percentage of service was increased from 40 per cent to 70 per cent.

One of the more significant aspects of this simulator study involves the scheduling algorithm. The first algorithms studied treated all jobs identically, whereas a second algorithm distinguished between jobs requiring small but infrequent amounts of service with fast response and those needing considerable processing time with relatively little user interaction. Debugging and gaming are examples of the former and compiling or production jobs are examples of the latter. Under the new scheduler which gave higher priority to those jobs requiring much interaction, system performance as measured by the simulator improved significantly. There was better response, throughput, turnaround time, and computer utilization. The machine utilization increased from 60 to 70 per cent and the number of users demanding service (those essentially waiting for service) reduced drastically. This shows that after maximizing the system with respect to the time quantum, a further significant increase in system efficiency can accrue by the use of a two-class scheduling algorithm.

Although much insight into the problem of system design can be gained by analytical techniques, the large number of parameters and variables involved in the design of a time-sharing system precludes closed form optimization techniques—those which yield a single answer as a result of directly calculating from formulas. At the time of the writing of this chapter, and to this writer's knowledge, the simulation performed by System Development Corporation was the only simulation of a time-sharing system employed, and therefore the only thorough, pragmatic approach to system design investigations.

4.9 The Scheduling Problem

One of the most important design problems in a time-sharing system is the scheduler. The scheduler is the important part of the executive program which decides on a real-time basis how the computer is to service the console station and how it is to carry out the production computation. Therefore, the particular characteristics of the scheduling algorithm which is utilized in time-sharing systems strongly influence the efficiency of the computer and the efficiency of the user. The economic consequences of the scheduler may be great, for there are implications here as to the entire responsiveness of the computer system to the organization or the agency which it is serving.

One of the best treatments of the scheduling problem has been provided by Greenberger,[5] who points out that there are conflicting objectives in the design of a scheduling algorithm. On one hand, it is desired that the average response time and the number of users waiting be reduced as much as possible. Another objective is that the scheduling algorithm must recognize customer importance and the urgency of the request. Often in conflict with the first two objectives is the desire to serve the users in a fair order and to limit the length of the wait. In the next paragraph, the general scheduling problem will be stated and discussed. Following this, a more specific discussion of the scheduler is presented.

The design of a scheduling algorithm to optimize cost and effectiveness functions is a complex operations-research problem. It involves the disciplines of statistics, queuing theory, and a practical knowledge of the way time-sharing systems are operated and used. However, a point of departure in all of this is a method of measuring the cost of waiting for computed results. Greenberger[5] points out that there are many different ways of relating the rate of accrual of costs and the waiting. Costs rate may be constant with respect to waiting time. It may be linear and increasing, or it may be nonlinear, complex function. The problem is difficult even with the simplest relationship of costs versus waiting time. However, with nonlinear relationships, the problem rapidly gets extremely difficult. Figure 4.4 shows some of the possible relationships between the rate of accrual of costs versus the waiting time. Each customer or each job may have a different cost function. The overall objective of the scheduler is to minimize the total costs accrued by all customers.

The scheduling problem for a time-sharing system is similar to the classical problem of job-shop scheduling. A job consists of many tasks. Each of the tasks must be performed on different machines. Therefore, there are priority decisions with respect to each one of the tasks of a job.

To better understand the complexity here, consider two tasks from two different jobs competing for service at a machine. The first task requires less machine time than the second, but the second job is in greater danger of missing its deadline. If priority is given to the first job, then the interests of high throughput and short wait are served. However, this may cause an increase in the probability of the second job going past the deadline. Therefore, a balance must be struck between these two conflicting points of view.

One of the most straightforward ways of scheduling is simply to pro-

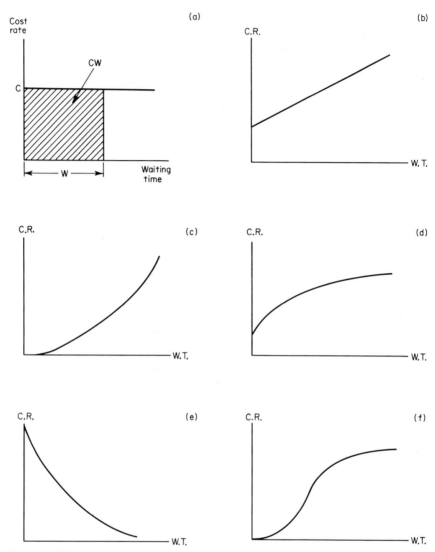

Fig. 4.4   Examples of cost curves.

vide a quantum of information to each user in turn.   This is called "round robin scheduling."   If the quantum of service is small, it will tend to satisfy the user who required only a short amount of computation, and will therefore serve the objective of reducing the waiting time.   Greenberger[5] points out that the more uncertainty there is with respect to the amount of computation required, the greater the benefits of round robin scheduling compared to a "first come, first served" scheduling algorithm.

In the event that the computation time is known a priori (which is seldom the case) then the "shortest job next" type of algorithm yields the least total wait. The disadvantage of the "first come, first served" rule is that the person with a very short amount of computation may have to wait as long as the person with a large amount of computation. Therefore, the sum total of these considerations yields round robin scheduling as an attractive technique.

However, there is an important modification to the simple round robin scheduling technique which can improve the total system service greatly. This is a scheduler with more than one level of priority.* Under this system of scheduling, computing requests which are known, either a priori or by machine experience, to be ones which require relatively large amounts of computation are placed in a lower level of priority than those which require short amounts of computation. If the scheduling can be done on a continuing basis of introspection, wherein adjustments are continuously made, advantages in system performance accrue.

Corbato[6] has proposed such a multilevel scheduler. Under his proposal, if a request is not completed within its quantum, its balance falls to the next priority level and is not served until everything ahead of it has been served, including new arrivals at the higher levels. Each level may have a different quantum of processing associated with it and quantum sizes increase for the lower levels of priority. Corbato also suggested that the quanta associated with each level of priority also be allowed to change as a function of the state of the system. For example, if few consoles are active, or if few users at the consoles are active, the quantum may be increased, thus providing a reduction in overhead while continuing the response times at appropriate low levels.

But there *is* a priori information which can be utilized in the scheduling. Certainly the programmer or user who approaches the console has an idea of how he will use the computer and, in fact, has an idea of how much computer time he will use. This information is available to the scheduler, and should be used in the scheduling process. Therefore, some of the degree of uncertainty which Greenberger refers to can be removed. In the following paragraph, a scheduling system is discussed which makes use of this a priori information.

Consider the following approach to a scheduling algorithm. Active programs in a time-shared system can be considered to be one of three types: conversational, standby, and deposited. There may be additional administrative programs such as those which collect data on the time-shared system itself, programs for bookkeeping or accounting, and programs for diagnosing machine operation. However, the three types refer

* This type of scheduler, in simplified version, is that discussed in the previous section as having been studied by simulation at System Development Corporation.

to user programs—those which provide the end product of the time-sharing system.

In this classification of time-sharing jobs, those which are conversational are jobs where the programmer or user is giving information to the computer very much in the way a supervisor communicates with his staff assistant. He gives the computer instructions or asks the computer questions which require a small amount of computation. He may ask what is in a certain register. He may supply to the system a FORTRAN statement, or he may inquire of the system the status of his computer program. What characterizes the operation here is that the user expects to receive a response within a few seconds—in fact, usually within less than five seconds. This means that the time-sharing system must, with high frequency, turn attention to the console. Since the amount of processing is small, the amount of attention given, in turn, will be small. In other words, the quantum of processing required at each turn can be small.

Jobs of the standby type are those requests of the computer system which require significantly more computation, but where the response to the user is required within a short time because the user awaits the results at his console. A primary example of this type of operation is the processing of part of a computer program during checkout to determine whether that part of the program works correctly. However, this type of operation could be extended to production runs where useful answers are provided, but which require small amounts of computing.

The third type is the production-run or the deposited type. The job is given to the computer or is deposited with the computer along with certain directions on how it is to be run; that is, the number of parameters involved in the computation and the entry point of the program. The important point with deposited jobs is that they do not require the person to stand by the console and, in a sense, they are off-line or batch jobs.

The scheduling process for this breakdown of job types for the time-sharing system would go as follows: The user would register in at the console and inform the system which type his job is.* The scheduler essentially places the conversational jobs in the highest priority, the standby jobs in the next highest priority, and the deposited jobs in the lowest priority. Round robin scheduling is done for each of the jobs; however, it is done within the framework of a multilevel priority system. Quanta of computer time for the three types of jobs are determined in advance. For example, the quantum for conversational jobs might be as low as 20 milliseconds; whereas the amount of time given to the standby jobs might be as great as 200 milliseconds. The quanta are determined

---

* This is not necessary in sophisticated systems where the executive program discerns, by the type of console action, what type of job is being processed.

on the basis of whether a meaningful amount of computation can, on the average, be provided with respect to the aims and objectives of the type of job, or the processes which are normally carried out in the type of job.

The scheduling process then is performed as follows: All consoles which have been registered in as the conversational mode are first attended to on a round robin basis. Following the completion of one cycle of all of the conversational consoles, the system turns in a round robin fashion to the standby jobs. Each standby job is given the appropriate amount of attention as determined by the quantum assigned to that priority level. Any remaining time before attention must again turn to conversational jobs is devoted to processing deposited jobs.

Let us consider an example to fix the ideas. Let us suppose that analysis has shown that responses to consoles in the conversational mode must be no greater than 3 seconds. This implies that every 3 seconds, the system must cycle through the conversational channels (consoles). Suppose that 20 consoles are in the conversational mode.* This would imply that if the quantum for this highest priority level were 20 milliseconds, the 20 consoles would be serviced in 400 milliseconds, leaving 2.6 seconds for other tasks before attention must be again returned to the conversational jobs.

Let us assume that the response time for jobs in the standby mode must be no greater than 20 seconds. Let us further suppose that 20 consoles are in the standby mode of operation, and that the quantum of processing reserved for these jobs is 200 milliseconds. Within the 20-second response cycle, the conversational cycle is traversed approximately four times. Therefore,

	Response time, seconds	Quantum, msec	No. of consoles
Conversational......	3	20	20
Standby............	20	200	20

Of the basic response cycle for the standby jobs of 20 seconds, approximately 2.8 seconds has been used by the system in the servicing of conversational jobs, leaving 18.2 seconds for the attention of jobs which are not in the conversational mode. For the 20 consoles in the standby mode, 4 seconds would be used, which allows 14.2 seconds of the 21-second

* Note that "the number of consoles in a certain mode" is a time varying, random quantity and, in referring to the number, the average number of such consoles over some period of time is implied in the discussion.

period to be made available for "deposited" jobs.   The quantum for the
deposited jobs might be as great as 4 or 5 seconds.*

Obviously, because of maximum response times for conversational and
standby programs, there is a maximum number of these jobs which can
be serviced at any one time.   If, for example, there are 100 jobs in the
conversational mode, then the maximum number of jobs in the standby
mode would be 95 since 95 jobs at 200 milliseconds would use up the
remaining 19 seconds of the 21-second response time for the system.

There are many modifications of this basic system.   For example, one
can define additionally an input mode which would simply be the computer system responding to the input of certain characters or the completion of certain lines of input commands.   Since these commands could
be handled by a computer completely outside the main time-sharing processor, these would not affect the example described above.   However, in
the event that such an input processor were made available, the system
design would probably require a different definition of the conversational
and standby modes and different quanta would be assigned to these
modes.

Still another modification of the system would have more than one
priority level for deposited jobs.   One could adopt the technique of Corbato[6] which drops the jobs to lower levels of priority in the event they are
not completed within the quantum, or within a given number of quanta
of computer service.   Another possibility is that a deadline might be
established for the job.   As the time remaining until the deadline got
within a certain multiple of the expected running time (supplied by the
programmer), the priority would be raised.   Raising the priority level
might happen a number of times before the job was completed.

Implicit in such a scheduling scheme is the fact that the user is charged
according to the time used at the priority level.   Each channel or console
is kept track of in terms of the amount of main frame processor time
devoted to it over a given period of time.   Charges for conversational
jobs are at a rate higher than charges at standby or deposited priority
levels.   This scheme would also prevent the user from registering in at a
higher level than his usage would indicate.

It should be noted that the above processing scheme is not offered as a
serious candidate for a scheduler.   Rather, it is offered to improve our
understanding of the scheduling process and to stimulate thinking on the
subject.   Furthermore, it is advanced because it illustrates the use of
a priori data on the job which the user can supply to the system, and
thereby increase the efficiency of the scheduling process and the efficiency

---

* The scheduling problem for deposited jobs is basically different from that for
other jobs since waiting time is not a factor.   Another factor, "time left before deadline," becomes significant in the process.

of system use. Since there is always a finite, nonzero possibility that the machine will be idle in any given period of time (assuming that the demand is random), there should always be a supply of lowest priority utility jobs which are performed to fill in this otherwise idle time. Examples are auditing, recording, and diagnostic jobs. It is appropriate that these nonrevenue-producing jobs be given the lowest priority.

A final observation on schedulers and scheduling algorithms: There is virtually no limit to the complexity which can be introduced. Complexity introduced in the system is costly and there is the lingering question of that cost incurred as compared with accrued savings in other factors. There is little doubt, however, that schedulers will become increasingly complex since, with increasing improvements in implementation techniques, that complexity will become steadily less costly.

4.10 Computer Configuration Aspects

There are a number of implications on the economics of on-line systems which involve the configuration of the computer. Configuration, here, applies to the type, amount, and interconnection of the various modules which comprise the computer.

Even before on-line systems came into the limelight and had such a great deal of professional interest turned to them, multi- and modular computer systems were becoming increasingly prevalent and popular. Most of this early interest stemmed, in fact, from a number of command and control military systems which had important on-line features. Some of these were the systems for SAC Control, Air Force Command Post, and the Department of Defense Damage Assessment Center (now called National Military Command System Support Center). The military people designed these systems with the advantages of multicomputer systems, and these same advantages are now apparent and becoming more accepted in the nonmilitary areas where time-sharing is important.

Multicomputer system has become a generic name for a system that is modular in concept and design. It allows the interconnection of various modules such as processors, input-output channel handlers, high-speed memory devices, and peripheral equipment in ways which allow the computer to be reconfigured both on a millisecond basis and, in the case of adding or deleting modules, on much longer time scales such as weeks or months. Some of the motivations and characteristics of multicomputer systems have been described in a paper[7] published in 1962.

Although there are a number of economic advantages to modular computer systems' use in on-line systems, two salient characteristics are reliability and expandability. In a monolithic computer system, a failure in an on-line system application can be very costly—more costly than it would be in a batch environment. This is true because of the large number of people who have been counting on using the computer and who are suddenly denied the opportunity and cannot adjust their schedules. In a batch system, there is often enough buffering and elasticity in the requests for service that equipment failures do not have nearly as disastrous an effect. The hour's worth of computation lost in the afternoon can be added to the midnight shift with no serious consequences since most of the people would not expect answers before the next day anyway. With an on-line system, an hour's outage of the machine could inconvenience several hundred people.

A significant amount of reliability can be achieved in a multicomputer system with only a modest cost for equipment redundancy. As has been explained in a paper on multicomputers,[7] equipment redundancy in the neighborhood of 20 to 30 per cent can buy the same reliability that 100 per cent equipment redundancy buys in the nonmodular systems. If the on-line system is designed for 100 users, and is currently being used at the 75 per cent capacity, one of the four processors could be lost without degrading system performance. Alternatively, if it were being used to capacity, and one processor went down, only the lowest priority 25 per cent of the work would suffer.

Expandability is probably an even more clear-cut characteristic of some of the advantages in on-line systems. Figure 4.5 shows that a modular system can be expanded to meet the needs and not incur the costs of a superfluous computer capability. Processors, more high-speed memory, and more input-output channels can be added to accommodate the growing numbers of on-line users. It is true that this imposes some additional desired requirements on the software. The executive, for example, must be written in a way that it need not be altered greatly with the addition

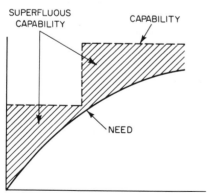
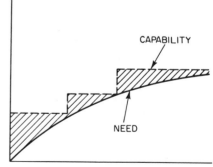

MONOLITHIC COMPUTER ECONOMICS   MULTICOMPUTER SYSTEM ECONOMICS

Fig. 4.5

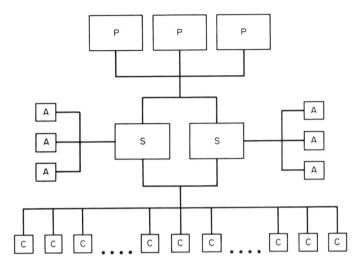

P PROCESSORS
S SEQUENCING OR SWITCHING COMPUTERS
A AUXILIARY MEMORY
C CONSOLES

Fig. 4.6

of the extra modules. However, this should not be an inordinately costly software factor.

It is likely that many on-line systems will be designed with a separate input-output computer which interfaces between the basic processor system and the consoles as well as between these two types of equipment and the auxiliary memories (see Fig. 4.6). This concept is the one currently employed for SDC's time-sharing system and M.I.T.'s Project MAC. The computer is frequently called a "sequencing" computer, and it handles the bits and pieces communication between the console and the main computer. It can, for example, accept the character by character input from the consoles; check it for format, syntax, and the like; make certain initial decisions on priority of the message and at the appropriate time; and transmit the composite command to the main processor. The economic advantages are that a simpler computer can be used for this task. Also, simpler executive can be designed since the executive of the sequencing computer need not interact in detail with that of the main processor, and the main processor can be utilized with greater efficiency since it will be interrupted with less frequency.

The concept of the sequencing computer described above is frequently used in communications systems and is referred to as the "local loop" concept. The basic principle here is to use a simple loop for the local traffic, low bandwidth activities, and allow for multiplexing the information to provide high bandwidth transmission to the main processor. An example of this approach can be found in the paper by W. F. Bauer and W. L. Frank.[8]

Perhaps, most significantly, it is interesting to observe that the modern computers being developed expressly for on-line operations utilize modularity to a very great extent. Examples of this are the GE645 and the IBM360/Model 67.

HARDWARE AND SOFTWARE COSTS

4.11 Hardware Costs

For quite a large number of reasons, information on the cost of implementing on-line systems is sparse. In particular, this writer has found no references which quantitatively present information on hardware and software costs, especially compared with batch systems. The newness of the field probably is the best explanation of this dearth of literature and analyses. Those sufficiently knowledgeable about on-line systems to make such contributions are deeply engaged in analyzing and designing, where the attention is turned to the technical factors only and the economic implications are given less emphasis.

Hardware manufacturers, at this point, undoubtedly regard on-line systems as prototype in nature, even though many copies of some systems are being built. Pricing will be done on the basis of factors other than the precisely derived costs of the hardware and software implementation. Manufacturers adapt software, for example, from batch systems to operate with on-line systems. Therefore, there arises a question of how much of the batch software costs should be assumed in amortizing the on-line system costs. There will probably be no clean break from batch to on-line from the manufacturer's point of view, and there will probably be no parallel activity in these two types of systems to enable a dependable comparison of costs.

However, there is much which can be done. For example, a knowledgeable person can study the extra costs of dynamic storage relocation or the extra costs of conversational compilers over conventional compilers. Hopefully, such incisive analyses will be made soon. The scope of this chapter precludes such incisive analyses. However, the following paragraphs present the salient factors of costs, both hardware and software.

As was frequently mentioned in earlier sections of this chapter, increases in user efficiency and certain other improvements will be balanced against increased costs in on-line systems for the future. Certainly the hardware costs for a system capable of efficient on-line operation will exceed those of batch processing. Some of the reasons for this increase in cost are:

1. Additional working storage features
2. Multiaccess to and independent operation of working storage
3. Large internal high-speed memory
4. Increased storage capacity of auxiliary memories
5. Hardware speed degradation

The following paragraphs discuss each one of these points in turn.

The working storage features necessary for on-line systems result from the needs of the executive to have the wherewithal to determine the instantaneous status of the computer system where attention is being turned very rapidly from one user to the next. Perhaps the most important feature here is the dynamic relocatability hardware. This is hardware which allows part of a program (frequently referred to as a "segment" or "page") to be read in from auxiliary memory into any portion of the physical working storage. Since that part of working storage may not be the same part of the program operated from before, and since there is a requirement that the programmer (user) need not be concerned with the location of his program each time it is to be executed, the modification of the addresses for relocation must be handled automatically. Therefore, in the interpretation of an address, a table look-up is accomplished by hardware to determine in which portion of the memory the address is to be found, and then the proper modification to the address is made to determine the effective address. Essentially, therefore, there is an associativity process which is carried out—the address of the program must be associated or correlated with the portion of the actual memory in which it is contained; a small associative memory must actually be included in the machines.

Still other working memory features are deemed desirable. Although it is becoming quite common to have memory protection on computers, some of these features have been extended in the case of time-sharing hardware. For instance, it is common to have a memory protect feature which prohibits writing into any unauthorized memory space. This feature has been extended to the prohibition of *reading* from any unauthorized space as well. This affords an extra degree of assurance that the hardware-software combination is doing what it is supposed to do.

Still another feature being added to time-sharing systems is one which indicates whether the portion of memory of a portion of the program has been used or whether it has been referred to or changed. Two bits are added to a memory block: one which would indicate whether the block has been referred to, and another one which would indicate whether the information in the block has been changed. The uses of this feature are

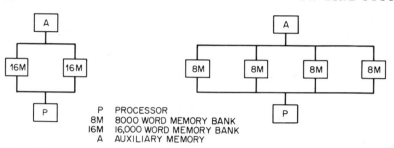

P   PROCESSOR
8M   8000 WORD MEMORY BANK
16M   16,000 WORD MEMORY BANK
A   AUXILIARY MEMORY

Fig. 4.7

manifold.   For example, one could conceivably design an executive which would shift out a portion of the memory if it has not been referred to or changed for a given period of time.   The assumption is made that this is not an "active" portion of the program.

In order to reduce the nonproductive period where the main processor is awaiting new portions of the program which must be transferred from some auxiliary memory ("swap time"), considerable changes must be made in hardware over conventional systems.   In conventional systems, at least the ones of a few years ago, the main frame is held up while transfers are made from auxiliary memories to core.   Or, at best, memory accesses of the input-output transfer are interleaved with those of the main processor, thereby degrading the performance of the processor.   In time-sharing systems, it is desirable to provide a sufficient independence of action between the memory devices and the auxiliary memory and input-output devices to allow a large amount of transfer to take place independently of the main frame.

Consider, for example, a time-sharing computer which has 32,000 words of memory organized as two independently operating 16,000 word banks (see Fig. 4.7).   After the completion of computing on one job (at the end of a time quantum) which has been operating from one of the two banks, the new program which will run during the next time quantum must be resident in the other bank, so that a transfer from auxiliary memory into the first bank can be effected and thus replace the "used" program. Thus, the process continues; one bank is connected to the processor while computing is in process with that bank while the other bank is undergoing replenishment through transfer-in from auxiliary memory.   Of course, the process is random.   Two successive time quanta may, for example, use the same memory bank.

Clearly, however, it would frequently occur in the case of the two 16,000-word memory banks described above, that processing stops because the alternating scheme of compute-swap-compute for each bank cannot be continued, since neither bank contains the next program segment.

(Realizing that a modern executive program, which must reside in the memory at all times, may be 8,000 to 16,000 words in length itself, makes it easy to appreciate the likelihood.) If the memory were organized into four 8,000-word independently operating banks (see Fig. 4.7), the probability of the process continuing would be increased, assuming that most programs are in the range of 2,000 to 6,000 words in length, as opposed to much larger programs of 10,000 to 14,000 words in length.

Therefore, it is desirable for the memory to be divided up into large numbers of small units, each of which can communicate with the main processor, and each of which can communicate with other devices if it is not connected to the main processor. One immediately sees that this represents a considerable amount of extra hardware. Instead of having address circuitry which addresses 32,000 words, there must be independent address circuitry for much smaller pieces, say 4,000 words. Also, there must be a switching capability which allows the processor to be switched to one of the many memory units, and similar circuitry to allow the switching from any one of a number of peripheral units to any one of the memory units. Furthermore, the input-output channels, when not connected to a processor, must have the capability of controlling themselves. In other words, they must have a stored program capability. Although an analysis of the costs on a quantitative basis is a sizable problem, it is easily seen that these capabilities represent additional costs over more conventionally organized processors and memories.

Larger high-speed storage memories are required for a number of reasons. The most obvious reason is that a complex executive resides in working storage and cannot, because of the high frequency of its usage, be kept even in part in auxiliary store. The SDC executive for their time-sharing system is 16,000 words in length and does not represent a complex executive as compared with ones currently being planned. Still another reason for large amounts of high-speed memory is to increase the probability that the part of the program of data which is required next is on hand in high-speed storage. Ideally, it is desirable to have in the memory all possible parts of all programs which could potentially be activated next; the larger the high-speed core is, the more likely it is that the program part is ready for execution.

A significant observation about high-speed memory is that it represents the most costly part of the machine. Frequently, memory costs more than the main frame. Another significant point is that in comparing batch and on-line hardware systems costs, one must realize an additional amount of high-speed memory—probably as much as 50 per cent more—is needed; therefore, it is a significant increment in cost.

Those programs which are not active must be kept in electronic storage devices so that they can be made ready on short order to be transferred

to high-speed memory and used.   There are probably at least three levels
in the auxiliary memory hierarchy.   First of all, there is the magnetic
drum which stores program data which can be transferred in at high-
speed rates to the main memory.   These are programs which are currently active—probably programs of users currently at the console.
There should probably be as much as 16,000 words of storage for each
console station, which implies on the order of 1,000,000 words of drum
storage for a 50-console station system.   The next level in the auxiliary
memory hierarchy are those programs and data which have been active
during the day or week which are likely to be brought to action.   They
may also represent portions of a program which overflow allotted drum
space.   Those programs can be stored on random access disk devices.
The third level of hierarchy is now frequently considered archival in
nature—magnetic tapes.   Magnetic tapes will be used as a general
backup for providing an additional reservoir of active programs.

The last item mentioned above on hardware costs refers to lowering of
efficiency of the usage of the hardware system rather than an increase in
the basic cost of the hardware.   In the process of interpreting addresses
when programs are relocated, that is, in the action of the relocatability
hardware, certain extra time is required above and beyond the normal
operation of the main frame and the memory.   The process of associating
the address of each executed instruction with one of the various portions
of the program, and then modifying its effective address, requires an
additional 15 to 20 per cent of computer time.   In other words, the basic
memory cycle is slowed down by this amount.   This is not incurred by
poor programming, but is part of the wired-in characteristics of the computer.   Any additional overhead or inefficiency in the machine starts
from this point, and must be considered.   This is a subtle point, frequently
not fully appreciated by time-sharing advocates.   It is, for all practical
purposes, like adding 15 to 20 per cent rental to a machine, and again,
comes in addition to any other total system inefficiencies.

Communications and console costs are likewise important in time-sharing systems.   Communications costs are not always a factor in time-
sharing systems for the consoles may be within the cable connection distance of the computer.   Communications costs and usage is a far-ranging
subject which will not be touched upon here.

The main cost item in peripheral equipment is the user station itself.
This may vary from a teletypewriter station costing in the neighborhood
of $1,000 to an elaborate console costing in the neighborhood of $100,000.
Whatever the amount, the increased costs here are clearly in excess of
those required for batch-processing systems.   Furthermore, it becomes
increasingly clear that typewriter stations will not provide the flexibility
and speed required.   The minimum-capability user station is a full key-

board plus a cathode-ray tube with the ability to "print out" approximately one-page worth of information. This raises the question of whether hard copy print-out stations will be necessary, and whether they are above and beyond the costs of the cathode-ray-tube-type user station. Any costs of buffering and communicating with the user station are, again, extra.

4.12   Software Costs

The general factor which leads to increased programming and analysis costs is that of increased system complexity. Some of the factors, in turn, involved in the increased complexity of the system are:

1. The programmer must make allowances for the manifold of "simultaneous" occurrences. Part of this is a design problem, and another part is a programming execution problem. It involves building the proper networks to react to the various random occurrences in the computer system which result from human inputs which, in turn, provide a multitude of interrupts to the system operation.
2. There is a basic problem of working storage overlay in such a system since there is a very large amount of programming data swapping between working storage and auxiliary storage. The systems must be properly developed to enable this swapping with a maximum of user efficiency or program execution productivity while, at the same time, giving all users a sufficient number of time slices within a given period of time to allow the system to be responsive. In more recent systems, there are hardware features ("relocatability hardware") which facilitate memory overlay operations. However, the executive must be properly designed to make good use of such hardware features.
3. The memory management problem becomes far more complex since there will be many levels of data storage depending upon the frequency of usage. There will also be communication among the various storage levels and a logic of describing the data which is consistent from the point of view of the many users and consistent from the point of view of the many storage levels.
4. The design of a scheduler which takes into account the various conflicting objectives of the system and its users is a continuing factor. To ensure a near-optimum system requires considerable paper analysis and system simulation. Unfortunately, the large number of parameters and the environmental anomalies make a unique solution to the scheduling problem a near impossibility.
5. The development of conversational mode languages and debugging aids is likewise complicating. These languages break down into two general classes: conversational compilers which are essentially adap-

tations of existing or off-line compilers, and new utility languages for man-machine communication and command.

Despite all of these apparent increases in software costs, a number of highly respected systems people with experience in both batch and on-line systems insist that an on-line system is no more complicated than a sophisticated batch system and, therefore, no more costly. It is doubtful, however, if this opinion would hold up under scrutiny. Even if the sophistication and costs of the executive were a standoff, the costs of adding conversational capability to the compilers might well upset the balance. Another factor is the real-time capability which must be added to the system, which is certainly not a factor in batch systems.

However, the fact that respected experts argue that the on-line software costs are no greater does augur well for the future of on-line systems. For one thing, much of the design and programming being done for on-line systems today is new. The professionals are greatly increasing their ability to produce systems of this kind.

4.13 Costing and Pricing

Early sections of this chapter dealt with questions of the relative merits of batch and on-line systems from economic standpoints. They have dealt also with the relationship of technical factors to economic ones. The previous section dealt with costs of hardware and software. This aspect of the economics of on-line systems—costing and pricing—is more closely related to business aspects. Costing and pricing refer to how one should account for costs and how charges should be made to customers—these are important aspects of any on-line system whether it be for commercial usage or to implement in-house capabilities or requirements. Large amounts of money will be spent in the daily operation of on-line systems. Costs ranging from $100,000 to $300,000 per month, and perhaps higher, are to be expected in systems of this type. The centralized aspects of these systems implies directly that total costs will be high and growing, thus making costing and pricing considerations of primary importance.

Anyone familiar in detail with the accounting and pricing procedures for large-scale batch systems should have no difficulty in developing accounting and charge policies for on-line systems. However, an understanding of the technical and administrative aspects of the on-line systems is essential. Administrative procedures for the batch systems are relatively straightforward, at least as they have usually been applied. The system equipment costs are well known for the first shift rental and for marginal additional rental on second and third shifts. Usually each job uses the entire system, or at least for simplicity it is assumed the entire system is used. One simply keeps account of the amount of time the job runs on the computer, and charges the person appropriately.

On-line systems will be more complex. However, the gap between the accounting and pricing for a modern batch system is probably not a great deal more troublesome than the accounting and pricing for an on-line system. However, there are some differences. The on-line system user will use a very powerful computer for shorter periods of time; perhaps accumulations of time slices ranging from 50 to 200 milliseconds. There will be the introduction of the concept of "overhead computing," where the computer system is performing computations—perhaps extensive—in support of all users. Certain sophistications may be introduced in pricing, such as charging the customer according to the priority he has been given in servicing the problems in the queues.

4.14   Cost Accounting Procedures

As with any kind of accounting procedure, there are two types of cost: "overhead" type and "direct charge" type. The former is not attributable to any given user, but benefits all users; the latter is directly attributable to the user. Although most of the identifiable costs clearly fit in one category or the other, there are a number which could fit in either category, depending upon the accounting philosophy. As with all accounting systems, the question is whether keeping account of small costs and attributing them to specific users is worth the extra cost of the required monitoring and handling. On one hand, it is desirable to give the customer a complete accounting of just what system capability he used, and thereby reduce the overhead costs to an absolute minimum. However, cost accounting can be excessive if carried to a very low level of data-processing functions.

A third type of cost can be regarded as a "one time" cost. Examples of this type of cost are the system design and systems programming costs which are done either initially with a system, or at periodic intervals as the system is being modified or upgraded. These costs are not usually regarded "overhead" and, of course, they are not direct charges to the customer. In general, they are amortized over a given period of time, and the prices charged for the services must, of course, take these amortization rates into account.

The following are examples of direct costs: processor time on tasks, console costs, local communications costs, line transactions, auxiliary storage usage. Processor time on tasks refers to the accumulation of the various time slices which are granted on behalf of specific tasks. In the case of a multicomputer system, there might be a number of different types of time charges, depending on which processor was used. If a console is dedicated to one user, then the entire console cost is directly chargeable to that user. Similarly, any local communications costs which can be regarded as dedicated to a single user are a type of direct charge. In certain types of systems, line transactions will be of considerable importance. An example is an on-line invoice system. This type of charge is not, of course, appropriate in a general-purpose scientific on-line system. Auxiliary storage usages might be considered a direct charge. However, the costs of accounting for auxiliary storage may be a very difficult problem.

A number of costs, as described above, are not attributable directly to any one customer, but support all of the system's customers. Examples of overhead uses are processor time on the executive, idle time, swap time, high-speed memory usage, and auxiliary storage usages not considered direct. Clearly, the time that the system spends in the executive processing is of the overhead type, as are swap time and idle time. High-speed memory could be considered a direct charge; however, it is probably not feasible to keep track of all of the bits and pieces of memory usage on the very small time slices which may be involved. Auxiliary memory usage is most likely to be regarded as overhead since, as with high-speed memory, it will not be practical to keep track of auxiliary memories. It is conceivable, however, that one could dedicate a number of tracks or disks of a random-access disk file to one customer to store his program data. Higher-speed auxiliary storage devices such as magnetic drums are not likely to yield to this accounting treatment since the costs of keeping track of such usage would be prohibitively large.

4.15 Customer Charges—Profit and Loss

Normally the basis for charges to the customer is the direct costs described above. In the simplest case, the customer is charged according to processor time used, which includes an allowance for a normal amount of overhead costs, such as those described in the previous section. Some specialized on-line systems are such as to allow a charge per transaction. Some charge procedures will involve keeping track of time to the nearest millisecond for the main frame and for the peripheral devices, and will charge different rates depending upon which of a half dozen or so priority levels are used.

One of the most interesting ways of charging for the usage of on-line systems is to charge according to the amount of console time used. The console, incidentally, can be either a dedicated console, where all of the costs are borne by the user, regardless of how much he uses the console or the system, or it can be a "utility" console where different customers use the console and are charged accordingly. The charge to the customer can be made in terms of the amount of time used at the console plus the amount of time the computer is used, or the charge might be made only on the basis of the console time used. The latter way of charging raises the interesting question of two users who use the system so differently that the amount of main processor time used in equal periods of console time is widely different. It appears that any reasonable way of charging by console time only would imply that a given amount of processor time is guaranteed over a given period of console time; then if the computer time is exceeded, the customer pays an additional amount, depending upon the overage.

The unsophisticated buyer should be aware, however, of any costs which relate only to console time. In the first place, he may be deluded into some belief that console time equals processor time. Even if he has no such delusions, he should realize that the amount of processor time he gets for a given period of console time may vary greatly, depending upon a host of conditions such as number of other users, types of other problems in the system, and the like. The computation of the price for service will, in principal, not vary from the price of any other service or product which, just as in manufacturing, is based on a certain expected usage or sales rate. If, for example, the charges were based on main processor time only, the price will be based on a certain number of hours of usage per day—say, six hours of billable or chargeable main processor, usage. All overhead costs will be added in such a way as to make the six hours of billable a break-even point in the system. If the usage goes below the six-hour level, the overhead rate goes up and the system "loses money." If the system is utilized more than six hours per day, the system "makes a profit."

Once the break-even point is passed in an on-line system, the operation can, of course, be very profitable. If the break-even point is sufficiently low to allow usage beyond that point without adding equipment, then the profit leverage can be great. However, the profit leverage can be good even if certain peripheral equipment or high-speed memory units have to be added to keep the system from downgrading in the quality of the service as the service amounts are increased. As the quality of the service deteriorates, that is, as response times get intolerably large, a processor can be added. The system should be of the multicomputer nature to allow for the efficient addition of such extra capability. Also, the programming system should allow the addition of an extra processor; if designed correctly in the first place, this will be possible. It is clear that many one-time costs are independent of the number of users. Among these are likely to be physical space, programming system, and most of the computing system. Therefore, as the amount of usage rises, and it can rise almost indefinitely in a well-designed centralized system, the profit leverage gets extremely attractive to the entrepreneur or to the organization implementing a system for service in a large company or agency.

REFERENCES

1. Patrick, R. L.: So You Want to Go On-line, *Datamation*, October, 1963.
2. Rosenberg, A. M.: Computer-usage Accounting for Generalized Time-sharing Systems, *Communications of the ACM*, no. 7, pp. 304–308, May, 1964.
3. Kaufman, D. J.: Monsantos' Conversational Mode Computer Network to Increase Engineer's Efficiency, *Data Processing Magazine*, no. 7, p. 48, August, 1965.
4. Fine, Gerald H., and Paul V. McIsaac: Simulation of a Time-sharing System, SDC Professional Paper SP-1909, Santa Monica, Calif., December, 1964.
5. Greenberger, Martin: The Priority Problem, Project MAC Technical Report (unpublished), M.I.T., October, 1965.
6. Corbato, F. J., et al., An Experimental Time-sharing System, *Proceedings of the SJCC*, 1962.
7. Bauer, Walter F.: Why Multi-computers? *Datamation*, September, 1962.
8. Bauer, Walter F., and Werner L. Frank: DODDAC: An Integrated System for Data Processing, Interrogation and Display, *Proceedings of the FJCC*, 1961.

ADDITIONAL REFERENCES

Beierle, John D.: Communications Switching and Buffering Networks, *Datamation*, vol. 9, pp. 24–27, July, 1963.
Blumenthal, Sherman C.: Management in Real-time, *Data Processing Magazine*, vol. 7, pp. 18–23, August, 1965.
Edwards, James D.: On-line Business Data Processing, *Datamation*, vol. 11, pp. 42–48, September, 1965.
Fano, R. M.: The MAC System: The Computer Utility Approach, *IEEE Spectrum*, vol. 2, pp. 56–64, January, 1965.
Frank, Werner L., W. H. Gardner, G. L. Stock: Programming On-line Systems, Part One, *Datamation*, vol. 9, pp. 29–34, May, 1963.
Gallenson, Louis, and Clark Weissman: Time-sharing Systems: Real and Ideal, SDC Professional Paper SP-1872, Santa Monica, Calif., March, 1965.
Licklider, J. C. R.: Man-computer Partnership, *International Science and Technology*, pp. 18–26, May, 1965.
Patrick, Robert L.: Measuring Performance, *Datamation*, p. 25, July, 1964.
Tonge, F. M.: Some Reflections on a Survey of Research Problems in Computer Software, Rand Memorandum RM 4467-PR, Santa Monica, Calif., April, 1965.
Wallace, V. L., D. W. Fife, and R. F. Rosin: A Study of Information Flow in Multiple-computer and Multiple-console Data Processing Systems, Technical Documentary Report No. RADC-TDR-64-427, Griffiss AFB, New York, December, 1964.

PHYSIOLOGICAL
AND
PSYCHOLOGICAL
CONSIDERATIONS

V

Edward E. David, Jr.

Bell Telephone Laboratories
Murray Hill, New Jersey

5.1 Introductory Remarks

In discussing on-line systems there is a temptation to overlook the fact that man and computers are equal partners and that the characteristics and efficiencies of each must receive due emphasis. Preceding chapters have emphasized the technical aspects of on-line system hardware and software. Chapter III, in particular, has stressed graphical displays attainable with present-day technology. The present chapter is intended to complement that discussion by describing the variety of physiological and psychological considerations which must enter into the design and the successful utilization of such on-line systems.

Despite superficial similarities, computers and people are organized quite differently. Men are logically deep; they deal with the world on many conceptual levels. Computers are logically shallow; their basic operations are few and primitive. Computers perform their operations serially in nano-or microseconds; man, in parallel, in milliseconds. Computer memory is small but precise compared with man's. Computer Gestalt is "bit"-oriented, whereas man's is mediated by learned or innate pattern constraints. Man's languages are imprecise and context-oriented; computer languages are unambiguous with minimal context modification. Thus, the interface between a man and a machine must incorporate recoding and buffering so that the requirements of both can be met.

This fact has had lip service for a long time, yet one tends to wonder just how basic these man-machine disparities are. Since man has great flexibility and can learn the most startling skills, is it not possible that interface problems can be eased by asking man to adapt? The answer is not entirely clear-cut. Certainly man can learn to manipulate controls, perform feats, and take information from displays remarkably well even under what appear to be very unfavorable conditions. Who would have thought, before it was demonstrated, that almost anyone could learn to read manually sent Morse code, with its impreciseness, at rates of over 100 characters per minute, or that aircraft could be identified consistently from a photograph viewed for only 200 milliseconds under poor illumination? On the other hand, clearly there are some tasks man can never learn. He cannot, for example, reduce his reaction time below some limiting value of the order of 100 milliseconds.

There is no clear-cut separation between these classes. However, in dealing with man-machine interactions, the designer must have some concept of what to expect of man, which of his characteristics and limitations are immutable and which are plastic. A knowledge of the underlying anatomy and physiology can be helpful. This chapter will examine some of man's characteristics and, where possible, the mechanisms responsible. Needless to say, it would be futile to attempt to be exhaustive; rather this chapter will try to supply a representative overview of a very extensive but not simply organized field of knowledge.

MEASUREMENT OF PERCEPTION

5.2 Subjective versus Objective Quantities

In perceptual measurement, a basic distinction is that between subjective and objective quantities. Take, for example, *sound intensity* and *loudness*. Sound intensity is a physical quantity which can be measured with a microphone and meter. Loudness, on the other hand, is the *perceived* magnitude of a sound. It cannot be measured with physical apparatus. We can, however, ask about the relation between physical quantities, in this case sound intensity, and subjective quantities, in this case loudness.

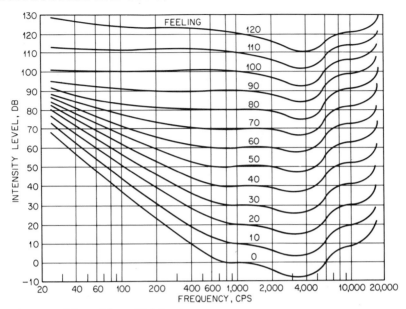

Fig. 5.1 Adapted from Fletcher.[1]

Harvey Fletcher[1] played a prominent role in quantifying the subjective-objective relationship. Initially he was cautious and merely aspired to match the loudness of different frequency sounds. He knew, for example, that a 1,000-cycle/sec tone of a given physical intensity sounds much louder than a 20,000-cycle/sec tone of the same physical intensity. In fact, not many people can hear a 20,000-cycle/sec tone no matter what the intensity. Thus, Fletcher asked how intense do tones at various frequencies have to be in order to sound as loud as the tone at 1,000 cycles.

To find out, he asked subjects merely to match the loudness of different frequency tones. The subjects listened to a 1,000-cycle/sec reference tone and adjusted the intensity of a second tone until it was equally loud. From this experiment, Fletcher, aided by Munson, derived the famous curves which bear their names and appear in practically every treatise on "hi-fi." These curves are shown in Fig. 5.1. Note that these contours of equal loudness are labeled with the unit *phon*. The phon scale is identical to a decibel intensity scale for a 1,000-cycle/sec tone. Thus, a 40-phon sound is equal in loudness to a 1,000-cycle/sec tone which is 40 decibels above the threshold of hearing.

Later Fletcher became bolder and began to ask how much louder a 40-phon sound is than a 20-phon sound. Is it twice as loud or ten times as loud? To investigate this matter, Fletcher made one crucial assumption, namely, that a sound consisting of two tones of equal loudness when

SOUND A = SUM OF 2 SINE WAVES
           SAY 500 AND 2000 CPS
SOUND B = 1000 CPS SINE WAVE
I IS AN INDEX = 0 INITIALLY

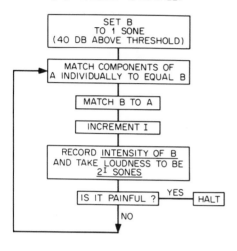

Fig. 5.2 Sound A = sum of 2 sine waves, say 500 and 2,000 cps. Sound B = 1,000 cps sine wave. I is an index = 0 initially.

heard together is twice as loud as either tone heard in isolation. With this assumption, Fletcher constructed an experiment whereby he could find the relation between the subjective loudness and objective intensity of a sound. The experiment involved merely matching the loudness of the two-tone complex to one tone in isolation. The scheme of the experiment is shown as a flow diagram in Fig. 5.2, and the data from that experiment are shown in Fig. 5.3.

In recent years, investigators have become even bolder and asked about the relationship between subjective and objective quantities for any one of a large number of dimensions. Indeed, one can ask if there is any underlying *law* which describes the relationship between subjective and objective quantities. Furthermore, does the relationship, if it exists, vary according to how it is measured? The answer is "yes" to both questions.

Prof. S. S. Stevens[2] of Harvard has developed a measurement method known as *magnitude production*, which gives nearly the same loudness function as that found in Fletcher's experiment. Here subjects are merely asked to adjust the intensity of a sound until it is twice or half as loud as a standard. In other words, the subject is producing a sound of subjective magnitude.

Professor Stevens has found that for a large number of sensations, the subjective-objective relationship follows a power law. That is, if we denote the subjective intensity as S, the objective intensity as I, and the

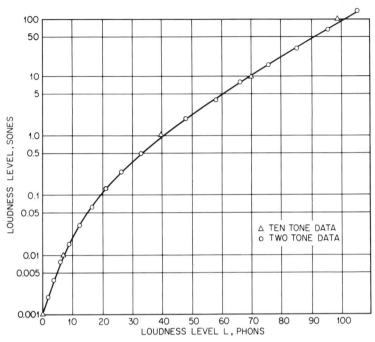

Fig. 5.3 Adapted from Fletcher.[1]

threshold intensity as Io, then

$$S = K(I - Io)^n \qquad \text{where } K \text{ and } n \text{ are constants}$$

For sound, the value of the exponent n is about 0.3. For the objective intensity of a light and its subjective brightness, the exponent is nearly the same. The corresponding relationships are shown in Fig. 5.4. However, for other sensations the power law has different exponents. Some are shown in Fig. 5.5. These curves are plotted on a log-log scale, and so the slope of the straight lines gives the exponent of the power law. The largest exponent so far discovered is 3.5, which applies to electric shock. The lowest is for sound and light.

Thus, to *double* the brightness or loudness of a display, the physical intensity must be increased *ten times* (10 decibels). However, to double electric shock, the voltage need be turned up only by a factor of 1.22. Note that all of the quantities discussed so far are "more of the same" quantities. That is, when the physical intensity of any of them is increased, the subjective intensity merely grows larger but does not change in quality. Such quantities are called *prothetic* by Professor Stevens. There is another class of quantities which he calls *metathetic*. In these cases, when the physical quantity is increased, a change in

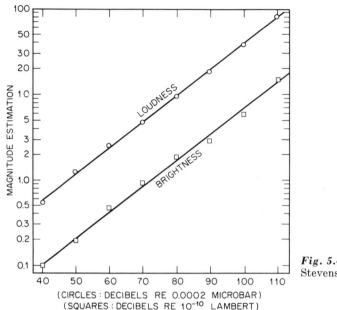

Fig. 5.4 Adapted from Stevens.[2]

quality results. An example is the physical frequency of a sine wave and its subjective pitch. When the frequency is increased, the pitch goes up. The sound does not change in magnitude but rather the quality of it changes. In the case of metathetic quantities, the subjective-objective relationship in general follows a logarithmic law:

$$S = K \log (I/I_0)$$

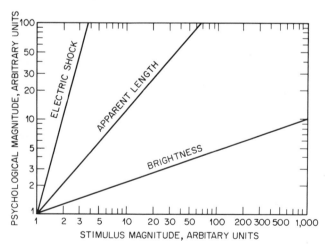

Fig. 5.5 Adapted from Stevens.[2]

PHYSIOLOGICAL AND PSYCHOLOGICAL CONSIDERATIONS *113*

5.3 Discrimination

Thus far we have been concerned with the relation between objective and subjective quantities. We have not, however, asked about the smallest discriminable change in a quantity. That is, we often ask: Are two things different or the same? To answer, we usually try to compare on a "side-by-side" basis. The accuracy of this process involves the smallest perceivable step-size in a physical quantity. Such a limiting step-size is known as a "just noticeable difference," or *jnd*.

As one might expect, the jnd of intensity turns out to depend upon the intensity itself, and in the case of sine wave sound depends also upon frequency. For a more intense quantity, or stimulus, the jnd is larger than for a weak one. Measurements show that the jnd is nearly a constant fraction. That is, ΔI, the jnd, is $\Delta I = KI$. This relation is known as Weber's law, and it favors measurement based on ratios rather than differences. Thus, the decibel is a convenient unit. (Jnd's are a fixed number of decibels.)

If Weber's law were strictly true and if each jnd were the same subjective size, then subjective magnitude would be logarithmically (approximately) related to physical magnitude. This can be shown very simply by mathematical proof.

If each jnd is the same subjective size, then

$$\Delta S = C$$

where ΔS is the change of sensation occasioned by a jnd, ΔI, in the physical stimulus. From Weber's law, then,

$$\Delta S = K \frac{\Delta I}{I}$$

where C is a constant. Summing both sides,

$$\sum_{s=0}^{s=s} \Delta S = C \sum_{I=I_0}^{I=I} \frac{\Delta I}{I}$$

Allowing ΔS and ΔI to pass to infinitesimals, the summations become integrals,

$$\int_0^s ds = K \int_{I_0}^I \frac{dI}{I}$$

or

$$S = K \log (I/I_0)$$

Actually, we know today that this law is true only for metathetic quantities, not prothetic ones. Thus, while Weber's law is a reasonable approximation, it is not exact for many quantities. Nevertheless, decibels and other ratio units are quite appropriate, for the power law implies that to double sensation (or, in general, multiply it by a constant) requires a fixed number of decibels increase, regardless of the starting point (so long as it is above threshold).

5.4   The Physiology behind the Laws

The nonlinear characteristic between subjective and objective quantities is probably the result of transducer action in the end organ (eye or ear).   The jnd of a physical quantity may well be determined by statistical fluctuations in the neural impulse train generated at the end organ. Thus, perceived magnitude and the jnd are both basic attributes of the sensory mechanism involved.

However, the exact physiological mechanisms responsible are not very well understood.   There are some obvious correspondences.   Take as an example the ear.   We know that sine waves have two perceptual attributes—loudness and pitch.   One of these is prothetic, the other is metathetic.   These distinctions are clearly related to the physiology of the ear.   If we look at Figs. 5.6 and 5.7, we can see this.   When a sine wave impinges on the eardrum, the vibrations are transmitted by the bones of the middle ear to the inner ear.   There the basilar membrane is set into vibration.   The auditory nerve senses the vibrations of the basilar membrane much as the surface of the skin senses the vibration of any object.

The vibration response of the basilar membrane can be approximated

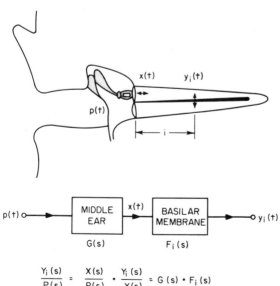

Fig. 5.6

$$\frac{Y_i(s)}{P(s)} = \frac{X(s)}{P(s)} \cdot \frac{Y_i(s)}{X(s)} = G(s) \cdot F_i(s)$$

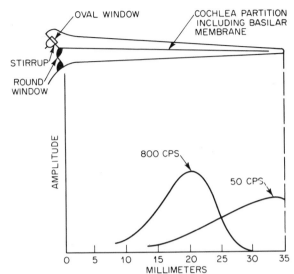

Fig. 5.7 Adapted from Bekesy.[18]

by a linear passive system.   A sine wave stimulates a particular place on that membrane.   An increase in its intensity merely increases the intensity of vibration at the same place, while a change in the frequency of the sine wave changes the place of vibration.   This model shows a correspondence between loudness as a "more of the same" quantity and frequency as a "substitutive" quantity.

It has been thought for many years that the *number* of nerve impulses initiated by the stimulus is closely related to the subjective magnitude of that stimulus.   This relationship, the number of nerve impulses versus the stimulus intensity, has been measured for many sensory modalities. For sound, the relationship has been measured using an electrode attached to the auditory nerve.   Typically, the relationship between number of nerve impulses and stimulus intensity is more nearly logarithmic than it is a power law.

For this fact not to be a fatal defect requires a logarithmic-to-power transformation in the auditory system.   Prof. D. M. Mackay[2] has shown a plausible mechanism for accomplishing this transformation.   It involves an internally generated matching response to the stimulus. This response is generated within the organism, and in the model, the subjective magnitude is not reflected by the number of nerve impulses but by the activity required to counterbalance that number of nerve impulses.   Again, the properties of this model can be derived mathematically.   Mackay's model is interesting and somewhat satisfying. There is, however, no evidence that it represents an actual physiological mechanism.

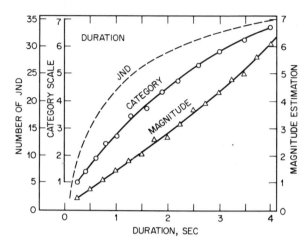

Fig. 5.8   Adapted from
Stevens.[2]

5.5   Effect of Measurement Techniques and Context

Results from scaling experiments do depend upon the measurement
technique.   We have said that the technique of magnitude production
gives results which are in concert with the Fletcher method.   It was also
said that if one merely counts the number of jnds above threshold, the
subjective-objective curve turns out to be approximately logarithmic in
shape.   However, if one establishes categories, designated by either
numbers or adjectives, into which subjects classify physical stimuli, the
result is somewhat different.   Take, for example, *apparent duration* as the
quantity to be scaled.   As in the case of *apparent length*, the exponent
turns out to be nearly one from magnitude production experiments.
Actually it is between 1.05 and 1.2, as shown in Fig. 5.8.   In the category
scale, shown in this same figure, 16 subjects classified 15 stimuli into 7
categories designated by numbers.   The curve is concave downward
because discrimination is better at the low end.   That is, it is easy to
tell a half- from a one-second signal, but it is not so easy to tell a 3.5-
from a 4-second signal.   Thus, the subject tends to put the latter in the
same category while he usually puts the former two in a different category.   Therefore, results of scaling experiments are sensitive to the
measurement technique.   However, Stevens feels that the magnitude
estimation results, that is, the power law and logarithmic law for prothetic
and metathetic quantities, respectively, are reflections of basic physiological mechanisms near the periphery of the nervous system, whereas
category scales are influenced by higher level factors.

Perceptual intensity or quality of a stimulus depends very much on
context.   It has been long known, for example, that the color of a disk
appears differently depending upon the surrounding color.   This phe-

nomen has been called simultaneous contrast. R. N. Shepard[3] has shown how the pitch of a musical tone can be strongly affected by its context. He has been able to construct a sound which appears to rise continually in pitch as a listener compares it with its nearest neighbors. However, the pitch actually does not rise. It is only local comparison that makes it appear so. There are other effects of contrast on perception also. Though the laws discussed earlier are indicative, they must be applied with care where context or contrast is involved.

5.6 Multidimensional Scaling

Thus far we have been talking about only one subjective dimension. The perception of speech sounds cannot be described along a single dimension. In fact, where complex stimuli are involved, the number of dimensions in which they are perceived and the corresponding physical dimensions are not at all obvious. An analytical method[4] for treating experimental data has been developed to determine the subjective space for complex stimuli.

The technique is based on the idea that stimuli can be assigned a position in a Euclidean space where distance determines similarity. Stimuli that are close together are similar, those that are farther apart are less similar, but the explicit relation between distance and similarity is not assumed a priori. It is assumed that subjects tend to confuse stimuli in proportion to their spatial proximity. That is, the closer together stimuli lie, the more often one is mistaken for the other when, for example, they are presented in pairs to a subject.

The method is as follows: First, the confusability of the stimuli is measured. A typical set of data from such an experiment is shown in Fig. 5.9. Those data were obtained by playing Morse code signals in pairs to subjects who were not familiar with these signals. They were merely asked if the members of the code pairs they heard were the same or different. Sometimes the subjects called some signals different, and sometimes they called different signals the same. These data specify the confusability of the signals which is assumed to be related in a monotonic way to the distance between the signals in the Euclidean space (subjective).

A method of successive approximations (e.g., the method of steepest descent)[4] is used to fit the signal points in a multidimensional space to fit the confusability data. This iterative procedure is implemented on a digital computer and converges rapidly in most instances. An additional step is to examine the subjective space and try to identify the physical correlates. The Morse code space obtained by this method is shown in Fig. 5.10 with the physical correlates indicated. By this method very complex perceptual spaces can be explored by experimenta-

	A	B	C	D	E	F	G	H	I	J	K	L	M	N	O	P	Q	R	S	T	U	V	W	X	Y	Z	1	2	3	4	5	6	7	8	9	0
A	92	04	06	13	03	14	10	13	46	05	22	03	25	34	06	06	09	35	23	06	37	13	17	12	07	03	02	07	05	05	08	06	05	06	02	03
B	05	84	37	31	05	28	17	21	05	19	34	40	06	10	12	22	25	16	18	02	18	34	08	84	30	42	12	17	14	40	32	74	43	17	04	04
C	04	38	87	17	04	29	13	07	11	19	24	35	14	03	09	51	34	24	14	06	06	11	14	32	82	38	13	15	31	14	10	30	28	24	18	12
D	08	62	17	88	07	23	40	36	09	13	81	56	08	07	09	27	09	45	29	06	17	20	27	40	15	33	03	09	06	11	09	19	08	10	05	06
E	06	13	14	06	97	02	04	04	17	01	05	06	04	04	05	01	05	10	07	67	03	03	02	05	06	05	04	03	05	03	05	02	04	02	03	03
F	04	51	33	19	02	90	10	29	05	33	16	50	07	06	10	42	12	35	14	02	21	27	25	19	27	13	08	16	47	25	26	24	21	05	05	05
G	09	18	27	38	01	14	90	06	05	22	33	16	14	13	82	52	23	21	05	03	15	14	32	21	23	39	15	14	05	10	04	10	17	23	20	11
H	03	45	23	25	09	32	08	87	10	10	09	29	05	08	08	14	08	17	37	04	36	59	09	33	14	11	03	09	11	54	37	05	17	04	03	03
I	64	07	07	13	10	08	06	12	93	03	05	16	13	30	07	03	05	19	35	16	10	05	08	02	05	07	02	05	08	09	06	08	05	02	04	05
J	07	09	38	09	02	24	18	05	04	85	22	31	08	03	21	63	47	11	02	07	09	09	09	22	32	28	67	66	33	15	07	11	28	29	26	23
K	05	24	38	73	01	17	25	11	05	27	91	33	10	12	31	14	31	22	02	02	23	17	33	63	16	11	08	05	09	17	08	08	18	14	13	05
L	02	69	43	45	10	24	12	26	09	30	27	86	06	02	09	37	36	28	12	05	16	19	20	31	25	59	12	13	17	15	26	29	36	16	07	03
M	24	12	05	14	07	17	29	08	08	11	23	08	96	62	11	10	15	20	07	09	13	04	21	09	18	08	05	07	06	06	05	07	11	07	10	04
N	31	04	13	30	08	12	10	16	13	03	16	08	59	93	05	09	05	28	12	10	16	04	12	04	06	11	05	02	03	04	04	06	02	02	10	02
O	07	07	20	06	05	09	76	07	02	39	26	10	04	08	86	37	35	10	03	04	11	14	25	35	27	27	19	17	07	07	06	18	14	11	20	12
P	05	22	33	12	05	36	22	12	03	78	14	46	05	06	21	83	43	23	09	04	12	19	19	19	41	30	34	44	24	11	15	17	24	23	25	13
Q	08	20	38	11	04	15	10	05	02	27	23	26	07	06	22	51	91	11	02	03	06	14	12	37	50	63	34	32	17	12	09	27	40	58	37	24
R	13	14	16	23	05	34	26	15	07	12	21	37	14	12	12	29	08	87	16	02	23	23	62	14	12	13	07	10	13	04	07	12	07	09	01	02
S	17	24	05	30	11	26	05	59	16	03	13	10	05	17	06	06	03	18	96	09	56	24	12	10	06	07	08	02	02	15	28	09	05	05	05	02
T	13	10	01	05	46	03	06	06	14	06	14	07	06	05	06	11	04	04	07	96	08	05	04	02	02	06	05	03	03	03	08	07	06	14	06	12
U	14	29	12	32	04	32	11	34	21	07	44	32	11	13	06	20	12	40	51	06	93	57	34	17	09	11	06	06	16	34	10	09	09	07	04	03
V	05	17	24	16	09	29	06	39	05	11	26	43	04	01	09	17	10	17	11	06	32	92	17	57	35	10	10	14	28	79	44	36	25	10	01	05
W	09	21	30	22	09	36	25	15	04	25	29	18	15	06	26	20	25	61	12	04	19	20	86	22	25	22	10	22	19	16	05	09	11	06	03	07
X	07	64	45	19	03	28	11	06	01	35	50	42	10	08	24	32	61	10	12	03	12	17	21	91	48	26	12	20	24	27	16	57	29	16	17	06
Y	09	23	62	15	04	26	22	09	01	30	12	14	05	06	14	30	52	05	07	04	06	13	21	44	86	23	26	44	40	15	11	26	22	33	23	16
Z	03	46	45	18	02	22	17	10	07	23	21	51	11	02	15	59	72	14	04	03	09	11	12	36	42	87	63	13	08	10	08	19	32	57	55	
1	02	05	10	03	03	05	13	04	02	29	05	14	09	07	14	30	28	09	04	02	03	12	14	17	19	22	84	63	13	08	10	08	09	19	32	57
2	07	14	22	05	04	20	13	03	25	26	09	14	02	03	17	37	38	06	05	03	06	10	11	17	30	13	62	89	54	20	05	14	20	21	16	11
3	03	08	21	05	04	32	06	12	02	23	06	13	05	02	05	37	19	09	07	06	04	16	06	22	25	12	18	64	86	31	23	41	16	17	08	10
4	06	19	19	12	06	25	14	16	07	21	13	19	03	03	02	17	29	11	09	03	17	55	08	37	24	03	05	26	44	89	42	44	32	10	03	03
5	08	45	15	14	02	45	04	67	07	14	04	41	02	00	04	13	07	09	27	02	14	45	07	45	10	10	14	10	36	90	42	24	10	06	05	
6	07	80	30	17	04	23	04	14	02	11	11	12	06	02	07	16	30	11	14	03	12	30	09	58	38	39	15	14	26	24	17	86	69	14	05	14
7	06	33	22	14	05	25	06	04	06	24	13	32	07	06	07	36	39	12	06	02	03	13	09	30	30	50	22	29	18	15	12	61	85	70	20	13
8	03	23	40	06	03	15	15	06	02	33	10	14	03	06	14	12	45	02	06	04	06	07	05	24	35	50	42	29	16	16	09	30	60	89	61	26
9	03	14	23	03	01	06	14	05	02	30	06	07	16	11	10	31	32	05	06	07	06	03	08	11	21	24	57	39	09	12	04	11	42	56	91	78
0	09	03	11	02	05	07	14	04	05	30	08	03	02	03	25	21	29	02	03	04	05	03	02	12	15	20	50	26	09	11	05	22	17	52	81	94

Fig. 5.9 Adapted from Shepard.[4]

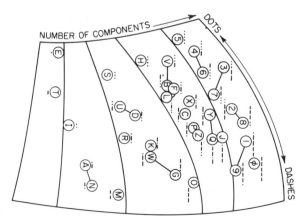

Fig. 5.10 Adapted from Shepard.[4]

tion and the perceptual factors influencing subjects' judgment can be ascertained.

5.7 Dynamic Range

The dynamic range of the senses is remarkably large when compared with electronic or electromechanical sensors. In hearing, the range is over 130 decibels and in vision, it is over 100 decibels. The basis of this fantastic performance is not well understood. However, it is known that regulatory mechanisms set the sensitivity of the nervous system at many different levels, depending upon the intensity of the observed stimulus. A familiar regulator is the pupil of the eye which contracts in bright light. Clearly, such regulatory mechanisms contribute strongly to the wide dynamic range.

5.8 Temporal Resolution

The temporal resolution of the senses is limited. They cannot resolve independent events if these events are more closely spaced in time than some minimum. In other cases, the senses act like an integrator. For example, the brightness of a flash of light whose duration is about 200 milliseconds or less is perceived according to its area or the intensity-time product.

This integrating characteristic shows up in the perception of temporal stimuli, for example, in viewing a flickering light. If the flicker rate rises above about 20 flashes per second (in the ordinary range of intensities), the light appears to be on steadily. There are many data relating the flicker-fusion frequency to the intensity of illumination.[5] Suffice it to say that the senses are low-pass, and fusion and temporal integration effects occur at low levels in the nervous system.

5.9 Summary of Concepts Relative to Perception

1. Perceived quantities are not linearly related to their physical counterparts. For prothetic, or "more of the same," quantities, a power law holds. For substitutive continua, a logarithmic law seems to hold. Though these basic perceptual relations are sensitive to context and measurement conditions, they can be usefully applied. For example, to double the brightness of display or the loudness of a sound, the light or sound intensity must be increased by about ten decibels.

2. Taking the idea of a subjective scale further, it is possible to define subjective multidimensional spaces in which objects are perceived. Objects appear as points in the space. Those close together are similar and confusable. The dimensions of these spaces can often be identified with the physical properties of the display and the dimensions themselves can be found through measurement.

3. The senses have a very large dynamic range and are low-pass in character.

INFORMATION TRANSMISSION

5.10   Discrimination versus Identification

In considering information flow across the man-machine interface, we note that the concept of information necessarily involves choice of one from a set of alternatives. Operationally a person might accomplish this choice by attaching a name (or label) or otherwise *identifying* the presentation. For example, a person might attempt to name musical notes as they were played on a piano one after another. Here the set of alternatives is merely the set of musical notes on the piano keys. Clearly, the person must be able to discriminate between all pairs of notes if he is to name them. This necessity for discrimination, however, is far from the limiting factor.

In man, discrimination (the ability to perceive changes) is ever so much more acute than the ability to identify items in isolation. A person can hear the difference between tones only 1 cycle per second apart at 1,000 cycles per second. Between 1,000 cycles per second and 2,000 cycles per second there are some 400 to 500 discriminable steps in frequency. Yet the usual subject cannot assign a label or otherwise tag more than some six tones over his whole range of hearing when these tones are presented singly.

At first this fact appears almost unbelievable. Yet you can believe, perhaps, that if you had photographs of a half-million faces, you could learn to distinguish between any two at a time by comparing them. This does not mean that you could learn to recognize and name them one by one.

Let us examine data from an experiment by Irwin Pollack.[6] Subjects tried to identify the pitch of a tone by assigning a number to it. The tones were presented singly, that is, there was an interval of 25 seconds between successive presentations. By changing the number of stimulus tones in the set that was presented to the subjects, stimulus information could be changed. The information per presentation was $\log_2 n$, where n was the number of alternative tones. The results, shown in Fig. 5.11, indicate that the information transferred as a function of the number of alternatives was at most about 2.2 bits per stimulus. This number corresponds to about five tones accurately identified. In other words, the average subject can identify accurately only five tones on the frequency scale from 100 to 8,000 cycles, while he can discriminate some 1,400 different tones on that very same interval. This was a surprising

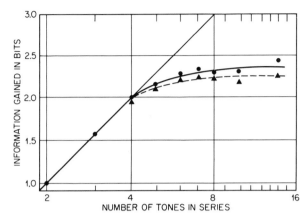

Fig. 5.11 Adapted from Pollack and Ficks.[6]

result, and Pollack varied the parameters of his experiment to try to maximize the information transmitted. With various frequency ranges and spacings of the tones, he was never able to do substantially better.

In fact, for most single perceptual dimensions, it is, in general, true that the average subject can perceive or can identify at most *seven plus or minus two* stimuli presented on that interval. Prof. George Miller[7] of Harvard has called this "the rule of seven plus or minus two."

On more than one dimension, more information can be transmitted. Note that here we are referring not to subjective dimensions but rather to the physical dimensions of the stimuli, that is, stimulus parameters which can be manipulated independently. As indicated in Fig. 5.12, Pollack was able to concoct auditory stimuli which had up to eight different dimensions. Using these dimensions, he was able to transmit about

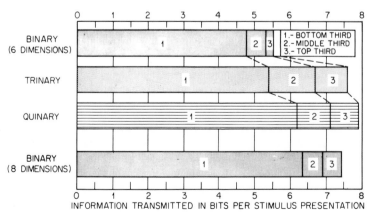

Fig. 5.12 Adapted from Pollack and Ficks.[6]

one bit per stimulus dimension to the subject. Pollack's results indicate, and subsequent studies have confirmed, that a large part of the total possible information can be absorbed by a subject from a multidimensional display with a binary choice on each dimension.

This striking limitation on identification is closely associated with the observer's tendency to place stimuli into, at most, a few categories. For example, American listeners tend to classify all speech sounds as one of the 40 or so phonemes in common use in the English language. Though such categories can be modified by training, as in learning a foreign language, they are highly resistant to change. Preformed categories, either acquired or innate, strongly bias perception and limit the information an observer can absorb.

5.11 Information Rates and Reaction Time

Thus far we have been concerned with information per stimulus presentation. What about the *rate* at which information can be transmitted across the man-machine interface? Here we are asking about the speed of perception and human reaction times.

Clearly the speed of perception is limited first of all by the transmission time of nervous impulses from the periphery of the nervous system to some central point. Measurements show that the minimum reaction time is somewhat greater than 100 milliseconds for merely indicating "yes" or "no." If we require the subject to push a button when a light comes on, his minimum reaction time would be about 150 milliseconds. The importance of this "hard core" reaction time shows up clearly in "delayed feedback" experiments where additional delay introduced in the stimulus-response path can be compensated only by a change in strategy, not by a shortening of reaction time. The most advertised example occurs when a talker's speech is played back to him with about 0.5 seconds delay through earphones. Many people find themselves unable to speak under this condition. Similar effects become evident in writing or drawing, when a delay is inserted between the manual act and the appearance of the result.[8]

What happens to reaction time when some processing is necessary or some choice is involved? Does the response time go up in proportion to the number of choices? There is conflicting evidence on this point. Hyman's[9] measurements seem to show that the reaction time does go up with information in the stimulus. He presented a matrix of 36 lights in a six-by-six array to subjects. Eight patterns were presented on that array requiring eight distinct responses, that is, button pushes. The patterns were presented with equal probability, weighted probability, and contingent probability in three separate sessions. Thereby the information in the presentations was varied. Fig. 5.13 shows the results

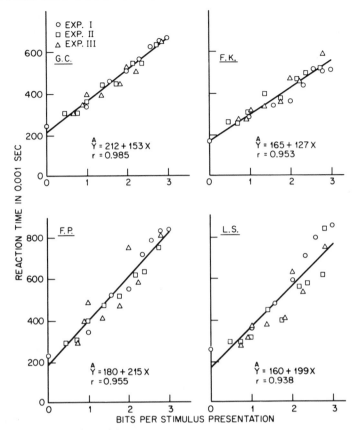

Fig. 5.13 Adapted from Hyman.[9]

and indicates that the reaction time increases with the amount of information in the stimulus set.

Things are not really this simple, however. Another measurement,[10] where naming responses were required, is shown in Fig. 5.14. Ensembles of faces, animals, colors, symbols, and letters were used and, while the reaction time for most of these increased with information content, the reaction time for letters did not increase. The reason appeared to be that letters are so familiar. A similar experiment by Mobray[11] measured the reaction time for naming the one-digit numbers. No increases in reaction time with number of alternatives for well-practiced subjects were found. Apparently "very familiar" objects or displays can be perceived more rapidly than "unfamiliar" ones. Therefore, to maximize the information rate transmitted to a person, choose a familiar stimulus set.

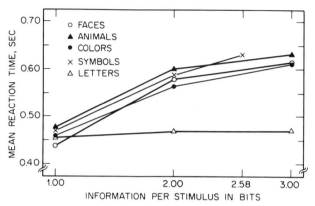

Fig. 5.14 Adapted from Morin-Konick-Troxell-McPherson.[10]

Using this approach, how high an information rate can be achieved? The answer turns out to be about 30 to 40 bits per second as the maximum limit. This rate has been measured in very many ways, but a representative experiment was performed by J. R. Pierce and J. E. Karlin.[12] They had people read aloud lists of words arranged randomly. To control familiarity and word length (long words take longer to read and pronounce than short ones), lists were chosen from the 500 most common words. The results are shown in Fig. 5.15. Reading rate was *independent of vocabulary size* except for the first and last points. The last point illustrates the effect of familiarity and word length, because with the 5,000-word dictionary there were many long and unfamiliar

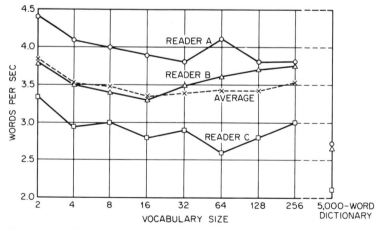

Fig. 5.15 Adapted from Pierce and Karlin.[12]

words. The first point was based on a perceptual anomaly in which two words from a two-word vocabulary could be read in pairs. Since information rate goes up with vocabulary size, the larger the familiar word vocabulary, the greater the information-transfer rate. In order to maximize the information rate, Pierce and Karlin took 2,500 of the most often used words which were short. Here the maximum information rate that the subject could achieve was about 40 bits per second.

To prove that the act of speaking does not limit this rate, Pierce and Karlin presented the subjects with word lists composed of very familiar sayings. Subjects could speak these much more rapidly than they could speak the random word list. Therefore, speaking rate was not a limitation in these experiments.

5.12 Learning

How easy is it to become familiar with, or to learn a display set, so large amounts of information can be transmitted? The answer is that it is not very easy. For example, House and Stevens[13] generated three groups of stimuli, each of which was intended to be more speechlike than the one preceding it. The subjects' tasks were merely to identify stimuli taken from these sets. The more speechlike the stimuli were thought to be, the harder they turned out to be to learn to identify. This result held except in the case of real speech, which turned out to be much easier to learn than any other set.

Thus, there are strong effects of familiarity and dimensionality among other facts in the rate of perception and in learning. Miller[14] has found, for example, that the ability to understand speech in large amounts of interfering noise depends upon very subtle structure, well-learned struc-

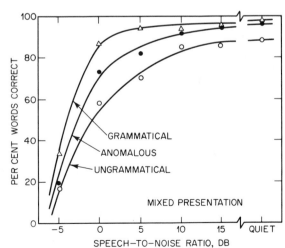

Fig. 5.16 Adapted from Miller and Isard.[14]

ture, namely, the grammar of the language. Grammatical sentences can be heard correctly in much larger amounts of noise than strings of ungrammatical words as shown in Fig. 5.16.

5.13 Summary of Concepts Relative to Information Transmission

1. Discrimination, that is, the ability to perceive differences, is much better than the ability to identify single stimuli. Subjects can identify only "seven plus or minus two" objects on a single dimension, corresponding to a little over 2 bits per stimulus. Multidimensional displays help the situation. However, subjects can absorb only somewhat less than 2 bits per stimulus dimension.

2. Human reaction times have a bottom limit of some 100-plus milliseconds for the most elementary tasks. For more difficult tasks involving identification, reaction time increases linearly with the number of choices, unless the identified objects are drawn from a very familiar set such as letters or numerals. In this case, the reaction time is not a function of the number of choices.

3. To maximize the information transmitted across a man-machine interface, choose a large familiar alphabet. If this is properly done, rates up to 40 bits per second can be achieved.

4. The rate of learning or the ability to identify from a set increases with the familiarity of the set, and it is not always obvious from the physical dimensions of the stimulus what is familiar. However, objects or displays which are in habitual use often turn out to be good choices.

5.14 Pattern Perception

One might summarize what we have said up to now as follows: There are certain favorable *patterns* for the transmission of information across a man-machine boundary. Pattern perception is an often-heard term of discussion among psychologists and other people. However, it is difficult to define. For our purposes, we may call it perception in which the perceived object is more than the perception of its individual parts.

There is some good evidence to say that pattern perception is strongly determined by an overall organization in the nervous system. For example, in ambiguous patterns, those with more than one interpretation, such as shown in Fig. 5.17, a viewer cannot see both patterns at the same time. What perceptual mechanisms are behind such phenomena we do not really know, but there are some intriguing hints.

In many lower animals, octopus and frog for example, there are simple mechanisms which are tailored to select certain features from the environment.[15,16] For instance, the octopus can learn easily to discriminate between horizontal and vertical lines, but not between diagonal lines to the right and left. The reason is that the retinal structure of the octopus

Fig. 5.17

eye is such that information is not available about diagonal lines. In the octopus retina, the photosensitive elements run horizontally and vertically; thus pattern perception in the octopus must be some function of the horizontal and vertical extent of the figures projected onto the retina. Thus, all information on which oblique discrimination could be made is discarded before the nervous system. In the frog, similar specific pattern-perception mechanisms in the nervous system itself have been found. The frog's eye is set up to be a fly catcher.

Do mechanisms of this kind exist in man? It is dangerous to extrapolate from lower animals to man. It seems reasonable to suppose that as one goes up the phylogenetic scale, animals can afford less to throw away information irretrievably by decision making early in their systems. The frog can afford to do this—man cannot. Thus, if such mechanisms exist in man, they are much less rigid and must be invoked via some central control.

For example, there is some anecdotal evidence that man can set up his peripheral nervous system so that it is selectively sensitive to certain patterns or tasks. If one ear is trained so that it becomes highly adept at discriminating small-frequency differences, this training does not transfer to the other ear.[17] Similarly, if a subject knows the frequency or pattern to listen for in noise, he can pick it out at much lower signal-to-noise ratio than if he is ignorant of the frequency or pattern. Such phenomena might be mediated by the descending or efferent nervous system. However, such central control or programming of the periphery, if it exists, can probably be carried out only for well-learned or innate patterns.

5.15 Conclusion

In conclusion, man is flexible but not infinitely so. We must take into account his idiosyncrasies when designing displays. Actually none of the characteristics that we have described in this chapter are surprising in retrospect, but they are often ignored by designers of displays.

REFERENCES

1. Fletcher, H.: *Speech and Hearing in Communication*, Van Nostrand, 1953.
2. Stevens, S. S.: The Psychophysics of Sensory Function, *Sensory Communication*, edited by W. Rosenblith, Wiley, 1961, pp. 1–33. Also, D. M. Mackay; Psychophysics of Perceived Intensity, *Science*, no. 139, pp. 1214–1216, March 22, 1963.
3. Shepard, R. N.: Circularity in the Judgments of Relative Pitch, *J. Acoust. Soc. Am.*, no. 36, pp. 2346–2353, 1964.
4. Shepard, R. N.: The Analysis of Proximities: Multidimensional Scaling with an Unknown Distance Function, *Psychometrica*, vol. 27, nos. 2 and 3, pp. 125–139, 210–245, 1962.
5. deLange, H.: Research into the Dynamic Nature of the Human Fonea-Cortex Systems with Intermittent and Modulated Light, *J. Opt. Soc. Am.*, no. 48, pp. 777–784, 1958.
6. Pollack, I., and L. Ficks: The Information of Elementary Auditory Displays, *J. Acoust. Soc. Am.*, no. 26, pp. 155–158, 1954.
7. Miller, G.: The Magical Number Seven, Plus or Minus Two: Some Limits on Our Capacity for Processing Information, *Psych. Rev.*, no. 63, pp. 81–97, 1956.
8. David, E. E., and W. A. Van Bergeijk: Delayed Handwriting, *Perceptual Motor Skills*, no. 9, pp. 347–357, 1959.
9. Hyman, R.: Stimulus Information as a Determinant of Reaction Time, *J. Exp. Psych.*, vol. 45, no. 3, pp. 188–196, 1953.
10. Morin, R. E., A. Konick, N. Troxell, and S. McPherson: Information and Reaction Time for "Naming" Responses, *J. Exp. Psych.*, vol. 70, no. 3, pp. 309–314, 1965.
11. Mobray, G. H.: Choice Reaction Times for Skilled Responses, *Q. J. Exp. Psych.*, vol. 12, no. 4, pp. 193–202, 1960.
12. Pierce, J. R., and J. E. Karlin: Reading Rates and the Information Rates of the Human Channel, *Bell System Tech. J.*, vol. 36, pp. 497–516, 1957.
13. House, A. S., and K. N. Stevens: On the Learning of Speechlike Vocabularies, *J. Verbal Learn. and Verbal Behav.*, vol. 1, 133–143, 1962.
14. Miller, G., and S. Isard: Some Perceptual Consequences of Linguistic Rules, *J. Verbal Learn. and Verbal Behav.*, vol. 2, no. 3, pp. 217–228, 1963.
15. Sutherland, N. S.: Visual Discrimination in Animals, *British Med. Bull.*, vol. 20, no. 1, pp. 54–59, 1964.
16. Lettvin, J. Y., H. R. Maturana, W. H. Pitts, and W. S. McCulloch: What the Frog's Eye Tells the Frog's Brain, *Proc. IRE*, vol. 47, 1940–1951, 1959.
17. David, E. E., and G. Shodder: Pitch Discrimination of Two-Frequency Complexes, *J. Acoust. Soc. Am.*, vol. 32, no. 11, pp. 1426–1435, 1960.
18. Bekesy, G. von: Uber die Resonanzkurve und die Abklingzeit der verschiedenen Stellen der Schneckentrennwand, *Akust. Z.*, vol. 8, pp. 66–76, 1943.

Part II

APPLICATIONS

SOLVING
MATHEMATICAL
PROBLEMS

VI

Burton D. Fried

University of California
Los Angeles, California

6.1 Introductory Remarks

The following four chapters are devoted to exploring the application of
on-line computing techniques in a variety of technical disciplines. The
conventional approach to the solution of the problems arising in each of
these areas is governed to a large extent by the limitations imposed by
man's computing capability and by the limitation of conventional batch-
type digital computing. The advent of on-line computing systems,
particularly those with graphic input-output, promises to revolutionize
existing analyses and design philosophies. The present chapter is
devoted to a discussion of the power and utility of on-line computing
techniques when applied to the mathematical problems arising in scientific and engineering work. Specific reference is made to the On-Line
System for Mathematics developed by Prof. Glen Culler, the general
features of which are described in the Appendix. Familiarity with the
basic concepts of this type of on-line system, with the nature of the

131

capabilities provided, and with the principal features ("console pro-grams," "x and y registers," "operator levels," etc.) is assumed in this chapter.

By deliberate choice, the structure of Culler's system closely parallels that of classical analysis (calculus, functions of a real or complex variable, etc.). Like its mathematical counterpart, the system is very powerful, but just as a student who has been taught differentiation, integration, functional substitution, and the other basic processes of analysis must still learn to employ these effectively in solving problems, so an on-line user must learn (or develop for himself) techniques which allow him to take maximal advantage of the facilities available.

We shall begin with a discussion of elementary on-line techniques, useful in a wide variety of problems, and then discuss briefly a *simple* example of the use of the on-line system for mathematical problem solving. The real usefulness of such a system can be conclusively demonstrated only by illustrating its application to a variety of really difficult problems. Unfortunately, a description of these would entail a level of detail intolerable to anyone who is not a specialist in the par-ticular problem area involved. We must simply ask the reader to extrapolate from the elementary examples given here to significant problems in his own area. (References 1 through 16 describe typical problems of varying degrees of complexity which have been solved during the period 1961–1965 using such an on-line system.)

In particular, from the dozen or so typical console programs, which are given here in full detail, the reader can judge how much, or how little, effort is required on the user's part in constructing the elements which go to make up a problem, and in composing these into more complex combinations, as required. We have not attempted to illustrate, or to discuss, the intellectual processes—analysis, invention, induction, etc.—which are required for successful problem solving. These are in no wise unique to an on-line system; the best the latter can do is to make it easier for the user to carry out these processes at a speed limited only by his own capabilities.

The general criteria for deciding whether or not a given problem is appropriate for on-line solution have been cogently stated in the Appen-dix. Once a problem has been chosen as appropriate for on-line solution, the basic task is to devise a constructive algorithm of some kind for com-puting the desired quantities. The difficulty of doing this will vary from case to case, and we can distinguish three broad categories of tasks:

1. *Elementary Techniques.* These are simple console programs, com-mon to a very large class of problems, some examples (to be discussed in detail below) being the choice of a suitable independent variable, integra-tion and differentiation to a given order of accuracy, inversion of func-

tions, and three-dimensional displays for viewing functions of two variables.

2. *Explicit Calculations.* These are somewhat more specialized and less simple, but in each case explicit, analytic procedures for constructing the desired quantities are known. The evaluation of the special functions of mathematical physics, for general functional arguments, provides good examples of these, and we use as illustrations below the Hermite polynomials, and Bessel functions of complex argument. In each such case, there are generally three steps to be followed:

a. Choose (perhaps tentatively) an appropriate analytical formulation—power series, integral representation, asymptotic series, etc., or some combination thereof.

b. Make any necessary numerical analysis decisions—method of integration, domain and mesh spacing of independent variable, etc.—again on a tentative basis.

c. Construct the appropriate console programs and try them. Depending on the user's experience, he may find that his choices for *a* or *b* were unsatisfactory; he can then experiment with other alternatives.

3. *Implicit Solutions of Problems.* This, of course, is where the real payoff comes, and is the end for which 1 and 2 really constitute means, although explicit calculations are sometimes valuable in their own right, as in a study of the effects of varying input parameters in a complicated formula or analytic expression. Whether the problem is one of finding complex roots of a transcendental function, solving nonlinear or singular differential equations, or solving integral equations, we are given certain conditions satisfied by the "unknowns" and must devise a technique for finding these.

As already noted, if the problem is of a standard type, it may be best to use a conventional computational approach rather than on-line methods. In general, the latter have proved particularly advantageous for problems which are in, or can be put into, the form mathematicians call "fixed point." The simplest example of a fixed point problem is an equation like

$$x = \cos x$$

where x is a number to be found. More generally, if y denotes any member of some "function space" and T a mapping of that space onto itself, then the solutions of

$$y = T[y] \tag{1}$$

are clearly "fixed points," or invariants, of that mapping. The display capabilities of the on-line system make it easy to determine whether any trial y agrees with $T[y]$; if not, we can readily see the nature of the disagreement, which can be of help in making an intelligent next choice.

Straightforward iteration, in which the $(n + 1)$st choice for y is determined from the nth by

$$y_{n+1} = T[y_n] \tag{2}$$

will converge if the appropriately defined "norm" of T at y is less than 1. When T is complicated and y unknown, this theorem is of little help; but once the console programs which calculate $T[y]$ from y (and which will, typically, involve a number of examples of categories 1 and 2 above) have been made, we can immediately investigate the convergence properties experimentally. If these prove unsatisfactory, we can then easily construct console programs for some of the infinite class of operators, S, having the property that the solutions of (1) and of

$$y = S[y] \tag{3}$$

coincide, while the norms of S and T are quite different. For example, S might be taken as

$$S[y] = \lambda y + (1 - \lambda) T[y] \tag{4}$$

where λ is any member of the function space. In some problems, an appropriate choice of λ leads to excellent convergence, albeit different λ may be required at different stages in the iteration; in other cases, this choice for S is of no help for any λ, and we must try a different S. For instance, if y and $T[y]$ are positive definite, then the choices

$$S[y] = \sqrt{y \cdot T[y]}$$

or, more generally,

$$S[y] = \exp \left(\lambda \log y + (1 - \lambda) \log T[y] \right)$$

are sometimes successful. Other examples are given below, but in general it seems fair to say that just here the ingenuity, intuition, and experience of the problem solver are what is required in finding the choice appropriate to a given problem.

In the following sections, we expand upon the points raised here and give examples of each of the three categories of problems. While the sections treating elementary techniques and explicit calculations may not seem particularly relevant to the more recondite subject of problem solving, it must be realized that the process of solving any problem will commence with the construction of such simple elements as those illustrated here, and that these account for a significant fraction of the user's total effort; their subsequent combination, via console programming, into the more complex routines required for a particular problem is relatively easy, albeit deciding how to use finally these routines in actually solving the problem may entail considerable intellectual effort. The discussion in the next two sections, although at an elementary level, is quite detailed, and presumes a *very* careful reading of the Appendix of this book. The impatient reader may wish to skim lightly over these and go on to the subsequent section, where some general remarks on problem solving itself are illustrated with a particular example, and to the final section, where a summary and evaluation are presented.

ELEMENTARY TECHNIQUES

From the large class of these, we have chosen a very few, representative simple examples. As will be clear from these, creating such techniques requires no skill of a programming character but may sometimes call for more experience with numerical methods than a typical user enjoys. However, the system makes it so easy to experiment at a numerical level that anyone with sound mathematical training will quickly rediscover standard numerical techniques or invent new ones.

6.2   Choice of an Independent Variable

In any problem involving functions of a single real variable, we must begin with some choice for the range of that variable and the distribution of mesh points within that range.

Since a uniform distribution is often appropriate, a useful console program is one which generates an independent variable t on the range $A \leq t \leq B$, with n equally spaced mesh points (the dimensions of the current "array" being $m \times n$, meaning that it accommodates m vectors, each having n points, with $1 \leq m, n \leq 125$). This program is simply

$IND. VAR.$:   II ID $+ 1 \cdot 0.5$ STORE t LOAD $B - A \cdot t +$
$\qquad A$ STORE t

In many problems, however, a uniform spacing is inappropriate. If the functions involved have rapid variation over some portion of their domain, we will want a higher density of mesh points in that region. In the simplest case, some of the given functions (coefficients in a differential equation, kernel of an integral equation, etc.) may have this character, and thus provide a basis for a satisfactory choice of the independent variable *ab initio*. In other problems, however, this structure may arise only in the (initially unknown) functions obtained as

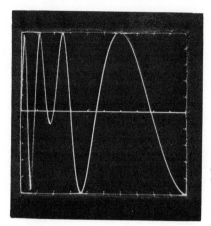

Fig. 6.1 Plot of $y(t)$, normal display (data points connected with straight line segments).

a final solution. In such a case, we might first solve the problem using a uniform mesh and then, having seen the character of the solution, make a better choice for the independent variable and repeat the solution procedure.

As a simple example of this, consider the curve $y(t)$ shown in Fig. 6.1, which arose as the solution of a certain problem. The rapid variation of the left-hand portion of the curve suggests that it is poorly represented there; this is confirmed by using the "dot" mode of display (Fig. 6.2) in which only the actual data points representing the function in question are shown. (In the normal display mode, these are connected by straight line segments, as an aid to the eye.) In the calculations leading to this curve, the independent variable t, with $0 \leq t \leq 1$, was constructed using the IND. VAR. routine described above, with $A = 0$, $B = 1$. Since we want more mesh points near $t = 0$, a simple way of improving the numerical representation is to use as independent variable $\bar{t} = t^2$. Both t and $\bar{t}$,

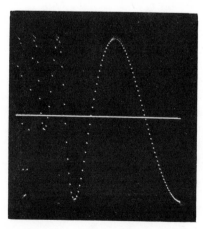

Fig. 6.2 Plot of $y(t)$, dotted display (straight line segments suppressed).

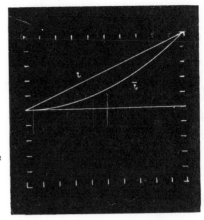

Fig. 6.3 Plot of t and $\bar{t} = t^2$
versus the ID vector.

plotted against the identity or ID vector,* are shown in Fig. 6.3.   If we
repeat the calculations, using $\bar{t}$ in place of t, we obtain the result shown in
Fig. 6.4, in which the variation at the left end is clearly less rapid.   Of
course, the shape of the new curve is qualitatively different from that of
Fig. 6.1, but that is simply because in Fig. 6.1 and Fig. 6.4, y is plotted
against the ID vector, which is a linear function of t, but *not* of $\bar{t}$.   If we
want a plot of the new solution comparable to Fig. 6.1, we simply put in
the x register a vector, say $\bar{t}$, which is a linear function of $\bar{t}$ and runs from
-1 to 1.   The result of doing this (II LOAD $\bar{t} - 0.5 \cdot 2$ STORE W
SUB W DISPLAY y) is shown in Fig. 6.5, using the dot mode of display.
It is clear that the rapidly oscillating part of the solution is now well

* That is, the x register contains a vector which runs from -1 to 1 in n equal steps.
It is usually convenient to have this ID vector in the x register when doing displays
associated with Level II operations, but we shall presently see an exception to this.

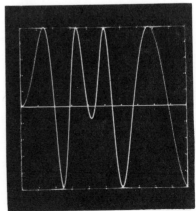

Fig. 6.4 Plot of $y(\bar{t})$ versus
ID function, normal display.

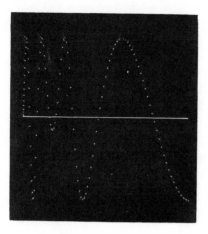

Fig. 6.5 Plot of $y(t)$ versus t, dotted display. Comparison with Fig. 6.2 shows the improved representation resulting from concentrating mesh points where they are needed.

represented, thanks to the concentration of mesh points at the left end, which is obvious in the figure.

6.3 Integration and Differentiation

The DIFF and SUM operations on Level II provide a capability from which it is easy to construct any of the innumerable numerical representations for differentiation and integration. We confine ourselves here to the case of a uniform independent variable; any book on numerical analysis may be consulted for algorithms appropriate to the general case.

From the Taylor series formula

$$\Delta f(t) = f(t + h) - f(t) = \sum_{n=1}^{\infty} D^n f(t) h^n / n! \tag{5}$$

we deduce the relation between the derivative operator, $D \equiv d/dt$, and the first difference operator, Δ,

$$\Delta = e^{hD} - 1 \tag{6}$$

or

$$D = h^{-1} \log (1 + \Delta) \equiv h^{-1} \left[\Delta - \frac{\Delta^2}{2} + \frac{\Delta^3}{3} - \cdots \right] \tag{7}$$

The simplest approximation to D is Δ/h; a better one is $\Delta(1 - \Delta/2)/h$; etc. Thus, a console program for the first derivative of the vector in the y register, correct to terms of second order, would be

$DERIV$: II STORE W DIFF $\cdot$ $-0.5 + W$ DIFF $/\, h$

corresponding to the representation

$$Df = \frac{df}{dt} = \frac{\Delta(f - \Delta f/2)}{h}$$

It is clear how to go on to higher-order representations (provided some appropriate extrapolation procedure is used to take care of the right-hand end point).

Since indefinite integration is the inverse of differentiation,

$$\int\! f\, dt = g$$

implies

$$f = Dg = [1 - \Delta/2 + \Delta^2/3 - \cdots]\Delta g/\Delta t \qquad (8)$$

Formally inverting the power series in Δ, we have

$$\Delta g/\Delta t = [1 + \Delta/2 - \Delta^2/12 + \Delta^3/24 - \cdots]f \qquad (9)$$

whence

$$g = \Delta t \cdot \Sigma[1 + \Delta/2 - \Delta^2/12 + \Delta^3/24 - \cdots]f \qquad (10)$$

where Σ is essentially the SUM operation of Level II. Stopping at the $\Delta/2$ term corresponds to the trapezoidal rule for integration, while the higher terms give more accurate representations. Keeping the first three terms, for example, we have

$$g = \int\! f\, dt = \Sigma[f + \tfrac{1}{2}\Delta(f - \tfrac{1}{6}\Delta f)] \cdot h$$

leading to the console program

$$\int : \quad \text{II STORE } W \text{ DIFF } / -6 + W \text{ DIFF} \cdot 0.5 + W \text{ RS} \cdot h \text{ SUM}$$

which computes the integral of the vector in the y register and leaves the result there. This console program assumes that h contains a vector with all elements equal to Δt, save the first, which is zero. (A little thought shows that whereas SUM is not precisely an inverse of DIFF, the last three operations of the above console program, with h so chosen, constitute an exact inverse of the operation DIFF $/ \Delta t$, which is just what is required for finding g from (9). This neat procedure for inverting DIFF is due to Dr. Glen Culler.)

Note that in arriving at the above console program for something as simple as indefinite integration, a number of user's decisions are involved. We have chosen to settle for the accuracy of the first three terms of (9); to have the vector initially in the y register and to leave the result there; to assume a suitable Δt vector is in h; to use location W as a working space; etc. None of these choices is unique in any sense, and different users will almost surely differ in some or even all of these. For this reason, SUM is provided as a basic subroutine of the system, while integration is left to each user to console program according to his needs and taste. Similar considerations are responsible for the fact that formalized sharing of console programs has not, so far, proved to be very important. The time and intellectual effort involved in communicating to another user the procedure for using even this simple console program and the associated restrictions and cautions ("Have the vector initially in the y register"; "Put Δt, with zero for the first point, in h"; "Note that W gets used as a working space"; etc.) is at least equal to that required to simply tell him the general ideas involved (i.e., Eq. (9) or (10) plus the correct inversion of DIFF via RS $\cdot$ h SUM as described above) and let him make a console program, tailored to his own desires, within his user system.

6.4 Functional Inversion

Given $r = f(s)$, over a range of s where f is monotonic, we want to find the inverse, $s = g(r)$, such that $f[g(r)] = r$.
Since

$$\text{II SUB } s \text{ DISPLAY } r$$

gives a plot of f, it might be thought that

$$\text{II SUB } r \text{ DISPLAY } s$$

should give a plot of the inverse function g.

In fact, it does, but for most purposes this is not a satisfactory *numerical* representation of the inverse function because we have no direct control over the mesh spacing of r. Typically, we want the variable which we think of as independent to have a certain mesh spacing, either uniform or variable according to some chosen pattern (as described in Sec. 6.2). If s is uniform, for example, r will generally not be. However, it is easy to use the EVALUATE on Level II to produce a version of g with uniform (or any other desired) mesh spacing for the independent variable. We simply construct a variable t, whose limits are the same as those of r but which has the desired mesh spacing; put r in the x register; and EVALUATE s at t (see Fig. 6.6). If we want $g(r)$ with a uniform mesh spacing for r, for example, we can use the following "simple inversion" console program:

SI: II LOAD r MAX STORE B LOAD r STAR MAX STAR
      STORE A USER I IND. VAR. LOAD s SUB r EVAL t USER I

where we have assumed that the console program IND. VAR. for generating a uniformly spaced independent variable, described in Sec. 6.2, is on User Level I. (We shall henceforth make this assumption for all console programs described in this chapter.) Given any other specification of the mesh spacing for r, we would simply use it in place of IND. VAR. in the SI program.

The resulting inverse function is the best we can do, given only the two vectors r and s and restricting ourselves to linear interpolation. However, it is often the case that we have a console program, GEN f, for f, i.e., one which computes $r = f(s)$ for any given s; then we can find g with much

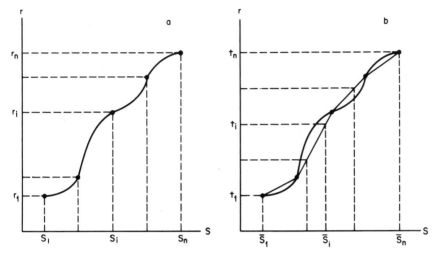

Fig. 6.6 Given the vectors $s = \{s_1, \ldots s_i, \ldots s_n\}$ and $r = \{r_1, \ldots r_i,$
$\ldots r_n\}$, with $r_i = f(s_i)$, we construct the vector $t = \{t_1, \ldots t_i, \ldots t_n\}$, with
$t_1 = r_1$, $t_n = r_n$, and the spacing of the t_i chosen as desired (e.g., uniform).   Then
the operations II LOAD s SUB r EVALUATE t will generate, in the y register,
the vector $\bar{s} = \{\bar{s}_1, \ldots \bar{s}_i, \ldots \bar{s}_n\}$ shown in b above; the $\bar{s}_i$ are a first approximation to $g(t_i)$, g being the function inverse to f.   Note that the $\bar{s}_i$ are determined
by the chords which approximate the curve; this is a consequence of the fact that
EVALUATE uses linear interpolation.   Better accuracy is obtained by using the
iterated inversion described in the text: taking $f(\bar{s}_i)$ gives points $\bar{r}_i$ which have
nearly the desired spacing (i.e., approximate the t_i better than do the r_i given to
us originally) so the linear interpolation involved in the next use of EVALUATE is
more accurate.   The vector (s_i) converges rapidly to $g(t_i)$ with an accuracy
limited only by the computer roundoff.

more accuracy by a process of straightforward iteration.   We use SI to
compute g at the points t and then compute $r = f[g(t)]$.   The resulting
points will have a nearly uniform spacing in r, and if we use them in SI,
a more accurate g will result.   To characterize the process mathematically, let $\mathcal{L}$ be the operator which corresponds to SI, i.e., which generates from a given s and r a new s vector, using linear interpolation
(cf. Fig. 6.6),

$$\bar{s} = \mathcal{L}[s, r]$$

Then, starting with a given s vector, say $s^{(1)}$, the iteration process is
described by

$$r^{(n)} = f[s^{(n)}]$$
$$s^{(n+1)} = \mathcal{L}[s^{(n)}, r^{(n)}]$$

As in many cases, the console program for this "iterated inversion" is
more succinct than the verbal description:

IT. INV.:   USER I GEN f SI STORE s USER I

By repeatedly pushing IT. INV., we generate a sequence of vectors, $s^{(n)}$, which converge (typically very rapidly) to a representation of $g(r)$ whose accuracy is limited only by the number of points per vector and the number of bits per word.*

6.5 Functions of Two Variables; "Three-dimensional" Display

A function $y = K(x, t)$, defined for n_1 values of x and n_2 values of t, can be represented as an array of n_1 vectors, each giving y as a function of t, for fixed x; or, conversely, as an array of n_2 vectors, each giving y as a function of x for fixed t. The choice will be determined by the use to be made of K. If it is to be the kernel of an integral transform, for example,

$$g(x) = \int dt\, K(x, t) f(t)$$

then we would choose the first of these. (Once K has been constructed in this way, the integral transform is quickly evaluated, using a basic system subroutine which performs a matrix by vector multiplication.)

In many cases, it is desirable to have a graphical representation of a function of two variables more sophisticated than simply plots of y versus t for several values of x. This is easily achieved if we can make "three-dimensional" plots (i.e., isometric, or, more generally, axonometric, projections) of a curve in space.

The underlying mathematics, and hence the associated console program, are elementary. Given a parametric representation of a space curve,

$$[x(s), y(s), z(s)]$$

where, of course, s may coincide with x, y, or z, and a choice for the projection angle θ, defined in Fig. 6.7, we need simply compute

$$X = x - z \cos \theta$$
$$Y = y - z \sin \theta$$

and then plot Y versus X. Thus, the console program for this projection is simply

PROJ: II LOAD θ COS $\cdot z$ STAR $+ x$ STORE W LOAD θ SIN $\cdot z$ STAR $+ y$ SUB W STORE U DISPLAY U

---

* The alert reader will have noted that each time SI is executed by IT. INV. it needlessly recomputes the same t vector. Thus, a faster version would be:

IT. INV.: USER I GEN f II LOAD s SUB r EVAL t STORE s USER I.

Of course, before using this version we must be sure that SI has been used once to give us a proper t vector.

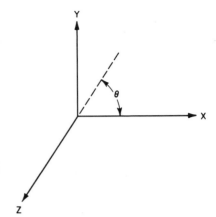

Fig. 6.7 X, Y, Z axes used in axonometric displays.

As a simple example, we use this to display Green's function for the one-dimensional diffusion equation

$$y = \frac{(e^{-qx^2/t})}{\sqrt{bt}}$$

in Fig. 6.8. Although the representation of such a surface is more comprehensible if constant x, constant y, and constant z contours are used, as shown, PROJ can, of course, be used for arbitrary space curves. The

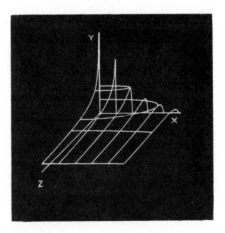

Fig. 6.8 The diffusion equation; Green's function,
$y = \exp(-qx^2/z)/\sqrt{bz}$, where $0 \leq x, z \leq 1$ and $q = 0.1$, $b = 100$.
One family of the curves shown is obtained by holding x fixed,
$x = 0, 0.2, 0.4, 0.6, 0.8, 1.0$. Two curves corresponding to fixed z,
$z = 0.5, 1.0$ are also shown. For given x the maximum value of
y is $y_{max} = (2bqe)^{-1/2}x^{-1}$; the two curves parallel to the xz plane
are obtained by fixing y as the y_{max} corresponding to $x = 0.4$
and 0.8.

projection of such a curve on any of the coordinate planes is also easily obtained. A console program to give the xy projection consists simply of putting zero in z and then doing PROJ. A program to make projection lines parallel to one of the axes, say, the z axis, at an arbitrary point of the curve, is likewise quite simple—it evaluates x, y, and z at the given point, to give constants x_0, y_0, z_0; puts x_0 in x, y_0 in y, and $z_0 t$ in z, where t is a vector with $0 \leq t \leq 1$; and does PROJ.

In closing this section, we note that the examples given represent a small fraction of the elementary techniques which one uses in practice. Most are more elementary than those described here, since we have deliberately chosen some which require a little thought on the user's part.

EXPLICIT CALCULATIONS

6.6   Orthogonal Polynomials

Many problems require the use of some family of orthogonal polynomials; we shall take Hermite polynomials as a simple example. Typically we need a sequence of the functions, rather than a single one, so for the first of the three steps described in Sec. 6.1 under the heading "Explicit Calculations," i.e., the choice of an appropriate analytic representation, we may use the recursion relation,*

$$H_{n+1}(x) = xH_n(x) - nH_{n-1}(x)$$

which together with $H_0 = 1$, $H_1(x) = x$, completely characterizes the functions. The simplicity of the example makes step b (numerical decisions) unnecessary and we can proceed directly to step c (the construction of console programs). The principal one constructs and displays H_{n+1}, assuming H_n and H_{n-1} known:

HERM: II LOAD $H_{n-1} \cdot n$ STORE W LOAD $H_n \cdot x - W$ STORE
H_{n+1} LOAD $n + 1$ STORE n LOAD H_n STORE H_{n-1} LOAD
H_{n+1} STORE H_n DISPLAY H_{n+1} USER I

Note that it also increments n and advances the H_n and H_{n-1}, so that, if repeated, it will generate a continuing sequence of the polynomials. In addition, it is convenient to have a "preparation" program which does the necessary setup:

PREP: II LOAD 1 STORE H_{n-1} n LOAD x STORE H_n

To try our programs, we choose some independent variable for x; push PREP; and then push HERM a few times. Some typical results are shown in Figs. 6.9 and 6.10. Since $H_n(x)$ behaves like x^n for large x, the structure in H_4 which is apparent in Figs. 6.9 and 6.10 is lost in Fig. 6.11,

---

* *Functions of Math. Physics,* Magnus and Oberhettinger, Chelsea Publishing Company, New York, 1954.

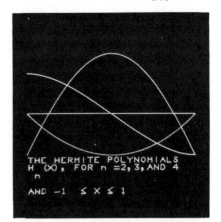

Fig. 6.9 The Hermite polynomials H_2, H_3, H_4 on the domain $|x| \le 1$.

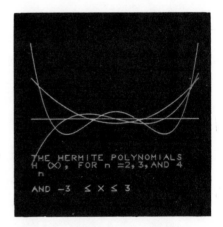

Fig. 6.10 The Hermite polynomials H_2, H_3, H_4 on the domain $|x| \le 3$.

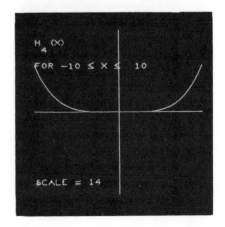

Fig. 6.11 $H_4(x)$ for $|x| \le 10$.

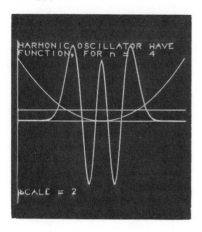

Fig. 6.12 Harmonic oscillator wave function $\psi_4 = e^{-x^2/4}H_n(x)$. The associated potential function $V(x) = x^2/4$ and energy eigenvalue $E = 4.5$ are also shown. The exponential decay of ψ in regions of negative kinetic energy $(E - V < 0)$ is apparent.

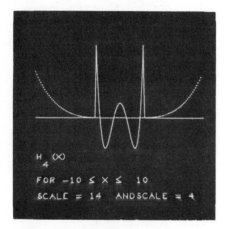

Fig. 6.13 $H_4(x)$ for $|x| \leq 10$ (dotted) and enlarged 10 times (solid curve). Dotted curve has binary scale 14, solid curve has scale 4. Points on the enlarged curve which would be "off the scope" are set equal to zero by ENL. (While this choice for ENL was made in the on-line system at TRW, where this photograph was taken, in the UCSB system ENL puts such points at the upper edge of the display field (if they are positive, or the lower edge, if they are negative); i.e., it replaces such "overflow" points by $\pm 2^s$, where s is the binary scale of the enlarged curve. This latter choice appears to be a more convenient one, particularly for Level III, since it eliminates the somewhat confusing lines which occur in displays like those of Figs. 6.26 and 6.28 when the curve "overflows" in x (or y) and returns to the x (or y) axis, rather than simply staying at the limit (right, left, top, or bottom, as appropriate) of the display field.

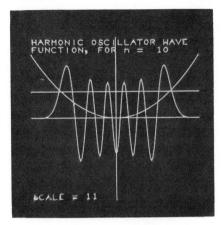

Fig. 6.14 Harmonic oscillator wave function $\psi_{10} = e^{-x^2/4}H_{10}(x)$; the potential function $V(x) = x^2/4$; and the energy eigenvalue, $E_{10} = 10.5$. The slightly polygonal character of the portions having highest curvature constitutes a warning to the user that over the range $-10 \leq x \leq 10$ the function oscillates a little too rapidly to be very well represented. The warning may be ignored, if one is satisfied with the accuracy thus achieved; or, the interval may be subdivided as required, with 125 points allotted for each subinterval.

which has, as shown, a binary scale of *14*; clearly a display which keeps $H_4(10)$ on scale cannot show this structure. However, if we multiply $H_4(x)$ by $e^{-x^2/4}$, thereby generating a harmonic oscillator wave function, we see (Fig. 6.12) that the structure has not been lost. This is also clear if we use ENLARGE on Level II to expand the function by 10 powers of 2, giving the display of Fig. 6.13. (ENL substitutes O wherever there would be an overflow in the expansion process.)

For larger values of n a similar behavior obtains. For example, Fig. 6.14 shows the harmonic oscillator wave function

$$\psi_{10}(x) = e^{-x^2/4}H_{10}(x)$$

as well as the total energy $E = 10.5$ and the potential energy $V = x^2/4$.

6.7 Bessel Functions of Complex Argument

Since the Bessel function $J_n(z)$ for complex z is tabulated for only a few values of n (save for the special cases where arg z is a multiple of $\pi/4$), a simple console program for this is worth having if one has any concern with, for example, wave or potential problems involving dissipative media in cylindrical geometry. In keeping with the functional organization of the system, we would like a console program to compute $J_n(z)$, not for a single complex number but for a given arc in the z plane. Thus, we will generate a mapping, $w = J_n(z)$, which carries each arc of the z plane into its image arc in the w plane.   This case provides a nice illustration of the three steps discussed in Sec. 6.1:

1. Choice of an analytic representation.   As usual, there are a number of alternatives.   We choose to use Bessel's integral representation,

$$J_n(z) = \pi^{-1} \int_0^\pi \cos\left[z \sin\phi - n\phi\right] d\phi \tag{11}$$

2. Choice of numerical procedures.   The principal question here is how to deal with the integrand

$$K(z, \phi) = \cos\left[z \sin\phi - n\phi\right] \tag{12}$$

which is a function of two variables.   We could construct K as a function of ϕ, for a fixed value of z; carry out the integration over ϕ, using the methods of Sec. 6.3; and repeat this for each point of the z arc.   If we did want J_n for a single value of z, or a few specific values, this would be a good method.   Alternatively, we could compute K as a function of z, for fixed ϕ, and sum these functions, for appropriate values of ϕ, $0 \leq \phi \leq \pi$, in order to get the integral, Eq. (11).   We shall choose the latter method here, and illustrate it for $n = 1$, in which case (11) becomes

$$J_1(z) = \frac{2}{\pi} \int_0^{\pi/2} \sin\left(z \sin\phi\right) \sin\phi \, d\phi \tag{13}$$

We use the trapezoidal rule for doing the integration on ϕ, and divide the interval $(0, \pi/2)$ into M equal parts, where M is a parameter to be chosen on the basis of subsequent experimentation.   Thus

$$J_1(z) = (2/\pi) \left[\tfrac{1}{2} K(0, z) + \sum_{p=1}^{M-1} K(p \, \Delta\phi, z) + \tfrac{1}{2}K(\pi/2, z) \right] \Delta\phi \tag{14}$$

where

$$\Delta\phi = \pi/2M$$

3. Construction of console programs.   We need two routines, one of an iterative nature to carry out the sum over p, the other to take care of various initial and final details.   The first, which we call INTERIOR, is

INTERIOR: III LOAD $\Delta\phi$ + ϕ STORE ϕ SIN STORE $W \cdot z$ SIN
              $\cdot$ W + J STORE J LOAD T $-$ ϕ REFLECT USER I
              TEST INTERIOR

Several comments are in order:

a. It is convenient to work on the complex vector level III; real vectors, like ϕ and $\Delta\phi$, simply have a zero imaginary part.

b. J is the location in which the results of the summation on p are accumulated. W is a "working space" location used for temporary storage of $\sin\phi$.

   c. Note that this program ends by calling itself. This would result in an unending "loop," save for the inclusion of TEST, which checks the first element of the y register and, if it finds it negative, skips the next key in the console program, thus ending the iterative cycle. By putting in location T the number $\pi/2 - 1.5\Delta\phi$, we ensure that the summation will include $p = m - 1$ but not $p = m$, as required.

The remaining chores—setting up T and $\Delta\phi$; adding to J

$$\tfrac{1}{2}K(\pi/2,\, z) = \tfrac{1}{2}\sin z$$

initiating INTERIOR; and finally multiplying the result by $2\Delta\phi/\pi$ are taken care of by

BESSEL: III LOAD 0, 0 STORE ϕ LOAD 1.5708, 0 STORE T / M
               STORE $\Delta\phi$ · -1.5, 0 $+$ T STORE T LOAD z SIN · 0.5,
               0 STORE J USER I INTERIOR III LOAD J / 1.5708, 0
               · $\Delta\phi$ STORE J

We have only to choose M; select an arc in the z plane; and push BESSEL. The transformed arc $w = J(z)$ is left in location J.

    At this point, we are in a position to experiment with the effect of M on the accuracy of the calculation. Choosing an arc for which the results are tabulated (arg $z = 0$ or $\pi/2$), we find that for $0 < |z| < 2$, for example, $M = 5$ gives a maximum error of 2 in the 5th decimal place! For cases where comparison with tabulated values is either impossible or inconvenient, we can observe the sensitivity of the results to a change in M. For example, using a semicircle

$$z = 4e^{i\theta} \qquad 0 \le \theta \le \pi$$

we find the curves $J_1(z)$ for $M = 10$ and $M = 20$ indistinguishable; both are shown in Fig. 6.15. Their difference, shown in Fig. 6.16, has a binary scale of -18, whereas that of the $J_1(z)$ curves in Fig. 6.15 is 5. Thus, we can use $M = 10$ for arguments of this order and count on an accuracy of one part in 2^{23}.

    We can expect that if we attempt to use this routine for an arc with $|z|$ too large, the accuracy will be poor. However, for large $|z|$ the asymptotic form

$$J_1(z) = \sqrt{\frac{2}{\pi z}}\,[\cos{(z - 3\pi/4)}A(z) - \sin{(z - 3\pi/4)}B(z)/z] \qquad (15)$$

where A and B are series in $1/z$, is useful, retention of a few terms in A and B giving an accuracy of better than 1 per cent for $|z| > 5$. It is straightforward to write a console program which uses the integral representation (13) for the part of the arc where $|z| < R$ (where R is a real

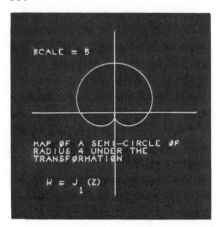

Fig. 6.15 Mapping, under $w = J_1(z)$, of the semicircular arc $z = 4e^{i\theta}$, $0 \le \theta \le \pi$, using the trapezoidal rule, Eq. (14). The curve obtained using 10 intervals ($M = 10$) is displayed, as is also the $M = 20$ result; the two agree to the accuracy of the display.

number chosen by the user) and the asymptotic form (14) for the part where $|z| \ge R$. (The program computes $\theta = \dfrac{\big||z| - R\big| + |z| - R}{2(|z| - R)}$ and $\bar{\theta} = 1 - \theta$; uses BESSEL to compute $\bar{\theta}J_1(\bar{\theta}z)$; uses the console program corresponding to (15) to compute $\theta J_1(\theta z)$; and adds these two results.)

Having constructed these console programs, we can use them for any problem involving Bessel functions. We can also use them to get familiar

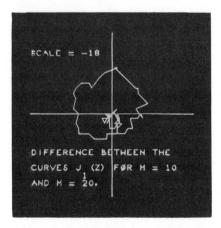

Fig. 6.16 Result of taking the difference between the $M = 10$ and $M = 20$ curves of Fig. 6.15. Taking account of the relative binary scales we see that the $M = 10$ and $M = 20$ curves differ by about 1 part of 2^{23}, a surprisingly small error in view of the fact that the computer used for this system has only 27 bits per word.

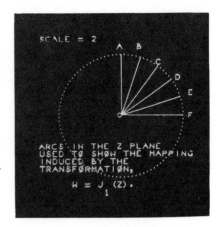

Fig. 6.17 Region of the z plane to be mapped by $w = J_1(z)$. The circle has radius 3 and the radial lines are equally spaced at angular intervals of $\pi/10$.

with particular properties of J_1 which may be relevant for certain applications. For example, we show in Figs. 6.17 through 6.19 the mapping, induced by J_1, of the interior of a circle of radius 3 about the origin. Figure 6.17 shows the boundary circle in the z plane and several radial lines. (Because of the obvious symmetry of the mapping, lines with arguments larger than $\pi/2$ would not give additional information.) When each of these is used as argument for the Bessel subroutine just

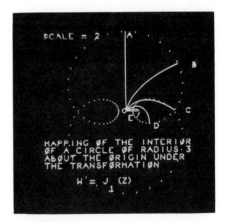

Fig. 6.18 The w-plane images of the arcs of Fig. 6.17 under $w = J_1(z)$. The circle of radius 3 is mapped into the dotted curve; the radial lines OA, . . . OE go into the similarly labeled arcs OA, . . . OE; and the origin is seen to be a fixed point of the mapping, as is obvious from $J_1(0) = 0$. The horizontal line segment is the map of OF, but the former is doubly covered; the map of point F is not labeled but lies at the intersection of the dotted curve and the horizontal line segment. (The double covering arises from the vanishing of $J_1'(z)$ at $z = 1.84$, and the consequent nonconformal character of the mapping at that point.)

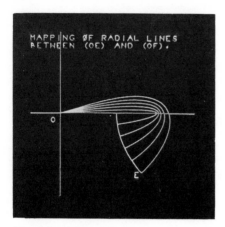

Fig. 6.19 Enlarged view of the transformation $J_1(z)$ in the neighborhood of the real axis, obtained by mapping five equally spaced radial lines between *OF* and *OE* (at angular intervals of $\pi/50$). (The images of the origin and of point *E* of Fig. 6.17 are labeled.) The tendency toward double covering as we approach the real axis is clear.

described, the result shown in Fig. 6.18 is obtained. As usual, we can take a more detailed look at any portion which shows interesting structure. For example, choosing radial lines between the line *OE* of Fig. 6.17 and the real axis, and transforming these with J_1, we obtain the enlarged map of this sector shown in Fig. 6.19. The tendency toward double covering of the w plane, as we approach the image of the real z axis, is associated with the zero of J_1' at $z = 1.84$.

IMPLICIT CALCULATION

6.8 Experimental Problem Solving

Although an on-line system of this sort may be quite useful for explicit computational tasks like the examples described above, its greatest value is as a tool for solving problems of such a nature that an experimental approach is desirable or even necessary. This is the case when the general structure of the problem or the character of the solution is unknown a priori, or when we cannot specify an analytic or numerical procedure which will certainly yield a solution.

A well-posed problem generally has the form of an implicit statement concerning the quantities to be found. Our first task is to reformulate the problem so that it has, superficially, the form of an explicit calculation. This generally leads to a fixed point problem

$$y = T[y]$$

where y is the unknown (number, function, set of functions, etc.) and T is some mapping of the space containing y onto itself. Sometimes the problem as originally stated is already of fixed point form, as with many integral equations, thus saving us one step. Often the reformulation involved appears completely trivial, but it is no less valuable. Two elementary examples illustrate the procedure:

1. Root location

Given $f(z)$, a function of a complex variable z, we want to find its zeros, i.e., the solutions of

$$f(z) = 0 \tag{16}$$

One possible reformulation is

$$z = T(z) \equiv z + \lambda f(z) \tag{17}$$

where λ is an arbitrary function of z. As compared with (16), (17) has the great advantage of being, at least superficially, explicit. It gives us a "handle" on z and allows us to set up an orderly procedure in which we guess a value of z; substitute it into $T(z)$ and see if the result (or "output") agrees with our initial guess (or "input"). If so, we have a solution; if not, the difference between z and $T(z)$ provides some measure of our error.

As a next "guess" for z, we may use $T(z)$ itself. In this way, we generate a sequence of values, $z_0, z_1, z_2, \ldots$, with

$$z_{n+1} = T(z_n) \tag{18}$$

If the sequence converges, the result is a solution of (17) and hence of (16). The criterion for convergence is easily found. If z_n is close to a true solution, z, then the error in z_{n+1} is

$$\epsilon_{n+1} = z_{n+1} - z = T(z + \epsilon_n) - T(z) = T'(z)\epsilon_n + \theta(\epsilon_n^2) \tag{19}$$

If $|T'(z)| < 1$ and second order terms can be neglected, $|\epsilon_{n+1}|$ will be less than $|\epsilon_n|$ and the sequence converges. With proper choice of λ, this can always be arranged. In fact, the optimum choice of λ is clearly that which makes $T'(z) = 0$, i.e.,

$$\lambda = -1/f'(z) \tag{20}$$

(provided $f'(z) \neq 0$), since we then have second order convergence ($\epsilon_{n+1} \propto \epsilon_n^2$). Since we do not know z a priori, we cannot really calculate λ, but we can approximate it by $f'(z_n)$. Thus, (17) becomes

$$z = T(z) = z - f(z)/f'(z)$$

and the iterative procedure (18) is

$$z_{n+1} = z_n - f(z_n)/f'(z_n) \tag{21}$$

The antiquity of this root-finding algorithm is indicated by its name: Newton's methods of successive approximations. We have included it here only as a simple example of the reformulation of an implicit problem, and the fixed point problem which results. This example is atypical only in that we are able to find a specific constructive algorithm, namely (21), which not only converges but, at least in the neighborhood of the fixed point, converges quadratically. In more complicated problems, we are often thankful if we can find a formulation which converges at all!

2. Ordinary differential equations

These can always be reduced to a set of simultaneous first order equations, which we can write in matrix form as

$$A(y, t)y' = B(y, t), \qquad y(0) = y_0 \tag{22}$$

where y represents n functions of the scalar variable t. If A is non-singular, a possible reformulation, which also brings in the initial conditions, is just

$$y = y_0 + \int_0^t dt\, A^{-1}B \tag{23}$$

resulting in a set of integral equations, again a fixed point problem. We shall discuss some methods of solution of these a little later. Here we simply remark that in specific problems something better than the "brute force" approach represented by (23) is frequently possible. When it is, it should always be used.

For example, suppose we have a single first-order linear equation, so that A and B are scalars not matrices,

$$A(y, t) = a(t) \qquad B(y, t) = a(t)[-b(t)y + c(t)]$$

with $a \neq 0$ over the t range of interest. Then multiplication of (22) by the integrating factor $\exp \int_0^t b\, dt$ leads to the well-known *solution*

$$y = E^{-1}(t)\left[y_0 + \int_0^t dt'\, E(t')c(t') \right] \tag{24}$$

where

$$E(t) = \exp\left[\int_0^t dt'\, b(t') \right]$$

The point is that this may be worth doing even if a, b, and c are functions of y. In that case, (24) is not a solution but, like (23), simply an integral equation. However, if the y independence of a, b, and c is not too strong, then (24) has an advantage over (23) in that a number of iterations of the latter would generally be required just to reproduce the exponential factor already contained in (24). We note that (24) is also valid in the general case of simultaneous equations, where b and c are matrices, provided one uses for E the "time-ordered" exponential

$$E(t) = \sum_{n=0}^{\infty} \int_0^t dt_1 \int_0^{t_1} dt_2 \cdots \int_0^{t_{n-1}} dt_n \, b(t_1) \cdots b(t_n)$$

Of course, it is not necessary to approach differential equations in this way, and, particularly if one has many to solve, it may be advantageous to simply construct a console program for one of the many standard algorithms for solving differential equations, such as that of Runge-Kutta. The global method described here may still have merit, however, for equations with singular coefficients.

6.9 Application to Linear Stability Theory

In analyzing the properties of complex physical systems, it is often useful to consider small deviations about an equilibrium configuration and to retain only terms linear in these deviations. The resulting set of linear equations can then be Fourier-analyzed in space and time, or, in more physical terms, we can study plane wave solutions, varying as $\exp i(k \cdot x - \omega t)$. This leads to a dispersion equation (or set of equations)

$$F(k, \omega, a_1, a_2, \ldots a_n) = 0$$

where the a_i are parameters describing the equilibrium solution. This dispersion equation has a simple significance in the case of an initial value problem for disturbances with wave number k: the dependent variables of the system will have a time dependence at long times which is, in general, dominated by terms of the form $e^{i\omega_n t}$, where the ω_n are, for given k and a_i, the roots of (11). If all the roots are in the lower half ω plane, then small disturbances from equilibrium die away eventually, and the system is *stable*. If, however, $Im \, \omega_n > 0$ for one or more roots, ω_n, then the disturbances grow. While the linear analysis eventually becomes invalid, we can be sure in this case that the equilibrium is an *unstable* one.

For given k and a_i, determination of the ω_n (at least those with largest imaginary part) is a classic root-finding problem, albeit not necessarily an easy one if F is a complicated function. Nyquist or similar methods can be used to locate the ω_n in a general way, and something like the Newton method, described above, can then furnish precise values. The graphical and topological character of the Nyquist diagram, and of similar techniques, makes this approach particularly appropriate for an on-line system with graphic output, like Culler's, even when F is a transcendental function of ω. (When F is an algebraic function of ω, standard methods for finding the roots exist, which are suitable for conventional off-line computation.) We simply construct a console program which, for given

k and a_i, and for a given arc in the ω plane, constructs F, i.e., gives a mapping from the ω plane to the F plane. We then choose a closed arc C in the ω plane, perhaps a circle, for convenience, although this is not necessary, and look at its map $\bar{C}$ in the F plane.

If $\bar{C}$ encircles the origin once and F is nonsingular inside C, then $F(\omega)$ has one root inside C, and we can proceed to shrink C (by multiplying it by a real number $r < 1$) and translate its center (by adding a complex number) to locate the root accurately enough so that Newton's method can be used.* If $\bar{C}$ encircles the origin n times, there are n roots of F inside C and we would shrink and translate C until it encloses only one, and then proceed as before. If $\bar{C}$ does not encircle the origin, then F has no roots inside C, and we can exclude that portion of the ω plane from further consideration. Various means can be devised to guide us in the translation of C. For example, we can calculate and display the minimum distance of $\bar{C}$ from the origin (III LOAD $\bar{C}$ MOD II STAR MAX STAR DISPLAY 1) at each step, and choose translations which minimize it. In fact, more elaborate routines can be devised to semiautomate this, and even (using ARG) to decide when, because of too much shrinking or injudicious translation, $\bar{C}$ no longer encircles the origin. The user must decide to what extent he wishes to retain direct control. In general, it is best to at least incorporate displays which will let him observe the search; using RESET he can always resume control of the process when necessary. Note that even after the transition from Nyquist to Newton, we can work with arcs in the ω plane, rather than the single number implied in the discussion under Root Location (see Sec. 6.8). If we have found a locally convergent formulation of the fixed point problem, then the arcs will tend to a single number, equal to the root in question; the size of the arc at any stage thus provides a convenient measure of our progress.

6.10 A Particular Example from Linear Stability Theory

The following example illustrates the general considerations of Secs. 6.8 and 6.9 (and also, perhaps, the aforementioned fact that detailed description of a complicated problem is of little interest to anyone but the problem solver!) A linearized treatment of electrostatic waves, with wave number k and frequency ω, in a gaseous plasma traversed by a beam of ions shows that k and $u = \omega/k$ are related by

$$2k^2 = D(u) \equiv Z'(u) + na^2 Z'[a(u - V)] - 2(n + 1) \qquad (25)$$

---

* A more elegant and much more satisfactory procedure which gives the root, ω_o, directly is simply to calculate $\omega_c = (2\pi i)^{-1} \int_{\bar{C}} dF(\omega/F)$. For further details, see Ref. 25.

where n is the density of the ion beam, V is its velocity, and a^{-2} is its temperature, all measured in suitable dimensionless units; for details, see Ref. 14. The complex function Z, whose derivative appears in (1), is defined, as in Ref. 17, by

$$Z(u) = -2e^{-u^2} \int_0^u dt\, e^{t^2} + i \sqrt{\pi}\, e^{-u^2} \qquad (26)$$

Thus, we have an example of linear stability problems described in Sec. 6.9, in which n, V, a correspond to a_i and $F = 2k^2 - D$. For fixed n, V, a, and k we could use the methods described there to determine whether $F = 0$ has roots with $Im\, u > 0$, i.e., whether the plasma-beam system is unstable. Of primary interest, however, is the question of *stability limits*: for n, V, or a sufficiently small, we know on physical grounds that the system is stable; as one of these is increased, we want to determine when the system first becomes unstable, irrespective of the value of k or u.

The technique we use is a variant on that of Sec. 6.9. We just examine the image of the real u axis under the mapping $w = D(u)$, for given n, V, a. In the stable case, e.g., $n = 0$, the map, C, of the real u axis does not intersect the positive w axis, i.e., there are no (real) values of k and u which satisfy (25). As n is increased, with fixed V, a, the curve C will change. The lowest value of n for which C first crosses the positive w axis gives the critical density above which the plasma-beam system is unstable. Repeating this procedure for other values of V and a determines the *stability limits* in the n, V, a parameter space.

A Subproblem. In implementing this strategy, our first task is the computation of the function Z for real arguments. The imaginary part presents no difficulty but

$$y = -\operatorname{Re} Z = 2e^{-u^2} \int_0^u d^{t^2}\, dt \qquad (27)$$

is slightly unpleasant if u has a large range, due to cancellations of the exponentials with large arguments, and resulting loss of accuracy. Of the many ways available for dealing with this, we choose (for pedagogical reasons) one which also illustrates the discussion of fixed point problems in Sec. 6.8.

Differentiating (27) gives the differential equation

$$y' = 2(1 - uy) \qquad (28)$$

which can be written in integral form as

$$y = 2u - 2 \int_0^u dt\, ty(t) \qquad (29)$$

[Of course, (28) can be solved immediately, via an integrating factor, but that simply leads us back to (27)]. We write (29) as

$$y = X - P(y) = T(y) \tag{30}$$

where $X = 2u$ is the inhomogeneous term and

$$P(y) = 2 \int_0^u dt\, ty(t) \tag{31}$$

Much of the discussion concerning (30) applies, *mutatis mutandis*, to the whole class of fixed point problems which can be put in this form, *independent* of our specific identifications of X and P.

To solve (30), we first try straightforward iteration,

$$y_{n+1} = X - P(y_n) \tag{32}$$

The console program is

STF. ITER.:   II LOAD $t \cdot y$ USER I $\int$ II STAR $+ u \cdot 2$ STORE y
                 DISPLAY y

(Of course, locations u and t both contain the same vector, which is chosen to span the desired range.)

If we choose $0 \le t \le 1$; take $y = X$ as a first choice; and repeat STF. ITER. six times, we get the sequence of curves shown in Fig. 6.20. The

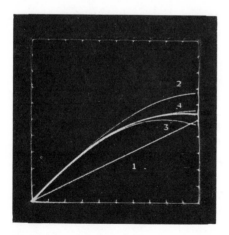

Fig. 6.20 First six passes in the iterative solution of Eq. (30), for $0 \le u \le 1$, starting with the initial choice $y = X$, labeled 1. The first pass yields $T(X)$, the highest curve, labeled 2. Using this as input yields curve 3; and this, in turn, gives rise to the curve labeled 4. The results of the next two iterations agree so closely that it was difficult to label them and the results of subsequent passes are indistinguishable on the scope (although we can always find and display the difference of two nearly equal curves, cf. Figs. 6.15 and 6.16).

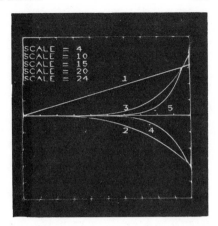

Fig. 6.21   First 5 passes in the iterative solution of Eq. (30), for $0 \leq u \leq 10$, starting from $y = X$.   The scales of the successive results, listed in the upper left corner, show that successive passes differ by an order of magnitude in size, in addition to the obvious differences in shape.

convergence is rapid, but this is no cause for complacency, since over this range the original explicit formula (27) gives the answer directly.

Next, choose $0 \leq t \leq 10$, which corresponds more nearly to the range required in our problem.   Again, take $y = X$ as a first guess and repeat STF. ITER. five times.   The resulting curves, together with their binary scales, are shown in Fig. 6.21.   The divergence is impressive, being exponential in character, and persists if we continue to iterate.*   To understand its origin, suppose that y_n is near the correct solution y. Then the error in y_{n+1} is

$$\epsilon_{n+1} = y_{n+1} - y = P(y) - P(y_n) = -2 \int_0^u dt \, t\epsilon_n(t) + \theta(\epsilon_n^2) \quad (33)$$

Although calculation of this requires knowledge of ϵ_n, we can get an approximate estimate by taking ϵ_n constant.   Then, to first order in ϵ_n,

$$\epsilon_{n+1} = -u^2 \epsilon_n \quad (34)$$

suggesting that if $u_{max} < 1$ the iteration will converge, while if $u_{max} = 10$, as here, it should diverge badly.   (The minus sign in (34) accounts for the

* The experts will observe that a Volterra equation like (29) always converges in principle, and that the divergence seen here is a consequence of our treating an inherently local problem globally and of the accuracy limitations of the machine functional representation. However, divergences like this are seen also in global problems, e.g., in integral equations which cannot be reduced to differential equations. Moreover, it is often convenient to use a global approach, even for local problems.

oscillating character of both the convergence, seen in Fig. 6.20, and the divergence, seen in Fig. 6.21.)

We are now in the situation described in Sec. 6.8, where we need to find a fixed point problem equivalent to (30) but with better convergence properties. Consider

$$y = S(y) \equiv y \cdot \frac{X - y}{P(y)} \tag{35}$$

Carrying out a calculation like that in Eq. (33), with ϵ_n taken as constant, we have

$$\epsilon_{n+1} = \epsilon_n \left[1 - \frac{y}{P} (1 - u^2) \right] \tag{36}$$

Since we have seen that the convergence difficulties are associated with large u, we use the asymptotic character of y,

$$y \to \frac{1}{u} \qquad \text{as} \qquad u \to \infty$$

which follows directly from (28), to deduce that

$$P = 2 \int_0^u dt \, ty \sim 2u, \, u \to \infty$$

and hence that

$$\epsilon_{n+1}/\epsilon_n \sim 1 - \frac{1 + u^2}{2u^2} = \frac{u^2 - 1}{2u^2} \tag{37}$$

Even for large u, this is smaller than 1 in magnitude, so we expect straightforward iteration based on (35) to converge.

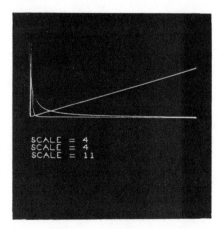

Fig. 6.22 First three passes in the iterative solution of (35), for $0 \le u \le 10$, starting with $y = X$. The first pass produces the broader of the two peaked curves, with binary scale 4; and taking T of this gives the very sharp curve, with binary scale 11.

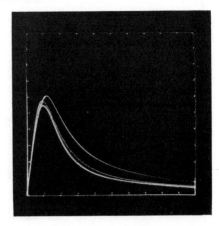

Fig. 6.23 First 5 passes in the iterative solution of (38) with $A = 1$, starting with $y = X$ (not shown here). The highest curve is $R(X)$, i.e., the result of the first pass; using it as input yields the curve below it; and after two more passes the curves agree to the accuracy of the display (but cf. caption of Fig. 6.20).

Upon trying it, again with $y = X$ as first guess, we get the curves shown in Fig. 6.22 for the first three passes. The troubles now occur at small argument rather than large, but the behavior is not much better. To analyze this new difficulty, we go back to the initial guess, $y = X$; observe that $P(X) = 4u^3/3$ is very small for small u; and conclude that our troubles now stem from division by these small numbers. We therefore try

$$y = R(y) = y \cdot \frac{X - y + A}{P + A} \tag{38}$$

whose convergence properties are essentially like those of (35), the function A simply providing protection against a vanishing or nearly vanishing denominator. Choosing $A = 1$, we get for the first five iterations, starting with $y = X$ (which is not shown), the curves of Fig. 6.23. The rapid convergence is in marked contrast to the behavior shown in Fig. 6.21.

Having now determined Re Z, we can get Re Z' by differentiation (as in Sec. 6.3) or calculate it directly, since it satisfies differential and integral equations similar to (28) and (29). In solving the stability limit problem, we will need Z' for a variety of arguments. Since it would be impracticable to go through the procedure described here each time, we use a simple table-look-up procedure based on the EVALUATE operation of Level II. Suppose we have determined Re Z' as a function of u for $0 \leq u \leq 10$, using the procedures sketched above, and stored it in

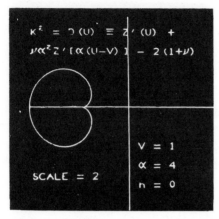

Fig. 6.24 The image C, of the real axis, $-3 \leq u \leq 3$, under the mapping $w = D(U)$, with $D(u)$ defined by Eq. (25), for the parameter values shown. The direction of traversal is such that the upper half of the u plane (corresponding to unstable waves) maps into the interior of C.

location R. To find Re $Z'(s)$ over some subportion of this range, e.g., for $2 \leq s \leq 7$, we simply

II LOAD R SUB u EVAL s

Finally, to allow evaluation for arguments which exceed the table, we use the asymptotic form

$$Z(u) = -1/u - \tfrac{1}{2}u^3 + \cdots$$

and join it to the $0 < u < 10$ range, using step functions θ, $\bar{\theta}$ as explained at the end of Sec. 6.7.

Determination of Stability Limits. The remainder of the original problem is now quite straightforward. We construct a console program which, given n, V, a and a section of the u axis, computes and displays the complex arc C which results from the mapping $w = D(u)$. In Fig. 6.24 we see the result of mapping the segment $-3 \leq u \leq 3$ for $n = 0$, $V = 1$, $a = 4$. (The rapid vanishing of $Z(u)$ for large $|u|$ makes this finite segment of the u axis quite sufficient for our purposes.) The upper half of the u plane maps into the interior of C; not only is there no real u satisfying (1), but we can also see that (1) has no roots in the upper half u plane. As expected, the system is stable.

As we increase n to 0.5, C expands and shifts, as shown in Fig. 6.25. On this scale it is not clear whether or not C encircles the origin, so we

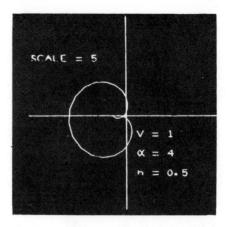

Fig. 6.25 Same as Fig. 6.24 with n increased to 0.5. The curve C appears to almost, but not quite, encircle the origin.

simply use ENLARGE (on Level III) to get the curve in Fig. 6.26. Ignoring the extraneous line segments (which appear because ENLARGE puts the curve on axis in those places where the indicated expansion would make it overflow),* we see that C crosses the real axis to the left of the origin, so the system is still stable. Further increase of n leads to Fig. 6.27. Again we can enlarge the curve, as shown in Fig. 6.28. The

* See caption of Fig. 6.13.

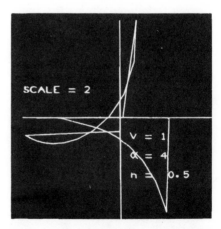

Fig. 6.26 The curve C of Fig. 6.25, enlarged three times. The straight lines running from extremities of the curve to the coordinate axes should be ignored (cf. caption for Fig. 6.13). This display establishes clearly that, as suggested by Fig. 6.25, C fails to encircle the origin.

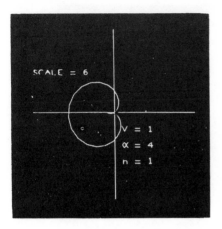

Fig. 6.27 Same as Figs. 6.24 and 6.25, with n increased to 1.0. It appears that C now encircles the origin.

polygonal nature of Figs. 6.26 and 6.28 indicates clearly that our numerical representation in the area of interest is poor, but this is easily remedied. Knowing the general topological character of the mapping, we need only map the small portion of the real axis whose image is near $w = 0$. Then, as shown in Fig. 6.29, we get a good representation of the region of interest and can determine the critical value of n quite accurately. The trial-and-error processes involved can be facilitated by various console programs, e.g., one which prints on the scope the values of the intercepts of C with the x and y axes.

Note that by restricting ourselves to the marginal stability problem (u real) we have eliminated the necessity for working in the complex u plane, as described in Sec. 6.8. *Nevertheless*, it is convenient to use complex representation, as illustrated, i.e., to observe Im D versus Re D instead of dealing with separate plots of these.

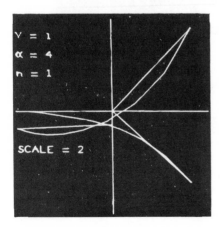

Fig. 6.28 The curve of Fig. 6.27, enlarged three times, confirming that for these parameter values C does encircle the origin and the beam-plasma system is unstable.

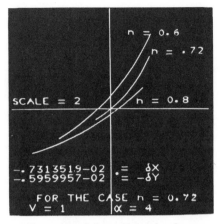

Fig. 6.29 Mapping of the small portion of the real u axis whose image lies near the origin of the w plane, for the parameter values indicated. From a knowledge of the intercepts of C with the axes (which the computer displays upon request), we can interpolate between the values $n = 0.6$, which is seen to be below the stability limit, and $n = 0.8$, which is above the limit. The result, $n = 0.72$, is seen to be correct, within the accuracy of this display. As usual, we can achieve greater accuracy by expanding the display or by restricting the range of u values used in the mapping.

SUMMARY, DISCUSSION, AND EVALUATION

6.11   Characterization of On-line Problem-solving Processes

The principle of "feedback" has proved to be a powerful one in many fields of application. If the computer and the originator of a problem are considered to constitute a single "system," then we might characterize Culler's work as providing a satisfactory feedback for this "system," wherein the mutual coupling between the user and the computer is close and, from the human viewpoint, convenient and even comfortable.

Implicit in this characterization are several assumptions: that the "user," meaning the man who originated the problem and wants to solve it, is actually at the console; that his problem is one which can be stated in mathematical terms; and that he has a sufficient competence in classical mathematical analysis to be able to take reasonable advantage of the facilities provided to him. If these assumptions are valid, then the user finds that he can explore the structure of his problem in an experimental way, making full use of his intuition for, and experience with, the particular field involved. He does not need to communicate with the computer through a professional programmer; nor does he need to invest the time and effort required to become an amateur programmer himself. It is possible for him to build a representation, in the computer, of those analytic tools he believes valuable for a particular problem or problem area. Without any necessity for learning conventional programming techniques, he is able, using only the concepts of classical mathematics, to create his own user's "language," one tailor-made to his own needs. He can freely manipulate the elements of this language, in precisely the same fashion one composes mathematical techniques, and can easily modify them to incorporate the knowledge gained from their use in problem solving, so that his computing capability grows with his understanding of the problems. Cut-and-try procedures, involving extensive interaction with the computer, which are possible but impracticable with most conventionally organized computer systems, become quite feasible, simply because the only limitations are the actual computing time and his own cerebral processes.

With the examples of the preceding sections in mind, let us analyze the activities actually involved in solving a problem using the Culler system. We would begin with some, probably tentative, mathematical formulation of the problem—tentative because in reducing most problems, whatever their origin, to mathematical terms a variety of assumptions, approximations, and idealizations are necessary. (The validity of these is difficult to estimate a priori when the problem is new, and usually we would like to proceed initially with its solution only far enough to be able to know whether the original formulation is a sensible one. This is not always easy to do in conventionally organized computers but comes quite naturally in the on-line system.)

If the problem is a complicated one, we may find it helpful to literally "look" at parts of it, i.e., to construct these elements (e.g., coefficients in a differential equation, the kernel of an integral transform, etc.) which are explicitly given in the statement of the problem and display them graphically. Often this will suggest further approximation procedures: If we see that a function is slowly varying, we may decide to replace it by a constant in a first treatment; if it has a single sharp peak, we might approximate it by a Dirac delta function; etc. (These simplifications may in some cases allow an analytic solution of the problem, or of a part of it, which, though approximate, can provide valuable guidance in subsequent numerical work.)

In any case, regardless of the value of such a visual inspection, we will need to construct the analytic elements in terms of which the problem is stated. This will involve work of the sort illustrated in Secs. 6.2 to 6.7, i.e., building the functions and other elements which make up this problem out of the basic capabilities furnished in the on-line system. This process may continue for several sessions of an hour or two if the problem is a complicated one. In the course of it we are really constructing a very special user's system, one tailored to the needs of this problem—or problem area, for if our choices are reasonably sensible, many of the console programs will be useful subsequently when we attack other problems in this field.

Especially important is our ability to check each console program, as soon as it is made, by executing it; examining the qualitative reasonableness, or, if appropriate, quantitative accuracy, of the result; and locating our error, or errors, if any.   Note that we thus detect, simultaneously, errors at many levels: in our mathematical formulation, in our numerical analysis, in our console programming, and in our mechanical key pushing.   If execution of the console program yields a wrong or suspicious result, we would go back and check each of these aspects, in whatever order seems appropriate.   On the other hand, if the result is correct or reasonable, we can be fairly confident that there are no errors at any of these levels.   Faithful adherence to this principle of checking each console program as it is made ensures that when, after some hours spent in this activity, we have accumulated a number of the console programs we need, there is no time-consuming and frustrating "debugging" procedure awaiting us.

Our next step is to devise some constructive procedure for solving the problem.   As illustrated in Secs. 6.8 to 6.10, one good rule is to bring the problem to a form in which the unknown appears explicitly on one side of an equality sign, even though it may also appear on the other side as well; but just how to proceed must depend on the details of the particular problem.   Whatever our choice here, it is likely to be tentative, since we usually lack a priori information on existence, uniqueness, convergence, and other basic properties of the desired solution.   In fact, this is just what makes an experimental approach so valuable.   Having assembled (and checked!) the component parts of the problem in the form of appropriate console programs, it is easy to combine and permute these as desired.   In a fixed point problem,

$$y = T[y]$$

for example, we would have arrived at the point of having a console program for the operator T, which, given any y, computes $T[y]$.   (If T is complicated, a number of console programs may be involved; but that is irrelevant, since we would finally combine them all into a single one, perhaps including a display of y and $T[y]$, etc.)   It is then a very simple matter to see whether straightforward iteration, $y_{n+1} = T[y_n]$, converges well; and, if it does not, to construct some of the related operators S with the property that $y = T[y]$ and $y = S[y]$ have some, or all, of their solutions in common.   (Cf. the examples given in Secs. 6.1 and 6.10.)

Note that, once we have the console program for $T[y]$ and have made a choice for S, it is easy to construct the associated console program and see if $y_{n+1} = S[y_n]$ has satisfactory convergence properties. However, to make a good choice for S, or, having made a few choices and found them unsatisfactory, to make intelligent use of that information in choosing a new one, may be quite difficult. In such a case, it is our own lack of ingenuity or insight which paces the problem-solving process, rather than man-computer communication problems, and this is all one can sensibly ask of an on-line system. (The utopian notion of a computer which accepts the statement of a problem and automatically finds a way of solving it is clearly chimerical, save for those "problems" whose structure has been thoroughly understood and for which methods of solutions are well known.)

In the above description, we have distinguished the synthetic process of constructing the required console programs from the experimental, problem-solving activity which uses them. We should emphasize that this distinction is not a firm one. To be sure, initial constructive work, involving the kind of things illustrated in Secs. 6.2 to 6.7, is analogous to the straightforward programming tasks which are required to attack any problem with a computer. However, even at this stage, one may find experimentation desirable or even necessary. If Bessel functions of complex argument are required as part of the problem, for instance, then one would probably work through some of the considerations of Sec. 6.7, in choosing a method of doing the integral transform, deciding on an appropriate value for M, etc. Even if the constructive steps are quite elementary, the on-line checking of each program as it is made proves exceedingly valuable.

Finally, and most important of all, once we have completed the preliminary work and start the actual problem-solving process, we invariably discover the need for additional console programs or for modifications in those we have. The ability to generate immediately, at the console, these new programs, or modify the old ones, and then go on to use them in the problem-solving effort is the *sine qua non* of a really powerful on-line system.

To continue with our description of the problem-solving process, consider the happy moment when we have found a constructive method of attack upon the problem; have generated a solution, say, for a particular choice of parameter values; and have convinced ourselves that the solution is at least reasonable, and very likely correct. We may now elect to go back and improve parts of the formulation or analysis of the problem, dropping some of the grosser approximations or simplifying assumptions; using more accurate numerical representations (e.g., higher-order differentiations or integrations); choosing a new independent variable to concentrate mesh points where, according to the solution at hand, they are needed; etc. We can make variations in the parameters to obtain solutions for other cases; in particular, if the solution has been difficult to obtain (requiring, for example, delicate control of a convergence-producing parameter like the λ of Eq. (4)), we will be well advised to make relatively small changes in the parameters and carefully "follow" the solution as we move through the parameter space.

Finally, when we have solved the cases of interest, we will want to generate suitable output. It is a minor but nontrivial feature of this on-line system that it enables us to avoid an annoying aspect of most computational efforts. Typically, one generates a "print-out" of the data and then has it plotted on a graph. (In high-class systems, one can have the plot made directly by the computer.) Unless one is very foresighted or quite experienced, however, the plot turns out to be not quite right; one really wanted a different choice of scale, or a semilog plot, etc. While it is always possible to go back and make the trivial program modifications required to put the results in the desired form, one often ends up having the necessary points recomputed by hand and then replotted. The geometric outputs continually available in the on-line system of course eliminate all this. We simply look at the scope plots of our solution curves; change scales, representations, etc., as desired until the display is to our liking; and *then* output the data, either directly in graphical form (via a polaroid photograph* of the scope or on a plotter attached to the system, which can accept display outputs in place of the scope, when desired) or in numerical form.

In many problems of the class appropriate for an on-line system, a qualitative understanding of the nature of the solution is all we require. It is clear that the system makes it easy for us to call a halt whenever we are satisfied. However, we sometimes want to solve a given problem for many different cases or parameter values. Having discovered on-line as a successful method of solution, we would like to go over to an efficient "production" basis for running additional cases. There are several possibilities. Using our knowledge of the correct method of approach to the problem, we may turn it over to a professional programmer and conventional off-line execution, on a totally different computer. Alternatively, we may modify our console programs slightly (eliminating displays, data requests by the program to the user, and other features inappropriate for off-line operation) and then construct one console program which, if run, would generate, and store in suitable locations, solutions for all the cases of interest. In the presently implemented Culler systems, the best we could do would be to initiate this extensive console program and let it run, say during hours of low demand. What is clearly desirable, however, is a provision for executing this extensive console pro-

---

* All of the figures in this chapter, with the exception of Figs. 6.6 and 6.7 are reproductions of polaroid photographs of the console oscilloscope face.

gram on a strictly off-line basis, either on the same computer used for the normal on-line work, or on a completely separate one, equipped of course with the same basic software structure as the on-line system.

6.12 Historical Background

Before attempting an evaluation of on-line problem solving and commenting on its future development, we should say a little about its history to date. The developments leading to the Culler on-line system began in July, 1961, in the Research Laboratory of the RW Computer Division of TRW. The first phase involved the solution of a specific problem—a nonlinear integral equation occurring in J. R. Schrieffer's extensions of the BCS theory of superconductivity. In that work, carried out from July to December, 1961, all subroutines were programmed (in machine language) in a conventional way. Using the control and display capabilities of a keyboard-oscilloscope console, the user could, according to his selection of these subroutines, vary his problem-solving strategy on-line; but he could not, of course, alter or add to these subroutines without the conventional time-consuming programming and debugging operations. This approach proved highly successful for this particular problem (a detailed description of the work, now only of historical interest, is contained in Refs. 18 and 19, and the physical results are to be found in Ref. 1), and at the conclusion of the work the direction to be followed was clear. Quoting from the April, 1962 report,[19]

> To gain experience with these other problem areas, one could consider additional specific examples beyond the one (BCS problem) described here. It appears more efficient, however, to create a more general facility, namely to carry out such programming as will permit the user, at the console, to perform the operations of classical analysis. In the BCS example certain subroutines were specified by the programming and the user could select one of several options at each stage of the solution process. The additional freedom to modify the subroutines themselves during the solution process (without, of course, going through the tedious procedures of programming and checkout) is clearly desirable. If the user can, with the console keys, call up any of the standard functions of mathematical physics; combine these algebraically; substitute functions into one another; perform analytical operations (differentiation, integration, integral transforms, etc.); examine any of these on the scope; rescale them where necessary; and store or recall them in a convenient way, then he will have the freedom not only to modify the subroutines of a particular problem but actually to construct those needed for a new one. The work required to create this capability is now in progress.

Thus, in these first experiments a sophisticated capability (for a particular problem) was provided, but the ability to do the kind of tasks described in

Secs. 6.2 to 6.7 was totally missing. It was clear that provision of this would yield a quite general system, in which one could construct on-line, from the basic subroutines, the more sophisticated and specialized programs needed for any particular problem.

The "work required" was carried out during the first half of 1962 under the direction of (and also by) Glen Culler, and a variety of users* experimented with, and constructively criticized, the system during the summer of 1962. During the next two years the system was used for a number of problems (see Refs. 2 to 6), and many changes and improvements were made in response to user reactions. A description of the system circa the fall of 1962 is given in Ref. 20, and a later version is to be found in Ref. 21.

In January, 1965, a Culler system exploiting all of the accumulated experience, with four simultaneously operational user consoles, came into operation at TRW Systems,[22] and has been available to all members of the technical staff since that time. In the fall of 1965, the still more advanced version described in the Appendix went into operation at the computer center of the University of California at Santa Barbara. In addition to the 16 classroom consoles at UCSB, this system also provides service, via phone line, to consoles in the physics department at UCLA and the computation laboratory at Harvard University.

6.13 Evaluation

In describing the first on-line problem-solving experiments, Culler[18] stated that "the basic philosophy of on-line computation is principally that the originator of the problem shall, in a fairly detailed fashion, actually direct its solution by the computer, thereby bringing to bear his own insights and knowledge based on the problem's structure or physical significance." As presently implemented, the system does provide this capability, for problems within that area of mathematics generally designated as classical analysis. One can go directly from conventional analytic expressions, in terms of functions of a single real or complex variable, to numerical representations of these, entirely skipping the chore of composing a series of single numbers into a vector representation. It is this descent to tedious arithmetic which constitutes a large portion of conventional mathematical programming, regardless of the language used. Aside from the time consumed thereby, this arithmetic detour constitutes a kind of mental obstacle, which makes it inordinately difficult to employ a combination of analytical and numerical techniques in solving problems. By using a software organization which is fully compatible with the structure of classical analysis and with the central role of functions therein,

---

* This group included Robert W. Christy, Richard P. Feynman, Karl Menger, J. Robert Schrieffer, John Ward, H. W. Wyld, as well as the author of this chapter.

Culler's system removes this barrier, and gives the user a very convenient facility for constructing numerical representations of analytical methods.

a. Limitations of the Culler System. One of the principal limitations of the system as presently implemented (January, 1966), both at UCSB and TRW Systems, concerns the handling of larger blocks of data, and is principally a consequence of current hardware inadequacies. For example, problems involving more than one independent variable—hydrodynamics, electrodynamics, field theory, etc.—require a capability for dealing with a matrix in the same way that one now operates on individual vectors. This is easily incorporated into the software structure of the system. On Level VI (or Level VII) one provides operations on matrices which are the analogue of those Level II (or Level III) operations on vectors which make sense for matrices, together with those operations (diagonalize, find eigenvectors, etc.) which are only defined for matrices. However, to handle several large (125 × 125) matrices simultaneously would require a larger mass memory capacity than is available in the small computers currently being used for Culler systems; and to execute routines like matrix inversion or diagonalization in a time short enough to preserve the dynamic character of the on-line response would require a faster computer. Since both the required memory and speed are readily available in the computers which have become available during the past year, we can expect this kind of limitation to be only temporary.

A different kind of limitation arises from the orientation of the system toward classical analysis. For example, it is incapable of doing even the simplest algebraic tasks, involving the transformations of literal (nonnumeric) expressions. This, in contrast to the deficiencies described in the preceding paragraph, is a consequence of the lack of appropriate software, and the remedy is clear. While the basic subroutines of the system are those appropriate to classical analysis, our ability to combine these into more sophisticated, and arbitrarily complicated, operators via console programming is independent of their nature. Thus, by simply adding to the system new basic subroutines for manipulation of, and algebraic operations on, literal symbols, for example, one could extend the capabilities of the system to encompass difficult algebraic problems; in fact, a good start has already been made by Blackwell.[23,24] The same comment applies to extension to other mathematical, or even nonmathematical problem areas. Note, however, that to make a good choice of basic subroutines in a new area is a nontrivial matter, requiring a good deal of experimentation. The present choice of Level II and Level III operations in Culler's system represents a quite satisfactory compromise between a set of operations which is complete, but too austere, and one which is overly redundant and, in trying to increase user convenience, actually diminishes it. However, this choice is a consequence of very extensive experience with critical users, with the system evolving in response to their needs and desires. Similarly, Blackwell has found it necessary to experiment with several versions of the basic symbol manipulation operations.

b. Economic Considerations. These are quite different for on-line systems than for conventionally organized computers, and while an extended discussion of this would be inappropriate here, a few comments on this subject and the related general question of equipment requirements are in order.

We may assume that an optimum system is likely to be one in which the charge per hour to use a console is comparable with the wages of the person using it. As is well known, this can be achieved only by some time-sharing or multiuser organization within the computer. While the power of the Culler system derives chiefly from the software structure, the computer must have a minimal size (particularly as regards mass memory) and speed if the on-line facilities provided are to be really useful. (A mass memory of 10,000 to 20,000 words per console and a multiply time of 50 microseconds are representative minimal figures.) In the versions currently in operation (at UCSB and TRW Systems), small computers just satisfying the minimal requirements are used exclusively for on-line operation, with a number of consoles simultaneously active to provide the multiuser economies.

However, as noted in the discussion of hardware limitations, there are classes of problems for which one really needs support from a more powerful computer. We might therefore anticipate systems in which a number of on-line consoles receive service equivalent to that provided in the present Culler systems, while the computer simultaneously executes off-line jobs; *provided,* however, that the overall organization of the software does not compromise the dynamic nature of the response to each console. It cannot be overemphasized that a sluggish on-line system is absolutely worthless. The current systems are so arranged that a request from any console for execution of a basic subroutine of Level II or III is honored in a small fraction of a second, *regardless* of the tasks being carried out for any other consoles. Thus, to every user it always appears that his trivial requests (multiply two vectors, display a vector or a numerical value, etc.) are completed immediately, while execution of a long console program requires a time commensurate with the amount of work to be done. All of our experience indicates that this character of the system *must* be preserved. This is why the matrix operations planned for Levels VI and VII will really be feasible only with a fast computer.

So far as the console equipment is concerned, the present keyboards and storage oscilloscopes are quite satisfactory. The small size of the display (3.5″ × 4.5″) causes no difficulty when, as is typically the case, one or two people are using the console. For group use, of course, a larger display tube or a closed-circuit TV presentation would be necessary. Technological improvements in the display field are to be expected but do not appear to be vitally needed in this application.

In addition to the scope and keyboard, it proves very desirable to have also a facility for producing hard copy versions of the scope displays. At present this is done by photographing the scope; or by diverting the display signals to an electromechanical plotter or, for purely alphanumeric information, to a printer. Because the user can instantly examine any part of his data graphically or alphanumerically on the scope, the need for hard copy is, of course, entirely different than in conventional systems and a single plotter or printer can easily be shared by several users.

Finally, it appears that a graphic input device, allowing a curve sketched or traced with a suitably instrumented pen to be converted to digital form and input to the computer, will be valuable. Having a numerical representation of the curve (as two of the usual Level II vectors) we can, of course, make use of all of the mathematical and display facilities of the on-line system to analyze it; approximate it with curve-fitting procedures; use it as a trial function or other input to a problem-solving technique; etc. Since the curve in question could represent experimental data, this represents, in a minor way, a union of experimental and theoretical on-line capabilities which is discussed below. Both digital and analogue devices for accomplishing this graphic input exist, and although none of the existing systems is so equipped at the present writing (January, 1966), the UCLA physics department console of the UCSB system will shortly have such a device. As with the printer and plotter, it can be expected that one graphical input device could be shared by several consoles.

Taking account of these various hardware requirements, using the existing systems as a bench mark, and estimating the costs involved in the use of the more powerful computers now available, it appears that a charge of the order of $10 to $15 per hour to use an on-line console of a Culler system (and the auxiliary input-output equipment) can be achieved, *provided* there is sufficient demand to keep several consoles busy eight hours per day. This comes close enough to the requirement suggested at the beginning of this discussion to indicate that widespread use of such systems is feasible.

c. Pedagogical Implications. As explained in Sec. 6.12, the primary motivation for development of the Culler system was its use as a research tool. However, one cannot use such a system very long without being struck by its considerable potential as an educational device.

Consider it first as an introduction to computer programming. As we have emphasized above, some effort has been expended to make the system convenient for users with no programming experience, but this does not imply that programming has been eliminated. In fact, constructing console programs, as illustrated in Secs. 6.2 to 6.7, involves the very essence of programming. It is relatively "painless," since so many of the tedious aspects are taken care of by the system, but the logical structure is clearly evident. (Without attempting to make any judgment concerning the virtues or shortcomings of the console programming as a "language," we simply note that to be really on-line one *must* have a means for generating new programs and modifying old ones *at the console* without great effort. Culler's console-programming procedure amply meets this need and does so in a way which requires no prior programming experience.)

In a different direction, the on-line system lends itself nicely to instruction in applied mathematics or theoretical physics. Again, this is a consequence of the extreme simplicity of the programming aspects. Instead of emphasizing these aspects, as one would do in teaching programming, one can minimize them, explaining to the students only as much as they need in order to solve problems in the area of interest. Experimental use of the UCSB system for instruction in mathematical and numerical analysis (at the UCSB mathematics department), in differential equations (at the Harvard applied mathematics department) and in theoretical physics (at the UCLA physics department) is currently in progress.

d. **Comparison with Other On-line Systems.** Within the last two years, interest in and use of on-line systems of various sorts have enjoyed an almost explosive growth. Perhaps this can be understood in terms of the notion, advanced earlier, that the basic concept of feedback, applied to the man-computer relationship, is the essence of on-line computing. In any case, there are many different reasons for having an on-line system and various ways of structuring one, according to the nature and needs of the "user," as illustrated by the following examples.

The Project MAC work at M.I.T. is a prime example of an on-line system designed to serve users who are professionally concerned with computer programming, languages, etc. It is a powerful tool in the hands of such a user, giving him explicit control over computer operations at a fine-grained level of detail, as well as an extensive ability to transform and manipulate programs at a very sophisticated level, but it is not appropriate for problem-solving use by a physicist or mathematician unversed in programming skills. The work of the Lincoln Laboratory on Sketchpad and similar facilities is oriented toward the engineering designer, who is given a much more elaborate graphic display capability than that of the Culler system but essentially no mathematical or program-generating facility. The on-line system developed by D. Englebart at Stanford Research Institute is oriented toward the display, control, manipulation, updating, and analysis of textual material. Its capability for this work is so great that the alphanumeric and documenting features of the Culler system are, by comparison, quite primitive, but it has neither graphic displays nor mathematical capability of any sort. Finally, there is an increasing tendency for experimental physicists to use on-line methods. These give the results of a preliminary analysis and reduction of the experimental data rapidly enough to allow the experimentalist to act upon this information, if changes in the experimental conditions are indicated. (Although the application of on-line methods to large machines like particle accelerators is relatively new, they have long been used for analyses of bubble chamber data previously stored on film.) Such systems are characterized by an ability to accept data, in analog or digital form, at a high rate of input, and often have elaborate displays and some on-line control of previously stored programs. However, the generation or modification of the programs required to process the data, display the results, or carry out mathematical transformations of either is typically done in conventional off-line fashion.

As is indicated by this very brief, and by *no* means comprehensive, survey, present on-line systems tend to be quite specific in their orientation toward a given class of users and a particular kind of application. In a sense, all of them provide help in problem solving and vary only according to the nature of the problems. From an objective point of view, it does not seem that any one of these various kinds of on-line system is superior to the others. Since they are almost entirely complementary to one another, rather than competitive, it appears what is really needed is an on-line system which combines the capabilities of these different varieties. An on-line system having input channels for experimental data, the sophisticated graphics of the Lincoln Laboratory system, the text manipulation capability of the SRI system, the mathematical operations and console-programming features of the Culler system, and the Project MAC capability for improving and transforming its own programs is certainly feasible and would be useful for a greater variety of problems in any one of these areas than are the present, more specialized on-line systems.

We close this chapter with a strong hope for the early realization of such a general on-line system and with the prediction that, when implemented, it will further enhance man's capability for solving difficult problems.

16.4 Acknowledgment

The research in problem-solving techniques reported here has received partial support from the National Science Foundation; The Office of

Naval Research; The Rome Air Development Center, USAF; and the TRW Systems Independent Research Program. In addition it is a personal pleasure for the writer to acknowledge how much he has learned about problem solving from Prof. Glen Culler, as well as from his on-line systems.

REFERENCES

1. Culler, G. J., B. D. Fried, R. W. Huff, and J. R. Schrieffer: Solution of the Gap Equation for a Superconductor, *Phys. Rev. Letters*, vol. 8, p. 399, 1962.
2. Fried, B. D., and G. J. Culler: Plasma Oscillations in an External Electric Field, *Phys. Fluids*, vol. 6, p. 1128, 1963.
3. Schrieffer, J. R., D. J. Scalapino, and J. W. Wilkins: Effective Tunneling Density of States in Superconductors, *Phys. Rev. Letters*, vol. 10, p. 336, 1963.
4. Johnson, Kenneth, and Marshall Baker: Quantum Electrodynamics, *Phys. Rev. Letters*, vol. 11, p. 518, 1963.
5. Cheng, Hung, and David Sharp: Formulation and Numerical Solution of Sets of Dynamical Equations for Regge Pole Parameters, *Phys. Rev. Letters*, vol. 132, p. 1854, 1963.
6. Field, E. C., and B. D. Fried: Solution of Kinetic Equation for an Unstable Plasma in an Electric Field, *Phys. Fluids*, vol. 7, p. 1937, 1964.
7. Bullock, D. L.: Exchange Ratio in $CuF_2 \cdot 2H_2O$, TRW/STL Report 9891-6001-RU-000, April, 1965.
8. Dixon, W. J.: ΔV to Enter Orbit About Mars, TRW IOC VM-2, Apr. 9, 1965.
9. DeNuzzo, J.: On-line Solution of 2-D Trajectory Equations, TRW/STL Report 9801-6013-TU-000, May 26, 1965.
10. Nishinago, R. G.: Preliminary Design Considerations for a Gyro-damped Gravity Gradient Satellite, TRW/STL Report 8427-6005-RU-000, May 28, 1965.
11. Margulies, R. S.: Response of a Peak-reading Instrument to a Contaminated Signal, TRW/STL Report 9990-6963-TU-000, June, 1965.
12. Pate, N. C., and S. M. Zivi: An Analysis of the Efficiency of Elliott's Liquid Metal MHD Energy Conversion Cycle and Its Applicability to the Power Range of 3 to 30 KWE, TRW Systems Report 9806-6002-MU-000, July 28, 1965.
13. Fried, B. D., and L. O. Heflinger: Scaling Law for MHD Acceleration, TRW Systems Report 9801-6014-RU-000, July 20, 1965.
14. Fried, B. D., and A. Y. Wong: Stability Limits for Longitudinal Waves in Ion Beam-Plasma Interaction, TRW Systems Report 9801-6015-RU-000, Aug. 31, 1965; *Phys. Fluids*, vol. 9, p. 1084, 1966.
15. Fried, B. D., and S. L. Ossakow: The Kinetic Equation for an Unstable Plasma in Parallel Electric and Magnetic Fields, UCLA Report R-3 Plasma Physics Group, November, 1965.
16. Coward, D. J.: On-line Computer Test Cases for Computer Aided Design: Structural Design of Cylindrical Shells, TRW IOC 65-9715.9-110, Aug. 24, 1965; Design of Helical Springs, TRW IOC 65-9715.4-104, Dec. 3, 1965; Flexure Design Problem, TRW IOC 65-9715.6-22, Dec. 9, 1965; Structural Design of a Beam with Varying Loads, TRW IOC 66-9713.1-14, Jan. 12, 1966.
17. Fried, B., and S. Conte: *The Plasma Dispersion Function*, Academic Press, 1961.
18. Culler, G. J., and R. W. Huff: Solution of Nonlinear Integral Equations Using On-line Computer Control, Proc. AFIPS Spring Joint Computer Conference, National Press, Palo Alto, Calif., vol. 29, p. 129, 1962.

19. Culler, G. J., B. D. Fried, R. W. Huff, and J. R. Schrieffer: The Use of On-line Computing in the Solution of Scientific Problems, TRW Report, April 2, 1962.

20. Culler, G. J., and B. D. Fried: An On-line Computing Center for Scientific Problems, Proc. 1963 Pacific Computer Conference of the IEEE, March, 1963 p. 221. Published by IEEE, New York.

21. Culler, G. J., and B. D. Fried: The TRW Two-station On-line Scientific Computer: General Description, *Computer Augmentation of Human Reasoning*, Spartan Press, Washington, 1965.

22. Fried, B. D.: *STL On-line Computer*, vol. 1, General Description; C. C. Farrington and D. Pope, vol. 2, User's Manual, TRW Systems Report 9824-6001-RU-000, Dec. 28, 1964.

23. Blackwell, F. W.: On-line Computer Symbolic Manipulation, TRW Systems Report 5253-6001-RU-000, Aug. 27, 1965.

24. Blackwell, F. W.: An On-line Symbol Manipulation System, submitted to Comm. of the A.C.M.

25. McCune, J. E.: Exact Inversion of Plasma Dispersion Relations, *Phys. Fluids* (in press).

SOLVING DESIGN PROBLEMS IN GRAPHICAL DIALOGUE

Donn B. Parker

Control Data Corporation
Palo Alto, California

7.1 Introductory Remarks

Engineering design, as distinct from engineering analysis, involves invariably some form of trial-and-error procedure. On the basis of previous experience or perhaps a guess, a first design of a system, such as an electrical circuit, a mechanical component, or a complex array of components, is devised. This preliminary design is then subjected to analysis to determine to what extent its characteristics or performance fail to meet specified tolerances. On the basis of this analysis, a second and hopefully superior system is constructed. This second design is then subjected to analysis, and this analysis-design iteration is repeated until a satisfactory system is achieved. The analysis portion of the design process can usually make effective use of an automatic computer to obtain rapid and accurate excitation-response data. The modifications to be made in the prototype so as to improve its performance generally require human judgement, experience, and intuition. The design process with its

179

intrinsic dependence upon man-computer cooperation therefore constitutes a particularly fruitful field of application for on-line computing techniques. The present chapter is devoted to a detailed discussion of the hardware and software requirements of an on-line system for solving design problems, as well as to a description of applications of such a system in a variety of technical areas. A survey of current graphic projects, hardware, and software is made, and a hardware configuration and a general software approach are singled out and justified for use in a described range of applications. The more important user aspects of the software such as data structure, console servicing, console attributes, and an interface to application programs are described in some detail.

7.2 Current Graphic Activities

In order to place the present discussion in its proper perspective, it appears useful to review very briefly the variety of projects devoted to the development of on-line graphical systems. Among the most significant of current projects are the following:

1. Lincoln Laboratory, M.I.T. (Dr. Larry Roberts[1]). Extensions of Sketchpad developed by Dr. Ivan Sutherland, who originated many of the ideas currently being developed on the TX2 computer, including three-dimensional projections, more efficient data structures, and hardware innovations.

2. M.I.T. Electronic Systems Laboratory (Douglas T. Ross[2] and Dr. Steven Coons[3]). Ross is continuing his development of AED, a general computer-aided design language and information structure. Coons has developed a method of displaying and manipulating projections of curved surfaces he calls patches. These projects use the M.I.T. MAC System.

3. Control Data Digigraphics Laboratory, Burlington, Massachusetts (Ed Fitzgerald). The digigraphics system[4] is the result of a research and development project to produce a practical graphical hardware and software system for industry. It is in operation using a Control Data® 3200 computer. Figure 7.1 is a picture of this system in use.

4. General Motors Research Laboratory (E. L. Jacks[5]). The DAC1 system developed at GMR is an advanced and elaborate graphic system for automotive styling design applications. It consists of equipment especially designed for GMR by IBM and is on-line to an IBM 7094 computer.

5. International Business Machines, Kingston, New York (Dr. F. Skinner). Software development for the IBM 2250-2840 graphic data-processing system[6] for use with 360 computers is proceeding along the lines of the Sketchpad.

6. General Electric Computer Department (Dr. Marvin T. S. Ling[7]).

Fig. 7.1   Digigraphic system in use.

Dr. Ling's approach to automated design includes an on-line graphic terminal with a light pen and voltage-gradient stylus built into the same instrument.   The development is based on a sophisticated data-structure concept for a wide range of applications.

7.   RAND Corporation (T. O. Ellis[8]).   The Rand tablet has been developed as a unique stylus and slate system for on-line graphical input. Recognition of handwritten characters has been emphasized.

8.   National Bureau of Standards (D. E. Rippy[9,20]).   MAGIC, a machine for automatic interface to a computer, has been developed.   It consists of two large cathode-ray-tube display consoles and light pen connected to a specially   designed   data   processor   with   a   magnetic-drum   memory. Emphasis has been on hardware design.

9.   Itek Corporation, Lexington, Massachusetts.   Itek has been using prototypes of the digigraphic system with a DEC PDP1 computer and a Control Data 924 computer.   These systems have been used for several years on a practical basis for lens design.

10.   Lockheed-Georgia Company (S. H. Chasen.[10,21]).   A computer-aided design project has been in progress using a medium-size computer and graphic terminal.   Applications are in the areas of structural analy-

sis management systems, editing, electrical circuit layout, information retrieval, and automatic control of programmed tools.

Other organizations doing significant work in graphics include United Aircraft, Cambridge Research Laboratory, Lawrence Radiation Laboratory, Ford Motor Company, Lockheed Missiles and Space Company, Boeing Airplane Company, MacDonnell Aircraft Company, and Lockheed-Burbank Aircraft Company.

7.3 Software Approaches

Software development can be generally classified into three main approaches. The simplest and most straightforward approach is to develop independent programs for each application to run in existing computer-operating systems. Only basic subroutines such as cathode-ray-tube drivers are shared among programs. Data structures are different for each application. This approach should lead to the earliest realization of useful applications.

The second approach, at the other extreme, is the development of sophisticated graphical systems to encompass most applications. Elaborate data structures and programming languages to use them include multidimensional list processing. Time-sharing the computer among several terminals and batch processing strive to make the most efficient use of computers. Console features include animation, three-dimensional projections, and functions for drawing with topological constraints. This work is the basis for practical systems of the future, three to five years away.

The middle approach, between these two extremes, is to provide a basic software package. This should include freehand- and precision-drawing capability, display routines, linear graphics transformations, a data structure with no list structure or a simple one, standard input-output capability, storage and selection of drawings from large files, and facility to interface application programs and library routines to provide additional functions. A schematic organization is shown in Fig. 7.2.

7.4 Hardware Approaches

The vector-generating cathode-ray tube is the central piece of equipment in most graphic systems. In the future, it may be replaced by devices such as electroluminescent panels. The vector-generating cathode-ray tube is characterized by a picture generated from digital cathode-ray-tube beam instructions which direct the beam in an on or off condition to move from any X, Y coordinate position on the cathode-ray-tube face to another coordinate position. The rate of regeneration of the picture is usually 30 to 40 frames per second depending on the phosphor used.

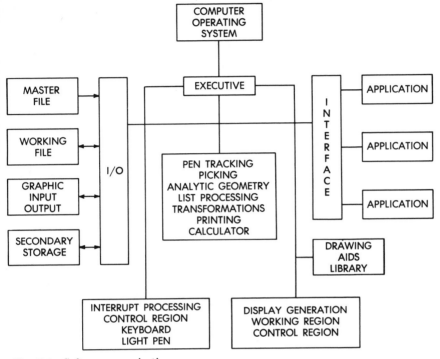

Fig. 7.2   Software organization.

There are important differences between two types of cathode-ray tubes based on the beam deflection used. The electrostatic cathode-ray tube is very fast, producing a line segment of any length in about five microseconds. The electromagnetic cathode-ray tube is slower, but it produces a much brighter and more accurately controlled beam. For example, a $\frac{1}{2}$-inch line segment might require two microseconds. The time varies with the length of line. The maximum line length generated by a single-beam instruction in most electromagnetic systems is from $\frac{1}{2}$ to $1\frac{1}{2}$ inches in a drawing area of 10- to 20-inch diameter. A longer line requiring more than one-beam instruction produces undesirable bright spots where the beam slows down, stops, and speeds up for the next segment. This problem is eliminated by a $\frac{1}{2}$-cycle delay between beam deflection and execution of the beam instruction. This produces continuous beam movement and two other advantages: very sharp end points by doubling back on the beam path and continuous curve-segment generation.

A controversial point is the precision required. Several graphical systems stress high-precision cathode-ray tubes with up to 4096 by 4096 beam positions and large relatively flat-faced viewing areas with extensive nonlinearity correction. Low-cost television-scan cathode-ray tubes of relatively low precision (500 lines) are being developed. However, high-precision, large-area cathode-ray tubes have a decided advantage in many design areas and should prove to be economically practical. Viewing requirements alternate between magnified detail views and wide-angle views with little detail. Each view change requires extensive computation. The large-area cathode-ray tube can reduce the frequency of view changes by as much as a factor of three. Reduction of computation, design aesthetics, and convenience of large, precision displays are strong arguments in convincing a design engineer that he should leave his drawing board and peer into the "end of a bottle."

Figure 7.3 is a J-size assembly drawing. Its complexity is staggering with almost 7,000 line and curve segments, 8,900 characters, requiring 54,000 words of computer storage. However, in a graphics system it would be represented by several drawings of the component parts which could be easily superimposed to see various aspects of the assembly. The rectangle near the center depicts the relative size of an 11- by 17-inch cathode-ray-tube viewing area which would make the smallest character readable.

A display-storage buffer system to hold the beam driving instructions and maintain the picture on these volatile cathode-ray tubes is essential to avoid excessive computer use. Magnetic drum, disk, and core storage devices are used. Some have extensive instruction sequencing controls and others are limited to simple invariant sequencing. The importance is in maintaining an off-line status to the large computer required for significant graphical work except when terminal servicing is required.

A pointing and drawing input device is essential. The three commonly used devices are the light pen, the voltage-gradient-surface stylus, and the capacitance-surface stylus. The Rand tablet[8] is a capacitance surface and stylus with precision compatible with a 1024 by 1024 cathode-ray tube. The surface is not transparent and must be used in independent physical orientation relative to the cathode-ray tube. The stylus controls the position of a dot* on the cathode-ray tube through a combination of software and hardware. A disadvantage is the extensive computation required to identify the graphic entity closest to the dot when the stylus is used to point. The stylus can be accurately controlled for detailed drawing, and an unimpaired view of the cathode-ray tube can be maintained. The voltage-gradient-surface stylus is used in the DAC1 system.[5] It has considerably less precision than the light pen and capacitance-surface stylus. The transparent stanous-oxide-conductor coating on glass makes the surface usable over the cathode-ray tube, but there are

* Often called a marker or cursor.

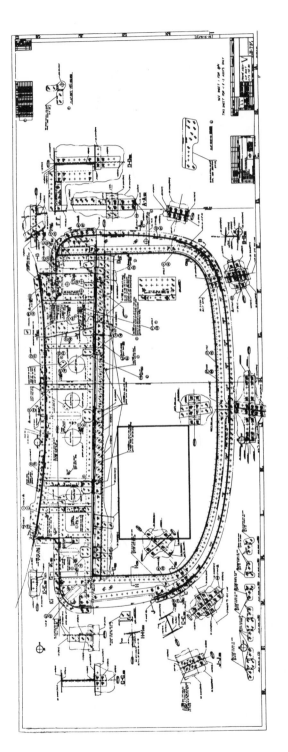

NUMBER OF ENTITIES	6945
NUMBER OF CHARACTERS	8912
DENSITY, ENTITIES PER ZONE	72
COMPUTER WORDS (field=24 bit word)	54,000
MAGNETIC TAPE STORAGE IN FEET (800bpi, 7 channel)	24

Fig. 7.3 Sample engineering assembly drawing.

185

severe stylus-position alignment problems with respect to the display. However, it is an inexpensive and simple device.

The light pen[11] is most popular and suffers few of the drawbacks of the other devices. Graphic entities pointed at are directly identifiable by the computer. Its major drawback is a slightly sluggish response and a dull point; that is, the focus area is usually uncomfortably large and is sometimes sensitive to the angle at which the pen is held. Great care must be taken to turn it on and off at the right time to avoid pen reaction to other light sources. Also the location of the pen can be determined by the computer only by identifying the entity being pointed at by the pen.

The exact point at which the pen is pointing can be determined only if that point is displayed by a unique beam-driving instruction; or if additional identification procedures are performed by the pen user. Dr. Marvin Ling[7] at General Electric has proposed combining the light pen and voltage-gradient-surface stylus into a single device. Improvements are continually being made to eliminate or reduce the drawbacks of these devices. An example is the experimental beam pen being used at M.I.T.[22] It detects the electron beam rather than the light produced by it.

Function- and character-keying devices are another important form of input. Where they are placed, the number of them, their form, and in particular how they are labeled are important human engineering considerations.

Fixed-use consoles have fixed-device labels since each device or feature has a constant function. Examples are the Control Data® 6060 Remote Calculator and Teletype terminals in some systems. A Teletype can be used in two distinct ways. User input can be in the form of typed words or mnemonics, or it can be in the form of pressing a single key where the key label identifies the type of input. In the former case, variable labels are unnecessary; in the latter, they could be highly desirable. A general-purpose console for use in many applications should have devices whose use is defined and labeled by software. Manually changing labels is not practical under dynamic conditions. The Digigraphics System partially solves this problem by putting many keying functions on the cathode-ray tube as light buttons[12] which require the use of the light pen to activate a button which can have a software-defined shape and location.

Consider the location of labels relative to the keys. The fact that a typewriter has labels on keys which are covered by the fingers is inconsequential since the typewriter was designed for touch-typing. However, the labels for function keys should be near the keys but not on them so that a user may read them at all times. Methods of supplying variable labels under these conditions are suggested as follows:

1. Fixed-label rotating bars, positioned by software control, placed at the base of each row of keys.

2. Labels from filmstrips light-projected onto frosted glass above each key.

3. Long-lever keys placed over an image-storage tube where the computer-controlled beam creates the labels on the tube face next to the keys.

4. A more novel approach is to use criss-crossing strips of stanous-oxide coating on the glass over the storage tube in place of keys. Voltage-gradient stylus-finger thimbles placed on intersection areas of the strips effectively activate keys. The computer can test each strip successively for the presence of a stylus. Capacitance buttons similar to those used in elevators might replace the oxide-coating and thimble method.

Registers for input and display of alphanumeric data are essential, especially in applications requiring precise, literal construction of graphics representing real objects. In fact, it is through the use of numeric input registers that graphics may be constructed and stored to the full precision of the computer even though viewed at relatively low precision on the cathode-ray tube.

Mechanical registers are too costly and inflexible. The cathode-ray tube can be used to advantage, as in the case of light buttons, to create software-generated light registers. A light register is a blank space for display of a number, label, or message; its name and outlining format can be displayed with it. A significant advantage is that light registers can be created, erased, moved, renamed, and modified to fit the needs of individual applications. They are convenient also because the user can limit his attention to just the cathode-ray tube and does not need to divert it to another part of the console to see a register.

The surface of the cathode-ray tube can be divided into two areas. Figure 7.4 shows a 20-inch circular cathode-ray tube with an 11- by 17-inch working region where graphics are constructed and manipulated and a control region constituting the remainder of the tube face. The control

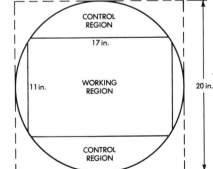

Fig. 7.4 Cathode-ray-tube organization.

region is used to display light buttons and light registers. In place of a keyboard, an array of alphanumeric and special characters can be displayed for light-pen selection. Also desk-calculator functions can easily be included in this region. It is practical to treat the displayed frame, dividing the two types of regions, as display data which can be modified to change the shape and area of the regions for different applications.

Several terminals are connected to a computer through one or more display-buffer controllers. The entire computer capability may be used to serve consoles in a dedicated system such as the Control Data® 3200 Computer Digigraphics System, or the computer graphics capability may be time-shared with other peripheral devices and batch-mode operation as in the General Motors Research DAC1 system. The computer requirements in speed, memory capacity, and secondary random-access storage capacity are considerable when one considers the need for storage of complex digitized drawings and minimum console-servicing response time.

The input of graphics from hard copy and output on hard copy is a major function but will not be considered in detail. Automatic methods of input by scanning techniques have been successful in some application areas such as bubble-chamber photographs in high-energy particle-accelerator research. However, considerable development is necessary for success in input of design drawings, especially dimensioned drawings. Current scanning techniques requiring human aid leave much to be desired. Instead, drawings can be quickly and accurately redrawn at the graphics console with computer-aided techniques. However, only experience yet to be gained will prove the practicality of this.

Hard copy of computer-stored drawings may be produced on paper, microfilm, or other media by one of many available plotter or microfilm systems now on the market. Configurations may include capability on-line, off-line, remote, or adjacent to a console. One objective in providing on-line graphic terminals, however, is to minimize the need for hard copy by making the consoles relatively inexpensive, easy to use, and readily available.

A PROPOSED BASIC SYSTEM

7.5 Basic Features

A basic graphics system is proposed here upon which will be based descriptions of advanced features and application-oriented functions. The console consists of a 20-inch, electromagnetic vector cathode-ray tube with a 4096 by 4096 beam position raster, a light pen, and a set of function keys with software-controlled and defined labels and functions. One or more terminals are connected to a display-buffer controller, which in turn is connected to a large, fast computer with a large, secondary storage such as a disk or drum system.

A light pen of normal pen size, with a microswitch on its shank to turn it on and off, is connected to a photomultiplier tube with a fiber-optics cable.

The keyboard is movable with a magnetic backing.   It may be set on a table surface to the left or the right of the user or adjacent to the cathode-ray tube.   The objective is to keep the mechanical features to a minimum, thereby reducing the cost and increasing the potential reliability of the system.   Two keys on the keyboard operate in parallel, one on each side of the keyboard, for symmetric availability of a major function.   One key operates in parallel with the light pen microswitch.   The number of keys is minimized to simplify operation.   Each key activates an interrupt line to the computer.   The keys are spring-loaded and non-latching.   Assignment of key functions is software-controlled.

Other possible mechanical features such as foot pedals, track ball, alphanumeric keyboard, or other keys are not included, since they complicate console operation and increase console costs.   Also, adequate features are easily introduced by software on the cathode-ray tube.

A concept of precise, literal drawing is employed.   Graphics are described in an analytic geometry representation, and topological freedoms are not allowed, with one exception.   When the pen is pointing close to a graphic element or to one of its parameters, it is assumed to be pointing at that element or parameter in an exact analytic geometric sense.   If the pen is pointing close to the end of a line segment, the computer assumes it is not pointing at the line but at the exact end point represented in the computer by coordinate values to the full precision capability of the computer.   This is one of the most significant features of the system.   Although a man instigates and views the construction of graphics at very low precision, the computer completes the construction and saves it at a precision far beyond the capabilities of man and console equipment.

The most primitive units of data are X and Y coordinate values, lengths, radii, angles, and alphanumeric characters.   These are combined with geometric, text, logical, and display codes to form entities such as straight line segment, circle, and text.   A distinction is made between a point entity, which is a temporary parameter for graphic construction, and the dot entity, which is a point entity formally introduced as part of the drawing.

7.6 Light-pen Picking

The selection of displayed entities as parameters for use in further construction is the most frequently performed function and should be the simplest to perform. The light pen is pointed at an entity, the micro-switch is turned on and then off, and the entity is picked. Entities in the working region and light registers in the control region may be picked. A successful pick is indicated by momentary light intensification of the entity picked, followed by the display of a character next to it or sur-rounding it (in the case of a dot). A light button is selected (as opposed to picked) by the light pen to cause an action to take place. Momentary light intensification of the light button shows computer acknowledgment of the selection. When an entity is picked, displayable parameters of the entity such as the center of a circle or focus of a parabolic arc are also displayed as small, low-intensity crosses.

A large number of entities may be picked before they are used in a last-in-first-used order. Picking groups of entities is performed by subsequent picking of already picked items. Picking a circle which has already been picked causes the group of entities which contains the circle as a member to be picked as a group (not as individual entities). The circle remains separately picked. The ERASE and other functions will change the status of items. Grouping is described in more detail in a later section.

TABLE 7.1 *States of Entities*

Erased..........	No longer exists
Nondisplayable..	Exists in the computer data list but is not displayable
Displayable.....	Exists and is available for display
Parameter-picked	Is currently displayed, and one of its parameters is in picked status
Picked..........	Is currently displayed as picked and is in picked status
Group-picked....	Is currently displayed as picked, is not itself necessarily picked, but the group or higher-level group of which it is a member is picked

7.7 Entity Types

An entity may be created in many ways, but only the basic parameters are used to store and define the entity. These parameters are chosen on the basis of minimizing storage requirements and making equation repre-sentations easy to derive. The entity types available in the system and the basic parameters which describe them are listed in Table 7.2.

The geometric entities are limited to planar conics. Higher-degree curves may be described by fitted conic arcs or by the straight-line-segment string. Three-dimensional graphics may be described by their two-dimensional projections.

Several line intensities and standard line types may be selected by light buttons. Several extra line-type buttons are unassigned for user or application-program designation. Other light buttons provide for non-display and redisplay by line type or line intensity. For example, a

TABLE 7.2 *Entity Types*

Geometric

Dot.....................	X, Y
Straight line segment......	$X_1, Y_1; X_2, Y_2$
Horizontal line segment....	$X_1, Y_1; X_2$
Vertical line segment......	$X_1, Y_1; Y_2$
Circle..................	X, Y (center); R (radius)
Circle arc...............	Circle parameters; X_1, Y_1 (beginning point, counterclockwise); X_2, Y_2 (end point)
Ellipse..................	X, Y (center); A (semimajor axis length); B (semiminor axis length); L (angle of major axis)
Ellipse arc..............	Ellipse parameters; X_1, Y_1, X_2, Y_2 (circle arc sense)
Parabolic arc............	X, Y (vertex); L (axis angle); F (focal distance; X_1, Y_1, X_2, Y_2 (circle arc sense)
Hyperbolic arc...........	X, Y (center point); A (transverse radius); B (conjugate radius); L (angle of major axis); X_1, Y_1, X_2, Y_2 (circle arc sense)
Straight-line-segment string	$X_0, Y_0, X_1, Y_1, \ldots X_n, Y_n$
Text....................	X, Y (lower left corner of first character); string of BCD characters

Logic and Control

Group..................	List of pointer addresses of group members
Register................	Register name, contents, location
Light button............	Light-button name, location
Frame..................	X, Y (center point)
Application..............	Parameters assigned by application programs

drawing may be studied with all center lines or all dimension lines temporarily nondisplayed.

7.8 Transformations and Constraints

Transformations provided by the basic software and directly available to the console user and application programs are similitude (uniform compression or expansion on a given point), translation, and the linear, orthogonal transformations, rotate and reflect. This provides the user with the facility to change the scale of drawings or parts of drawings. Entities and groups of entities may be moved, rotated and reflected. Only one-half of a symmetric drawing need be drawn; and with the selection of a button, it may be reflected to produce the completed drawing. A transform causes an original form to disappear and reappear in its final state. A transform-a-copy operation retains the original form and the new one appears.

The light pen can be used in freehand-drawing mode using a tracking cross on the cathode-ray tube. Semiprecision drawing can be accomplished by imposing constraints on freehand light-pen usage. With the horizontal HOLD key depressed, the user can pick the tracking cross in the working region; the drawing point normally traveling with the cross is constrained to move in a straight line as the pen is moved at the angle specified in the base-angle register. The vertical HOLD key and angle HOLD key work similarly, one normal to the base angle and the other at an angle specified by an angle register. The straight line is created by selecting a second key and accepting or rejecting that which is displayed.

7.9 Drawing Surface

While considering the transformations, it is logical to introduce the concept of the drawing surface (see Fig. 7.5). This is the two-dimensional, imaginary surface on which all graphics are described. It is limited in size and detail by the range of the number representation and precision of the computer. In engineering-design applications involving the drawing of objects, the drawing surface is virtually unlimited in size and precision when the computer has a 48-bit word, floating-point number representation. The working region of the cathode-ray tube is used to view parts or all of the graphics on the drawing surface just as a variable magnification glass might be moved over a map to view parts of it in

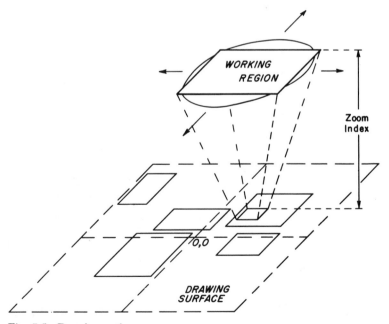

Fig. 7.5 Drawing surface.

detail. The zoom register, frame-location registers, frame picking, and the translate transformation are used for this purpose.

The drawing surface can be looked upon as an imaginary two-dimensional computer storage where the contents of specified X, Y locations are points. The concept of drawing or subdrawing (groups of entities) relocatability is useful. Relocatability is simply defined by the translate transformation. A drawing may be stored in secondary storage, such as magnetic tape, and located any place on the drawing surface. After it is brought into computer memory, it may be moved to a convenient location. A drawing overlapping another is not prohibited. It is important to keep in mind the distinct difference between moving graphics on the drawing surface and moving the working surface frame of view on the drawing surface. Both actions are performed with the translate transformation; but the graphics to be moved are picked in the former case, and the working surface frame is picked in the latter case.

There is danger in loss of accuracy due to relocation. A drawing could be moved to a region of very high X and Y values and then returned to a region closer to the origin with complete loss of accuracy. Scaling could be of assistance, but it adds unnecessary complexity in most cases which can be controlled by working close enough to the origin to maintain required accuracy. A nonlinear drawing surface might solve this problem without significant additional complexity, but it is not considered in this chapter. Overflowing the range of the number representation is indicated as an error in the message register. However, modulo treatment of the number range makes the drawing surface cylindrical in X and independently cylindrical in Y.

7.10 Drawing Scale

Drawing scale is normally an unnecessary consideration except when hard-copy output is being prepared. Drawings are usually made in actual dimensions without any difficulty because of the vast range of the drawing surface as compared to the real world of objects to be drawn. The zoom function changes the scale of drawings, but only for visual purposes on a temporary basis which does not affect the data list. When a drawing is to be output in hard-copy form, the user must change the scale of auxiliary views with the similitude transformation as needed, add scaling notes to the drawing, and indicate the scale to be used by the output program.

7.11 Printing

Alphanumeric printing capability deserves an important place in a graphical system. Engineering drawings can contain very large volumes of notes, labels, and dimensions. Printing capability is provided in the form of a raster of alphanumerics displayed in the control region. The procedure consists of picking a starting point, picking an angle if other than the base angle, and then employing a hunt-and-pick mode of character selection, all done with the light pen. Associated light buttons are also needed for margin control, font selection and roll-up or roll-down "carriage return." All characters are placed in a single-text entity until an end-text light button is selected. The alphanumeric raster is displayed in the control region only when selected by a key, and it disappears when the end-text light button is selected. Erasure is done at the character level by the erase function. Numeric information is put into a picked light register from the right end and shifted left for each new digit or decimal point selected. The sign is entered independently in a fixed location.

Advantages of this type of software-provided printing feature in contrast to a hardware keyboard include economic savings in hardware, reduced maintenance problems, and increased console reliability. Another advantage is found in having all of the user's attention remain on the cathode-ray tube and light pen. He does not have to put the pen down and turn to a keyboard. Printing and drawing graphics are highly intermixed in design, making it an asset for the two types of operations to be compatible.

7.12 Input and Output

Input and output between secondary mass storage and the computer memory (drawing surface) for temporary and permanent storage is accomplished in the basic software by a two-file system. A permanent file of drawings available to the user is based on drawing titles. The file is updated by an editing program from the working file. Each console user has his own working file in which are stored reference drawings, partially completed drawings, and possibly drawings awaiting approval for transfer to the permanent file. A region of the drawing surface is reserved for a list of names of drawings in the working file. An arrow points to the name of the first or last selected drawing. The arrow may be moved by the light pen to a name of a drawing; selection of a light button causes the drawing to be deleted or placed in the computer (on the drawing surface). New names are added automatically as drawings are filed by the user.

Many of the functions of this basic system were derived from the Sketchpad work of Dr. Ivan Sutherland[11] and the development of digigraphic-system prototypes by Itek Corporation, Adams Associates, and Control Data Corporation.

CONSOLE ATTRIBUTES

7.13 Basic Console Characteristics

It is of utmost importance that a terminal system appeal to potential users, since these users will be in intimate contact with terminals for varying amounts of time in their use of computers. Some users will have already had extensive experience in the use of computers; but more important, many potential users are people who have not had direct contact with computers in their work. This makes the challenge of providing successful interfaces all the more difficult, important, and potentially rewarding. The general attributes which apply in most cases are as follows:

Application Orientation. Systems must have the versatility to "talk the same language" as the user for the range of applications desired. A user must be able to use the vocabulary of his trade or profession. A graphic console for manipulating points, lines, and circles, which recognizes the graphics by these names is appropriate for the geometer or draftsman. However, it must recognize those items as events, activities, and critical paths for the project planner; and for electronic engineers, they must be called terminals, wires, and transistors. A terminal system with many different application capabilities would be complex and costly, but flexibility in the basic software and data structure to accommodate customer-generated programs which can provide specific application orientation is a reasonable approach.

Programmed Instructional Characteristics. A primary application could be an instructional program. It should provide two levels of instruction, a course in basic system usage and usage reference. When a user forgets the method for a specific function, he could ask the system for aid in recalling the necessary steps. The neophyte could take a basic course. This capability could become very complex when application programs drastically alter the console characteristics. Then a programmed instruction feature would have to be built into each major application to describe the changed characteristics.

The graphics system is ideal for instructional purposes. The flexibility of the program-controlled light buttons and registers provides a means of leading the student through the steps of performing functions. Buttons and registers to be used can be highlighted and others made inactive. Messages and arrows can be displayed any place on the cathode-ray tube.

Confidence. A user's confidence in a terminal system is a function of several variables. Hardware reliability is important, from little things like keys that do not stick to recovery from mass-storage wipe-outs. Confidence is built up with stable software and controlled modification of console characteristics. Reference documents must be comprehensible, comprehensive, and correct. The user must have optional isolation. When he desires to work alone and isolated, he must not be aware of computer or console activity other than his own; and other activities must not conflict in unexpected ways with his.

Security. Security and privacy must be maintained at least to the same level as with current hard-copy security systems. Acceptable storage of classified documents consists of metal containers and combination locks. The equivalent is easy to provide to protect data and programs in storage as long as the computer room is classified. One drawback is that the computer could be used to "pick" a combination by trial and error. A possible solution is to put time and method limits on user responses to combination requests from the computer.

However, the real problem is not so much how to protect classified information as it is to identify breaches of security and where to put the blame.

Optimum Response Times. Two kinds of response times are to be considered: user to computer and computer to user. The former is easy to dispose of by simply stating that the user must be allowed all the time he needs between computer actions; after all, he is paying for it. However, the software must be designed to minimize high-speed memory requirements and machine cycles needed for an idle terminal.

Computer response time to user action is the single most important property of a terminal system; there are two types: time-to-acknowledgment and time-to-completion. A number of experienced people recommend that ideally time-to-completion should always be less than one second. However, optimization with cost, significance of response, and method of acknowledgment—all as variables can produce far different conclusions. Continuous acknowledgment or continued discrete acknowledgments can result in smaller rates of increase in the user fidget factor thereby increasing allowable time-to-completion.

The user can be legitimately deceived, in some cases, to increase overall performance of the system. One acknowledgment device is a terminal light or noise indicator which gives a continuous signal during the periods that the computer is truly serving that terminal. This is a poor technique because of the above considerations; it is distracting and becomes a point of argument concerning system performance. Artificial acknowledgment techniques are far more flexible and can be more effective.

It is reasonable to expect the user to be willing to wait for a significant amount of time for what he thinks is a major function to be performed for him by the computer. Unfortunately, some functions appearing to be minor in nature require a great deal of computation. For example, moving the working region frame of view on the drawing surface could require a complete search of a large data list testing for intersection with the frame. This could require from five to fifteen seconds. It can only be hoped that the total value of using a graphic system and the adaptability of the people using it will offset the serious problems of excessive response time.

7.14 Optimum Control Dynamics

Control dynamics is concerned with the relationships between user action at the terminal and system responses. Optimum control dynamics is based on the principle of reasonable request–reasonable response. If a user makes a reasonable request (input), he should receive a reasonable response (output). This requires software flexibility and sophistication, but much can be done at little or no extra cost. Some techniques result in reduction of software and hardware cost.

The principle of reasonable request–reasonable response can be more fully expressed. If a potential user is given a general statement concerning the capability of the graphic system, he should then be able to decide logically what operations he should perform to accomplish a task based on the labeled devices and display. The system should then correctly and clearly respond to his reasonable requests and inform him of unreasonable ones. This generality can be achieved by defining the minimum necessary limitations. For the performance of any specific function, a set of parameters must be picked and function keys pressed. It should be possible for the system to extract information from the picked parameters and the order in which they are picked, in some cases, to partially determine what the user's request is going to be. The final function-requesting keys may then be made very general.

A concept of order-dependent parameter specification can be employed in ambiguous cases to impart necessary meanings. The order in which parameters are picked determines how they are to be used when more than one way is possible. If two points are picked and the construction of a circle is requested, the first is the center and the second is a locus point. If the user forgets the order-imposed meaning, he guesses and if wrong, erases and starts over. This avoids the necessity for parameter descriptor keys for center, locus, end point, focus, vertex, radius, and axis. Table 7.3 shows all the allowed combinations and ordering of parameters to construct a circle in the described basic system. The numbers indicate order dependence, and X's indicate order independence. Combinations are read vertically.

It is impossible to specify too many parameters for a construction because only the first set of meaningful parameters encountered are used in a last-in-first-used basis. Based on the first acceptable parameter encountered in this order, all other nonmeaningful parameters are ignored.

TABLE 7.3 *Circle Construction Parameters*

Point or X, Y registers	1	X	X	X			
Point or X, Y registers	2	X					
Point or X, Y registers		X					
Length register				X		X	
Straight line segment					X	X	X
Straight line segment						X	X
Straight line segment							X

Table 7.4 shows several push-down-from-the-top lists for the circle construction.

TABLE 7.4 *Push-down Parameter Lists for Circle Construction*

* Point	(2)* Point	* Point	* Line
* Point	(1)* Point	* Line	* Point
* Point	Line	Point	Point
* Line	* Line	* Point	* Line
Line	* Point	* Line	* Line
* Point	Line	Line	* Line
* Point	* L. register	* Line	* L. register
* L. register	* Point	L. register	Line
		* Point	* Point

* Indicates the chosen parameters.

If not enough meaningful parameters are given when the construction is specified by a light button, MORE appears in the message register. Construction proceeds when enough parameters have been picked. Thus, it does not matter when the construction button is selected relative to the parameter picking in this case. Entities are constructed independently of the limiting frame of the working region. An entity can be constructed without appearing in the working region, or it may only partially appear. An exception is open conics (hyperbola and parabola); only the arcs which lie inside the working region are created. Generally, arcs are constructed by creating the whole conic (in the working region) and then picking the conic and end points as parameters to the arc construction.

When three intersecting lines are used as parameters to construct a circle, several choices are possible: the inscribed circle tangent to the lines, the three exterior circles tangent to the lines, and the circle with the three line intersections on its locus. When a construction is requested, one of the possible cases is displayed. The user must press the ACCEPT key to make the entity permanent, press the REJECT key to make it disappear, or press the ALTERNATE key to display another case for acceptance or rejection. Only one case may be accepted for any one construction procedure.

Another example of applying this principle is in the design of transformation features in the graphic system. The user is provided with the capability to move, rotate, reflect, and change scale of graphics displayed on the cathode-ray tube. A straightforward way of accomplishing this is as follows (NOTE: Commas allow permutation of terms but periods do not; parentheses delimit punctuation effectivity):

Move (Graphics from Point $(X1, Y1)$ to Point $(X2, Y2)$) =
(Pick Graphics, Pick Point $(X1, Y1)$ and identify as "from" point, Pick Point $(X2, Y2)$ and identify as "to" point, Press MOVE key). *Computer performs move . . .*
Rotate (Graphics about Point by Angle) =
(Pick Graphics, Pick Point and identify as "about" point, Pick Angle and identify as "by" angle, Press ROTATE key). *Computer performs rotation . . .*

Another approach is based on the idea that the type of transform may be deduced by the system from the parameters chosen, and the order in which the parameters are chosen (order dependence) determines how they are to be used. This is illustrated as follows:

Transform (Graphics according to Parameters) = Pick Graphics, Pick Parameters. Press TRANSFORM key. *Computer performs transform . . .*

The transform type is chosen on the basis of deducing from the parameters ΔX and ΔY for MOVE, a point and angle for ROTATE, a straight line segment for REFLECT, and a point and scalar for SCALE. There are a few ambiguities among all parameter combinations which could produce the basic parameters and identify the transform, but four keys have been replaced by one key and several parameter identification actions have been eliminated. However, one limitation has been introduced by imposing an ordering of operations to separate parameters from graphics to be transformed. This limitation can also be eliminated when the graphics by their nature cannot be interpreted in any way as parameters.

These particular techniques complicate the software slightly but reduce the complexity of the console, reduce the amount of information the user must acquire and retain, increase his speed of operation, and make the terminal system more appealing and sophisticated. Also, isolating the software deduction logic and the parameter reduction facilitates system expansion to allow more powerful functions to be specified for producing a multiplicity of combinations of transformations.

7.15   Console Lockout Protection

Since both the user and computer are using the console, it is important that they do not interfere with each other. The computer should have the facility to lockout the user to prevent unexpected actions during the computer servicing of the console. Selected user lockout from specific console devices is desirable in certain more complex console configurations. Since the user instigates all computer actions, it is not necessary to have the reverse lockout—the user locking out the computer—to prevent conflicts of simultaneous use. However, computer lockout is convenient to prevent unintended console usage either by the user or other persons.

7.16   Forgiveness and Fail-softness

These are buzz words which have important meaning in man-machine systems design. Two types of user errors are of most concern: errors inherent in his own work of which the system is not aware and errors in system use which are recognized by the system. A third type, misuse not recognized by the system as an error, can only be handled by external methods until repair can be accomplished. Another solution is to change the specifications of the system to conform to the deviation.

Fail-softness is the system capability to let the user down easy when he uses incorrect procedures. The system must discover incorrect procedures before harm is done, recover as far as possible, and gently and politely inform the user of his error. The use of the terms "gently" and "politely" may sound facetious, but it is important. Such flip comments to the user through a message register as "you goofed" or "Dunderhead, try again" are very bad. The users develop a camaraderie with terminal systems through experience and look upon them as having human qualities; and as learned long ago, proper etiquette and politeness go a long way in human relations. Potential users may think such comments are funny in some circumstances, but they are going to resist acceptance of a system that calls them a dunderhead.

Forgiveness is the ability to recover from both inherent user errors and system errors. A good rule of thumb is to have a system capable of restoring conditions to the state which existed prior to the last computer action and facility for the user to request restoration. The graphic system provides this feature in the following way (NOTE: Dollar signs delimit comments and computer responses to user actions are italicized):

> Accept/Reject (Action) = $ Computer has just completed Action $
> *Computer ((Message Register) = ACCEPT/REJECT)*. IF User presses ACCEPT Key THEN (*Computer (Makes action permanent, erases parameter references used, clears Message Register)*. Terminate). IF User presses REJECT Key THEN *Computer (Restores conditions to state before Action, erases parameter references, clears Message Register)*. . . .

Forgiveness not only implies that a means for recovery be provided but also suggests that the user be given instructions and assistance in recovery.

7.17   Macro Function

One of the more annoying console operations is performing the same sequence of operations very frequently.   The normal console features are micro in nature to provide flexibility.   Application programs can be written to provide automatic execution of sets of operations but not so easily and quickly as sometimes needed.   A drawing-aid subroutine is provided with which the user may define macro console operations as he needs them from sequences of basic operations.

The sequence of operations to define and use a macro might be as follows:

1. Pick the input parameters.

2. Select the macro definition button.

3. Select two characters and place in a box to be used as the macro button.

4. Step through the sequence of operations to be defined.

5. Select the macro definition button to terminate the definition.   The box disappears leaving the macro button displayed.

6. The macro may now be used by picking the appropriate parameters and selecting the macro button.

Note that no parameters may be picked intermediate to the macro operation.   When this is required, several macros must be defined and used in sequence and separated by parameter picking.

An example shows the usefulness of this feature.   A copy of a template pattern such as a standard screw (represented by a group of entities in a standard template drawing on the drawing surface) is to be placed at the proper angle into the drawing under construction.   A point at the base of a displayed screw head is picked, the point of final position in the drawing is picked, and another point is picked such that the angle defined by the last two points is the desired angle for the screw centerline.   The macro definition button is selected, and the letters SC are placed in the macro button box in the control region.   The operations performing the translate-a-copy are now performed.   The first picked point is picked again to cause the whole group defining the screw to be picked, the X, Y registers containing the coordinate values of the second point are picked; the copy of the screw is moved to overlay the translate parameter points, the copy of the screw and the last two points are repicked, and the screw is rotated through the required angle.   The macro definition button is selected to complete the definition.   A copy of any group of entities may now be moved and rotated by picking the three prescribed points in order.

7.18   Animation

Animation as used in the Sketchpad-type systems is a spectacular and desirable console attribute in some cases.   The ability to guide pictures around with the light pen and see transformations performed in small incremental steps can be extremely helpful. However, the cost in computer time and programming should be carefully considered. A likely conclusion is that animation is an attribute which cannot be afforded except in essential applications. A transform function can cause an original form to disappear and reappear in its final state without animation. An additional function, transform-a-copy, can retain the original form and produce a new one. Applications in dynamic mechanical design such as linkage-clearance studies where animation is important can use the move, rotate, rotate-a-copy, and move-a-copy transformations with the erase function repeatedly in small increments to create animation.

SOFTWARE CONSIDERATIONS

7.19 Application Interface

Principal features of software unique to graphics are pen tracking, display generation, console servicing, data structure, and the application interface (see Fig. 7.2). The last three items will be treated in detail.

The most important feature of the basic system described earlier should be an application interface. Its purpose is to make the current data list available and provide all the system features in a form easily used by application programs. This makes the system a versatile design tool and problem solver, not just a drafting machine. The interface consists of an executive application-call routine and a set of subroutines. All application-program activity is carried out through the interface in a relatively nonchanging environment to minimize the need for recoding programs when basic software changes are made.

One interface function allows an application program to perform all functions available to a user and in the same way. A program may pick parameters, fill registers, select light buttons, and effectively press keyboard keys. In addition, the program may inhibit the use of most console features, change their meanings, or, in the case of control region features, change their positions and add new ones. Finally, a pause-until-console-action function provides an interrupt before or after action making the application program operable in the console user's real time. These features combine to provide a close working relationship between the user and computer, allowing the best characteristics of both to be brought to bear on problems. A master switch allows the user to turn off the application and return control to the console. This capability is unalterable by an application program.

A practical application program using this first function of the interface is one which records every action taken by the user in a time history.

It produces a printed list naming each action and the time consumed. This is most valuable in studying the man-machine interaction to make improvements in the system and to evaluate the skill and difficulties of the user.

Another interface function provides features more suitable to programming. Routines are included to translate and add program-generated entities to the data list, to search the data list for entities based on any combination of characteristics, and to use the entity construction and manipulation facilities without going through the external console. For example, a call to the intersection subroutine with two entity relative addresses as parameters would return the intersection point(s) as values assumed by a second pair of parameter names in the calling statement.

The system becomes a versatile tool with this capability. Many existing programs run in a batch-mode computer operation can be fitted with preprocessors and postprocessors, thus adapting them for on-line graphics capabilities. Another important program executed outside of the system provides a data structure and language translation for punched-card input of graphics to work files from handwritten coded sheets.

Application programs are brought into memory from secondary storage by the executive application-call routine at the request of the console user. An application program is executed until ended, until an interrupt for a higher priority console request is received, until a pause statement is executed, or until a time limit expires. If control is to be returned to the application at a later time, it is kept in memory; or it is temporarily dumped into secondary storage, preserving its current state, when memory space is needed.

7.20   Application Example

A concise application demonstrating many of the system capabilities is the calculation of the area and centroid of a closed polyconic forming a simply or multiply connected domain and/or a system of dot-area centroids (see Fig. 7.6). The program steps and algorithm are as follows:

1. The randomly ordered, user-picked entities describing the simply or multiply connected domain and/or the dots each followed by its associated area value are accepted.

2. A closure check is made. If lack of closure is discovered, the unconnected end points are displayed in small triangles and MORE appears in the message register. The user may press the REJECT key, in which case, the displayed triangles and message disappear and the program terminates. The user may also pick one or more entities which complete the closure, in which case, the triangles and message disappear and step 2 is repeated. If only a single closed conic has been chosen, the

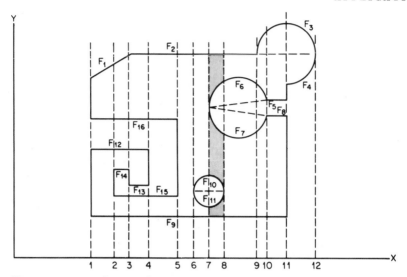

Fig. 7.6 Area and centroid calculation application.

centroid is set to the center point, and the area is calculated by standard formula. Go to step 8. Step 2 is ignored if all parameters are dot-area centroids.

3. Divide each double-valued entity in X into two single-valued entities. Discard vertical straight-line-segment entities, and divide straight-line-segment string entities into straight-line-segment entities.

$$Y = F_j(G, X, \{XY, S\}), X_1 \leq X \leq X_2$$
$$j = 1, 2, \ldots p$$

are the p remaining entities where G is the geometric descriptor taking on one of the values: straight-line segment, horizontal straight-line segment, circle arc, ellipse arc, parabola arc, or hyperbola arc. XY, S is a set of fixed coordinate points, and scalars, and X_1 and X_2 the X coordinates of the end points. Thus a circular arc with center at h, k, radius R, and end points at X_1, Y_1 and $X_2, Y_2(X_1 < X_2)$ would be represented by the equation

$$Y = k - \sqrt{R^2 - (X - h)^2}, X_1 \leq X \leq X_2$$

where the sign of the radical was chosen negative because $X_1 < X_2$ and X_1, Y_1 is the beginning point of the arc in a counterclockwise direction.

$$\{X_c, Y_c, A_c\}_i, i = 1, 2, \ldots, L$$

are the dot-area centroids.

4. Divide the range of X, from smallest to largest encountered, among the end points of the p entities into subranges of X so that all end points of entities lie on subrange boundaries.

$$X_1 < X_2 < X_3 < \cdots < X_n$$

X_i, $i = 1, 2, \ldots, n$ are all the distinct coordinate values of end points of the p entities.

5. In each subrange, order, from the highest to lowest Y values, the entities included in that subrange by highest Y value each entity assumes in that subrange.

$$\{F_{j_1}, F_{j_2}, \ldots, F_{j_m}\}_i, \quad \mathrm{Max}_{(X_i, X_{i+1})} F_{j_k} > \mathrm{Max}_{(X_i, X_{i+1})} F_{j_{k+1}}$$

for the m entities in the subrange X_i, X_{i+1} and for each i,

$$i = 1, 2, \ldots, n - 1$$

Note that if $\mathrm{Max}_{(X_i, X_{i+1})} F_{j_k} = \mathrm{Max}_{(X_i, X_{i+1})} F_{j_{k+1}}$, it must be at X_i or X_{i+1} for $p > 2$. If this is the case, say at X_i, then the ordering is based on $F_{j_k}(X_{i+1}) > F_{j_{k+1}}(X_{i+1})$. For $p = 2$, it is based on

$$F_{j_1}\left(X_1 + \frac{X_2 - X_1}{2}\right) > F_{j_2}\left(X_1 + \frac{X_2 - X_1}{2}\right).$$

6. Working from smallest to largest values of X_i and largest to smallest values of Y, compute contributions to the total area and first moment using the appropriate algebraic expressions which are based on the geometric property of each entity. Area contributions come only from alternate regions bounded by the X subrange boundaries and ordered entities in pairs. This correctly chooses the inside area contributions. The area and moment equations are derived analytically from the definite integral equations. (This is a tedious but straightforward task.)

$$\mathrm{Area} = \sum_{i=1}^{n-1} \int_{X_i}^{X_{i+1}} [F_{j_1} - F_{j_2} + F_{j_3} - \cdots + F_{j_{m-1}} - F_{j_m}] \, dX + \sum_{i=1}^{L} A_{c_i}$$

$$\mathrm{Moment} = \sum_{i=1}^{n-1} \int_{X_i}^{X_{i+1}} X[F_{j_1} - F_{j_2} + F_{j_3} - \cdots + F_{j_{m-1}} - F_{j_m}] \, dX$$

$$+ \sum_{i=1}^{L} X_{c_i} A_{c_i}$$

$$X_c = \mathrm{Moment}/\mathrm{Area}$$

where X_c is the X coordinate of the centroid.

7. Step 3 through Step 6 are repeated interchanging X and Y.

8. The centroid point is displayed contained in a small box, the X, Y values of the point are placed in the X, Y registers and the properly

scaled X-calculated area and Y-calculated area are stored in the second set of X, Y registers. REJECT/ACCEPT is put in the message register.

9. The user may activate the ACCEPT key, the point is made a dot, the box and message disappear, and the program terminates. If the user presses the REJECT key instead, the point, box and message disappear, but the contents of the X, Y registers are not changed, and the program terminates.

During steps 1 through 7 the message register contains COMPUTATION PROCEEDING. If the parameters chosen are limited to point-area centroids instead of closed polyconics, then the program computes the centroid of the system of these centroid points.

7.21 Console Servicing

Part of the resident monitor provides for acceptance of input from the terminals and decides on performance of functions based on that input. Service requests are recognized on an asynchronous interrupt basis when data input is available, or input devices are scanned, usually on a periodic basis. Each terminal requiring service can be allotted a specified period of main computer time. The methods make no difference to the user except as reflected in service time for his requests.

A general terminal servicing program is described in Fig. 7.7. All console attributes described earlier are either provided or, at least, not denied by this approach. At box 2 in the flow chart of Fig. 7.7, it is decided whether incoming data are parametric or requesting action. A parameter could be an implicit action if it is the last parameter needed for a pending action identified in box P11. An action could be an implicit parameter if a macro were being defined; the macro capability is not shown in this flow chart.

The process accepts actions and parameters in random and intermixed order. It is left to the logic in box PA12 to make sense out of the current contents of the parameter list and decide whether they satisfy the needs of the particular action request. A table lists each action and possible parameter combinations. The ACCEPT/REJECT routine is entered after exit from the action subroutine at box PA17. Conditions at boxes P5 and A4, "list full" and "double action," should result in display of the particular condition and also suggest what the user might do next.

An application program in active status at the time of the service request may be given control at one of three points: A9, P10, or PA16. The application can control user activities or perform services directed by him after a parameter has been received and accepted, before a pending action is executed, or after execution of an action. It is important that the basic software not limit even the unanticipated requirements of application programs. Toward this goal, it might also be advisable

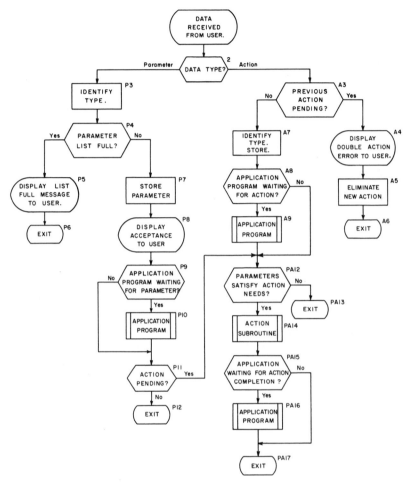

Fig. 7.7   Terminal servicing.

to put a conditional exit to an application program between boxes 1 and 2 before data are analyzed.   An application program should be allowed to change completely the nature of a terminal to anticipate as yet unknown types of graphic terminal usage.

7.22   Data Structure

A data structure is the context into which data are placed for storage and use by a computer program or system of programs.   It is concerned with format, ordering, and interconnection or association of data.

The basic or generic unit of data is called a block, item, or entity.   It has a specified format and is composed of fields for atomic or primitive

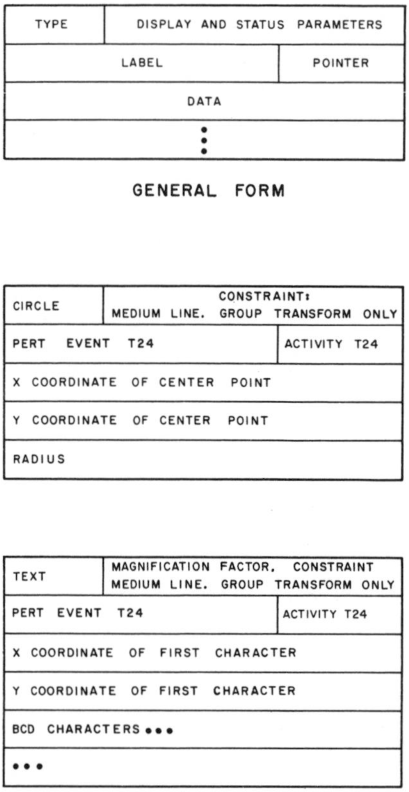

TYPE	DISPLAY AND STATUS PARAMETERS
LABEL	POINTER
DATA	
⋮	

GENERAL FORM

CIRCLE	CONSTRAINT: MEDIUM LINE. GROUP TRANSFORM ONLY
PERT EVENT T24	ACTIVITY T24
X COORDINATE OF CENTER POINT	
Y COORDINATE OF CENTER POINT	
RADIUS	

TEXT	MAGNIFICATION FACTOR. CONSTRAINT MEDIUM LINE. GROUP TRANSFORM ONLY
PERT EVENT T24	ACTIVITY T24
X COORDINATE OF FIRST CHARACTER	
Y COORDINATE OF FIRST CHARACTER	
BCD CHARACTERS •••	
•••	

Fig. 7.8 Block structure.

data—data which are not expected to be further subdivided. An example of blocks in the basic graphic system are shown in symbolic form in Fig. 7.8.

Various generic types of blocks are interconnected to complete the data structure. The contents of blocks and their interconnection is dependent on a specific application. There are a variety of ways in which blocks may be ordered, associated, and addressed. Also blocks may be of variable or fixed length. These variations are determined by how the data are to be collected and used and the environments in which they are stored.

One of the simplest forms of data structures is a block consisting of a single computer-memory word containing a single number. A set of M blocks (numbers) is stored in sequentially addressed computer-memory words starting with address N and ending with address $N + M - 1$. This structure is adequate for many purposes, but more complex structures are required when multiple atomic elements comprise a block, when blocks are of different or variable sizes, when more than one ordering or association (multidimensional) must be simultaneously and dynamically imposed, and when the volume of data causes manipulation complexity in time and storage space.

The need for more complex structures became apparent when computers were first used for applications outside of the realm of numerical analysis. The development of compilers required text manipulation and parsing of statements in programming languages. Symbol-manipulating or list-processing languages[13] have been developed to manipulate data in applications such as artificial intelligence, simulation of human and other processes, information retrieval, and operations research.

One of the earliest list-processing languages is FLPL,[14] which was followed by COMIT,[15] IPL-V,[16] LISP,[17] and SLIP.[18] All use some form of list structure representing an association of ordered sequences of elements called strings. The most important feature of these structures is that address pointers, which tie strings together in a specified order, are included as part of the list or are in a separate list. Thus, when strings are removed, reordered, or added inside the ordering, data need not be physically moved in storage but only the linking pointers are changed. An example of this is shown in Fig. 7.9 using a SLIP-like structure. SLIP has a symmetric structure, so called because the top of a list points to the bottom and the bottom points to the top, making each list circular. This is why it is often called a ring.

The digital representation of drawings introduced new data structure requirements. Dr. Ivan Sutherland[11] and Douglas Ross[2] introduced multidimensional concepts involving membership of an element in more than one symmetric list or ring. A circle represented by a block could belong to several subdrawings and have several properties at the same time requiring this multiple membership. The list structures of the list-processing systems were not adequate for graphic data representations because they lacked the multidimensional and variable block-size schemes.

The work of Sutherland has been refined by Dr. Larry Roberts[1] in a list-structure system and macro language called "CORAL." It is organized in a ring-structure form with variable length blocks. A block contains a pointer-pair element for each ring of which it is a member (Fig. 7.10). Each element of each block in a ring points to the next pointer-pair element in sequence. Two types of elements alternate in sequence, pointing to either the starter element or to the last element not pointing to the starter. The alternating elements scheme conserves storage, ties the ring elements together and ties each element to the starter (requiring one extra operation in half the cases). CORAL geometry is point- and picture-oriented in that point blocks and picture blocks are starters and line blocks are ring members as shown in Fig. 7.11. The

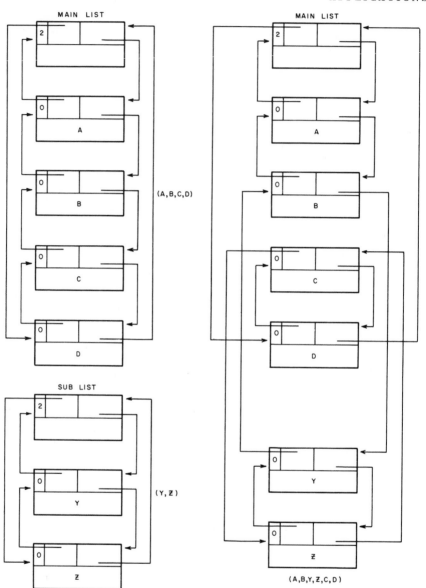

Fig. 7.9 Symmetric list structure.

points describing a line can be found by moving down the list of ring elements in its block rather than having to move around a ring if the lines had been made starters. CORAL has superimposed on this basic list structure a sophisticated class structure to attach properties to items.

Dr. Marvin Ling[7] at General Electric Computer Division has a

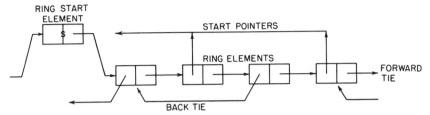

Fig. 7.10   Ring structure of CORAL.

scheme at least as complex and sophisticated as Roberts'.   An entity is anything in the real world having certain properties.   It is represented by a generic block of fixed format and has pointers relating other properties to it.   Each entity has associated with it three types of rings. The call-out ring ties together entities of lower level.   The where-used

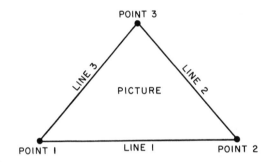

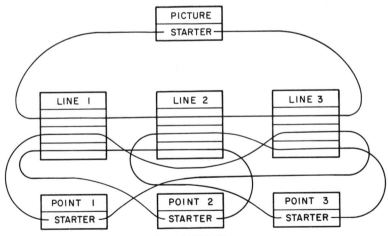

Fig. 7.11   Picture representation of CORAL.

ring ties together all entities of higher levels which contain this entity as one of their lower-level entities.

The third type of ring is the property ring which ties all other generic blocks that describe the properties of the entity. For example, the property ring of a triangle would contain three line blocks and three point blocks. A line is an entity only in very special cases, and most of the time it is a property of an entity. The rings and blocks are constructed in ways similar to Roberts' scheme.

The relationship between entities of different levels is represented by conjunctions. A conjunction block contains information such as quantity, location, orientation, and size. Figure 7.12 is an example taken from Ling's paper. The rectangles are entities, and the circles are conjunctions. It shows an entity A consisting of two entities B, one entity C, and four entities D. The entity B consists of three entities E and two entities F and so on. Thus, A has lower-level entities B, C, D and lowest-level entities E, F, and G. It also shows that B is not only a lower-level entity of A but also of D.

A simplified approach is taken in the Control Data Digigraphics System,[4] first developed by John T. Gilmore. A tree structure of blocks is formed; and a generic group block, with data consisting of pointers to its members, is used to organize blocks into groups (see Fig. 7.13). A

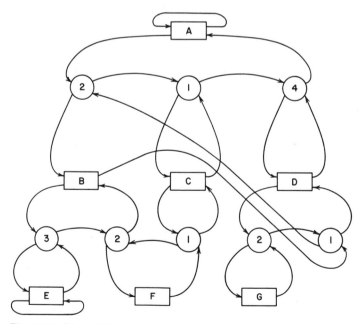

Fig. 7.12 Ling's list structure.

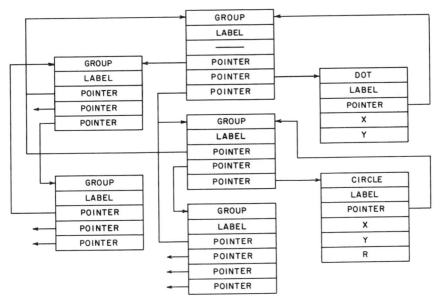

Fig. 7.13   Tree structure of groups.

group is logically equivalent to a ring and requires about the same amount of pointer storage space.

This system does not allow a block to be a member of more than one group. A block must be reproduced for each group membership. This causes problems of multiple display and additional storage requirements, but it simplifies the grouping logic software. However, an additional type of block could be introduced to represent multiple memberships.

The ring structure of CORAL is ideal when the entire data list or, at least, self-contained parts of it can be stored in the main computer memory. In many cases this is not possible, and a large data list must be stored in secondary storage with just random parts of it brought into memory. A ring structure is somewhat impractical in this two-level storage structure because of the numerous storage-to-memory transfers and the possible repeated transfers necessary to move about a ring. The tree-grouping structure guarantees that only one pass of the data is required to obtain the immediate group members, because all addresses are available at once. A paged addressing scheme is used to simplify the two-level memory structure data transfers.

An extra word, called a "label," is provided in all types of blocks in the digigraphic system and basic system. For example, in Fig. 7.8 the circle has a label identifying it as event T24 in a PERT diagram, and the text entity describes the event. The user need not be concerned with these entities as circle and text but can refer to them together as an event in a PERT diagram. The labels are made available through the interface to application programs. Thus, an application program may superimpose its own special structure of grouping, naming, and assigning properties to blocks. In this system, grouping can be completely eliminated or made as simple as desired for each particular application.

The geometric organization of the digigraphic system and the basic system are line-oriented rather than point-oriented as found in the other systems described. Roberts' and Ling's structures are organized to represent three-dimensional graphics and take advantage of three-line vertices by making points separate entities. It can easily be shown that in two-dimensional representations nothing is gained by doing this. Therefore, points are stored as primitive data within line blocks. A special dot block is provided to represent unattached points.

The two-point representation of straight-line segments is adequate when line and points are used extensively in graphics manipulation and construction. However, computation becomes critical as the terminal user changes the magnification and position of his view of the drawing. Frequent searches of the entire data list for the drawing are made testing blocks for inclusion, partial inclusion, or exclusion in the field of view. In this case, representation of straight-line segments in normal form rather than stating the coordinates of the end points seems more desirable. The parameters A, B, D, D', D'' are stored representing the normal form $AX + BY + D = 0$ where $A = \cos a$, $B = \sin a$, D is the normal distance from the origin, a is the angle of the normal and D' and D'' mark off the end points by specifying the length along a line through the origin parallel to the line segment (Fig. 7.14). Potential inclusion of the line segment in the field of view is determined by simply making the test $|AX_1 + BY_1 - D| < R$ where R is the radius of field of view and X_1 and Y_1 are the coordinates of the center point of the field of view. The

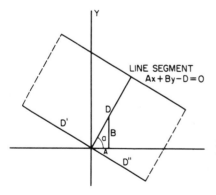

Fig. 7.14 Normal form of line representation.

choice of line representation is one of the many choices which can be optimally made only after considerable experience is gained in practical use of graphic systems.

APPLICATIONS

7.23 Parts Programming for Numerically Controlled Milling Machines and Lathes

The tedious job of encoding cutter movements to shape a part from its drawing is an obvious potential application. A description of how this might be done using a graphic system is well explained by Mr. C. H. Chasen in an article concerning the computer-aided design project (C.A.D.) published in the *Lockheed-Georgia Quarterly*[10] as follows:

> In our manufacturing process, many items are milled automatically by numerical tape-controlled milling machines. The creation of this tape is a laborious task. To produce the numerical control tape for a part or tool, an accurate drawing of the item must be produced. Then a part programmer must painstakingly go through the drawing and define the intersection points for each distinct line, curve, or other significant features. A series of computer instructions are then written to represent the path that the cutter must follow to mill the item according to the part programmer's specifications. The computer program which interprets the instructions is called APT (Automatically Programmed Tools). The APT language has been developing for many years, and the task of producing it has been a formidable one.
>
> Still, the various steps leading to the production of a numerical control tape require many man-hours. It was recognized that the application of new techniques in automation might significantly reduce the manual effort. It is estimated that about 80% of the items produced by means of numerical control at Lockheed-Georgia are of a two-dimensional line and circle geometry. Therefore, the desirability of using the early C.A.D. capability to assist the 2-D N/C problem became apparent. First the item would be defined directly on the scope using the various input media—light pen, buttons, and keyboard. The geometry of the item would be stored in computer memory on a permanent file.
>
> Figure 7.15 is a two-view representation of a part. Figure 7.16 is a drawing of the completed part. The cross at the center of the cylinder is the arbitrary origin to which all coordinates are referred. The starting point, *S*, for the center of the cutting tool is entered on the keyboard.
>
> To create the part, the part programmer must describe a linear coordinate path for the cutting tool. In general, there is no way to determine the optimum path. The part programmer only knows that he must consider the plate surface, the lug, the cylinder, and the outer dimensions of the part.
>
> To illustrate the creation of a typical path and the application of Com-

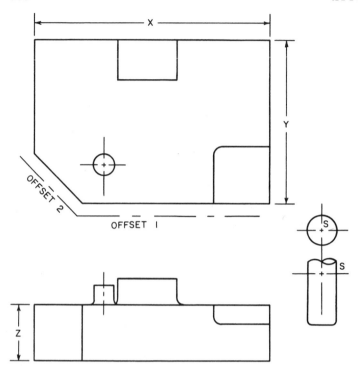

Fig. 7.15 Two-view part drawing.

puter-Aided Design, the console operator will set in a desired depth coordinate, Z, through the computer keyboard.   The cutter will cut to the indicated value of Z for all X, Y until a Z change is requested.   The operator will point the light pen to the line in the top view that represents the front face of the part.   He will push the appropriate function button to establish a parallel offset, Offset 1 in the figure.   The amount of the offset, the cutter radius, is keyed in.   This offset line is the initial path over which the part programmer wishes the center of the cutter to move.   Then the operator

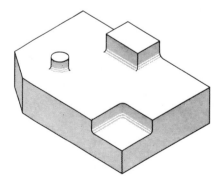

Fig. 7.16 Completed part.

will move the tracking cross from the starting (X, Y) position towards the offset line. A function button will permit the computer and the tracking cross to "lock" on the offset line. This will establish the next (X, Y) coordinate location for the cutter.

Now the operator desires to move the cutter left along the offset line to where it intersects with another offset line, Offset 2, which he constructs. This second offset will be a diagonal line in the example. The tracking cross will be moved towards the intersection of the offset lines. Function buttons will be employed to "lock" on the intersection. This will establish the next set of (X, Y) coordinates with Z remaining unchanged.

In a similar way, the part programmer may establish successive coordinates to cut out the outside dimensions. Then by keying in a change in Z, he may wish to move to the lug at the rear of the plate. Using the same function buttons, he can cut around the lug. Additional function buttons and the lock-on feature will permit the cylindrical cut-out. It is also necessary to mill the top of the plate, the top of the cylinder, the top of the lug, and the surface cut-out at the right front. The C.A.D. feature that displays the milled areas will greatly facilitate the description of successive coordinates to swath surface areas.

With successive coordinates thus described, an output tape can be generated that describes the necessary cutter motion and completely bypasses the APT programming requirement—the C.A.D. application is GAPT (Graphical Automatically Programmed Tools). It is estimated that the average part programming time for approximately 1500 parts (lines and circles) was 60 hours per part for the C-141. The estimate for the same requirement using C.A.D. is 10 hours. Considerable savings will also be manifested in tooling and template manufacture. In addition to the greatly reduced lead time, estimated cost savings substantially outweigh computer-display system costs.

7.24   Newspaper Page Layout

Whole pages of newspapers may be typeset with the advent of photographic typesetting. Computers are being used extensively for line adjustment and production of punched paper tape to drive hot-metal typesetting machines. The entire text of a newspaper edition and symbolically represented pictures and display ads can be stored in a computer. Pages may be made up from this material by viewing it in scaled size at a graphics console and using the light pen to place it column by column in a page frame. The computer would keep track of the ratio of news space to ad space to aid in conforming to newspaper standards. One problem in this application is to identify news items and ads when they are scaled down to the size necessary to make the whole page visible on the cathode-ray tube at once. This can be solved by having the computer automatically replace text too small to read with large labels superimposed over the text area.

7.25 Numerical Analysis in Engineering Design

The trend has been to make the most automatic use of the computer as possible. For example, many design problems reduce to searching for maxima and minima of mathematical functions of several variables. Direct minimum search procedures have been developed[19] using variants of gradient and other methods on the basis of using a computer's great speed to do great numbers of searches automatically, because it is inefficient for human beings to intervene in any practical way to help things along. Now it is possible for the designer, directly without the programmer intermediary, to view cross-sections and contours of a function and even three-dimensional projections of it on-line at a graphics console. Using short bursts of computer time, he can see the actual path traced by one of a variety of search algorithms and can participate in the search. The designer gains new insight into his problem; and with this insight might develop new, efficient, automatic techniques to solve many variations of the problem without the need for the on-line system.

There is a danger of overuse of graphic systems which is even greater than the danger of overuse of computers in batch-mode operation. The use of a graphic system could degenerate into unproductive play, and it could be used for tasks obviously more effectively accomplished in other ways. The criteria for efficient, useful employment of graphic systems can only be learned through experiments and experience in specific application areas.

REFERENCES

1. Roberts, L. G.: Graphical Communication and Control Languages, *Lincoln Laboratory, MIT*, Reprint MS1173, November, 1964.
2. Ross, D. T., and Rodriguez, J. E.: Theoretical Foundations for the Computer-aided Design System, *AFIPS Conference Proceedings*, Spring Joint Computer-Conference, 1963.
3. Coons, S. A.: An Outline of the Requirements for a Computer-aided Design System, *AFIPS Conference Proceedings*, Spring Joint Computer Conference, 1963.
4. *Control Data Digigraphic System 270 System Information Manual*, No. 60146600, Control Data Corporation.
5. Jacks, E. L.: A Laboratory for the Study of Graphical Man-machine Communication, *AFIPS Conference Proceedings*, Fall Joint Computer Conference, 1964.
6. Use of the IBM 2250 Display Unit, IBM Data Processing Application, E20-0080-0, IBM Data Processing Division, White Plains, N.Y.
7. Ling, M. T. S.: Man-machine Communication with Graphical Console. General Electric Company, Phoenix, Ariz. (presented at the Engineering Summer Conference on Computer Graphics, University of Michigan, June, 1965).
8. Davis, M. R. and Ellis, T. O.: The Rand Tablet: A Man-machine Graphical Communication Device, *AFIPS Conference Proceedings*, Fall Joint Computer Conference, 1964.

9. Rippy, D. E.: MAGIC: A Machine for Automatic Graphics Interface to a Computer, *National Bureau of Standards Report* 8665, December, 1964.
10. Chasen, S. H.: Man-computer Graphics, *Lockheed-Georgia Quarterly*, Lockheed-Georgia Company, a division of Lockheed Aircraft Corporation, Marietta, Ga., summer, 1965.
11. Sutherland, I. E.: Sketchpad: A Man-machine Communication System, *AFIPS Conference Proceedings*, Spring Joint Computer Conference, 1963.
12. Parker, D. B.: Graphical Communication in an On-line System, *On-line Computing Symposium Proceedings*, University of California at Los Angeles and Informatics, Inc., February, 1965.
13. Borrow, D. G. and Raphael, B.: A Comparison of List-processing Computer Languages, *Communications of the ACM*, 7, 4, April, 1964.
14. Gelernter, H., et al.: A FORTRAN-compiled List Processing Language, *ACM Journal*, 7, 2, April, 1960.
15. Yngve, V. H.: COMIT, *Communications of the ACM*, 6, 3, March, 1963.
16. Newell, Allen: Documentation of IPL-V, *Communications of the ACM*, 6, 3, March, 1963.
17. Berkeley, E. C. (ed.), et al.: The Programming Language "LISP": Its Operation and Applications, *Information International*, Maynard, Mass., 1964.
18. Weizenbaum, J.: Symmetric List Processor, *Communications of the ACM*, 6, 9, September, 1963.
19. Witte, B. F. W., and Holst, W. R.: Two New Direct Minimum Search Procedures for Functions of Several Variables, *AFIPS Conference Proceedings*, vol. 25, 1964 Spring Joint Computer Conference, Spartan Books, Inc., 1964.
20. Rippy, D. E., and D. E. Humphies and J. A. Cunningham: MAGIC: A Machine for Automatic Graphics Interface to a Computer, *AFIPS Conference Proceedings*, vol. 27, 1965 Fall Joint Computer Conference, Spartan Books, Inc., 1965.
21. Chasen, S. H.: The Introduction of Man-computer Graphics into the Aerospace Industry, *AFIPS Conference Proceedings*, vol. 27, 1965 Fall Joint Computer Conference, Spartan Books, Inc., 1965.
22. Haring, D. R.: The Beam Pen: A Novel High Speed: Input/Output Device for Cathode-ray-tube Display Systems, *AFIPS Conference Proceedings*, vol. 27, 1965 Fall Joint Computer Conference, Spartan Books, Inc., 1965.

COMPUTING IN
A STRATEGIC
COMMAND SYSTEM
ENVIRONMENT

William L. Wilkinson

Logistics Research Project
George Washington University
Washington, D.C.

8.1 Introductory Remarks

The rapid technological advances in weapons, vehicles, sensors, communications, and digital data-processing systems since World War II have had an aggregate effect on the composition of modern command and control systems. They have brought about some dramatic changes in the organizations, doctrines, procedures, and devices which provide a commander with the vital flow of information on which to base decisions in the exercise of effective command. In this pace-setting era, the role of automated military information systems has been equated to the role of weapons in the maintenance of peace and the insurance of national survival in the advent of war.[1] That the problems of command and control are recognized as significant in the United States defense posture is supported by the conservative estimate that 10 per cent of the annual Department of Defense (DOD) budget has been devoted to this area.[2]

Concomitant with the available production of automatic data-processing equipments, the middle 1950s experienced an intensified concentration on the automatic information processing aspects of command. These early efforts in automated systems design were guided by little experience, less theory, no seasoned doctrine, nor even a clear definition of terms. Lessons have been learned largely the hard and expensive way through the installations of systems which were, upon reaching operational status or being rejected, found to be in some measure short of the mark. Through this progression there has evolved a loose body of discipline in the design and development of such systems and an even looser body concerning the management and implementation of such systems. Currently, three principles appear to enjoy almost universal acceptance among command system developers.

1. System growth should be evolutionary and this evolution must take place within the context of the user command.

2. User participation in all phases of system development is essential.

3. Compatibility among subsystems comprising the total national command and control system is an important consideration in the design of a given system, but not necessarily a clearly defined objective which must be achieved in all respects.

The fundamental problems of command and control are not new, of course, and the structure of military command has been, as it is today, tailored to carry out its basic responsibilities. The commander's staff, one of the most powerful tools ever devised, is a group of men attuned to their chief's desires, augmenting and expanding his capacity to do his job. In the hierarchy of military commands, there is embedded a large capacity, highly developed, efficient information system which is a product of the military command structure and its communications and quite distinct from the information-handling mechanics of any hardware system.[3] While the system may be less than adequate in some respects for the problems of today and the future, it is important that we understand and improve it rather than attempt to ignore and replace it. When we refer to an "advanced" command system in a design sense, it should be as a coherent array of supporting subsystems which can be understood and controlled by the people who are responsible for advising the commander. It is the "fitness" of these subsystems into the command environment and its "people" system which will largely determine their usefulness, acceptability, and survival as an integral part of the command system.

The design, development, and integration of digital data-processing systems into command and control systems should be viewed as modifying or augmenting an existing system, not as a new system from which all else must evolve.

From a different point of view, the fuller development of military information systems in consonance with our national needs is facilitating some changes in our concept of command and control. The historically recent and current breed of international conflicts involving the use of our Armed Forces is characterized by a need for maintaining a delicately controlled response to military, diplomatic, political, economic, and social implications. It is often necessary that this control be exercised at a high national level based on detailed information from tactical forces in order to minimize the inadvertent escalation to a point where the survival of the sovereign powers is at stake, on the one hand, and to maximize the fulfillment of our international responsibilities on the other. We have experienced occasions where a high-level commander has directly commanded forces several levels below his because of the rapid pace of events and the serious implications of what would otherwise be a minor clash. The continued need on the part of top echelon commanders for this capability appears inevitable; however, the exercise of this option is a serious departure from the principle of chain of command operations which can easily lead to confusion on the part of operating forces as to "who is running the show" and a mismatch in the supporting activities required to carry the directed action forward. In view of the antithetical nature of this capability, it requires great wisdom on the part of top echelon staffs to distinguish between "need" and "desire" in the exercise of direct control.

Within the strategic staff, the continued development of improved information systems has had its impact. First, the collection, organization, and convenient accessibility of vast quantities of data have opened the door to more intimate interactions between staff elements in the evaluation-recommendation-decision process. In the past, certain bodies of quantitative information were more or less the exclusive property of particular staff elements, primarily because of the manpower effort required to collect, interpret, and assimilate the information. The flow of information within the staff upward to the commander resembled a tree with cross-coordination carried out as experience and judgment indicated. Recommendations were stratified and consolidated into recommendations at the next level up until the appropriate level for decision had been reached. The aggregated information on which each level of recommendations was reached generally remained at that level. In exploiting the full potential of high capacity, quick response automated information systems, the flow of information becomes more of a network where detailed information in support of a higher-order decision may be called up at any time by any level in the staff hierarchy. The tree structure of the recommendation-decision process is maintained, but the forced stratification of information-filtering no longer obtains. The vertical and horizontal staff interactions become more complex and comprehensive in detail, e.g., a common definition of data elements and universal understanding of their meaning must exist. Second, the advent of advanced information systems creates a need for a sharp increase in the technical capability within the staff in order to control and promote the evolution of its system to assure that it continues to meet the command's specific needs. In part, the increase in capability must be acquired within the command line and, in part, through coordinated outside technical assistance.

In the following descriptions, discussions, and observations, our system of reference will be a particular, large-scale, integrated multicomputer system which is designed to fulfill the automatic data-processing requirements for the command systems of a joint strategic commander and designated subordinate commanders. These supported commands will be referred to, collectively, as the end user of the system. The system will be referred to throughout as the OPCON ADP system. This is the third and largest system to be installed for this purpose, replacing an IBM 704/1401 combination which replaced an IBM 305 installed in April, 1960. The system is not considered a basically on-line system wherein the user of the system interacts directly with the system, although there are limited on-line capabilities of this kind. The addition of on-line facilities is considered a natural extension of the system and was, indeed, considered in the system design. In describing the system's characteristics, its functions, the environment in which it is being implemented, and certain problems associated with implementation, the details are intended to present an illustrative example of environmental conditions under which the relative merits of more sophisticated on-line capabilities may be assessed by those engaged in research and development in that area.

THE HARDWARE SYSTEM

8.2 System Design Philosophy.[4]

In 1959, discussions were held within the Navy concerning the merits and feasibility of an integrated, multicomputer data-processing system which would serve the needs of Navy and Navy-supported command systems. It was recognized that there was a requirement for a complex data-processing system of major proportions which was both modifiable and expansible to take unforeseen requirements and future loading into account. Additionally, there were two needs, each very important in its own right but, oddly enough, apparently contradictory to one another. The first was the need for subsystem isolation to divorce specific parts of the system for an indefinite period of time. The second was for system integration with centralized control of all subsystems.

Translating these system needs into a system's design involved a number of steps, including those of following the traditional requirements of policies, economics, time-scale, system life, and compatibility with existing co-located equipment. Taking the traditional requirements, first-order needs, and other factors into account, the functional requirements could be summarized as follows:

a. **Computation.** The system will be called upon for a variety of tasks for a broad spectrum of computational and processing capability. Both large- and small-scale computers are indicated as long as proper integration into one system is feasible. During the course of the program, in line with the traditional requirements given above, the concept of a multicomputer system was established, and four large-scale computers were chosen for major computing tasks and five small-scale computers were chosen for minor tasks.

b. **Files.** An enormous volume of data must be accessible to the computing elements. Some of these data are made use of frequently, while other data go unexamined for weeks at a time. At first, magnetic tapes will carry the major burden of file storage, but, as time goes on, disk files will be used for much of the system files.

c. **Input-Output.** Input and output equipment must be both varied and versatile. Both on-line types of operations, involving fast human responses which might be classed as real-time processes, and off-line types of operations, such as medium-to-medium transfers, are required. Not only magnetic tapes and disk files are involved but also cards, paper tape, and high-speed printers. Central control input-output equipment, including a console, cathode-ray display, and typewriter, must be provided so that operators can monitor the system operation and provide system control as required.

d. **Facility Integration.** The major system components must be able to work together in complete harmony. Independent tasks must be capable of being executed concurrently, and yet simple communications for centralized management by an operator must be provided.

e. **Subsystem Operation.** For the purposes of security, administrative considerations, maintenance, and program checkout, the data-processing system must be capable of being divided into several independent computing subsystems. The requirement for isolation of subsystems falls generally into two categories: (1) where, under integrated operation, subsystems are set up and controlled automatically and (2) where more positive isolation is desired and subsystems are set up and controlled manually. Under integrated operation, subsystems may be of practically any combination of equipment contained in the full system.

f. **Equipment Availability.** The equipment should be designed for continuous operation of the system. Any section of equipment must be capable of being effectively isolated from the rest of the system for maintenance as well as administrative, security, and other purposes.

g. Expansibility. At some time in the future, new equipment, both of the same kind and of new kinds, may have to be added to the system. The original design should anticipate reasonable growth and allow expansion with minimum interference to the operation of the facility.

Solving the problem took both traditional and functional requirements together to form a set of design goals. Four such goals emerged as being of primary importance: modularity, system balance, coordination and control, and switching. Of course, as the design progressed, interim results were considered against the system requirements, but by meeting the design goals, a major step was taken toward the design solution.

8.3 System Description.[5,6]

Pursuant to the established major design objectives, specifications for the system were written in 1960. Among the design objectives which strongly influenced engineering design and implementation were the maximum use of existing "off-the-shelf" solid-state hardware and the extreme system's flexibility which had to be achieved with an optimum man-machine interface. A contract for the system was awarded in 1961 but was suspended later that year because of a divergence in opinion on the switching system to be used. In early 1962, reconciliation of these views was achieved and the contract continued with firm specifications. The following is a description of the resultant system.

The OPCON ADP system consists of nine general-purpose computers as the driving force, coupled to a wide variety of peripheral equipment (over 100 devices) through a large "matrix" switch, and controlled from a central control console. A simplified block diagram of this installation is shown in Fig. 8.1.

Four CDC 1604A computers comprise the large-scale facilities for major information processing and computational tasks. Each 1604A provides 32,768 48-bit words of magnetic core storage, three buffered input-output channel pairs, where each pair is capable of parallel mode operations, and a highly versatile interrupt system.

Each 1604A channel pair is connected to a horizontal of the subsystem selection switch, i.e., the "matrix" switch, via a 1604A bus adapter. This is an adaption unit which (together with the design of the 160A and the 160A bus adapter) enables both the 1604A and the 160A computers to present the same interface to all input-output equipment. A 48-bit 1604A output word is disassembled into 12-bit words plus parity and sent to output equipment. Input data to the 1604A is assembled from 12-bit to 48-bit words, parity checked and sent to the 1604A.

Five CDC 160A computers, each with 16,384 12-bit words of magnetic

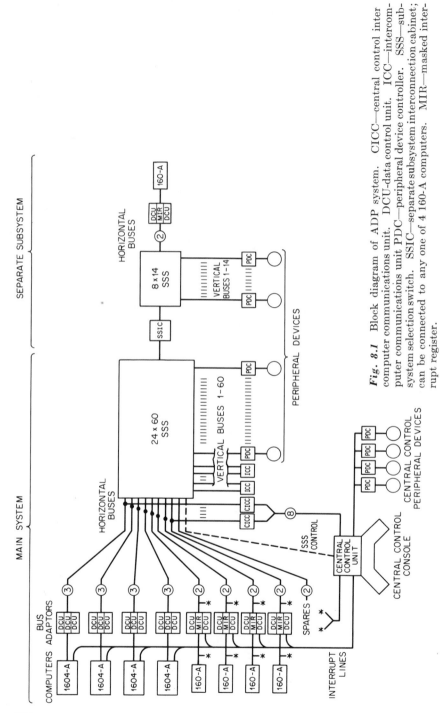

Fig. 8.1 Block diagram of ADP system. CICC—central control inter computer communications unit. DCU-data control unit. ICC—intercomputer communications unit PDC—peripheral device controller. SSS—subsystem selection switch. SSIC—separate subsystem interconnection cabinet; can be connected to any one of 4 160-A computers. MIR—masked interrupt register.

core storage, two input-output channels and interrupt features, provide the facility for input-output processing, smaller data-processing tasks, and centralized system control.

Each 160A has a bus adapter consisting of two data control units (DCUs) and a masked interrupt register (MIR). The DCUs couple the 160A internal buffer channel and the external buffer channel to the subsystem selection switch horizontals. The MIR couples preselected interrupt signals originating in other system equipments to the 160A and allows the 160A to utilize these interruptions efficiently. The primary purpose of the MIR is to provide additional interrupt capability to the 160A so that the consistency of the computer-switch interface for both 1604A and 160A computers is preserved.

The subsystem selection switch (SSS) is the device which allows interconnection between system computer and system peripheral devices. It is a matrix switch in which any horizontal (computer input-output channel) may be connected to any vertical (peripheral device). Each of the possible connections in the SSS is called a "crosspoint." The SSS is used by central control to select and connect from all available system equipment the computers and peripheral devices which will operate together as a smaller data-processing system called a "subsystem." Under program control with a manual alternative or override, a subsystem can be made up of one or more computers and a number of peripheral devices subject to the provisions that no more than five verticals be coupled to a horizontal, and no vertical be coupled to more than one horizontal at a time. The SSS in the main system has 24 horizontals and 60 verticals; the SSS in the separate subsystem has 8 horizontals and 14 verticals.

Each peripheral device, or set of devices, is coupled to the vertical through a peripheral device controller (PDC). The PDC matches the standard interface of the bus adapter to the peculiarities of the peripheral device by providing the timing, control, and data-buffering memory for the device. In addition, each PDC provides high-speed switching which allows a computer to select and activate one PDC out of all units connected to that particular horizontal. Selection and activation of a PDC is responsive only to the computer to which it is connected via the SSS. This latter feature may be considered as the second level of switching provided by the system.

Two of the peripheral devices are of particular interest and design as they provide some special on-line properties to the system.

1. Intercomputer communication units (ICC) provide the necessary hardware for two system computers to arrange and consummate a buffered, program-controlled data transfer. Every ICC unit has a data-transfer path for each of the two computers connected to it. ICC units

are used for both system computer-to-system computer communications and for system computer-to-control computer communications. The latter are designated as central control intercomputer communication (CICC) units.

2. Remote paper-tape stations provide both on-line and off-line paper-tape read-and-punch operations. On-line operations use a Teletype BRPE-11 punch and a Control Data 350 reader. Off-line operations use a Friden flexowriter for both reading and punching. These stations are intended as remote query terminals which can be located anywhere within 1,000 feet of the main system.

The overall system management and control capabilities are provided by central control, permitting automatic (computer-programmed) or manual supervisory control of the system. Once a subsystem is assembled and connected by central control via the SSS, it can operate with its assigned equipment independent of other subsystems. However, all subsystems operate under the supervision and control of central control to help provide the necessary operational, planning, and summary data. A 160A computer is used in conjunction with central control and is called the Control 160A. Through the use of a manual selector switch on the central control console, the system operator may select any one of the four 160As in the main system to serve as the Control 160A.

As seen in Fig. 8.1, the OPCON ADP system has two parts: the main system and a smaller equipment area referred to as the separate subsystem. The smaller system is adjacent to, but physically separated from, the main system for the purpose of handling extremely sensitive information. The equipment in the separate subsystem is available to the main system and functionally the two areas can operate as one large system. Also, equipment in the separate subsystem can operate independently from the main system or may use some of the equipment in the main system as needed.

The separate subsystem interconnection cabinet (SSIC) allows personnel in the separate subsystem area to interconnect equipment manually in the separate subsystem with equipment in the main system. The separate SSS is not under control of the main system central control; therefore, all crosspoints in the separate SSS must be manually set.

Equipment contained in the OPCON ADP system.
  4 CDC 1604A computers with bus adapters
  5 CDC 160A Computers/169 auxiliary memories with bus adapters
  1 central control console with CRT display, typewriter line printer, control unit
17 switch modules (8 × 12)
38 729 IBM tape units
  7 remote paper-tape stations

4 1402 IBM card punch-read units
8 1301 Mod 2 IBM disk-storage units
5 intercomputer communications units
2 cathode-ray data displays
1 separate system interconnection cabinet
3 OPCONCTR card readers
4 OPCONCTR line printers
1 CDC 501 line printer
1 CDC 670-564 plotter
   plus all the necessary PCDs

8.4   Installation Schedule

The short-delivery schedule for equipment was a significant factor in system design and production.   While the major system was of primary importance, the phasing in of two truncated systems appeared advisable. These truncated systems contained a 1604A, two 160As, and a proportionate share of peripheral devices.

In the fall of 1962, a truncated system was installed in Washington, D.C., as a vehicle for developing and testing the system software packages.

In the spring of 1963, a similar system was installed at the OPCON site for the purpose of advanced operating experience.

On June 1, 1964, the truncated OPCON installation had been expanded to full size and accepted for operational use.   This was one month ahead of the installation date established early in 1962.   Hardware production schedules had been met.

SYSTEM SOFTWARE

8.5   Design Considerations[4]

The considerations made in designing such a large data-processing facility certainly had to contain the system software which included control programs, operating systems, input-output utility programs, use of programming languages, and use of other programming systems as well. The crux of the programming consideration involved the automatic control of the system.   If the system was to be productive at anything more than a fraction of its full capacity, full use of centralized management had to be made.   This was defined as integrated operation, i.e., completely automatic control of subsystems formation, job sequencing, and job monitoring.

8.6   A Generalized View of Integrated Operations

One of the computers, the Control 160A, has the system control function for the integrated portion of the system and contains a master control program. Changing the designation of the Control 160A is a manual operation. Thus the removal of any particular 160A from the system does not destroy the ability to control the system.

The master control program provides for centralized bookkeeping, job scheduling and status, security controls, automatic switching of equipment, and centralized response control of queries in the system.

Each subsystem computer contains a subsystem executive program which provides for localized control and services. There is one type for the 1604s and another for the 160As. Thus, for example, the Control 160A might assign a 1604A the job of performing a compilation, but the sequencing between successive passes of the compiler would be handled internally by the 1604A subsystem executive program.

For an overview of this process, the general sequence of operations to perform a job may be as follows.

1. An incoming job request, i.e., an organization of control cards containing one or a sequence of tasks to be performed, is received by master control.

2. Master control constructs tables, performs scheduling functions, and issues instructions to the system operator for the mounting of specific magnetic-tape reels that might be required.

3. Master control assembles a suitable subsystem in accordance with the requisites of the job to be executed.

4. Master control calls up the subsystem computer, activates its subsystem executive, and furnishes information pertinent for the execution of the job.

5. The job is performed by the subsystem through control of its subsystem executive.

6. Following job execution, the subsystem executive sends information relating to the task performance to master control.

7. Master control transmits this information to the operator.

The possible flow of information during the above sequence is delineated in Fig. 8.2.

8.7 Isolated Subsystem Operation

For a number of reasons, a group of equipment may have to operate as an isolated subsystem without communication with master control. In these cases, the normal 1604A or 160A consoles rather than the central control console are used. The same subsystem executive program is retained in the isolated computer. The operator-subsystem executive program interface is filled by a master control simulator program which provides the control for the operation of an isolated subsystem and simulation of some of the master control program facilities.

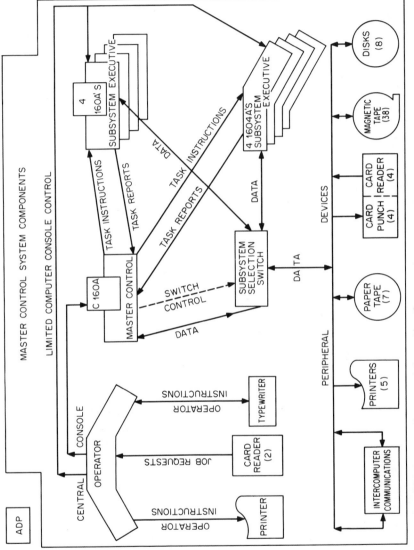

Fig. 8.2 Master control system information flow.

8.8   Master Control System Characteristics

Having described in the broadest of terms the general functioning of master control, it is now more meaningful to set forth some of the necessary performance characteristics of a master control system in a command and control environment.[7,8] Such a system includes the subsystem executive programs.

a. **Job Scheduling.** The scheduling scheme must be responsive to the user's priority requirements while maximizing the total system throughput. It is recognized that a trade-off is involved here for job throughput and system efficiency will decrease as the complexity of priority scheduling is increased.[9]

The system must be capable of recognizing several distinct levels of priority when scheduling equipment and files against job requests. These category levels form an ordered sequence for the scheduling of jobs. The user assigns the priority and thereby controls the sequencing of his work by categories, but the recognition and subsequent processing of the priority are a system control function.

In accordance with the scheduling algorithm, the system provides for program interruption, rescheduling of interrupted programs, preservation of restart points and dumps taken on interrupted programs, initiation of jobs by predefined times, the collection and reservation of equipment and files, and ensurance that no job is continuously shunted aside.

The system provides for manual interrupts and for modification of the priorities of jobs in the queue.

In the prosecution of a particular task, the availability of the necessary files is as vital as the availability of the necessary equipment. Therefore, neither equipment nor files are tagged as "in use" until both are assigned. The system provides for the use of duplicate files.

A suitably designed scheduling algorithm provides the means for fully flexible management of desired system performance over a wide range of conditions. Recall that the user always designated the priority for a particular job. Through his use of, or more exactly, his nonuse of certain priorities, he directly influences the mode of system operation. For example, one priority category, called "routine," is especially designed to maximize the efficient utilization of the equipment and to minimize the average throughput time of submitted jobs. Within this category, the position of a job in the queue is not paramount in scheduling it, although the queue scan always starts from the first job in the queue. Instead, a job is selected so as to utilize the most of the available equipment. Should the user assign only this priority to all his jobs for a period of time, then the system could be considered to be operating at a highly efficient level in the conventional sense of efficiency.

b. **Facility Allocation.** Attention is given here to the allocation of such facilities as core memory, disk storage, and 160A computers for use of the system support programs vis-à-vis the allocation for functional program use. The prime characteristic of such allocation is that it must be dynamically flexible to support the current demand. Work loads and hardware availabilities change from hour to hour. There is a natural tendency for the allocation requirements of the control system to grow in the interest of providing additional services. In a data-processing environment, the functional requirements are also quite large. Accordingly, there must be continuous consideration given to the interaction between services provided and the resultant loss in storage-working space for functional programs. The use of input-output library call to enable a functional program to control the core occupancy of only those input-output programs required by the functional programs is an example of techniques that are exploited toward this end.

c. **Subsystem Formation.** Performance characteristics in this regard are closely related to the scheduling scheme. In addition to the capability of matching available equipment to jobs in the queue and rapidly forming the required subsystem through use of the SSS, there is a requirement for dynamically releasing equipment within a task using parameters furnished by the functional program.

d. **Security Requirements.** The condition of maintaining adequate security for a wide spectrum of classifications being processed simultaneously on an integrated multicomputer system introduces another full dimension to the problem of system control. The requirements for processing programs of mixed classifications were considered in the hardware system design as they were known at that time. However, security regulations do change over time to meet new requirements and new developments. Those concerning the precautions for data-processing storage media have a particular impact on a software control system.

It is essential that the control system provide meticulous software safeguards in recognizing the several distinct levels of security classifications and handling them as separate entities. Complementary operating procedures are also necessary.

In summary, it is the interactions of an electronics system, programs, and data files that compound the problem as contrasted, say, to a communications center which also processes mixed classified matter, but there is no interaction between messages from input to output. As data-processing systems become more "on-line," these problems become the more formidable.

e. **User Interface.** The system is designed to provide the maximum of service with a minimum of user intervention. A permanent file of control cards for production of standard jobs is maintained. These can be retrieved and modified by parameter-card techniques. Prestored and scheduled production runs can be automatically initiated. The system has the ability to recognize predefined query inputs, to generate the control cards necessary to process such a query, and to schedule the run required to process the query. Hard copy summary history of the execution of each job is provided the user at his option.

f. **Programmer Interface.** This interface can be subdivided into two sections: external and internal. The external interface attempts to minimize the number of task and file cards for multitask jobs. A flexible format allows the programmer considerable leeway in preparing his control cards. The programmer also receives information concerning the task running time, the physical equipment involved, and any errors on peripheral devices that occurred during his job. Wherever possible, this summary report is provided on the stacked output medium used by the job. The internal interface, such as the calling sequence, is kept intact during any modification of the control system, so that existing functional programs do not have to be changed internally to accept the change. Diagnostic and debugging aids, such as error messages for errors in calling sequences, normal termination and abnormal termination postmortem dumps, and dynamic or snapshot dumps are provided by the system.

g. **Operator Interface.** The operation of the system is made as automatic as possible wherein the operator is assigned the role of monitoring the system and is called upon to act in only those circumstances which the control system cannot automatically regulate. The system is designed to be operated by personnel with limited training and experience. Within reasonable limits, master control detects all procedural errors and if automatic corrections are not possible, appropriate corrective instructions are given the operator. Corrective procedures are initiated as early in the processing flow as possible so as not to cause the abortion of a job unless absolutely necessary. The operator is informed of procedural errors that stop the functioning of the computer, e.g., the operator is alerted when a needed device senses "not ready." At all times, the operator can determine the status of jobs, equipment and file allocation, assigned priorities, and the security classification of jobs and files.

h. **Management Interface.** The system provides management with timely and pertinent computer-generated reports on each job and how computers and other equipment are being utilized in the system. The primary purpose of these reports is to assist in the day-to-day administration of the system and to measure and compare its operational effectiveness over different periods of time such as shifts, days, and weeks. A directory of data files and storage media, their date of creation, date of release, and devices used for creation is maintained by the system. A system history and log record is maintained of all events taking place under the master control system.

i. **Utilities.** Utility programs required for operation of the master control system and those common utilities needed for successful execution of functional programs are considered part of the master control system.

j. **Diagnostics.** The purpose of the diagnostic function within the master control system is not to isolate machine failures to the level of logic cards, but rather to provide sufficient information to the operator and maintenance personnel to permit them to isolate equipment that appears to be failing. The diagnostic function does, in most cases, provide an indication of the nature and history of the failure or error detected. The operator then uses master control to isolate a subsystem for maintenance purposes without having to manually set the SSS and then maintenance personnel exercise their own diagnostic programs on the isolated subsystem in order to determine the precise cause of failure.

k. **Degraded Operations.** Any operation of the system not utilizing the optimal properties of the master control system is considered a degraded operation. Subject to constraints of storage device allocation, the master control system contains secondary methods for operating the system. Primary input-output central control devices have substitute devices in the event of failure. Interchangeability of computers and storage devices used for system control and services is provided on a selective basis.

An alternate source of file-directory information is provided in case the storage device containing the system file directory fails after a large number of automatic changes have been made to the files.

Provisions have been made for normal shutdown of master control where all information is retained for a restart from point of shutdown. Functional and system support programs which use input-output services provided by the master control system are also operable at the subsystem level under the master control simulator as described earlier.

Under emergency conditions, immediate back-up procedures are provided in the event of equipment failure affecting the control system. These procedures provide for the continued operation of a few, preselected functional programs. For these, master control produces an identification of the status of each and its associated files, and the storage medium on which the data bases are stored whenever they are run or their files updated.

l. **Expandability.** The subsystem selection switch (SSS) has been equipped with spare horizontals and verticals. Additional equipment may be added and the master control system is designed to accommodate them.

8.9   Other Programming Packages

The system support programs contain two other major packages: (1) the program production system and (2) the information processing system. These will be described in the following paragraphs. There are two other generalized support programs which properly belong to this group, but they will be mentioned only briefly.

a. **Generalized Sort-Merge Program.**[10] A generalized variable record-length sort-and-merge program with special provisions to handle uniquely formatted files produced by the information processing system. Also, this program provides for interaction with the user's own code contained in his program.

b. **Generalized Input Processor.**[11] A 160A program system designed to permit automatic entry of formatted teletype messages into the data base.

8.10   The Program Production System[12]

This system provides facilities for compiling, assembling, modifying, and testing programs; building and updating master tapes; and performing all attendant utility functions. The major parts of this system are the OASIS utility system and the JOVIAL compiler, each with its own control program. The entire program production system performs all of its input-output and peripheral device manipulations through the subsystem executive programs and, like all systems in the OPCON ADP system, is monitored by the master control system. Provision also is made in the program production system for operation under the master control simulator.

8.11   The Information Processing System[13,14]

This is a set of general-purpose programs designed, first, to provide the means whereby the large volumes of information contained in the data bases may be structured and maintained in the form of files and, second, to provide the means whereby information contained in these files may be retrieved when needed. The use of the information processing system is not restricted to a particular set of files with a rigid content and structure, but rather the user must describe to the system the content and structure of the files to be processed.

In developing the information processing system, great emphasis was placed on minimizing the requirement for ADP experience on the part of the user. Consequently, the methods employed by the information processing system are not necessarily the most rapid, but represent a compromise between flexibility, ease of use, and speed.

The information processing system is composed of three major parts:

file maintenance (FMS), information retrieval system (IRS), and library maintenance system (LMS).

8.12 The File Maintenance System

All data processed by the information processing system are organized as files of information stored on a device to which the computer has access. The file maintenance system generates and updates these files. Here two basic capabilities are required:

1. To allow the user to refer to data fields, i.e., logical pieces of data, irrespective of how many computer words or binary bits they occupy

2. To provide an easy means for instructing the system as to what operations must be performed without the necessity of writing computer instructions

The first of these capabilities is achieved through a mechanism called the "file format table." This table specifies the file structure and the characteristics of each logical piece of data called an "item." A combination of one or more consecutive items which have some logical relationship is called a "set"; a combination of one or more sets forms a "logical record." The next step upward is the "file." The second capability is achieved through the manipulation of these items through a technique similar to that of a procedure-oriented programming language. The operators or statements of the language are called "macros."

Conceptually, FMS simulates a two-address variable word-length computer which has a memory consisting of master, transaction, and summary records. This simulated computer has various "registers" which may be set and tested, and operators or macros which may be executed. In updating a master file it is presumed that each record has a unique identifier or key field, and that the file is sequenced in ascending order on this field. The transaction file is similarly sequenced. Master and transaction records are read sequentially and if there is a key field match, a macro list is executed in order to update the master record with the transactions. Where there is no key field match, a new record may be generated on the master file under an "add-a-record" mode. When all transactions have been exhausted, a new master file is generated.

During the skeletal processing procedures described above, one has many variations or options. There is the capability for the first-pass generation of a file when there is no old master; similarly, no new master need be written if one merely wants to scan, correlate, or synthesize data. The occasion also arises which necessitates the same changes to or operations performed on every record in a master file. Here, no transaction file is needed and the same macro lists are executed against every record in the file. Frequently there is a need to annotate or summarize runs, subdivide files, or generate reports, thus the purpose of the summary files. The summary files are outputs and are written only on request from the user. Consequently, he may summarize over many master and/or transaction records, or he may generate many summary records from a given master and/or transaction. The summary files are comparable to master files in every respect. There are two additional files in the system: a library file which contains partially or completely assembled groups of tables for processing various files in the data base, and the parameter file which provides a means of entering control information and "more dynamic" tables "on-line." There is also a code conversion table which allows data to be placed in the file in an encoded form. Basically, the code conversion table is a set of arguments with corresponding values which are manipulated by a special macro. The same macro operating on an inverse map of the table will enable decoding.

8.13   The Information Retrieval System

The information retrieval system is a set of programs which operate on a master file generated by the file maintenance system; its purpose is to retrieve selectively, synthesize, and edit information from the file. The inquiries are made in a series of statements which resemble "ordinary" English called the "query language." There are eight types of statements.

FILE   designates the file that is to be queried.
SECURITY   specifies the security classification of the output which is generally the classification of the file.
TITLE   contains header information for output which serves to identify it.
SEARCH   prescribes the retrieval criteria.
OUTPUT   gives the items to be outputted and the manner in which they are to be manipulated and edited.
SORT   designates the items on which the output should be sorted.
LIBRARY   references a query which has been prepared beforehand and prestored on a library tape.
VALUES   allows "run-time" insertion of parametric values in a library query.

The two most critical and difficult statements are SEARCH and OUTPUT. The first of these, generally called the "IF" statement, may consist of a combination of item names, values, logical and relational operators, and functions. Function here is used to connote arbitrary operations on items which produce values. The language defines these logical and relational operators.   The OUTPUT statement identifies the items to be retrieved and the type of edit required.   There are various output statements such as LIST, COLUMN, COUNT, SUM, etc.

An example:

NOTE FROM COMMANDER PARRISH

Request names of all US-controlled merchant ships transporting aviation gasoline located within 500 mile radius of Point ZULU.   List quantities, grade and destinations.   Report CONFIDENTIAL.

FORMATION OF QUERY BY OPERATOR JONES

FILE MERSHIP$
SECURITY C$
TITLE 6/28/65 CDR PARRISH'S REQUEST$
IF SHIP TYPE EQ (TANKER) AND CONTROL EQ (US) AND CARGO EQ (AVGAS)
    AND LOC EQ (500R ZULU) $
COLUMN NAME, QUANTITY, GRADE, DESTINATIONS
SORT GRADE$

8.14   The Library Maintenance System

The information processing system makes use of parameter tables to describe the inputs to be used and the actions to be taken when processing files of the system data base.   These tables may be entered by the system and processed when needed or may be retained by the system in processed form to be used at some future time.   The function of the IPS library file is to provide storage for the processed tables.

The following tables are maintained on the IPS library file.

Library Queries.   These are prestored queries which are used by the information retrieval system.

Summary Format Tables.   These tables are used to define the structure and content of summary files produced by the file maintenance system.

Transaction Format Tables.   These tables describe the structure of transaction files using the file maintenance system to maintain files of the system data base.

Macro Lists.   These tables describe the actions to be taken by the file maintenance system in converting coded information to uncoded form and vice versa.

The IPS library file is generated and maintained by a special-purpose program.   The function of this program is to read tables which are acceptable to the information retrieval system and the file maintenance system, process these tables, and place them in their proper sequence in the library file.

FUNCTIONAL APPLICATION OF THE ADP SYSTEM

8.15   Staff Mission

The descriptions given in the preceding section were confined to the system software which may be viewed as the "white-collar" programs. They perform the control function and provide the necessary services for the programming, operation, and management of the system but produce no useful end product in themselves.   We now turn our attention to the functional or "blue-collar" programs which use the system hardware-software combination to produce useful end products.

The primary purpose of ADP support to a command headquarters is to provide the commander and his staff an improved method of collecting, disseminating, manipulating, retrieving, and displaying information necessary to exercise command and control of operational forces.   In discussing the way in which the ADP system is employed to fulfill this role, it may be well to review the mission and function of a commander's staff:

1. To gather and evaluate detailed and accurate information on all phases of the existing situation—strategic, tactical, and logistic
2. To prepare plans, schedules, directives, and reports based on this information
3. To disseminate rapidly, accurately, and completely the appropriate information and directives to subordinate commanders and reports to higher authority in order to assist the commander in the discharge of his duties

The traditional organization of a staff has included the administration, intelligence, operations, logistics, plans, and communications divisions.

8.16   Functional Programs

The first generation of functional programs are substantially data-processing programs which concern themselves with the organization of large data bases or files, the maintenance of the data base, the production of routine reports and retrieval capabilities against which queries can be levied.   Each program can usually be identified with the primary functions of one of the traditional staff divisions.   While this is largely true, there are some notable exceptions.

If we analyze the staff mission, certain explicit functions can be derived which are common to all the staff divisions:

1. Resource and situation monitoring
2. Plan generation, evaluation, modification, and implementation
3. Plan execution monitoring

The first generation of functional programs makes available the necessary large computer-based automatic files so that a second generation of programs can provide the tools for automated, fully integrated staff support to carry out the above common functions in a simulated environment or on a real-time basis for the conduct of actual operations. The functional design of these programs requires a combination of the highest technical competence, the most mature professional experience, and the finest coordination of interests that can be brought to bear on the problem. The requirements for a comprehensive, coherent methodology representing the interactions of the planning process place severe demands on research. A well-documented approach to formalizing this process has been described by J. C. Emery.[15] On-line system capabilities which facilitate a symbiosis between man and the computer will be essential to complete realization of this potential. It is during this stage of development that we will bring the full force of automation to bear on the dynamic development and interaction of command contexts which F. R. Thompson[3] so clearly sets forth as the essence of command and control.

RESPONSIVENESS, PROCEDURES, AND ORGANIZATION

8.17 Response Requirements

As any other tool of command, the ADP system must be responsive to the command and all its staff elements which it supports. It must be responsive to the command and control concept of the commander and changes to this concept. It must be responsive through all escalation of situations, from cold war to general war. Whatever glowing attributes the system may have in providing services, if it lacks this essential property, it will be inadequate. Furthermore, the OPCON ADP system serves in a real-time capacity as given by the official definition of real-time systems adopted by the Joint Chiefs of Staff for command systems:

> Real-time System: The processing of information or data in a sufficiently rapid manner so that the results of the processing are available in time to influence the process being monitored or controlled.[16]

By way of contrast, there are other systems more readily identified as real time in that the response time between event and action is consistently much less than in a strategic command system. One such system is the Naval Tactical Data System,[17] developed primarily for shipboard installation in combat information centers. The system is made up of remote data-processing subsystems interconnected by automatic data links. Each subsystem makes extensive use of operators interfacing with computers in such a way that operator actions are processed with no perceptible delays and system response to asynchronous external stimuli is accomplished with no degradation of system operation. It consists of stored program computers, display consoles which permit communication between operators and computers, automatic data links which transmit data between subsystems, and various other peripheral devices for loading programs, entering static or slow-moving data, and monitoring system operation.

Similarly, the real-time data-processing requirements of air-traffic control are being served by general-purpose computers in advanced centers such as the Northern Area Air Traffic Control Center, France.[18] The purpose of air-traffic control is short-term planning in real time, thus optimizing flights by making the most efficient use of the available air space and runways while providing adequate separation to avoid collisions. The real-time requirements on man are very exacting in such a system. Prompt response in the pilot-controller dialogue in position reporting and issuance of clearance imposed by traffic density rules out queuing for data processing. The automation of the system in France has proceeded stepwise, presenting currently an interesting man-machine relationship. Automatic input is confined to that intelligence which can be collected independent of the active, real-time participation of the controllers, e.g., digitalized radar data and flight-plan data. Many of the essential data cannot be fed to the system without the assistance of the real-time human processor; consequently, we have both man and computers partaking intimately in the acquisition and processing of data.

The common feature among these systems is that the information is *used* in some way as soon as it can be displayed following the processing of data on an event. The distinction between real-time systems appears in the amount of time lag between event and response that can be tolerated in a given system. We stated earlier that the functions of a command were already being performed and that the role of ADP was to improve the methods. While it may be argued that reports from the field on such matters as status of forces, bomb damage assessment, threat remaining, and similar data may take some time to reach the strategic level of command, the exercise of that command still requires timely decisive action based on *all* information available. Properly employed, ADP can reduce substantially the time-link between the receipt of large volumes of data and its selective display, assisting the commander in monitoring the situation and in influencing the action where his judgment deems it necessary.

Having stated that the OPCON ADP system serves in a real-time capacity, in the interests of balance it is necessary to point out that much of its operation is not in such a capacity. The essentiality of historical information in a strategic command system is unmistakable. Much of this information is routinely processed for such purposes as planning, reports to higher authorities, and query response. At the opposite end of the spectrum, certain computer outputs are based on predictive data, presenting the situation that will exist as a result of a particular time-table being followed. This extremely wide range in the age of the data to be processed and the time at which the computer output is valid or used somewhat typifies the heterogeneity of the entire information processing activity in a strategic command system.

8.18 Procedural Pattern

Another dimension to be considered is that the ADP facility is, in fact, in direct support of the various staff elements, not the commander. Even with the perfection of exotic displays, it is doubtful that the commander will ever be satisfied to accept quantitative advice directly from the computer—he will continue to want this information verified and evaluated by his key staff advisors. For the foreseeable future, we should consider the ADP system as serving multiple users in the broad sense. In the case of the OPCON ADP system, it also serves different echelons of major commands. The individual staff specialist within these commands has his individual requirements of the ADP system. To perform his assigned function, he depends, to some degree, on the system satisfying these requirements. The responsibilities are personally his, not the computer's. Priority schemes laid on the ADP system may well admit first things first from the grand view, but if the system does not support each individual user as he needs it to do his job, that individual user will go his own way, independent of the ADP system. It is true that he may be a forced contributor to the system in that he provides machine-usable data for reports going upward and outward, but he is not a bona fide user of the system.

Responsiveness to individual users is the key to system design for many of its applications. Considering the range, depth, and heterogeneous character of these applications, it is little wonder that we have trouble developing the ideal system. Alternatively, we might well consider a family of subsystems, each with its specialized characteristics yet sociable in the sense that data can be exchanged between subsystems. A large-scale, time-sharing, multiaccess system could be considered the equivalent of such configuration.

Considerations of the responsive characteristics of systems similar to the OPCON ADP systems should include the organization of people, responsibilities, and the necessary procedures of all technical and operational supporting agencies involved, as well as the hardware-software system capabilities. Through the early and intermediate stages of development and implementation, until an acceptable plateau of production capabilities exists and a minimum level of developmental activity is established to maintain that adequacy, there is a constant shift in the balance between the on-site developmental- and the production-activity levels. In the initial stages, when developmental activity is on a very high key, strong technical weight must be brought to bear requiring the support of agencies normally outside the command system itself. During this early phase, the available machine time is primarily used for program-development work, and shop conditions can be arranged to best promote that end. The culmination of development is a production program which implies that there exists a staff dependency on the output. It follows that production has a natural priority over development work when priorities have to be exercised.

As the ratio of production to development work increases, shop conditions are altered to meet the requirements of the production load. That set of procedures representing system management which is most efficacious for production activity is frequently in conflict with the best conditions for development activity. As the situation becomes more and more dominated by production standards, the less tenable it becomes for the program developer. In general, if a 24-hour turnaround can be maintained for his work, he can progress reasonably well; but during the first year of operating the OPCON ADP system we were not always able to do that. The staff user needs his production outputs and at the same time has target dates when current development projects are to become operational. Under these conditions there is a strong temptation to treat a program prematurely as being in a production status. This is invariably a mistake. Much time has been wasted in squeezing production out of a pseudooperational program in attempting to meet urgent staff requirements.

One may ask: Why mix development and production activity on an operational site? First, there is a need to utilize any available machine time in meeting the initial peak requirements for creative program development. Second, frequent coordination with the end user is required in writing some programs. Third, there is a need for each program to be given at least a preliminary checkout on the final hardware system prior to formal turnover proceedings. This often leads to a substantial amount of debugging.

An orderly plan for the development and turnover of a system of functional programs covering a long period of time suffers many disruptions. Some are due to changes in requirements both internal and external to the user staff. The completion of some programs depends upon the prior completion of others. A shift in one schedule has an accumulative effect on another. High-density periods of program turnovers sometimes result and there is a low-saturation level on the part of staffs to accept a number of new capabilities in a short period of time for they must continue to carry out their day-to-day responsibilities. The rate of developmental activity by the supporting technical agency may be on the increase at the same time that available machine time is decreasing. Throughout this process, compounded slippage in schedules is inevitable.

Two additional factors confounded our problems. First, the hardware system was accepted for operational use before a suitable system software package had been developed. Since the hardware had been developed by one technical agency and the system software was the responsibility of another, there appeared no fair alternative but to accept each in the sequence that they were installed and checked out. The resultant concurrent development of system and functional software gave rise to many problems for everyone concerned with the total effort. The performance properties of both system hardware and software are so inextricably dependent on each other that it would seem wise to place the developmental responsibility for both in the hands of a single technical agency, given that other important considerations are reasonably equal. The system, then, would not be offered, nor accepted, for operational status until both system hardware and software were ready as such. One notable success where this arrangement has been followed is the Naval Tactical Data System.[17]

The second factor was the necessary transition from the IBM 704/1401 system to the CDC 1604A/160A system. Many programs had to be converted and run in parallel before the load could be shifted to the new system. While it was mutually understood that this transition should be executed as quickly as possible, it actually took more than a year longer than planned. The older programs were not written in any common language. Furthermore, one-to-one program conversions simply do not occur for many reasons, some of which are not under the control of the development activity concerned with the particular command system. Significant program changes are made along the way. During this conversion period, the older system constitutes a substantial drain on personnel, funds, and available space. The systems are sufficiently different that shop procedures are further complicated and training operators to be proficient in both is not feasible. As the time required for program conversion expands beyond the planned period, trained operators are reassigned without replacement in kind.

As the new system moves to becoming more of a production facility, the requirement for outside assistance should diminish and a compact organization directly responsive to the user command then sustains and improves the capability. It is during this total transition period when the organization of effort, which is also responsive to the end-user command, acquires its deepest and most complex meaning. Sound principles of organization and management apply here as in any complex activity.

One characteristic worthy of note is that in the management of computer program development, the pragmatic span of control is exceedingly small.

In an apparent contradiction to system responsiveness, it is characteristic of the initial development of functional programs that a considerable lead time is involved. From the time a project request for a distinctively new and substantial program capability is initiated, it follows a prescribed procedural pattern. Specifically, the pattern is as follows.

a. **Project Request.** Submitted by the staff specialist to his command, a project request gives a brief but descriptive title of the completed capability desired. An objective is stated as to the purpose of the project, a concept of operations is given which describes in some detail the manner in which the desired products will be used to satisfy stated requirements, and tasks within the project request are delineated. Normally, the initial request contains only those tasks in the analysis area which are necessary to determine feasibility or to produce a preliminary functional description of the proposed program. The security classification, the priority, the data capability required, and reference data are also included in the project request. Each project request is coordinated with other project requests within the command and then, if approved, forwarded for further approval and action.

b. **Analysis.** This comprises a scientific investigation to define problems and determine the most feasible methods for solution, taking into consideration both cost and effectiveness. It normally includes a detailed review of existing procedures which locates weak points and highlights opportunities for improvement. This requires an analysis of user requirements and a tracing of the flow of information to, within, and from the user staff division to include the processes and procedures by which this information is acted upon or utilized to provide a desired intermediate or final product. The outcome of this phase should result in improved operations either by utilizing existing techniques or developing new procedures, or a combination of both. The results of the analysis phase are reflected in the preliminary functional description which provides a basis for obtaining concurrence from the user on the proposed design resulting from the analysis. When an analysis indicates that a capability cannot be satisfactorily obtained, the analysis results are reflected in a report designated as a feasibility study.

c. **Preliminary Functional Description.** This is an explicit and comprehensive description of the project to be fulfilled, written in the language of the user and representing the results of the foregoing analysis. Its primary purpose is to provide a coherent basis for concurrence between the staff user and the developing activity before actual detailed program analysis and writing proceeds. In general it will:

(1) Provide a complete statement of the problem, this statement to define precisely each aspect of the problem for which the particular ADP application is being designed.
(2) Provide a complete description of the ADP capability to be developed.
(3) Define the inputs which will be required to support the system, and specify data requirements by type, source, frequency, and expected volume. This will permit feasibility analysis of data collection requirements and provide the basis for initiation of data collection procedures.
(4) Define the outputs to be generated by the system, including report formats and item definitions, together with the uses for which the report is intended, in order that the proposed system may be evaluated from the viewpoint of satisfying stated requirements.
(5) Define the ADP files which will be required as a measure of the physical complexity of the system being designed.

d. **Modification of Project Request.** Upon concurrence of the preliminary functional description, the original project request is suitably modified and, upon approval, program development, test, and documentation proceed until the point of turnover has been achieved, whereupon the program is designated as a production capability when accepted by the user.

Such procedural steps as outlined above are essential if we are to minimize false starts, equitably distribute limited resources, avoid infeasible projects, provide orderly evolution, and prevent exaggerated expectations and consequent disillusionment on the part of the staff user. It is a necessary but costly and time-consuming process. It has been recognized by others and bears repeating here that it takes a large number of people a long time to prepare an ADP system to do in a short time what it would take a large number of people a long time to do. The end result is stored speed capable of unlimited repetition, an element of the responsiveness which we seek. What we cannot store is machine time, for that is highly perishable.

If during program development, the needs of the user are not understood or honored or the user is uncertain or ambiguous in stating these, the result will most likely be disappointing. To avert this condition, there is much coordinative cross-talk between user and developer throughout a particular project in sharing this common burden. There is a requirement that the operational man understand the technical problems and conversely, the technical man must have some feel for interpreting the operational man's needs into technical objectives. There is an overlap in indoctrination here where, in practice, one tends to be the stronger depending upon where the primary responsibility for a particular evolution in the process is assigned. In our present methods, it is usually the technical activity which creates the preliminary functional description in coordination with the user staff. This requires that a considerable number of new people, often contractor personnel, have to be schooled in the purpose, methods, and operating mechanics of staff procedures. These developed abilities are ultimately *lost* to the particular command system. On the other hand, if the user staff is to create the preliminary functional description in coordination with the technical activity, it requires a substantial understanding in depth of detail for the particular ADP system concerned. However, this ability is *retained* in the command system and can be gainfully employed to the continued enhancement of the system. Also, from an objective point of view, the user staff is best qualified to conduct the functional and operations analysis of its own problems as potential computer programs. As a product of this organic capability, projects for detailed analysis and programming by the technical supporting agency can then be submitted in the form of explicit functional descriptions. Where this capability does not exist or is inadequate during high developmental phases, the staff could be augmented by technically qualified personnel from the technical supporting agency on a "time and materials" basis until a self-sustaining inhouse capability has been established.

The technical supporting agency is best suited for the detailed analysis and programming by virtue of:

1. Having expert detailed knowledge of the programming features of the hardware system and the system support (white-collar) programs.

2. Having broad support responsibilities for other systems. The actual programs can be made to conform to total systems standards for compatibility and advantage can be taken of similar programming efforts for other systems.

3. Having a large pool of programmers available, either inhouse or contract, that can be allocated to support different systems in consonance with peak loads and priorities. The heaviest requirement comes in the initial development of programs. Once accepted for operational use, the burden of maintaining the capability should not be placed on the technical supporting agency as this would eventually sap the creative strength of that agency as well as virtually assign it a major continuing role in sustaining the capabilities of the command system.

8.19   Allocation of Responsibilities

Before proceeding further, it may be helpful to describe certain essential responsibilities in the context of implementing and operating a system such as the OPCON ADP system.

a. **Data Collection.** This includes the acquisition, assembling, and formatting of data for insertion in the data base, including the promulgation of any necessary instructions regarding the reporting of data. Formatted data will normally be in the form of a creation sheet. This is normally a staff function.

b. **Data Conversion.** This means the changing of formatted data into a form or language that the ADP system will accept as direct input. Data conversion requires absolute accuracy, but interpretive knowledge of the data itself is not required. This is normally an ADP system operations function.

c. **Program Maintenance.** This covers the activity required to modify or change an operational program to meet changing requirements or to correct deficiencies that were undetected prior to acceptance. In the user's eyes, program maintenance covers the responsibility for keeping an operational program operational. This is performed best as an ADP operation function. As a function, it is separate and distinct from that responsibility of data base management, i.e., maintaining the accuracy and timeliness of inputs in the updating of files or data bases, although the interplay between these two functions often requires the finest coordination. This latter function is normally a staff responsibility.

d. **Program Operation.** This is a mechanical function performed by a specialist who understands the operating characteristics of the hardware-software ADP system and the operating documentation of the particular functional program. This is an ADP system operations function.

e. **Program Turnover.** This refers to the formal procedure leading to a point in time when all concerned agree that the developed program is fully qualified for operational status. It is an important event in the evolution of a program which deserves a comprehensive plan for executing the necessary sequence of events. It includes the training of user, program maintenance and operation personnel, and demonstration of the program in an operational environment to exercise its capabilities as described in the functional description. The provision of complete documentation is part of the turnover. The developer, user, and operator all play key roles in the process.

The supporting operational ADP facility, whether organic to the command which it is serving or not, is held responsible for the timely production of documented outputs from a functional program once it is placed in production status. The user need not have to concern himself with the inner workings of how this is accomplished. The relationship is one of matching production by the operator to the requirements of the user. To pursue an analysis of this arrangement, we must examine the functions involved for the ADP facility to sustain this kind of support. They are:

1. System Management
2. Hardware Operation
3. Hardware Maintenance
4. System Software Maintenance
5. Functional Program Maintenance

In the running of production programs they can, and do, have abortive terminations. The cause is seldom obvious. It may lie with the condition of the hardware, its operation, a flaw in the system software, a bug in the functional program itself or even in some combination of these. In a large system which also is undergoing some degree of development, these functions are so inextricably interwoven that they must be administered at the lowest feasible level and in no instance higher than the command responsible for the management of the ADP facility. In an operational environment, only people who have intimate day-to-day responsibilities for these functions and have the common goal of maximum continuous system readiness can take adequate action in resolving current production problems. If these functions are fragmented in any way to organizations outside of the ADP facility, problem resolution becomes a joint organizational matter where discussions are frequently a cut above that required for a determination and solution of particular problems. We have something analogous to cannons shooting at sparrows, both overgunned and ineffective. What is required is a compact organization that can provide a comprehensive troubleshooting team ready to investigate and take corrective action in real time. In the above, production work has been considered specifically; however, in program developmental work, the same principle of compact organization becomes more binding except that functional program maintenance does not yet play a part.

Overall management, its policies and procedures, and security precautions play a very important role in the system's total productivity and these must be subject to the review and guidance of the user commands.

We have said quite a little about how efforts may be organized to support the user command. It is of equal importance that the staff structure of the user command provide for a working interface with the various supporting activities. It is of interest to note that the major user command recognized this requirement several years ago when he created within his staff a command and control systems group to coordinate the continuous development and implementation of his command and control system. The director of this group reports to a level above the staff divisions. This provides the organizational freedom to serve the interests of all staff divisions equally well and also provides a single point of contact with suitable status for liaison between the user staff elements and outside agencies which support the command system requirements of the staff. The efficacy of such an organization has been demonstrated by experience.

OPERATING EXPERIENCE

8.20   System Evolution

It was stated in the introductory section that the principles of evolutionary development, user participation, and compatibility were generally accepted by command system developers. While they may agree in principle, it is unlikely they agree on all the implications of these principles. Certain observations relevant to these principles can be made in the light of experience with the OPCON ADP system.

System growth should be evolutionary and this evolution must take place within the context of the user command. The dictionary gives this definition for evolution: "a process of continuous change from a lower, simpler or worse state to a higher, more complex, or better state: growth." This growth, of course, must be measured in terms of capability to the user, i.e., once a capability is accepted, then we can never take it away unless, at the same time, we replace it with something equal or better. Computer programs, on becoming operational and given a relatively stable hardware-software system environment, have a natural way of evolving under the function of program maintenance and changing user requirements.

Occasionally, a large program may never reach the production stage because, in the design, the evolutionary principle was violated in that it was an all-or-nothing design, i.e., the program was not partitioned properly. Through the long period of program development, the user gets no useful product to evaluate. Also, his own requirements may change or external forces may require fundamental program changes during this extended period of time, keeping the program in a state of flux which only extends the time further—a self-aggravating condition. The program never attains adulthood. Experience indicates that where some useful product, however imperfect, is placed before the user within six months following concurrence on the preliminary functional description, that program has a far better chance of success than those which take substantially longer. Some of the best sellers in the production inventory had their beginning as simple bookkeeping programs where updated versions were produced periodically and the frequency of updates was keyed to the rate of decay of the information. Updated versions can be used as a primitive, but acceptable, substitute for an automated query capability until the latter can be developed.

Given a production program, the essential factor is a relatively stable hardware-software system environment for smooth evolution. This can be a difficult condition to maintain during growth periods of the system. The OPCON ADP system was designed for growth. During the first year of operation, we added on-line equipment to the system. While the electronic and program interfacing of this new equipment introduced nontrivial problems, the solutions were relatively straightforward. This kind of evolutionary growth can be taken in a natural stride, for current capabilities remain firm while new ones are added. There is little risk of any discontinuity in processing capabilities while the change is taking place. As described earlier, evolutionary growth which involves transitions from one ADP system to another can be time consuming, awkward, and expensive.

We have stated that some degree of sustaining developmental activity was necessary and desirable in the continuous growth of ADP systems serving command. If, however, a new system is introduced prematurely into the operational environment, such that there is a high level of system hardware or software development, then the condition of instability will exist and many problems ensue. These may well include user disappointment, programmer frustration, operator harassment, and system management inhibitions. This was true in some measure of the OPCON ADP system. To most participants and all observers, the usefulness of an operational installation is viewed in terms of productivity, not the sophisticated level of developmental activity. The premature installation of these systems on an operational site should be avoided whenever possible.

8.21 User Participation in Development

User participation in all phases of system development is essential. This principle is closely allied to the first concerning evolutionary development. If the initial system design is to satisfy an original requirement and the subsequent orderly evolution of that system is to keep pace with the user's requirements, then his active participation in all phases is a necessary ingredient. Notwithstanding, the era prior to 1960 has been identified as one which lacked user participation in system design.[19] The evolution to and development of the OPCON ADP system has been a marginal exception to this generalization in that the user was involved as early as 1959. The record reveals that formal conferences were held in early 1959 concerning the development of this system. These meetings were held at frequent intervals until the end of 1960. In each, the user commands were principal participants. In fact, toward the end of 1959, the senior user command established the group which formed these meetings as an official organization under his aegis. In early 1962, when the

OPCON ADP hardware system philosophy and configuration reached final agreement, the user commands were a party to that agreement. Throughout this development, the user commands have been active participants and are continuing as such, for true development has no terminal date. Today, hardware extensions to the system are made on the basis of justified requirements specified either by the user or the supporting ADP facility. Changes do not come about hurriedly but are founded on completed staff work and technical evaluations, following an established recommendation-approval chain. As described earlier, there is a similar procedural path for software development. We have come a long way in creating sound methods for orderly system development, for recognizing the need for new organizations and placing the role of each participating activity in its proper perspective.

In October, 1963, the Secretary of Defense forcefully reaffirmed by directive[20] the requirement for balanced influence between user and developer in system design. This directive established new and decisive roles for the user commands on the unified and specified command level in the design, development, and implementation of their command and control system. On the one hand, certain actions on the part of the user command were specified, while on the other, his prerogatives to engage in almost any level of detail his judgment dictated as appropriate were spelled out. The directive went on to say that the commander's staffs would be augmented as necessary for implementation.

One closing remark on the user-technical support relationship in system development. When a system or any addition thereto becomes an operational part of the command's information processing system, however primitive or at whatever stage of development it may be, then the resources required to sustain and exploit the designed capability should be largely on-site and responsive to the user command. It does not follow that these resources must be organic to the user command, but they must be so located and organized as to be directly responsive to him. Time and distance can so buffer the exercise of his prerogatives that his constructive influence is diluted. On the other hand, the user command must organize his staff for participating in the development and management of this new capability, as we have seen accomplished for the OPCON ADP system. The single point of contact within the staff for all supporting technical and operating activities is most essential.

8.22   Compatibility

Compatibility among subsystems comprising the total national command and control system is an important consideration in the design of a given system but not necessarily a clearly defined objective which must be achieved in all respects. As the second principle of user participation is related to the first of evolutionary development, we find the third principle of compatibility related to user participation.

The command and control system of a unified commander is a subsystem of the Worldwide Military Command and Control System.[21] As such, it must be capable of providing information to that system. In turn, the unified commander must establish policies and provide guidance to subordinate commanders to ensure compatibility of their command and control systems with his system. Within this vertical structure of compatibilities, he must fulfill his functional ADP requirements. In practice, he finds that certain lateral compatibilities must prevail if his system is to give him full support as well as meet external requirements.

On the national level, active steps have been taken to cope with the compatibility problems as viewed at that level. These have been clearly described by the Honorable E. G. Fubini in an interview stressing compatibility.

> For example, at the functional level, the Joint Command and Control Requirements Group is responsible for the review of new command and control requirements of the Unified and Specified Commands to assure that requested capabilities, information to be interchanged, etc., are consistent with the current operational doctrine and the mission of the user.
>
> In addition, the Joint Command and Control Standards Committee of the JCCRG is doing excellent work in establishing functional standards such as data elements and coding abbreviations to assist in the problems of data exchange. In a broader context the OSD (Comptroller) has established an organization which will develop and maintain standard data elements and codes for DOD as a whole.
>
> At the technical level, the Defense Communication Agency establishes communication standards and provides much of the interconnecting digital and voice links between various command and control centers.[22]

Later in the same interview, Dr. Fubini describes how the Director of Defense Research and Engineering conducts "functional area reviews" as part of his procedures for handling technical reviews and funding decisions. Such a review takes a functional area as "command and control" and considers it as a consolidated package. With due representation by all services and offices involved, a particular program is considered with respect to its impact on related systems and on the overall functional area of command and control systems. The process reveals incompatibilities, inconsistencies, and areas of overlap between the various programs.

At the national level we have a mechanism for minimizing incompatibilities in design of large systems and for promoting standards. As we move to the implementation phase of such systems, a phase where the end user is most active, the influence of compatibility considerations is felt most keenly. At this point, the user command is primarily interested in bringing the ADP system into full productivity as soon as possible. For proper perspective, it must be remembered that the implementation of this particular system is not being accomplished within a total system where all else is fixed. There are developmental activities taking place in all directions. The combination of inadequate standards for compatibility and total system flux produces conditions which are generally poor for establishing and maintaining a good total system compatibility level. If total system compatibility considerations somehow inhibit our end user in his rate of functional program development, the tailored capabilities of these programs, or responsive modifications to these programs, then compatibility, in his view, is being achieved at a luxury price.

A practical level of total system compatibility may best be achieved through emphasis on standards as distinguished from standardization and by requiring any such standards to be intrinsically mission-independent. It is true that standards involve standardization, but requirements for standardization should be the subject of severe review. Standardization has its penalty in either subsystem flexibility or responsiveness, the balance being a function of the level in the total system hierarchy at which standardization is aggregated.[23] Our progress in establishing common data definitions and their codes is an excellent example of useful standardization which facilitates the transfer of information. In other instances, we have missed the point of practical compatibility in astonishing ways. We have somewhat outgrown our fascination for standardizing the program source language to the exclusion of all others. There are good and sufficient reasons for having different compilers in a system, e.g., the induction of foreign programs created outside the system or accommodating the use of highly specialized languages such as designed for simulation and war games. Standardizing a source language has, at best, only a cosmetic effect on our ability to transfer information, although the adoption of a language as a standard is useful for the creation of most subsystem programs and for facilitating their transferability between subsystems. In the same vein, the practicality of building and maintaining identical system support and functional computer programs for similar strategic subsystems in the interest of economy and compatibility is overwhelmed by technological progress, procurement policies, and changing individual user requirements. The facts are that there do exist fundamental differences in the hardware of the subsystems; where hardware is similar, there may be differences in the user's mission; and where both are similar, the commander, his staff, and the environmental conditions are different. Total system compatibility in any comprehensively precise sense would be enormously expensive to achieve and nearly impossible to maintain without an unacceptable degree of rigidity in most of the system.   On the other hand, we have neglected to set such system standards as the minimum number of print positions available on line printers in each subsystem.   If a data file is transferred which is structured for the full print capacity of the sender and this exceeds the print positions available on that of the receiver, it cannot be printed in an acceptable form.   A suitable standard would set a minimum.   Each subsystem could have as many print positions in excess of that minimum as needed for inhouse use, but it would be understood that for intersubsystem data transfer, file structure could not exceed an established maximum of print positions.

8.23 Large Versus Small Systems

A large integrated system, such as the OPCON ADP system, provides for the following capabilities.

1. The capacity of the full system when required.

2. The flexibility and efficiency of automatic tailoring of subsystems to fit the task.   The availability of all system peripheral devices for subsystem use, unless actually engaged in task execution, provides a total effective capacity larger than a fixed system of the same size.

3. Concurrent execution of independent tasks.

4. The flexibility of manually selecting a subsystem for independent operation.

5. The availability of massive data files to all subsystems and remote stations.

6. Fully automatic system scheduling and control with a minimum requirement for operators.

7. Expansibility in on-line extensions of the total system.

8. Interchangeability of similar system equipments and components.

The above capabilities were designed into the system to meet stated requirements.   With some experience in the development, implementation, and operation behind us, it is of some interest to draw a comparison between the fitness of such a system and the relative simplicity of smaller, independently operated ADP systems in a command and control environment.

1. The lead time required to develop a hardware system of this magnitude is considerably longer than required to produce smaller, duplicated systems.   Such lead time is in danger of being overtaken by the rapid advances in the state of the art in automation.

2. A long lead time is required in the development of the highly specialized system control programs necessary to realize the design capacity of the system.   System software development cannot keep pace with system hardware development, for the final stages of system software development depend on the availability of the hardware system in its final

configuration. In turn, the development of functional programs is heavily dependent on the operational capabilities of the system support software. Sequential implementation characterizes the entire process. Whereas with smaller, like-systems, particularly off-the-shelf systems, these problems are greatly simplified and sound production output commences at an earlier date. Additionally, the training of operators and programmers can be standardized and system documentation stabilized at an early date.

3. Compliance with all security precautions while processing data of mixed classifications in a large system adds another dimension to the problems of system management. In the fullest exercise of the system, only software safeguards prevent, in some instances, the accessing of a data file by an unauthorized program or prevents data from trickling down an incorrect and unidentified data channel. Firm standards for the adequacy of software safeguards have not been established. It is difficult to get wide acceptance that the system is, in fact, secure in all these respects. One has to admit that there does exist a finite probability, however remote, that such events could occur. Input and output are controlled, but the system operators are not users of the information they process and in most cases cannot identify the contents to be anything other than as labeled. Physically isolated systems get the warmest reception from those staff elements concerned with the processing of sensitive information.

4. The large system does not contain total redundancy of components and equipment. In the event of catastrophic failure in one of the non-redundant components or equipment, we must be able to shift quickly and smoothly to separate subsystems mode with only a loss in capacity and not in capability wherever possible. This resilience must be embedded in the master control program. Maintaining a state of readiness to shift from integrated to separate subsystems mode on a sudden, unscheduled basis involves a surprising number of complexities. In providing the necessary automatic control-management services, master control internally codes and indexes system information, e.g., the file directory. The constant maintenance of this information in alternate forms and locations consumes an extravagant amount of the system's capacity. Also, there are exceptional cases where equipment failure cannot be circumvented, e.g., the subsystem selection switch. Smaller, like-systems installation would provide the ultimate in redundancy as well as modular system evolution.

5. Each programmer engaged in developing a functional program has available to him the full capacity of the large system. This provides an open invitation for inefficient programming where the use of additional peripheral equipment makes the programming task easier. In a highly

flexible system where scheduled completion dates are important, efficient programming is difficult to ensure through direct supervision, for such supervision requires the services of the best programmers and the ratio of supervisors to programmers is high. On the other hand, smaller independent systems tend to force this kind of economy, for the challenge will be to see how large a program can be made to fit the fixed small system.

6. There is the complexity factor to be considered. The large integrated system is characteristically more complex than small, independent systems. It requires a higher level of training on the part of users, programmers, operators, and maintenance personnel. This remains a near constant for the life of the system. Each must understand the philosophy, structure, and capabilities of the total system to some degree, or individually they can defeat the full value to be realized through system integration. For example, if a programmer does not understand the benefits of modular program design in obtaining better utilization of peripheral equipment and does not program accordingly, then the system throughput and response time suffers.

7. When the integrated system was being designed, an educated guess had to be made as to the most suitable combination of computers and peripheral devices. Expansibility in both was provided for in the design. With the wide range in processing functions and the variability of work loads, it is not surprising that a perfect match between these two is a coincidence that has rarely been experienced under operating conditions. It is true that computers are sometimes idle for lack of available peripheral equipment. In fixed, small systems, the converse would be the usual case.

It should be made clear that this comparison between large and small systems is not intended as an indictment against this or any other large system, nor is it an endorsement for families of small systems for command and control support. It is a fact that any number of smaller systems could not have satisfied the original system design goals. The original functional requirements on which these design goals were based have proved to be quite valid during the implementation of the system. The comparison is used merely as an expository device which may be helpful in considering the design of follow-on systems. For example, the current research efforts in developing on-line, time-sharing systems accompanied by highly flexible problem-oriented user languages may provide the better computer support in command systems. Crude comparisons such as this could serve to delimitate the number of alternative systems under initial consideration for a particular command environment, much as the chemist uses litmus paper to point the direction for a finer analysis.

8.24 Problem Areas and Trends

The technical advances made in the higher-order automation of command and control information systems have introduced new problems and accentuated some older ones. In describing some of these below, it is not implied that these are not generally recognized nor that they are being ignored. In some areas, it is known that considerable emphasis is being placed and substantial talent is being brought to bear on the problem. However, since acceptable, more complete solutions are still being pursued at this time, it is of some value to identify them here. The list, of course, is certainly not exhaustive. It should be noted also that some parts of these problems are not, in the classical scientific or engineering sense, technical in kind. While system design must promote a symbiotic system-organization pair, it is a new capability and, as such, is an enemy of the *status quo* in many respects. The corollary is that we must improve our ability in profitable adaptations in management, methodology, and organization to exploit the new potential. While the latter may not qualify as true research, it deserves our sincere study.

We need a better understanding and definition of what the man-machine interface is and what it should be for a particular system. This relationship deserves the most exhaustive examination, for without this penetration we cannot systematically design and provide computing systems which will perform internally as the user requires, nor determine optimal, even satisfying, output links and terminal equipment including on-line displays. Earlier, we drew some comparisons between a large ADP system and a family of small, similar systems. In another section, the heterogeneous nature of automatic information processing requirements in a strategic command system was pointed out. There is a growing body of opinion that ADP support systems should have two major logical functions.

1. A highly efficient, quick response ADP system which accommodates and displays the data systems covering established invariants of command information requiring repetitive manipulations, i.e., a data system tailored to the specific stabilities of the processes to which ADP can bring efficiency. Perhaps the technique of microprogramming as now employed in computer emulations[24] is a profitable avenue in the pursuit of such highly efficient systems.

2. A system highly generalized at the expense of operating efficiency with a higher-order problem-oriented language which provides quick support to new or infrequent user problems. The on-line, time-sharing systems now under development appear promising in providing such service.

We need to determine, on a total military command and control system basis, those minimal *standards* required to achieve the lowest *acceptable* level of total system compatibility. Accent should be on standards for only those hardware components, transfer media, software considerations, and language which facilitate data exchange. The determination of the necessary minimal standards is a complex task and following that, the actual specification of these standards involves considerable negotiation between high-level organizations. Through such an effort, practical compatibility could be achieved, truly competitive bids for procurement would be possible, and each subsystem manager would know the bounds within which he can alter his system.

We need a taxonomy of data elements, one which in its abstract form would lead us to a mutually exclusive and exhaustive classification of data elements and their machine-sensible codes within well-defined contexts. With the achievement of total system compatibility and available high-volume data links, we could be transferring giant volumes of data and midget volumes of information if we do not have a common dictionary. Moreover, the misinterpretation of data and consequent decision could well be catastrophic in some instances. Additionally, a classification scheme for data elements is essential within a subsystem for proper data base management and for explicit statements of requirements for prospective data bases.

We need better measures of effectiveness for the support rendered by the ADP facility in command systems. The continuous requirements laid on the ADP system cover a wide spectrum of priorities, security classification, programming running times and scale of equipment required per job, as compared to a more orderly production system operating under a batching mode. On the one hand, a measure of system operating efficiency is needed, and on the other, a measure of the actual contribution the system outputs make to the overall staff function is needed. Either the commander or the staff user will make it known when one of these falls below acceptable levels, but above that level proper measures are difficult to formulate. The lack of adequate measures limits our ability to evaluate objectively such systems for purposes of internal improvement or to recognize and justify a requirement for system expansion or contraction.

We need algorithms, adaptable for efficient computer programming, which accurately represent the conditional interactions of the different staff functions in the integrated process of plan generation, evaluation, modification, monitoring and control. The objective behavior of these algorithms must be alterable in real time through parametric controls which reflect decisions made by the commander.

8.25 Conclusion

It has been the primary intent of this chapter to set forth a comprehensive set of environmental conditions, both tangible and intangible, in which a particular large-scale computer system—the OPCON ADP system—is being developed and implemented as a tool of command and control. In so doing, it is intended to provide a setting, a scenario, so to speak, in which advanced on-line concepts or designs may be imaginarily cast and their comparative fitness judged as to better serve command. While the general objective of automatic information processing in command systems is somewhat fixed, many of the environmental conditions described herein are not. With suitable follow-one, more advanced systems, there can be an adjustment, a settling, of these conditions to best exploit the potential of the new system. These adjustments evolve slowly and uncertainly, however, for we know little about the best methods of adapting large organizations to exploit radically new capabilities. Conventional ways are tested ways with an indisposition to change and herein lies a large measure of insurance. For the exercise of command is a demanding process in which the maintenance of readiness, and the execution, monitoring, and modification of plans, and the control of operations are continuous, nonterminating responsibilities. New capabilities which involve change to conventional methods cannot replace those methods until they have been satisfactorily demonstrated in parallel with the older methods. Our process of basic research and enterprising technology continues to develop ingenious computer-based information processing systems. Where these are intended as a part of a command and control system but cannot be reasonably assimilated into the command environment which exists, they will not be used by the commander's staff as an instrument to aid decision, and reliance on established methods will continue. New systems have a formidable, well-founded competitor in old systems. Clearly, the implementation of such on-line systems where the staff specialist, as a programmer, interacts directly with the computer will bring about some far-reaching interactions with the command environment. These relationships deserve our fullest and most deliberate consideration in evaluating the fitness of more sophisticated systems in command and control.

We have made frequent, almost constant, reference to command systems with specific attention given to the use of computers as automatic data processors in support of the total system. Because of this frequent reference and our narrow focus on the ADP aspects, it is worth some conscious effort to avoid equating large-scale computer systems to command and control systems. Within the definition of a command and control system there is contained all the facilities, equipment, communications, procedures, and personnel that provide the technical and operational support involved in the functions of command and control of operational forces.[21]

Where opinions have been expressed in the foregoing, these are the author's own and not necessarily the official views of any command or office. The author is indebted to many individuals who have been significantly instrumental in the development and implementation of the OPCON ADP system. They have patiently critiqued the first draft and otherwise made substantial contributions to the technical descriptions and to the formulation of the author's views.

REFERENCES

1. Speigel, J., and D. E. Walker (eds.): *Second Congress on the Information Sciences*, Spartan Books, Inc., Washington, D.C., 1965.
2. Bennett, E., et al. (eds.): *Military Information Systems*, Frederick A. Praeger, Inc., New York, 1964.
3. Thompson, F. B.: Design Fundamentals, *Military Information Systems*, Frederick A. Praeger, Inc., New York, 1964.
4. Hughes, A.: Multi-computer Data Processing System Design for a Navy Command and Control Center, *Conference Proceedings of the Seventh International Convention on Military Electronics*, Western Periodicals, N. Hollywood, Calif., 1963.
5. Gunderson, R. C., and J. D. Johnson: Engineering Design and Implementation of a Multi-computer Data Processing System for a Navy Command and Control Center, *Conference Proceedings of the Seventh International Convention on Military Electronics*, Western Periodicals, N. Hollywood, Calif., 1963.
6. Bureau of Ships: *Systems Manual; General Description Manual for Data Processing Set AN/FYK-1(V)*, Book 1, CDC Publication No. 302, Department of the Navy, Washington, D.C., July 15, 1963.
7. Naval Command Systems Support Activity: *System Design Concept for Phase 3 Master Control System for the AN/FYK-1(V) Data Processing* Set, NAVCOSSACT Report No. 194, Department of the Navy, Washington, D.C., August, 1965.
8. ————: *User's Guide to the OPCON Operating System, Phase 2.3*, NAVCOSSACT Report No. 96 (Revision 4), Department of the Navy, Washington, D.C., Apr. 30, 1965.
9. Patrick, R. L.: So You Want to Go On-line, *Datamation*, October, 1963.
10. Naval Command Systems Support Activity: *1604A Generalized Sort/Merge Program Phase II (Revision 1)*, NAVCOSSACT Report 89B, Department of the Navy, Washington, D.C., Mar. 12, 1965.
11. Naval Command Systems Support Activity: *160A Generalized Input Processor*, NAVCOSSACT Report No. 115, Department of the Navy, Washington, D.C., Apr. 15, 1964.
12. ————: *Phase 3 Program Production System*, NAVCOSSACT Report No. 243, Department of the Navy, Washington, D.C., Aug. 15, 1965.
13. ————: *Information Processing System for the AN/FYK-1(V) Data Processing Set*, NAVCOSSACT Report No. 123 (Revision 3), Department of the Navy, Washington, D.C., July 25, 1965.
14. Foster, D. C.: The Information Processing System for the AN/FYK-1(V) Data Processing Set, *Second Congress on the Information Sciences*, Spartan Books, Inc., Washington, D.C., 1965.
15. Emery, J. C.: The Planning Process and Its Formalization in Computer Models, *Second Congress on the Information Sciences*, Spartan Books, Inc., Washington, D.C., 1965.
16. Bureau of the Budget: *Automatic Data Processing Glossary*, Washington, D.C., December, 1962.

17. Ream, D. L., and E. C. Svensen: Design of a Real-Time Data Processing System, *Proceedings of the International Federation for Information Processing Congress, May, 1965, New York City*, Spartan Books, Inc., Washington, D.C., 1965.
18. Villiers, J.: Concept of a Real-Time System, Automating Air Traffic Control, *Proceedings of the International Federation for Information Processing Congress, May 1965, New York City*, Spartan Books, Inc., Washington, D.C., 1965.
19. Davis, R. M.: Design of an Information System, *Military Information Systems*, Frederick A. Praeger, Inc., New York, 1964.
20. Department of Defense: *Development, Acquisition, and Operation of the Command and Control Systems of the Unified and Specified Commands*, Secretary of Defense Memorandum of Oct. 26, 1963.
21. Joint Chiefs of Staff: *Unified Action Armed Forces (UNAAF)*, Joint Chiefs of Staff Publication No. 2.
22. Fubini, E. G.: Interview with Dr. Eugene G. Fubini, Assistant Secretary of Defense, Deputy Director of Defense Research and Engineering, *Data*, February, 1965.
23. Jacobs, J. F.: Communication in the Design of Military Information Systems, *Military Information Systems*, Frederick A. Praeger, Inc., New York, 1964.
24. IBM Systems Reference Library: *IBM System/360, Model 30 1401/1440/1460/ Compatibility Feature*, File Number S360-13, Form A24-3255-2, rev., January, 1965.

A THEORY FOR FILE ORGANIZATION *

IX

Robert M. Hayes

University of California
Los Angeles, California

9.1 Introductory Remarks

A most important application for on-line computing systems involves the storage and subsequent retrieval and display of technical, business, and a wide variety of other data. The problems inherent in such information storage and retrieval applications rank among the most challenging presently confronting computer specialists. The present chapter is devoted to a discussion of the theoretical aspects underlying this important field. The mathematical formulation of the communication problem, the pattern-matching problem, and the organizational problem are reviewed in some detail. The chapter concludes with a consideration of the implications of these concepts for man-computer systems.

"Information retrieval" is a term which has been used in a variety of ways, depending upon the particular concern of the individual using it.

* The work described in this chapter has been supported by the National Science Foundation under Grant GN-422.

It has been applied to the management of "data base" systems, to the processing of text for "information" content,[1,2] to the matching of "document descriptions,"[3] to the development of vocabulary structures.[4,5]   To an extent, each of these usages has overemphasized one or another aspect of a total problem.   As a preliminary to the detailed discussion of quantitative methods for design of retrieval systems, therefore, it is desirable to describe the retrieval problem in all of its aspects.

In summary, the retrieval problem is constituted of at least three different and equally significant aspects.   It is a *communication* problem,[6,7] a *pattern-matching* problem,[8] and an *organizational* problem.[9]   The first aspect arises because the data involved are significant as descriptions of things external to the system.   They may be descriptions of people, of signals, of ideas; but they are *descriptions*, not the things themselves.   In some way, therefore, mechanisms must be provided to facilitate the processes of selection and translation to arrive at adequate descriptions.   These constitute the communication problem.

The second aspect—pattern matching—arises because the intent of retrieval is the selection of "relevant" data from the file.   The problems lie both in the ill-defined meaning of relevancy and in the uncertainty or even actual error in description of both requests and stored data.

The third aspect—organization—arises because, as the file gets large enough, it is impossible, or at least uneconomic, to scan every item in the file to judge its relevancy.   It is therefore necessary to structure the file, to provide indexing mechanisms, and to provide intermediate measures of degree of match which are less sophisticated than the ultimate measure of relevancy.   It is this third aspect which really constitutes the technical problem in information retrieval system design, since it is here that the size of file, the requisite response time, the degree of selectivity, and the accuracy of response all interact.   It is therefore the aspect with which this chapter is particularly concerned.   The other aspects, however, have significant effects which must also be discussed.

9.2   The Communication Problem

While communication is an integral part of the entire man-machine interaction and not just of the retrieval problem, the concern here is solely with five topics of special importance in retrieval.

1. Descriptions must be expressed using "terms" recognizable to the computer in a more or less formalized manner.   In document retrieval systems, this is done by establishing a "glossary" of acceptable terms (which may even include nonacceptable ones, with reference made to the preferred alternatives).*   However, counterparts of a glossary are neces-

* For example, see *Thesaurus of Engineering Terms*, Engineers Joint Council, May 1, 1964.

sary in any retrieval system, and the name "glossary" will therefore be used more generally, i.e., we consider a collection G, called a *glossary*, of elements $(T_1, T_2, \ldots, T_n)$, called *terms*, which are acceptable for description of file items.

2. Although the more trivial retrieval systems can function with a glossary which is a simple list of terms, it is usually necessary to define various types of relationships among them. These include both "generic" relations and "degree of association" relations. The former is illustrated by the usual treelike structure of a hierarchical classification, but more generally it is complicated by the fact that a given term may have more than one term immediately more general to it. As a result, a glossary is usually considered as a lattice, with the relation "T_i is specific to T_j" as the defining relation.[10]   On the other hand, under appropriate conditions (specifically, that the lattice be "distributive," for example), lattices can be decomposed and the association relations provide the basis for doing so.[11]   In particular, there is a unique decomposition of a distributive lattice into the direct product of elementary, nondecomposable sublattices:

$$L = L_1 \otimes L_2 \otimes \cdots \otimes L_k$$

so that any term T in L can be represented by an ordered k-tuple of terms $T^1, T^2, \ldots, T^k$ from the respective sublattices:

$$T = (T^1, T^2, \ldots, T^k)$$

In this way, the inherent lattice structure is displayed in a particularly comprehensible form.

3. The resulting structures are then used to aid in the formulation of descriptions (of both file items and requests) by facilitating the man-machine dialogue. For example, they provide the means for definition of terms and for automatic "explosion" of them, using both generic and association relations.[12,13]

Among the problems raised by this are the following: How can we derive the relations defining the glossary's structure? How can we "decompose" the vocabulary for easier manipulation? How should the "dialogue" between the formalized vocabulary of the machine and the rich vocabulary of the external world of things and requests be carried out?

4. The relationship between the terms and their use in the description of items is determined by the number of defined formats, the *fields* or *facets* of data description within each of them, the number of *values* assignable to a given field and the degree to which a field is *repeatable*, and the number of *roles* which each field can be assigned.* Each of these affects the number of terms and interterm relations. In particular,

---

* IBM, *Generalized Information System*, Application Description, 1965.

the maximum number of terms which must be included in tables of definition for format and vocabulary is given by

$$N = F \cdot 2^n \cdot 2^{Fg} \cdot 2^f$$

where F is the number of fields in a format, n is the number of bits in each field, g is the number of bits defining roles, and f is the number of bits defining format.

5. As will be discussed later, it is necessary to distinguish "levels of description," i.e., subsets of the glossary G on which levels of "screening" can be defined. These may introduce additional elements in G and additional fields in the description of items.

In summary, the communication problem is represented by the following specifics:

1. A vocabulary of description must be defined.

2. A network of interrelationships, adequate to the needs of translation, must be defined.

3. Items must themselves be structured into formats and fields and then described in the given vocabulary.

4. These descriptions must provide for levels of pattern matching.

9.3 The Pattern-matching Problem

Just like the communication problem, pattern matching is an integral part of all man-machine communication and, in fact, of all machine processing. The particular aspects which result from the problems in retrieval relate to the necessity for a succession of rules for matching. We will think of these as successive "screens," of finer and finer detail and more and more sophistication, with the results accepted through one screen, then being examined by the next. The need for a succession of screens arises because, as the file gets large and the vocabulary gets complex and the item descriptions get less formalized, it becomes too expensive to apply the most sophisticated screening criteria to every item in the file.[14]

For example, in retrieving the descriptions of chemical compounds, we first screen by empirical formula, then by major subcompounds, then by atom-to-atom connections.[15] Similarly in document retrieval, we first screen on words, then on phrases, then on syntactic relations.[16,17]

Thus, one aspect of pattern matching which is of particular significance to the retrieval process is the succession of screens. Of special concern is the likelihood of missing desired items because they are rejected by coarse screens, even though they would be accepted by the sophisticated ones. This concern is complicated by the very real difficulties in description: Errors are likely; not all descriptive data can or will be included; and significant interrelations among descriptive terms may be missed. Usually, these difficulties are handled by introducing "weights" into the measures of degree of match to represent relative importance or extent of interterm relationship desired.[18]

In summary, the pattern-matching problem is represented by the following specifics:

1. A succession of measures of degree of match must be provided.

2. These must recognize the likelihood of rejecting items actually wanted.

3. They must accommodate the likelihood of error in description.

4. They must also accommodate desired interrelationships among terms, as they may be described by the glossary.

5. They must be sufficiently efficient so that processing time is not a combinatorial function.

9.4   The Organization Problem

In a sense, the organization problem is a specific illustration of a kind of screen which must be introduced; that is, with very large files or with a necessity for short response times, it is impossible or uneconomic to scan the entire file. Thus, one could not apply the most sophisticated screening process to every item, even if one wanted to. Less sophisticated criteria must be applied to surrogates, usually representing—at a coarser level of description—groups of items.[19]

The design of a file organization then is an attempt to provide an appropriate balance among (1) the required response time, (2) the degree of required reliability, (3) value of the information retrieved, and (4) cost. Quantitative methods for file design will be developed in three stages: First, the relation among response time, amount of information, and value will be discussed. Second, the definition of amount of information provided by a file will be discussed. And third, design criteria for file organization will be discussed.

The first issue is raised only to make the most cursory of comments and primarily to raise a set of questions.

The first question involves the relation between the value of an information system and its response time. It is suggested that this relationship is characterized by a logistic decay function based on a single parameter—the half-life of the value of the decision—and that virtually all of the characteristics of an information system are a function of that single parameter. We therefore raise the question, "Can we define the appropriate relation between time and value and determine the parameter of half-life?"[20]

The second question involves the relation between the value of an information system and the cost of it. It is suggested that the obvious criterion is the economist's dictum—"cost equals value"—but that apparently is not valid. All too many systems have been designed with virtually no concern for their cost. We therefore raise the question, "Can we define the appropriate relation between cost and value?"[21,22,23]

The third question involves the relation between the value of an information system and the information derived from it. It is proposed that this relationship is characterized by a logistic growth curve as a function of the amount of information provided. This obviously raises the question, "Is this the relationship?" but more fundamentally, it raises the question, "How do we measure the information from a file system?"[24,25,26]

These three questions are raised for two reasons: First, to derive an expression for the efficiency of an information system as a function of the three parameters—T, C, and N—with which these questions are concerned; and second, to suggest some approaches to the definition of the third of them—the measurement of information from a file.

Efficiency as a Function of T, C, and N. Consider the relationship between decisions and their value as a function of the time at which they are made and of the information entering them. The value of a decision should almost certainly be considered as at least a statistic of a probability distribution, as shown in Fig. 9.1. It is impossible to assign an absolute value to a decision, since a variety of results are all possible and the value of each of these results, if it could be measured, would be different. Therefore, we can only describe the relative probability of the different values which each would have. The most reasonable choice of a statistic for measuring the value of a specific decision is the expectation, so that

$$V = \int V(r)\rho(V(r))\, dV\ (r) \tag{1}$$

If the value of a decision is viewed as a function of the amount of information on which it is based, it is suggested that it is characterized by a normal growth curve:

$$V(I) = \frac{V_o}{(A2^{-I} + 1)} \tag{2}$$

This is shown in Fig. 9.2. The significance of this concept is illustrated by the following reasoning: Most decisions can be made correctly on the

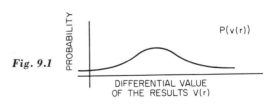

Fig. 9.1

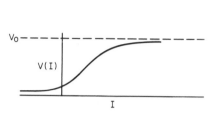

Fig. 9.2

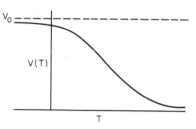

Fig. 9.3

basis of past experience (intuition) and a limited amount of data. Additional data are then usually used to support the decision and rarely to change it. The problem, which is evident even if this characterization is accepted as valid, is that of providing a consistent measure for information I.

On the other hand, if the value of a decision is viewed as a function of the time at which it is made, it is suggested that it is characterized by a normal decay curve, as shown in Fig. 9.3, where

$$V(T) = \frac{V_o}{(B2^{T/T_o} + 1)} \tag{3}$$

It is here, of course, that the overwhelming role of time becomes evident.* The time unit T_o represents, in a sense, the "half-life" of a decision and therefore of the information entering into it. To put this into perspective, view the spectrum of likely values for T_o for various classes of information storage system as shown in Fig. 9.4.

For a given decision environment, there is a range of speed of response over which the decision should be a "reaction," based solely on experience; there is another range of speed of response over which the decision

---

* Again the situation is represented by the necessity of *making* a decision, even if it is the "wrong" one.

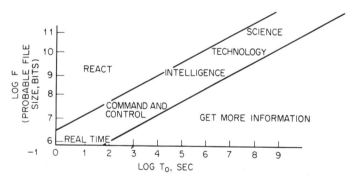

Fig. 9.4

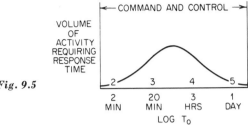

Fig. 9.5

should be delayed until more information can be acquired, perhaps through a less dynamic system; it is the middle range of response time over which the information system must be designed to function. Therefore, in a given system, say command and control, the design must be in terms of the expected value of the activity as a function of the half-life T_o, which might be distributed as shown in Fig. 9.5.

Finally, can we characterize the operation of an information system as a function of both time and information? If we assume that the value of a decision is a product of the two functional relations—one a growth curve based on information and the second a decay curve based on the ratio of response time T to expected value T_o of the half-life of the decision—then

$$V = V_o \left(\frac{1}{A2^{-I} + 1} \right) \left(\frac{1}{B2^{T/T_o} + 1} \right) \tag{4}$$

We must now define the relationship between the size F of data base on which a decision is based, the two parameters I and T of information and actual response time, and the cost C of the information system.

Measurement of File Information. The obvious approach to measurement of I, the information provided by a file, is to apply communication theory. So picture a file system as though it were a communication channel with an associated decoder. As input to the channel, we have requests and as output we have the file records for relevant documents, including selected content as stored for the document.

Consider a file of F bits consisting of F/N *different* items x, each of N bits. Suppose that a request y is input and matched against each item in the file over a specified n bits of the N, and that the item which matches most closely is output. We are concerned with measuring the information from the file, in response to the set of requests y, as a function of F, N, and n. We consider it in three parts: (1) assuming that the search process is noiseless, (2) assuming that the significance is dependent upon the relevancy of information, and (3) assuming that the search process is noisy.

Noiseless Communication. There are 2^N possible x's and 2^n possible y's. Assume that each x is equally likely,* and similarly each y, and consider any pair of them, say x and y. If we measure the relevancy† or degree of match between x and y by the number $i = n - (x \oplus y)$ of bits of the n over which x and y agree, the total number F_i of files from which x might be the response is derived as follows. Let

$$\alpha_k = 2^{N-n} \binom{n}{k} \tag{5}$$

be the total number of possible x's which match y over k bits. Assume

$$\alpha_0 = 2^{N-n} > 2^n > \frac{F}{N} \tag{6}$$

Define

$$\sigma_i = \sum_{k=0}^{i-1} \alpha_k, \; i \geq 1, \; \sigma_0 = 0 \tag{7}$$

as the number which match on fewer than i bits and α_i as the number, including x, which match on exactly i bits.

Since

$$(1 + t)^{\alpha_i}(1 + t)^{\sigma_i} = (1 + t)^{\alpha_i+\sigma_i} \tag{8}$$

then the relation among binomial coefficients yields

$$\sum_{k=0}^{F/N-k} \binom{\alpha_i}{k}\binom{\sigma_i}{\frac{F}{N} - k} = \binom{\alpha_i + \sigma_i}{\frac{F}{N}} \tag{9}$$

and thus

$$F_i = \frac{1}{\alpha_i}\left\{\binom{\sigma_i + 1}{\frac{F}{N}} - \binom{\sigma_i}{\frac{F}{N}}\right\} = \sum_{k=1}^{F/N} \frac{1}{\alpha_i}\binom{\alpha_i}{k}\binom{\sigma_i}{\frac{F}{N} - k}$$

$$= \sum_{k=1}^{F/N} \frac{1}{k}\binom{\alpha_{i-1}}{k - 1}\binom{\sigma_i}{F/N - k} \tag{10}$$

* This is an enormously simplifying assumption. For example, if we consider that the identifier portion of the item x consists of a set of n bits representing the assignment to the item of terms from a vocabulary of n terms, we know that the probable assignment is on the order of, say, 30 terms from a vocabulary of, say, 3,000. Thus the probability of a 1 at any given bit position is perhaps $\frac{1}{100}$. Introducing this probability, although it can be done, at this stage merely complicates the analysis without changing the crucial results. However, in applying the techniques in a practical situation, it would be essential to include the effects of skewed probabilities.

† "Relevancy" is of course an intuitive term, highly oriented by the view of the evaluator of it. We use the term here because of the descriptive content it has. The particular choice of measure (number of bits of agreement) given here is almost certainly not that which would truly represent the criterion for match in a complicated situation. However, it must be recognized that it is the typical choice in almost all operational coordinate representation systems.

is the number of files from which, on the average, x might be selected, (assuming that, if j items in the file match over i bits, each has a probability $\frac{1}{j}$ of being selected). Since there are a total of $\binom{2^N}{F/N}$ possible files, the a priori probability of selecting x/y is given by

$$p(x|y) = \frac{Fi}{\binom{2^N}{F/N}} = \frac{1}{\alpha_i}\left\{\binom{\sigma_{i+1}}{F/N} - \binom{\sigma_i}{F/N}\right\} \bigg/ \binom{2^N}{F/N} \tag{11}$$

Note that

$$\sum_x p(x|y) = \sum_{i=0}^{n} \alpha_i \frac{F_i}{\binom{2^N}{\frac{F}{N}}} = \binom{\sigma_{n+1}}{\frac{F}{N}} \bigg/ \binom{2^N}{\frac{F}{N}} = 1 \tag{12}$$

The measure of information, provided by the usual entropy measure for such a communication channel with this probability distribution, is given by

$$H(X|Y) = -\sum_{j=1}^{2^N} \sum_{k=1}^{2^n} p(x_j|y_k) \log p(x_j|y_k)$$

$$= -\sum_{i=0}^{n} \alpha_i \frac{F_i}{\binom{2^N}{\frac{F}{N}}} \log \frac{F_i}{\binom{2^N}{\frac{F}{N}}} \tag{13}$$

To bound this, we must bound $\dfrac{F_i}{\binom{2^N}{\frac{F}{N}}}$.

Define

$$P(t) = \prod_{j=0}^{\frac{F}{N}-1} (t-j) = \sum_{j=0}^{\frac{F}{N}} a_j t^j, \ a_{\frac{F}{N}} = 1 \tag{14}$$

Then, using the mean-value theorem of differential calculus,

$$\frac{F_i}{\binom{2^N}{\frac{F}{N}}} = \frac{1}{\alpha_i}\left\{\frac{P(\sigma_{i+1})}{P(2^N)} - \frac{P(\sigma_i)}{P(2^N)}\right\} = \frac{1}{P(2^N)} \frac{P(\sigma_i + \alpha_i) - P(\sigma_i)}{\alpha_i}$$

$$\tag{15}$$

$$= \frac{P'(\sigma_{i+z})}{P(2^N)}, \ 0 < z < \alpha_i$$

Consider the polynomial $P'(t)$: its roots separate those of $P(t)$, so

$$P'(t) = \sum_{j=1}^{\frac{F}{N}} ja_jt^{j-1} = \frac{F}{N} \prod_{j=0}^{\frac{F}{N}-2} (t - t_j), j \leq t_j \leq j+1 \tag{16}$$

For the values of t we are considering

$$t > t_{\frac{F}{N}} \tag{17}$$

since we require

$$\frac{F}{N} < 2^n \tag{18}$$

Therefore,

$$P'(\sigma_i + z) \leq \frac{F}{N} \prod_{j=0}^{\frac{F}{N}-2} (\sigma_{i+1} - j), i > 0 \tag{19}$$

This yields then

$$\frac{F_i}{\binom{2^N}{\frac{F}{N}}} \leq \frac{F}{N}\left(\frac{\sigma_{i+1}}{2^N}\right)^{\frac{F}{N}-1} \cdot \frac{1}{2^N - \frac{F}{N} + 1} \leq \frac{F}{N} \cdot \frac{1}{2^N - \frac{F}{N} + 1} \leq 2\frac{\frac{F}{N}}{2^N} \tag{20}$$

Therefore,

$$H(X|Y) \geq -\sum_{i=0}^{n} \alpha_i \frac{F_i}{\binom{2^N}{\frac{F}{N}}} \log \frac{2\frac{F}{N}}{2^N} \geq N - \log 2\frac{F}{N} \tag{21}$$

Incidentally, we can improve the estimate by using known results for bounds on the sums of binomials:*

$$\frac{\sigma_{i+1}}{2^N} \leq \begin{cases} 2^{-n\left[1-H\left(\frac{i}{n}\right)\right]}, & \frac{i}{n} \leq \frac{1}{2} \\ 2^{-1}, & \frac{i}{n} \leq \frac{1}{2} \\ 1, & \frac{1}{2} \leq \frac{i}{n} \leq 1 \end{cases}$$

* These are standard results from information theory, where $H(P) = -p \log p - (1 - p) \log (1 - p)$ is the entropy function.

Finally, by a similar analysis, we can estimate from above, and arrive at the result

$$H(x|y) \approx N - \log \frac{F}{N} \tag{22}$$

The mutual information contained in $x|y$ is given as

$$I(x; y) = \log \frac{p(x|y)}{p(x)} = \log \frac{2^N F_i}{\left(\dfrac{2^N}{F/N}\right)} \tag{23}$$

The average mutual information from the file and all its usage is then

$$I(X; Y) = \sum_x \sum_y p(x|y)p(y) \log \frac{p(x|y)}{p(x)} \tag{24}$$

If we assume that, on an a priori basis,

$$p(y) = \frac{1}{2^n}, \ p(x) = \frac{1}{2^N}, * \tag{25}$$

$$I(X; Y) = 2^{N-n} \sum_{i=0}^{n} \binom{n}{j} \frac{F_i}{\left(\dfrac{2^N}{F/N}\right)} \log \frac{F_i}{\left(\dfrac{2^N}{F/N}\right)} \tag{26}$$

$$= N2^{N-n} \sum_{i=0}^{n} \binom{n}{j} \frac{F_i}{\left(\dfrac{2^N}{F/N}\right)} - H(X|Y) = N - H(X|Y)$$

Thus, given the file as a communication channel to which the set of requests Y is input, the set of outputs X consists of sets of N bits (one x in response to each y) of which $I(X; Y)$ are already "known" and $H(X|Y)$ are essentially new information.

The approximation (22) implies that $H(X|Y)$ increases with N but that it decreases with F/N. This seems counterintuitive with respect to F/N. One feels that the "information" should increase as the size of the file increases. Why the apparent paradox? It seems that it arises in the following way: We are looking for a balance between $H(X|Y)$, the new information provided by the file, and $I(X; Y)$, the extent of agreement with the known information input to the file by the request. In a sense, a file is not simply a communication channel, and disparity between input and output is not solely a result of noise, as we will discuss in detail. We are thus faced directly with reconciling the problems in combating noise, on the one hand, and in maintaining the agreement

* This of course is simply the assumption of equal likelihood for each x and similarly for each y.

with the requested information, on the other.   As we increase n or F/N, we increase the likelihood of finding a good match, but we decrease the new information obtained.   Of course, the decrease is due to the necessity of using $\log F/N$ bits to distinguish the F/N file items, but this does not mitigate the fact that the "information" as measured by the entropy function would be a maximum for a file of just one item.

Significant Communication. Communication theory normally confines itself to models that are statistically defined, the only significant feature of the communication being its predictability. We wish to extend this to include, as an equally significant feature, the relevancy of the information received—determined, for example, by the degree of similarity to a request.*   To extend communication theory in this way, consider a collection of 2^n items

$$X = \{x_1, x_2, \ldots, x_{2^n}\} \tag{27}$$

each x with an associated probability $p(x)$ and an associated relevancy $r(x)$.†   We define the concept of the significance of x as a function of $p(x)$ and $r(x)$:

$$S(x) = f[p(x), r(x)] \tag{28}$$

If, for example, we assume that each item is a set of n bits, that each item is equally likely, and that $r(x)$ is measured by the ratio to n of the number of bits k_x of match with some particular item, then

$$S(x) = f\left(\frac{1}{2^n}, \frac{k_x}{n}\right) \tag{29}$$

Similarly, if there is an independent set of items

$$Z = \{z_1, z_2, \ldots, z_{2^m}\} \tag{30}$$

each of which is a set of m bits, each equally likely, and $r(z)$ measured by the ratio of j_z to m,

$$S(z) = f\left(\frac{1}{2^m}, \frac{j_z}{m}\right) \tag{31}$$

We could make a selection of (x, z) in two ways:
(A) Selection of x and then, independently, of z

* This has been one of the principal difficulties in applying communication theory to "information" problems.   The effect of the communication upon the recipient falls outside the scope of the theory.   Some attempts have been made to treat this. Russell Ackoff, "Towards a Behavioral Theory of Communication," *Management Science*, vol. 4, no. 3, April, 1958, pp. 218–234.

† As we use the term "relevancy" here, it could be any function over the set of patterns x, although we will of course particularize it as the relevancy to, say, a request pattern y.

(B) Selection of x and z, among 2^{m+n} different pairs, with the relevancy measured analogously:

$$r(x, z) = \frac{j_z + k_x}{m + n} \tag{32}$$

We want to choose $f(p, r)$ so that the significance of the selection is the same in both cases (A) and (B):

$$S(x) + S(z) = S(x, z) \tag{33}$$

This functional equation has at least one solution, which we will define as the "significance" of a selection:

$$f(p, r) = -r \log p \tag{34}$$

In general, $\qquad f(p, r) = -\alpha \log p - \beta r \log p \tag{35}$

for all choices of α and β, not both zero.

For example, let $n = 3$, $m = 2$, and consider relevancy as related to the number of 1s in the corresponding bit arrays. If $x = 101$, $z = 11$, $(x, z) = 10111$

$$S(x) = \tfrac{2}{3} \cdot 3 \; S(z) = \tfrac{2}{2} \cdot 2, \; S(x, z) = \tfrac{4}{5} \cdot 5 \tag{36}$$

If we now consider the entire set X, the average significance per item is given by

$$S(X) = \sum_{i=1}^{2^n} p(x_i) S(x_i) = - \Sigma p(x_i) r(x_i) \log p(x_i) \tag{37}$$

We return now to the question raised at the end of the last section, concerning the importance of finding a good match and thus concerning the significance of the file communication. Define $r(x) = r(x/y)$ as the relevancy of x to y measured by the number of bits of agreement. Then

$$S(x|y) = -r(x|y) \log p(x|y)$$

and

$$S(X|Y) = - \sum_{x} \sum_{y} p(y) p(x|y) r(x|y) \log p(x|y)$$

$$= - \sum_{i=0}^{n} \frac{i}{n} \alpha_i \frac{F_i}{\left(\dfrac{2^N}{\dfrac{F}{N}}\right)} \log \frac{F_i}{\left(\dfrac{2^N}{\dfrac{F}{N}}\right)} \tag{38}$$

Noisy Communication. The standard information theoretic approach to noise is to assume a binomially distributed error, based on the probability, say p_o, that an error might occur at any one bit of the n over which the match is made. Such a source of error is combated by lengthening the signal (by increasing n). The comparable analysis for file systems has not been completed, so only some preliminary results can be presented here. The approach however is as follows:

To treat this type of error source for its effect on file operation, let x be the item output from the file in response to y and let them differ in $d = n - i$ bits. Assume that there is an error (in x or in y or in the match process) in d_o bits, due to the probability p_o of errors in single bits. Then x will be the correct output, provided no other x' in the file differs from y in $d' = d + d_o$ bits or fewer. On the other hand, since x was the output, no x' can differ by fewer than d bits. Thus

$$Pr(e|d = n - i,\, d_o = j) = Pr(\text{some } x',\, n - i \leq d' \leq n - i + j),\, i \neq 0$$

$$(39)$$

and the average probability of error is therefore

$$\overline{Pr(E)} = \sum_{i=0}^{n} \sum_{j=0}^{i} Pr(e|d = n - i,\, d_o = j)Pr(d_o = j)Pr(d = n - i) \quad (40)$$

For each x', the probability that x' and y agree in any bit is $\frac{1}{2}$, if we assume the set of file items has been selected independently at random (with replacement) from the set of all possible 2^n binary sequences of length n. The total number of items which differ from y on d' bits,

$$n - i \leq d' \leq n - i + j \quad (41)$$

is given by

$$\Delta_{ij} = \sigma_{n-i+j+1} - \sigma_{n-i} \quad (42)$$

We have found that x, the closest item in the file, differs from y by $n - i$, and therefore is in this set. The probability one or more additional items in the file have also been included in the file from this same set is given by

$$Pr(e|d = n - i,\, d_o = j) = \sum_{k=1}^{F/N-1} \frac{\dbinom{\Delta_{ij} - 1}{k} \dbinom{2^N - \sigma_{n-i} - \Delta_{ij}}{F/N - 1 - k}}{\dbinom{2^N - \sigma_{n-i} - 1}{F/N - 1}} \quad (43)$$

Bounds on this expression imply that merely lengthening the identifier (by increasing n) does not reduce the probability of error. However, if we output more than just the single response, say a total of β_i items, then the probability of error can be viewed as the probability that the set of β_i items does not include the correct response. This can occur only if the file contains, in addition to the closest items x, β_i or more items from the set Δ_{ij}. Such an approach is, of course, standard operating practice in file systems with error.

Preliminary results indicate that the number of items β_i which must be output increases only linearly for an exponential decrease in the probability of error.

Error in file operation as we have defined it will not be due solely to the type of noise resulting from an error in single bits in x or in y or in the comparison process. An equally significant—perhaps even more important—source of error arises from the failure even to examine the particular x which matches the request y over the maximum number of bits, and such an error can arise when any indexing structure is imposed upon the file.

Indexing Structures and Sequential Decoding. Consider then the nature of such an indexing structure. Let the item x be identified for matching purposes by a maximum of n_t bits out of the N. An index can be constructed by any one of three methods:

1. By establishing a "sequence of significance" on the bits (which we can take as the given one) and using successive bits (or groups of bits) as index criteria

2. By establishing class numbers, encompassing groups of bits, by factor analysis or a priori classification of terms

3. By establishing groups of items, on the basis of similarity, and using a representative item as a group identifier

Consider the first method, and let an index term be n bits of the n_t. The approach we adopt here is fundamentally that of Wozencraft and Reiffen in their work on sequential decoding. The process of index search can then be interpreted as one of successively screening items from the file on the basis of matching the request y with successive portions n_i of the n_t bits.

In particular, it is intuitively clear that almost all items in the file will differ from a random request y to a considerable degree. There may be a subset of items in the file that agree in many positions with y, but the size of this subset will be small. Even though it may be difficult to select the single most probable member of the file, it should be relatively simple, as we have discussed, to screen out the potentially relevant items for further analysis or, alternatively, to eliminate most of the items from detailed consideration. Concentration upon selecting the set of most probable x's, by discarding from contention all improbable x's, is the single key concept in the searching strategy that we now discuss. By "improbable" we mean that "the probability that x differs from y at length n in k_n or more digits is overbounded by 2^{-K}," where K is some arbitrary positive constant which we call the "probability criterion":

$$Pr(n - i \geq k_n) \leq 2^{-K} \qquad (44)$$

From our analysis of the probability that the file item x which should be output will match y on i bits, we derive (assuming no other source of error)

$$Pr(n - i \geq k_n) = \sum_{j=0}^{n-k_n-1} \frac{\binom{\sigma_{j+1}}{F/N} - \binom{\sigma_i}{F/N}}{\binom{2^N}{\frac{F}{N}}}$$

$$= \binom{\sigma_n - k_n}{F/N} \Big/ \binom{2^N}{F/N} \leq 2^{-\frac{F}{N} \cdot \frac{\alpha_{k_n}}{2^N}} \quad (45)$$

We therefore set

$$K = -\frac{F}{N} \cdot \frac{\alpha_{k_n}}{2^N} \quad (46)$$

and determine a value for k_n. The larger F/N, the larger k_n can be. With k_n specified in Eq. (46), our objective is to discard all file items that differ from y in k_n or more digits out of n.

For those items which pass through this screen for one value of n, we further screen for another value of n, and do so for every value n within the constraint length of the code n_t. Let us consider a randomly selected file, with identifier constraint length n_t, for which the size $|S(n)|$ of the index for each n is an exponential function of the variable n:

$$|S(n)| \leq A 2^{n(1-H(p_t))}, \ 1 \leq n \leq n_t \quad (47)$$

where A is some constant ≥ 1. An indexing structure that is consistent with Eq. (47) is a tree, as shown in the figure. In this case, $1 - H(p_t) = \frac{1}{3}$, $n_t = 15$, and 2 is clearly a large enough value for the constant A in Eq. (47). For any reasonably homogeneous tree, A can always be small.

The searching procedure for such an index file consists of instructions that direct the searcher along a path through S, the index. The surrogates then encountered along the way represent the accepted index terms which match the request y within the rejection criteria. An example is illustrated in the figure.

On account of the tree structure of the indexing system, the process is illustrated by the decision about the first index level. This level divides the entire file S into two subsets, S^o and S^1. The task of the searcher is to decide whether the answer to a request y should be found in S^o or S^1. Let us assume that a desired x belongs to subset S^o of our file. We can correctly identify this by using the discard function k_n to eliminate from consideration the entire incorrect subset S^1.

								Leaf
110	2	111	3*	000		101		100 / 110
						110		100 / 101
				001		010		011 / 001
						011		100 / 011
		000	4*	111		101		100 / 001
						110		000 / 001
				100		100		101 / 011
						000		100 / 110
100	3	**001**	6	001	7*	100		011 / 110
						011		011 / 001
				000	9	000	10*	100 / 110
						011	**12**	**010 15** / **110 14**
		011	5	011	6*	111		010 / 110
						100		100 / 101
				110	6*	101		010 / 110
						000		101 / 010

Random tree index structure, $n = 15$, $R_t = \frac{1}{3}$. The index terms in bold figures form the closest sequence in comparison with $y = (100, 001, 000, 011, 010)$. The values of k_n on which successive decisions are made are (0, 0, 2, 2, 2, 5, 5, 5, 8, 8, 8, 11, 11, 11, 14). The result is the output (acceptance) of two items, including the closest one. The number represents the successive degrees of match; the *'s represent the level at which an index term is rejected.

Consider a screening process that starts at $n = 1$ and attempts to trace every sequence $s(n)$ in S. As it proceeds, it compares $s(n)$ with the request identifier y over the same number of bits n, and counts the number $d(n)$ of 1's in $y(n) \oplus s(n)$. If $d(n) < k_n$, the process follows $s(n)$ from n to $n + 1$. If $d(n) \geq k_n$, the process discards $s(n)$ and considers the next sequence in S that has not yet been discarded at any n. The procedure stops when either subset S^o or S^1 is discarded in toto.

In summary, associated with an increasing sequence of criteria K_1, $K_2, \ldots, K_j \ldots$, the searcher has in storage (or is able to compute) a matrix

$$
\begin{array}{llccl}
K_1: & k_1(1) & k_2(1) & \cdots & kn_t(1) \\
K_2: & k_1(2) & k_2(2) & \cdots & kn_t(2) \\
K_j: & k_i(j) & k_z(j) & \cdots & kn_t(j)
\end{array}
\tag{48}
$$

The jth row in the matrix corresponds to criterion K_j. The following algorithm is employed to find the file item x.

1. The search process starts with the smallest criterion K_1 and proceeds as if to scan sequentially through the entire set S. The process discards any sequence that differs from the received sequence in $k_n(1)$ or more digits out of n.

2. As soon as the searcher discovers any item in S that is retained through length n_t, it accepts it as the relevant x.

3. If no sequence in S is retained through length n_t, the searcher starts again with criterion K_2. Whenever all items in S fail to satisfy criterion K_j, the procedure starts again with criterion K_{j+1} until an item is found that does satisfy a criterion.

Activity Organized Files. To reduce the expected average number of computations in such an index searching process, we can also resort to the methods of activity organizing the file. The aim of activity organization is to produce a hierarchical arrangement of nested "boxes," or levels of grouping, which will represent a compromise among the various distribution measures in such a way as to optimize the selected measure of efficiency (such as channel rate). These sets of boxes become quite analogous to the structure of a normal classification scheme, although their method of derivation is dependent upon the character of usage rather than a priori decision. Thus, they can be visualized in terms of the type of chart shown in Fig. 9.6.

Each box shown represents a grouping at some level of abstraction, the level being described by the relative size of the box in the diagram. Thus, four levels are shown here, of which the smallest or lower level might possibly be the original documents themselves. If the cover of any box is removed, as shown in the upper right hand corner, the interior of the box contains a nest of boxes of the same general character.

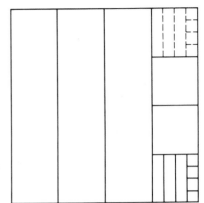

Fig. 9.6

Each box is "labeled" by a pattern obtained from its contents; in this way what can be seen at any time is a set of patterns representing various levels of abstraction.

The actual size of the box at any given level is of course determined from the distribution of the documents themselves and the logical relationship which they bear to each other. It can be determined on the basis of any of the distribution functions. On the other hand, the number of levels open at any time is dependent upon the distribution of probable activity. The aim is to produce boxes independent of their level of abstraction such that the probable activity of each box will be equal for all boxes which can be seen at any time.

We may further organize the sequence of scanning of these boxes— looking at them in their order of probable relevancy. In other words, given a measure of the probable activity, arrange the boxes in the order according to that measure. That means that, in scanning them, we will expect to come to the one of interest sooner than under an organization which ignores this distribution.

The determination of the actual relevancy of the given documents to an environmental situation and the selection of an adequate response involves the matching of the "request" (for example) against the available box patterns and/or the location of the position which the request occupies. To do this involves a scanning operation in which the pattern of the request is matched against the patterns of successive boxes. The selected box is then "opened," and the contents similarly compared.

It could be considered that such an operation takes place in parallel (with all available box patterns simultaneously matched), but this would beg the question. Instead, it could be considered that the scanning operation takes place sequentially, in a preferred order.

We define the levels of the file in terms of the number of box covers removed. That is, all items on the first level are those which can be seen without removing any box cover; items on the second level are those which can be seen by removing one box cover, etc. It is characterized by two parameters, k and m, which we interpret as the rate of growth and the number of levels in the file, respectively. From these parameters, k and m, we can define $\dfrac{F}{N} = k^m$ as the number of items contained in the file. A set of parameters b_1, b_2, . . . , b_m are defined by $b_i = (k - 1)i + 1$. This represents the number of boxes covered by a single cover at each level of the file.

Although this structure has been defined in a highly rigid form and has been characterized by the two parameters, k and m, it can be generalized by considering the b_i, each independently defined, as the fundamental parameters.

Given this structure, we can assume a corresponding activity distribution based on the following conditions. Each box within a box has an equal probability of being utilized if that box has been opened. In particular, each of the original boxes in the library has an equal probability of being utilized.

9.5 Implications for Man-computer Systems

The theoretical approach outlined in this chapter is intended to provide a methodology for the solution of some of the file problems involved in man-computer systems. Specifically, as such systems encompass large files which are interrogated by a wide variety of users, all the problems which characterize "information retrieval" become very significant. Of predominant importance is the degree of *uncertainty* which is involved in the operation of an information system: The likely usages are uncertain; the way in which needs will be expressed are uncertain; the relevancy of data is uncertain. How is the designer of the system to cope with these information retrieval problems in a world of uncertainty?

The focus of this chapter has been on file organization, as has been pointed out, because it is here that the issues of optimum operation must be finally resolved. In particular, as the size of the file gets larger, as the man-machine communication becomes more dynamic, and as the required response time becomes shorter—as all these become requirements, the kinds of indexing structure defined become essential.

To illustrate, consider the following hypothetical, but typical, sequence of storage equipment, all of which might be present in a system:

1. Computer associative memory   2. Computer addressed core memory   3. Disk memory   4. Data cells   5. Tapes

Given multiple users, with multiple access to multiple files, how should storage be allocated and how should access to it be provided? To an extent, this question has been answered almost completely by the indexing structures developed for disk memories—except for the overwhelmingly significant factor of uncertainty. Where stored data can be identified—uniquely, positively, and absolutely—those structures are completely adequate. But man-machine dialogues are, almost by definition, characterized by uncertainty.

To picture the possible application of the theoretical approach outlined in this chapter, consider a typical data base problem. Records in the system contain fields of data values and fields of identifiers (which may, in certain circumstances, be interchangeable). Both the set of values and the set of identifiers are expressed in terms from an allowable vocabulary, which includes ranges of numerical quantities, alphanumeric codes, and names. For example:

Record X:	Field A	Field B	Field C	$\cdots$	Field W	Field Y	Field Z
	A_x	B_x	C_x	$\cdots$	W_x	Y_x	Z_x

where A_x, B_x, C_x, $\ldots$, W_x, Y_x, Z_x are all from the vocabulary of allowable terms. Requests for retrieval from the data base are expressed by specifying values, also from the vocabulary of allowable terms, for the fields of identifiers.

A specific example is given in Fig. 9.7, drawn from the Department of Defense Federal Cataloging Program. The figure shows one of approximately 15,000 "descriptive patterns" which are the basis for the description of several million different items of Federal inventory. Figure 9.8 gives examples of two such descriptions. Requests for the Federal item identification number of parts satisfying given characteristics, or for other characteristics of such parts, are expressed in identical form and are matched against the stored descriptions.

Although some of the steps in organizing the file of stored descriptions are perhaps self-evident—for example, one might group together all descriptions based on the same descriptive pattern—others are not at all evident. Thus, one pattern—that for "wire-wound resistors" is used to describe over 34,000 different parts. In a real-time, on-line, interactive man-computer system, it would be unreasonable to search all 34,000 descriptions looking for those of interest. Furthermore, the request may have uncertainty with respect to one or more parameters. Finally, although the 34,000 descriptions of wire-wound resistors might conceivably all be stored in direct-access memory, it is not yet feasible to

Federal Item Identification Guides for Supply Cataloging—PART II

FSC Group 74

DP 1193A

23 April 1953

Superseded DP No. 1193a

1. Item name (obtain from Alphabetic Index of Names, Section A, Cataloging Handbook H 6–1)
2. Specify whether portable or nonportable (e. g., portable)
3. If noiseless, so state (e. g., noiseless)
4. If nonportable, give carriage size (e. g., 11 in. carriage size; 33 in. carriage size)

   NOTE.—*Carriage size is equivalent to maximum width of paper accommodated, disregarding fractions. For example, 11-¾ inch maximum width paper accommodated gives an 11 inch carriage size; 11.2 inch maximum width paper accommodated gives an 11 inch carriage size.*
5. Type data
   - a. Style (select from list below)
     - academic no. 21
     - bold face no. 16
     - bulletin
     - documentary no. 40
     - elite
     - executype no. 516
     - facsimile gothic
     - gothic
     - gothic no. 4
     - large vogue
     - large bulletin
     - modern no. 32
     - modern gothic
     - pica
     - pica gothic
     - pica double gothic
     - pica single gothic
     - small bulletin
   - b. Type of characters (select from list below)
     - upper-case and lower-case
     - upper-case only

     NOTE.—*Lower-case refers to small (noncapital) characters.*

1 November 1954

(Continued)

DP 1193A

6. Keyboard data
   - a. Type (select from list below)
     - air navigation
     - American Standard
     - French
     - Greek
     - Russian
     - Spanish
     - telegrapher
     - United States Navy telegraph
     - United States Weather Bureau
   - b. Number of keys (e. g., 42 keys)

     NOTE.—*Include character keys only.*
7. If electric, so state (e. g., electric)
   - a. State whether alternating and/or direct current (e. g., ac; dc; ac, dc)
   - b. Frequency (e. g., 60 cycles)
   - c. Voltage (e. g., 115v)
   - d. If shielded to prevent radio (electronic) interference, so state (e. g., shielded to prevent radio interference)
8. Special features (list in tabular form)
9. SR–1 Specifications data
10. SR–5 The manufacturer's data

A. *Deleted*

Fig. 9.7

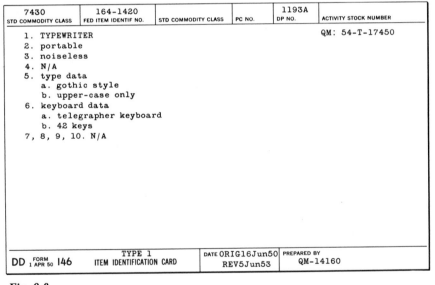

Fig. 9.8

store all 4,000,000 descriptions in this way. Therefore, since requests can involve any of the items of inventory, how should storage be allocated—which items on tapes, which on disks, etc?

These constitute the kinds of problems with which the methods of this chapter are concerned. In summary:

1. How should storage be allocated? The approach described is a combination of indexes with frequency of usage.

2. How should such indexes be searched, when requests are fragmentary and particularly when they are uncertain? The approach described involves a strategy of selection of groups of items, based on relatively limited criteria, for examination with more sophisticated ones. The number of groups to be examined is determined on the basis of the degree of uncertainty in description and the desired probability of success.

Although the results presented are at best preliminary, it is hoped that they will provide a direction for making such decisions in the organization of large files for man-computer usage in an environment of uncertainty.

REFERENCES

1. Rath, G. J., A. Resnick, and T. R. Savage: Comparisons of Four Types of Lexical Indicators of Content, *American Documentation*, vol. 12, no. 2, pp. 126–130, April, 1961.

2. Salton, Gerard: The Identification of Document Content: A Problem in Automatic Information Retrieval, *Proc. Harvard Symp. on Digital Computer Applications*, Harvard, pp. 273–304, April, 1961.

3. Salton, Gerard: Associative Document Retrieval Techniques Using Bibliographic Information, *J. ACM*, vol. 10, no. 4, pp. 440–457, October, 1963.

4. de Grolier, Eric: *A Study of General Categories Applicable to Classification and Coding in Documentation*, UNESCO, 1962.

5. Meetham, A. R.: Preliminary Studies for Machine Generated Index Vocabularies, *Language and Speech*, January–March 1963, vol. 6, no. 1, pp. 22–36.

6. Hill, L. S.: *Communication, Semantics, and Information Systems*, Rand, March, 1964.

7. Simmons, R. F.: Natural Language Processing and Information Retrieval Research at SDC, *SDC Magazine*, vol. 8, no. 3, March, 1965.

8. Goffman, William: On Relevance as a Measure, *Inform Storage and Retrieval*, 2, pp. 201–203, 1964.

9. *ADI-NBS Symposium on Statistical Association Methods for Mechanized Documentation*, Mar. 17–19, 1964.

10. Hillman, Donald J.: *Study of Theories and Models of Information Storage and Retrieval*, Lehigh, 1963.

11. Birkhoff, Garrett: *Lattice Theory*, American Math Soc., p. 25, 1961.

12. Doyle, L. B.: Semantic Road Maps for Literature Searchers, *J. ACM*, vol. 8, pp. 553–578, October, 1961.

13. Licklider, J. C. R.: *Toward the Library of the 21st Century*, Bolt, Beranek, and Newman, March, 1964.

14. Mesarovic, M. D.: Multi-level Systems and Information Problems, *Preprints; First Congress on the Information Systems Sciences*, Nov. 19, 1962.

15. Marden, E. C., and H. R. Koller: *A Survey of Computer Programs for Chemical Information Searching*, OTS, 1961.

16. Perry, James W., Allen Ken, and M. M. Berry: *Machine Literature Searching*, Interscience, 1965.

17. Rees, Alan: Semantic Factors, Role Indicators, et alia *ASLIB Proc.*, vol. 15, no. 12, pp. 350–363, December, 1963.

18. Maron, M. E., and J. L. Kuhns: On Relevance, Probabilistic Indexing, and Information Retrieval, *J. ACM*, vol. 7, no. 3, pp. 216–244, July, 1960.
19. Wyllys, Ronald E.: Document Searches and Condensed Representations, *Preprints: First Congress on the Information Systems Sciences*, Nov. 19, 1962.
20. Burton, Robert E., and R. W. Kebler: The Half-life of Some Scientific and Technical Literature, *American Documentation*, vol. 11, no. 1, pp. 18–22, January, 1960.
21. Anderson, Arthur: *Study of Criteria and Procedures for Evaluating Scientific Information Retrieval Systems*, March, 1962.
22. Kugel, P., and M. F. Owens: *Some Techniques to Help Improve Methods for Exercising and Evaluating Command and Control Systems*, Technical Operations Research 31, January, 1964.
23. Bourne, Charles P., and Donald F. Ford: Cost Analysis and Simulation Procedures for the Evaluation of Large Information Systems, *American Documentation*, vol. 15, no. 2, pp. 142–149, April, 1964.
24. Carnap, Rudolf: Meaning Postulates, *Philosophical Studies*, vol. 3, no. 5, pp. 65–73, October, 1952.
25. Kemeny, John G.: A Logical Measure Function, *J. Symbolic Logic*, vol. 18, no. 4, pp. 289–308, December, 1953.
26. Harrar, David: A Model for Applying Information and Utility Functions, *Philosophy of Science*, vol. 30, no. 3, pp. 267–273, July, 1963.

SOCIOLOGICAL CONSIDERATIONS

X

Louis Fein

Synnoetic Systems
Palo Alto, California

10.1 Introductory Remarks

In preceding chapters of this text we have treated various technical aspects of on-line computing. The advent of on-line computing and automatic computation in general constitutes one important impetus in the evolution of an automated society—a society in which tasks heretofore performed by human beings are economically and efficiently performed by sophisticated machines. The impact of automation upon our social and economic value systems and upon our society as a whole has received and continues to receive the attention of a wide variety of specialists including political scientists, economists, sociologists, psychologists, etc. Each of these specialists is in a position to make an important contribution to the eventual optimum social use of technological advances such as on-line computing. At the same time it is appropriate and important for the engineers designing computers and for the technically oriented users of these computers to become aware of and to participate in discussions of the problems and possibilities of an automating society.

It is the purpose of this chapter to stimulate in the reader just such interest in considering certain economic and social problems and possibilities of the automating society. To this end the key idea of the association between men and machines is first elaborated and used in the elucidation of both technical and social systems. The implications of the continuing replacement of man by machine upon such social objectives as "full employment" are then considered. The chapter closes with a survey of various suggested approaches to the alleviation of some of the indignities and hardships resulting from the replacement of a significant portion of the work force by computers or other machines. It is not the purpose of this discussion to suggest or recommend a specific solution; rather, it is hoped that the interested reader will be stimulated to read some of the references and to clarify his own views on the subject.

10.2 Classification of Man-machine Systems

"Render unto Man the things which are Man's and unto the computer the things which are the computer's. . . . What we now need is an independent study of the systems involving both human and mechanical elements."*

It will be useful to define certain key concepts that are important in understanding man-machine systems as well as the social implications of such systems.

Symbiosis† and Synnoesis. The advantageous (or disadvantageous or neutral) association of dissimilar entities such as a man and a machine, or a man with one kind of capability and another man with another kind of capability, or a machine of one sort with a machine of another sort has a striking parallel in the partnerships of dissimilar organisms that have become established by evolution. In nature, the association may exist between animal and plant, between animal and animal, and between plant and plant. Four types of coexistence between organisms may be distinguished: (1) commensalism, in which food or space may be shared without evident benefit or harm to either organism or in which the benefit relation is one-sided, without harm to the host; (2) mutualism, in which both guest and host are obviously or apparently benefited, (3) parasitism, in which the host is subject to varying degrees of injury; and (4) helotism, in which one organism functions as the slave of the other. One of the best known mutualistic relations is that between fungi and algae to form lichens, the discovery of which led Heinrich de Bary in 1879 to coin the term "symbiosis" to refer to the partnership phenomena of commensal-

* N. Weiner, *God and Golem, Inc.*, M.I.T., 1964.
† Article on Symbiosis, *Encyclopaedia Britannica*, 1957 edition.

ism, mutualism, parasitism, or helotism. The term "symbiosis" is derived from the Greek; *sym* is an assimilated form of *syn*, which is a prefix meaning together; *bio* is a combining form denoting relation to life. Each symbiotic partner is called a "symbiont"—or alternatively, a "symbiote." Symbiosis has been widely used in the restricted sense of mutualism.

The term "antibiosis"—*anti* is the antonym of *sym*—is used in biology to refer to the antagonistic association of organisms to the detriment of one or between one and a metabolic product of another. Each antibiotic partner is called an "antibiont."

The interrelationships of commensalism, mutualism, parasitism, helotism, and antibiotism are extremely complex; they are often difficult to distinguish. Parasitism may evolve from either external or internal commensalism; mutualism may commonly develop from the various types of commensalism. In the opposite direction, mutualism may arise by complete adjustment of host and guest in an originally parasitic relation. In helotism, it is possible that the roles of master and slave may be interchanged. Thus symbiosis, in its manifold external, internal, physiological, and social relations, appears as a biological relation of fundamental importance.

Let us draw parallels between symbiotic (and antibiotic) partnerships of living things and other kinds of partnerships of dissimilar things that may be living or not. What living partners share in symbiosis is food, locomotion, shelter, support, and other physical amenities required for development and survival. What living men and inanimate machines mainly share as partners in the man-machine systems that characterize our rapidly evolving society are intellectual capabilites—abilities to do and to learn to do cognitive tasks—to recognize, to plan, to decide, to control, to calculate, to deduce, to solve problems. Thus, if like Heinrich de Bary, we were to coin a general term for the advantageous, disadvantageous, or neutral intellectual partnerships of machines and machines, or machines and men, or men and men, the word "synnoesis" would obviously be a candidate. Synnoesis is derived from the Greek; *syn* is a prefix meaning together; *noe* is a combining form relating to the intellect. Furthermore, just as the term "symbiont" refers to an organism living in symbiosis, so does the term "synnoent" refer to a partner using his (its) "head" in synnoesis. The meaning of the terms "antinoesis" and "antinoent" is evident.

Biologists use the term "symbiotics" as the name of the science that deals with symbiosis, but they do not speak of a symbiotic society in the plant and animal kingdom. Nevertheless, it is natural and useful to speak of a synnoetic society in the United States, for instance, where there is an extraordinarily large degree of pooling of the intellectual resources of men and machines in various combinations to direct and to do the intellectual work that is important for the country's development and survival. (Presumably these man-machine combinations are forms of helotism, with the man as master and the machine as slave rather than the reverse). Hopefully, these man-machine associations are not in antinoesis, i.e., in association to the detriment of man.

Commensalism, mutualism, parasitism, and helotism in symbiosis have their parallels in synnoesis; they are thus types of symbiotic and synnoetic associations (see Table 10.1).

It is apparent that just as commensalism, mutualism, parasitism, and helotism in symbiosis may evolve one from the other, so may synnoetic commensalism, mutualism, parasitism, and helotism evolve in like manner. Indeed, such evolutions occur as combinations of people, computer programs, networks, and communication links are designed, redesigned, and debugged. Frequently, commensalism where men and machines do not seem to be doing each other any good evolves into mutualism, where the combination is mutually advantageous.

Thus synnoesis, in its manifold external and internal and cognitive relations, appears as a technological and economic relation of fundamental importance.

Synergesis. Another parallel may be drawn in the partnerships of discrete agencies such as man and capital goods (machines, land, buildings, equipment, and tools) that combine—not to pool their intellectual powers to do cognitive tasks as in the case of synnoesis—but to pool their muscle power or physical powers to do physical work. The term "synergesis"* (*ergon* is Greek for work) is here adopted to refer to the physical partnership phenomena of the four types: commensalism, mutualism, parasitism, or helotism. It should by now be apparent what the terms "synergetics" and "synergent" refer to (see Table 10.1). Synergesis, in its manifold internal and external relations, appears as a technical and industrial relation of utmost importance.

Where there is an extraordinarily large degree of pooling of the physical resources of machines and the muscle power of man, it is clarifying to speak of a synergetic society or of a synergetic economy. Thus, the industrial or automation revolution is largely a synergetic revolution; our modern cybernation revolution is largely a synnoetic revolution.

Synnoergesis. But our society and our economy are both synergetic and synnoetic. Men and machines, as well as labor and capital instruments, are collaborating to do both the physical and intellectual work of society. Thus, we will speak of the synnoergetic society, rather than the

* Synergism is used both in physiology and theology; in physiology, the cooperating agencies may be drugs, or muscles, or organs; in theology, the cooperating agencies are divine grace and human activity.

TABLE 10.1. *Classification of Interrelationships*

	Symbiotics Symbiosis *Symbiont–Symbiont* Plant–Plant or Plant–Animal or Animal–Animal	Synnoetics Synnoesis *Synnoent–Synnoent* Man–Man or Man–Machine or Machine–Machine	Synergetics Synergesis *Synergent–Synergent* Labor–Labor or Labor–Capital or Capital–Capital	Synnoergetics Synnoergesis *Synnoergent–Synnoergent* Labor–Labor or Labor–Capital or Capital–Capital
Commensalism				
Mutualism				
Parasitism				
Helotism				

automated society or the cybernated society or the technological society (see Table 10.1).

The preceding remarks are of a technical nature; they are made by one computer scientist to another.   If it is agreed that time-sharing in a conversational mode is an instance of synnoesis—of the intellectual (and advantageous) collaboration of a man and a computer; if it is agreed that on-line computing, retrieval, and control are instances of synnoesis; then just as biologists, since de Bary, in the interests of both conciseness and clarity of communication, deprecated awkward phrases such as fungi-algae interaction, or fungi-algae interface, or fungi-algae relationship, or fungi-algae coupling, etc., in favor of fungi-algae symbiosis—or just symbiosis, so should we no longer speak in awkward phrases such as man-machine interaction, or man-machine relationship, or man-machine interface, or man-machine coupling, etc., in favor of man-machine synnoesis— or just synnoesis.   Indeed, textbooks with subject matter similar to this one could concisely and unambiguously be called "Synnoesis."

10.3   Is Our Economy Labor-deficient?

As already indicated, this chapter is concerned with the design and rationale of man-machine synnoergetic systems that are popularly called social and economic institutions and about the corresponding ethical and psychological systems that are congruent and congenial with and meet the needs of a rapidly changing society such as ours, that presumably strives to continually enhance, as conditions permit, the dignity of every person in it.

What is the actual condition of our synnoergetic economy?   To what extent does this condition permit the enhancement of the dignity of every person in the society?   Without going into the ramifications of the meaning of dignity, it seems clear that the dignity of a person is closely associated with the way in which he earns his living and obtains his income and with the self-respect he enjoys from doing what he does.   We will examine opposite views of what the actual condition of our economy is. We will also examine the effects of these opposing views on the kinds of opportunities society provides for ways in which people can make a living and maintain an income and on the kinds of opportunities society provides for gaining dignity from the doing of what people have to do or choose to do.

People hold opposite views on the fundamental issue of whether the United States synnoergetic economy is labor-saturated or labor-deficient, i.e., whether there are more persons in the labor force (however trained and mobile they may be) than the economy can use productively on useful projects, even if all current job openings were filled (labor-saturated), or whether there are fewer persons in the labor force than the economy can use productively on useful projects (labor-deficient).

To be sure, the question is ordinarily formulated differently: Do automation and computers cause unemployment? Does technology make more jobs—or fewer? Does an increase in aggregate demand for goods and services require increased employment of people (rather than machines) to satisfy the demand? But, however the question is articulated, the American people are groping to determine their current economic condition: labor-saturated or labor-deficient?

The current generally accepted point of view is that the United States synnoergetic economy is now labor-deficient and will for the foreseeable future continue to be so. There are essentially three arguments in support of this position:

1. There is so much work that needs to be done in the United States in building and rebuilding cities, roads, parks, dams, hospitals, museums, theaters, schools, etc., and in defense, conservation, health, air and water pollution control, education, research, and all kinds of social and personal services, that it is unimaginable that we already have or will soon have more people than we need to do all this necessary and useful work.

2. The productivity of labor (defined as the dollar value of the gross national product divided by the man-hours paid for) has been rising only 3.5 per cent per year in the sixties, and even this modest rate of increase is probably not sustainable during the rest of the decade. This small rate of productivity is not at all indicative of the "disappearance of the job as an institution," or that we are advanced enough technologically, so that machines together with a fraction of an appropriately trained and mobile labor force can do all the work required to meet realistic demands for goods and services.

3. It is an established principle of Keynesian economics that if aggregate demand is increased, more persons must be employed and put on a payroll so that American industry can meet the new demand. Because needs are limitless, the potential demand (desire to buy and ability to pay for what one wants or needs) is limitless; therefore, the requirement for the employment of persons in order to produce the goods and services to satisfy the limitless demand is boundless.

Consistent with and following from the premise that the United States economy is labor-deficient is the policy that a stable and prosperous economy can be achieved by providing the opportunity for employment (and its consequent increase in personal income through wages and increase in dignity from having a job) to all those who do not have an adequate income. This policy is based on the expectation that with a fully employed, well-paid labor force and with prospering business, the effects of poverty could be eliminated and welfare minimized because most individuals would then have adequate incomes through wages, or dividends, or interest, or rents.

Naturally, then, the Congress has passed legislation, and the administration has decreed that monetary and fiscal measures (such as tax cuts, and interest rate adjustments) be used to increase aggregate demand (purchasing power) which will stimulate business to employ more persons who will thereby gain both income and dignity. For the unemployed who are insufficiently trained or educated, Congress has legislated and funded programs to educate, train, or retrain the people that in this view are needed in our labor-deficient economy.

10.4 Is Our Economy Labor-saturated?

The opposing view on the condition of our synnoergetic economy is that it is labor-saturated; that we already have more persons in the labor force than can be employed both usefully and productively, even if all job openings on useful projects were filled. This view is supported by three interrelated counter arguments that parallel the three arguments of those who hold that our economy is labor-deficient:

1. Granting that there is much work that needs to be done in the United States in building and rebuilding cities, roads, parks, dams, hospitals, museums, theaters, schools, etc., and in defense, conservation, health, air and water pollution control, education, research, and all kinds of social and personal services, the people of the United States will refuse to support spending programs on the necessary scale; they will not pay for (demand) all of this work. It is thus academic to say that if the people of the United States were to demand what is needed, it would take the whole labor force to do all the work.

2. No one knows, nor has anyone yet tried to measure, the amount and extent of unproductiveness among the employed. Nevertheless, many believe that an appreciable percentage of the average workday is spent unproductively. Thus, if the number of man-hours paid for in featherbedding, and other forms of unproductiveness were subtracted from the number of man-hours used in calculating productivity, then the adjusted figures would indicate that we have a labor-saturated economy.

3. Needs are limited. Demand never exceeds the need and is thus also limited. Therefore, the manpower and machine power needed to meet a limited demand is bounded.

10.5 Proposals to Provide Income in a Labor-saturated Economy

Individuals and families have three sources of income: (1) as employees, they receive wages or salaries; (2) as owners, they receive profits, or rent, or interest, or dividends; (3) as pensioners, dependents, alimony beneficiaries, charity or welfare recipients, subsidy recipients—they receive welfare. If one accepts the premise that the United States economy is labor-saturated, full employment no longer becomes a practical goal. Accordingly, it becomes necessary to devise means for assuring that all members of society have an acceptable income level, even if this income is not directly related to their productive labor. Some approaches to achieving this end are briefly outlined below. They are discussed in considerably greater detail in the references at the end of this chapter.

Deliberately Reduced Productivity.   John R. Bunting, in his book *The Hidden Face of Free Enterprise*, does not suggest that we sever the link between income and jobs. His proposal for reasonable featherbedding presumes that, while full employment is not economically necessary, it is not economically harmful and that it is certainly socially desirable and psychologically healthy.

> The challenge of the future will be for the American economy to provide the spending to enable a substantial rise in material well-being and, not incidentally, fully employ its work force. It is my thesis that these goals will go unfulfilled unless labor and business first stop acting as antagonists and begin behaving as though motivated by the public interest.
>
> On the other hand, we are in an economic position where not all in the labor force need work to produce enough for a good jump—if not universal affluence—in standards of life. The perplexing question is how to get enough income to those who need not work. The answer that I believe will evolve will be that they will be employed by a process best described— though it won't be so called—as "reasonable featherbedding."
>
> Jobs, in the traditional sense, are not increasing and will not in the future increase fast enough. In the recovery following the 1960 recession, it took maybe three or four times as much of an increase in total spending to result in a job as in the mid-1950's. Business and labor, as each becomes less inclined toward self-interest, will come to see the necessity of supplying additional employment. It is imperative, however, that it not be obvious that jobs are being created from whole cloth.
>
> Already this process has taken place on a fairly large scale. Many well paid corporate executives are working in occupations that hardly existed before the war. To some extent, new methods and processes have necessitated swollen executive ranks. Mostly, however, new corporate titles have come as a kind of subconscious response to the fact that the economy can afford them.
>
> Now, for everyone but the smallest corporation, the personnel department hires and fires instead of division chiefs performing the function. Before 1950 economists were a rarity in private companies; now they are a necessary status symbol. (Anthropologists seem to be replacing them for the company that wants to be unique.) Corporations have men at high levels who spend half or more of their time working for the United Fund, and other

civic enterprises. "Planning" departments with far-sighted thinkers are quite stylish. Two and three junior executives back up seniors where one filled the bill in the past.

What has happened so far is all to the good. More of the same is in order. The jobs that have come into being have much more dignity, therefore afford more social satisfaction in the world in which we live. Why pay someone to watch a machine half the day when he could be doing something all day that is interesting to him and useful to the corporation?

There is no need for this eventuality, fortunately. Values can be added, work can be made satisfying if good minds are put to the task. If abundance has replaced scarcity, those rising to business leadership in the future will be skilled at maintaining demand at levels sufficient to perpetuate affluence, not those able to produce more with less as in the past. Maintaining demand will involve getting money to those who would be unable to find traditional market jobs.[1]

Guaranteed Minimum Income Plans. While Bunting's reasonable featherbeds could probably not provide a minimum income to all persons living in poverty—some would be too aged, or too young, or too sick or unqualified—there are a variety of more comprehensive suggestions designed to assure a certain minimum income to everybody regardless of the cause of his poverty—to each according to his need. These go by various names: The Guaranteed Income (Robert Theobald); The Negative Income Tax (Prof. Milton Friedman); The Social Dividend (Lady Rhys Williams); The Individual Subsidy Plan (Joseph Farber). None of these suggestions would now sever any of the three links: between income and wages, between income and profits, or between income and welfare. Those individuals and/or families whose wages and/or profits exceeded a preestablished minimum amount would be taxed according to some preestablished rules in order to provide a certain minimum income to those families and individuals whose income fell short of a preestablished minimum.

The proposals differ as to what body would decide what the minimum income should be; who would qualify; how the program was to be administered; how financed.*

The economic philosophy and the spirit of some arguments made in favor of these plans by their proponents are captured in Robert Theobald's statement:

> The provision of a constitutionally guaranteed right to an income is the only way to prevent the emergence of a technologically dehumanized consumer society. This proposal for a guaranteed income is not a solution to problems

* See Eveline M. Burns, "Where Welfare Falls Short," *The Public Interest*, no. 1, pp. 82–95, fall, 1965.

but rather a precondition for solutions: in some ways it is rather like the introduction of limited liability in the middle of the nineteenth century. Limited liability allowed the company to take risks; a guaranteed income will allow the individual to take risks in order to promote his self-development in the interest of himself and his society.

The guaranteed income would provide everybody with an absolute right to resources and thus take the place of the personal property which Jefferson believed every man had to possess in order to be independent. Our society has changed so greatly that human dignity can no longer be based on the possession of land but must rather derive from the production of machines. Human dignity in a cybernated era can only be guaranteed through a constitutional right to a share in the production of machine systems.[14]

A U.S. Labor Department Commission[19] states that the United States economy can now afford guaranteed minimum income plans, and Friedman argues that the Negative Income Tax is a form of welfare that is cheaper to administer than present forms.

All these guaranteed minimum income plans presume that in a highly labor-saturated synnoergetic economy, a progressively smaller fraction of the gross national product will be allocated to the progressively smaller number of employed through their wages (the link between jobs and income will be weakening). These plans call for maintaining the welfare link as the only way to guarantee the constitutional right to a share in the production of machine systems.

The plans say nothing specific of the profit link. Some proposers (Friedman[5], for example) would presumably maintain the income-through-profit link and would foresee the day in the highly labor-saturated economy when a few had income through wages and most people had incomes either through profits or welfare, or both. Other proposers (Marxists, for example) would cut the income-through-profit link and would foresee the day in the highly labor-saturated economy when a few had income through wages and most had income through welfare according to some preestablished rules—to each according to his need.

Wider Dispersion of Industrial Ownership. A proposal that is fundamentally different from the aforementioned ones was made in Louis O. Kelso and Mortimer Adler's *The Capitalist Manifesto* and in other writings by Kelso. Recently, their proposal has been called the "Second Income Plan." Bunting's plan would maintain all three income links "forever"; the minimum income plans are designed around maintaining the income-through-welfare link "forever." The Second Income Plan would progressively eliminate the income-through-welfare link until it was gone "forever"; it would progressively reallocate the gross national product among the population as income was linked either to profit or wages, or both. Thus, the Second Income Plan would eliminate the income-through-welfare link "forever"; it would employ the income-through-jobs link when necessary; it would progressively strengthen the income-through-profit link.   The mechanism for achieving this involves the buying of stock in industrial enterprises by members of the population having a low-income level or who are displaced by automation or who are unemployable for any reason.   Each year industry raises a substantial amount of new capital through stock issues.   It is proposed that private banks give insured long-term loans to low-income members of society for the purpose of acquiring such shares in industrial enterprises, parallel to the way in which private banks give insured long-term loans to GIs for the purpose of buying homes.   The earnings or dividends from these shares would then furnish or at least supplement the income for a substantial portion of the population.   People receiving such income would be relieved from the stigma normally associated with welfare benefits or of the psychologically demoralizing consequences of featherbedding and other unproductive labor.

10.6   Concluding Remarks

Although this chapter is oriented toward the United States economy and social outlook, the ideas expressed are more or less relevant to many countries of the world.   Technologically advanced countries will soon have to face the problem of how to allocate income in a labor-deficient economy.   In many of these countries where the traditions of socialism are held in esteem, the feeling of indignity is not associated with government welfare.   Indeed, some already embrace both the idea of reasonable featherbedding and of government welfare as they break the link between income and profit.   The explicit identification of the three income links may nevertheless help to put in perspective what each technologically advanced country is already doing about income allocation.   It is believed that such an analysis may be of use to economists and sociologists of developing countries in determining fair and dignified ways of allocating income as their countries advance technologically and as they approach the time when their economy will become labor-saturated.

There have, of course, been more proposals on income allocation than have been mentioned in this chapter.   Certainly Henry George's idea of the government obtaining its revenue exclusively from taxes on the land and using the money for welfare and other public purposes deserves consideration in any complete work, as do the ideas of the technocrats, the freeholders, the various socialist plans, and of course the economic theories of Marx and of Lord Keynes.   Nevertheless, it is hoped that the interested reader will be encouraged to apply the analysis presented in this chapter to the evaluation of any proposal he decides to study.

REFERENCES

1. Bunting, John R.: *The Hidden Face of Free Enterprise,* McGraw-Hill, 1964.
2. Fein, Louis: Noology—The Science of Intelligence, *Computers and Information Sciences,* Chap. 20, Spartan Books, 1964.
3. Fein, Louis: Dear Mr. President, *Datamation,* January, 1965.
4. Fein, Louis: The Computer-related Sciences (Synnoetics) at a University in the Year 1975, *Am. Scientist,* vol. 49, no. 2, June, 1961; *Datamation,* September, 1961.
5. Friedman, Milton: *Capitalism and Freedom,* The University of Chicago Press, Chicago, 1964.
6. Heilbroner, Robert L.: Men and Machines in Perspective, *The Public Interest,* no. 1, fall, 1965.
7. Kelso, Louis O., and Mortimer J. Adler: *The New Capitalists,* Random House, 1961.
8. Kelso, Louis O., and Mortimer J. Adler: *The Capitalist Manifesto,* Random House, 1958.
9. Kelso, Louis O., and Walter A. Lawrence: The Second Income Plan, 1965 (an unpublished document).
10. Silberman, Charles E.: Is Technology Taking Over? *Fortune,* February, 1966.
11. Silberman, Charles E.: The Real News about Automation, *Fortune,* January, 1965.
12. Solow, Robert: Technology and Unemployment, *The Public Interest,* no. 1, fall, 1965.
13. Theobald, Robert: *The Challenge of Abundance,* Mentor Books, 1962.
14. Theobald, Robert: *Free Men and Free Markets,* Doubleday, 1965.
15. Employment Act of 1946. (An Act of Congress.)
16. Manpower Report of the President and a Report on Manpower Requirements, Resources, Utilization, and Training. A report by the U.S. Department of Labor, transmitted to the Congress, March, 1965.
17. *The Public Interest,* no. 1, fall, 1965. (Most articles in this issue of the magazine are relevant.)
18. Report to the Governor and the Legislature of the California Commission on Manpower, Automation, and Technology, 1964.
19. Final Report of the National Commission on Technology, Automation, and Economic Progress. (Available from Dr. Garth Mangum, executive secretary, National Commission on Technology, Automation, and Economic Progress, U.S. Department of Labor, Office of the Secretary, Washington 25, D.C.).
20. Toward Full Employment: Proposals for a Comprehensive Employment and Manpower Policy in the United States. A report by the U.S. Senate Subcommittee on Employment and Manpower, Joseph S. Clark, chairman, 1964.
21. The Triple Revolution: An open letter to President Johnson on March 22, 1964. (Available at the Center for the Study of Democratic Institutions, P.O. Box 4068, Santa Barbara, Calif.)

Appendix

Glen J. Culler

University of California
Santa Barbara, California

A.1 Introductory Remarks

This appendix constitutes a reproduction in its entirety of the user's manual designed to accompany an on-line computer system in use at the University of California, Santa Barbara, as well as at a number of other installations. The reason for its inclusion in this text is twofold: Chap. VI, "Solving Mathematical Problems," by Fried, describes in considerable detail an application of the Culler on-line system. Some of the material presented in this appendix is required for a complete understanding of that chapter. In addition it is hoped that this manual can serve as a model or guide to others preparing operating instructions for specific on-line systems. Portions of this chapter were compiled by Prof. Anthony G. Oettinger of Harvard University, while others were drawn from Culler and Fried[1] and from Farrington and Pope.[2]

A.2 Orientation of the System

The drive to produce more efficient systems which earlier led to the closed shop and batch processing approaches has more recently led to on-line computation and time-sharing. These more recent efforts attempt to combine some of the valu-

303

able assets of earlier modes of operation to create systems more readily related to user needs both in terms of problem language and computer response. Our primary interest is in human control of a computer at a rather sophisticated mathematical language level. In this user's manual we will suppress all details related to hardware and as much detail related to software as is consistent with our desire to make this manual self-contained.

One can characterize the system described here as a problem-oriented language which provides an on-line capability in the area of classical mathematical analysis. It is possible to do a variety of algebraic things with this system, but the basic constructs are those of analysis rather than algebra. There are many problems which are, so to speak, natural for this type of system, but there are also many which are utterly inappropriate and which violate the premises under which the system was designed.

To aid a prospective user in determining the appropriateness of his problem for this on-line system, we suggest the following check list:

1. Is your problem primarily analytic in nature?
2. Is your problem of enough direct interest to you to make you want to solve it yourself?
3. Is your problem difficult to do by conventional means?
4. Do you need to work through the problem to see how it goes?
5. Is the visual inspection of results of subproblems of benefit to you?

If most of your answers turn out to be "no," we recommend that you use some approach other than that presented here. You, as user of the system, must really provide the mode of problem solution, and problem solving—even with the best advantages—is always difficult enough to merit full consideration of the approach.

Taken altogether, the mathematical capabilities represented by the software lying behind this system are quite comprehensive; consequently, the user should be aware that to use the system, he need not understand everything that can be done with the system. A good operating philosophy is to pay detailed attention only to that part of the system required for the solution of your problem.

The description of the system in Sec. A.8 is arranged in sections which correspond to the levels of operations which are available in the basic system. Section A.6 on Operations for Program Control needs to be read and understood by all users.

When he leaves the on-line computer (OLC), the user may save the console programs and data which he has created. There are four files available for his use for this purpose. He may use two of the files for storing different versions of his console programs, and the other two for storing different versions of his data. The computer will store all the console programs and data on magnetic tape in a form suitably coded for loading back into the computer. When the user returns for another OLC session, he loads the desired files back into the computer.

A.3   User Control and Computer Feedback

Control of the computer is provided by means of the input keyboard as shown in Fig. A.1. This keyboard consists of two halves: the upper half permits access

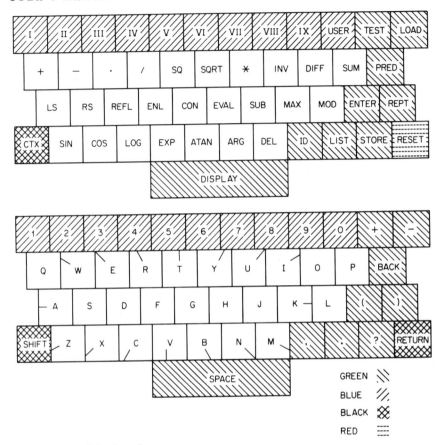

Fig. A.1 OLC keyboard.

to operators and the lower half to operands.   Thinking of each of these halves as separate keyboards we designate the types of keys as alphabetic, numeric, and punctuation.   The labels on the upper keyboard do not reflect this nature, but the color coding on the keys clarifies the correspondence.

The *white keys* are the alphabetic keys; they provide locations for storage. Programs and operations are stored under the white keys of the upper keyboard, and data may be stored under the white keys of the lower keyboard whether single numbers, one-dimensional or two-dimensional lists of numbers.

The *blue keys*, or numeric keys, provide a means for changing the reference to things stored under the white keys.   That is to say, on the operator keyboard the roman numerals I, II, . . . , IX provide nine different sets of operations that can be accessed by depressing white keys, and the numbers 1, . . . , 9 permit access to as many as nine different sets of data objects that can be stored under the white keys of the lower keyboard.

The *green keys*, as well as the *black* and the *red*, provide control of a nonmathematical and nondata type. Those of the upper keyboard provide what may be considered program control and those of the lower keyboard typewriter control.

The response of the computer to you as a user is provided by means of a display scope associated with each user station. This display scope is capable of presenting alphanumeric display as well as curvilinear display, and part of the system is designed to permit you rather easy means of using this scope for observing what the computer is doing with your problem.

A.4 Interrelationship of Levels

The 48 keys physically present on the operator keyboard are not sufficient to accommodate the necessary repertoire of basic subroutines, let alone the console programs constructed by a user. The totality of operators in the OLC are therefore grouped into "levels," those of a given mathematical or logical character being kept on one level. All of the basic subroutines are located on Levels I through IX. The level desired at any time is selected by pushing one of the keys, labeled I, II, . . . , IX, in the top row of the operator keyboard. Once a level is chosen, all subsequent key pushes are interpreted by the computer as belonging to that level (which we will term the "current level") until a different level changing key is pushed by the user. These nine levels comprise what is called the *basic system*.

An additional four levels, all of whose keys are initially null operators, are provided to accommodate the console programs created by a user. Access to these is provided by first pushing the USER key, followed by one of the keys I through IV: one may think of these as being Levels I through IV of the *user system*. After creating a console program and pushing STORE, you must go to one of the user levels, since console programs may not be stored in the basic system.

A change in level alters the meaning of all keys on the operator keyboard, save for a few, like LIST, which are common to all levels. The level changes are thus somewhat analogous to the shift operation on a normal typewriter, except that we have 13 different levels, rather than just 2. Thus, a single physical key may initiate any one of 13 different subroutines depending on the identity of the current level.

As you work with the OLC, you will build up, in your user system, a computing capability tailored to your own problems, needs, and interests, and expressed in a problem-oriented language created by you in the process of console programming. The user system thus created is a private one; whenever you leave the OLC, you may save your part of the computer—the data lists you have stored and the console programs you have created—on magnetic tape. When you return, you may load this data back into your console's portion of the computer, restoring it to the same state as when you left. In the interim, other people will use this console, or other ones, to create their own user systems, but these need have no intersection with yours.

A.5 Data Structures

Vectors and Arrays. The nature of the "data" referred to above is left to the choice of the user. In particular, you may wish them to be just single numbers, in which case the OLC will, essentially, function as a fancy hand computer and plotter, albeit with a much larger repertoire of operations than the usual desk variety. It is generally advantageous, however, to choose as operands not single numbers but rather a set, or list, of numbers, for in almost all mathematical and scientific applications, and in much of data processing as well, we wish a given operation to be carried out not on a single number but on a whole set. In mathematical terms, such a list of numbers is called a "vector," and that is the term we shall generally adopt here. It is equally correct, and, in some applications very useful, to think of the numbers as constituting the values of the dependent variable of a real "function," so we shall regard the two terms as synonymous. A *real vector with* n *components* is a list of n real numbers. A *complex vector with* n *components* is a list of n complex numbers, or equivalently, a two-column list, with n entries in each column.

You may choose the number of components of the vector to be anything from $n = 1$ to $n = 124$. With $n = 124$, you get a computer representation of a function which is satisfactory for a large fraction of problems. However, in some cases, one would like to deal with larger blocks of data. For this reason, the OLC provides for the use of "arrays." An array is just a collection of m vectors where m, like n, is chosen by you, subject only to the limitations imposed by the size of the portion of mass memory allocated to one console.

One benefit of organization of data into such blocks is that, from a practical point of view, it allows you to initiate a good deal of computing with a very small effort, in terms of the number of keys pushed. Each vector is "stored under" or "named by" one of the 26 letters of the alphabet on the operand keyboard. Thus, if vectors have previously been stored under keys A and B, then the 6 key pushes

$$\text{LOAD } A + B \text{ STORE } C$$

cause the following things to happen. The vectors stored under A and B are added, componentwise, and the resulting vector is stored under key C. A and B themselves remain unchanged.

In using the OLC you have the freedom to partition your share of the mass memory in any convenient fashion. If you wish to have storage space for m vectors, each with n components, you simply define an array with the dimensions m by n. Just as with the individual vectors, we use the letters A through Z to label the arrays. The CONTEXT key on the operator keyboard is used in defining arrays (see CTX operation in Sec. A.8, Level IX). If m is less than or equal to 26, then the first m letters of the alphabet will be the operand keys under which vectors can be stored. If m is greater than 26, then it is necessary to introduce the concept of "data banks." Thus, if m is 54, for example, the array will allow storage of vectors under keys A through Z on banks 1 and 2, and will allow storage under keys A and B on bank 3. Bank changes are specified to the computer by pushing the SHIFT key on the operand keyboard, followed by the appropriate numeric key, 1 through 9. Once a bank has been indicated it remains the "current" bank until some other bank is selected. After you have pushed SHIFT 1, the computer will interpret all operand keys thereafter as being references to vectors stored on bank 1.

New users will usually find it sufficient to work with a single array. In order to accommodate both real and complex vectors of any size up to the maximum of 124, you could simply define a complex array of dimensions 26 by 124. This would provide room for one bank of complex vectors which will suffice for simple problems. As you acquire more familiarity with the system, you can take advantage of the array capabilities to make more efficient use of the storage space, e.g., by defining one real array and one complex one, since it is wasteful to use complex arrays for storing real vectors.

Note especially that you have not only the freedom to define one or more arrays, but you have an *obligation* to do so, for until you have defined at least one array the computer will ignore any instructions you may give it to store a vector. Thus, when you first use the OLC, begin by defining and making "current" at least one real or complex array.

Scaling Considerations. The OLC uses a floating vector organization, whereby a vector with n components is actually represented in the machine as n numbers (the "mantissas"), all of magnitude less than 1, together with a single binary scale. Thus, if a is a vector of mantissas representing the vector A and $S[A]$ is the binary scale, then the actual components of A are the numbers

$$A = a \times 2^{S[A]}$$

All of the operations on vectors deal with the scales in an appropriate manner. However, when a curve is displayed on the scope, it is really the mantissas which are used to form the display points, and one can get information about the absolute magnitudes of the vector only by displaying also the numeric value of the binary scale (by using the combination DISPLAY O on Level II or III). If a curve has scale S, then the limits of the display area on the scope are $\pm 2^S$. Note that if two curves are displayed simultaneously, correct conclusions concerning intersections, etc., can be deduced only if both have the same scale. If this is not already the case, it can be accomplished using ENLARGE or CONTRACT.

All operations of Level II leave the result in the Y register in "standard" form, meaning that at least one of the mantissas lies between $\frac{1}{2}$ and 1, unless the vector is identically zero. Operations of Level III result in a "standard" form for the X or the Y register, or both; in addition, the scales of the two registers are made equal.

A.6 Operations for Program Control

LIST. The OLC provides a procedure for constructing new programs from those operations already defined in the system. A program consists simply of a list of operations to be performed. The LIST operator allows the construction, and subsequent storage, of a list of key pushes.

The kind of operation involved in pushing keys which the computer interprets and executes immediately may be denoted as the "manual" mode. When construction of a "console program" is desired, you push LIST and then push any sequence of keys on either keyboard just as though you were operating the computer in the manual mode. However, instead of responding to these key pushes in the usual way, i.e., by initiating the corresponding subroutines, the computer simply records, and also displays on the display scope, a list of the keys you push. When you push LIST a second time, it terminates the list and returns to the manual mode. If you now wish to store the program you have just created, you push STORE followed by some user level (e.g., USER II) followed by some white key of the *operator* keyboard. If, at any later time, you return to this user level and push that key of the operator keyboard under which the program was stored, the computer will execute the list of operations, just as though you were pushing the component keys manually.

This "console program" now becomes a part of the OLC so far as your use is concerned, and can be initiated with a key push in exactly the same way as any of the basic subroutines originally supplied. Note particularly that this console program can *itself* constitute one of the components of a subsequent console program; i.e., after pushing LIST you may push any key, including those which initiate other console programs. Given this pyramiding feature, it is possible to construct programs of virtually unlimited complexity.

You may cause the computer to display, on the scope, the list of key pushes which comprise any console program by pushing DISPLAY (on the appropriate user level) followed by the button under which the program is stored. This operation also "opens up" the program for addition of more operators and operands or for deletion of the ones already there (via the BACK key, see below). If no change is desired, push LIST to close the program.

The backspace key, BACK, can be used while creating a console program to correct errors by canceling keys previously pushed. No visual indication of the BACKSPACE action is given on the display scope: thus the user must count the number of backspaces carefully. All button pushes backspaced over are deleted from the console program. Each backspace removes one key from the list regardless of the number of characters displayed as the name of the key. When this program is stored and displayed subsequently (as described above), the buttons backspaced over will not appear in the program.

A comment concerning a console program P can be created by creating a console program in which Level IX DISPLAY is used. This "comment console program" can then be stored under the two button sequence CTX P on the user level on which P is stored. To recall the comment about P (i.e., to execute the "comment console program") simply go to the appropriate user level and push CTX P.

Normally, when a previously defined console program is used in the definition of a new console program, the symbol on the key under which the old program is stored is displayed on the display scope in the process of creating the new program. The user can change this symbol to any combination of special and alphanumeric characters he desires. We call the process involved "renaming the console program." This renaming is done by pushing LIST, then pushing a sequence of characters on the operand keyboard which comprise the new name, and finally pushing a closing LIST. The name is stored for console program P by pushing STORE USER (Level number) DISPLAY P. The characters in the name can be any of the alphanumeric characters on the operand keyboard, the SPACE, and any special characters created on Level IX. (Because names occur one after another when a program is displayed, it is usually well to begin and end a name with SPACE.)

DISPLAY. DISPLAY generates either a numerical display or a graphical display on the display scope depending on the current level and on the argument following it. For a detailed description of the effect of DISPLAY, see its definition on each level in Sec. A.8.

The scales of the X and Y registers are ignored by DISPLAY on Level II. On Level III, DISPLAY adjusts the X and Y registers so that their scales are equal.

When on Level II or III a display of a graph is desired, two modes of display are available. The first is *curvilinear* display which causes a straight line segment to be displayed between succeeding points, giving the effect of a continuous curve. This mode of display is entered by simply pushing DISPLAY and then the name of the vector whose display is desired. The effect of DISPLAY is "continuing" in the sense that all vectors specified after a DISPLAY button push will be displayed. The effect of DISPLAY is stopped by pushing any operator key.

The second mode of display is a *point* display, that is, no connecting line will be drawn from point to point when the display is generated. This mode is entered by pushing DISPLAY, then pushing the "period" key on the operand keyboard and then pushing the name of the vector whose display is desired. The effect of DISPLAY . is also continuing in that all vector names pushed after DISPLAY . until an operator button is pushed will appear on the display scope in point mode. The point mode allows the user to choose between two sizes of "dots" to be displayed; the smaller is specified as described above, i.e., by pushing the period key once between pushing DISPLAY and pushing the name of the vector. The larger dot is specified similarly except that the period key is pushed *twice* between DISPLAY and the vector name. Each display mode continues in its effect until some operator key is pushed.

REPEAT. REPEAT allows you to repeat any operation, in the basic or user system, any number of times. You simply call in the correct level, then push REPEAT, followed by the operator and the number of times it is to be repeated in one of two forms:

1. A number typed on the numeric keys (followed by RETURN to indicate that the number has ended), or
2. The name of a Level I storage position where the number of repetitions is stored

On Level IX, SPACE, RETURN, or any character may be repeated as though the SPACE, RETURN, or character were an operator as described above.

CONTEXT. On Levels I through VIII, if CTX is followed by an alphabetic key, say A, then the data array with name A is defined as the current array. If the structure of A has not been defined, the level is automatically changed to Level IX and the user is allowed to define the array requested. After defining an array on Level IX, the user still must designate the array as "current" by using CONTEXT on one of Levels I through VIII (see Sec. A.8, Level IX).

Use of CTX on user levels is described above under LIST.

RESET.   RESET is used to stop a console program.   When the computer comes to the next operation of the program it is running, it will be interrupted and will return to the manual mode.

Pushing RESET causes the current level of the OLC to become undefined. Consequently, the user must return to a desired level by pressing the appropriate level key.

When in the RESET state, pushing ID will cause the display scope to be erased. Thus, if you suspect that the computer may be "off the air," the simplest test is to see whether pushing RESET ID will erase the scope.

TEST.   TEST allows you to make a console program branch according to the sign of the first component, Y_1, of the Y register.   It is only for use in a console program and operates as follows.   If Y_1 is positive or zero, then the next instruction following TEST in the console program is carried out, in normal fashion. If Y_1 is negative, then the instruction immediately following TEST is ignored. Although TEST can be used anywhere in a console program, it is most conveniently used at the end in order to make a conditional loop of some kind.   For example, you might make TEST a part of a program, P, and have P conclude with the operators TEST P.   If the result of P is such as to leave Y_1 nonnegative, then P will be repeated.   Otherwise, it will come to an end.   Of course, if P is such that Y_1 never becomes negative, P will repeat itself indefinitely, but can be stopped with RESET.

If TEST k, where k is an integer typed on the numeric keys, occurs in a console program, then the next k key pushes will be skipped if Y_1 is negative.

ENTER.   ENTER is used only in a console program.   A console program containing ENTER will interrupt itself when it comes to ENTER and the computer will return to manual mode, allowing you to enter data or take any other action. Upon completion of the manual operations, you may push ENTER and the console program will resume where it left off, providing your manual operations have not included the command to execute some other console program.

ERASE.   The button pushes which cause the display scope to be erased vary from level to level.   The following list indicates which button pushes erase the scope on each presently defined level:

Level I: DISPLAY SPACE
Level II: DISPLAY SPACE
Level III: DISPLAY SPACE
Level IX: DISPLAY ID
User Levels: Same command as on the most recently used basic level.

Since the OLC uses a storage scope, no partial erase of graphic information is possible.

A.7   Basic Operator Names and Abbreviations

Add	+	List	LIST
Arctangent	ATAN	Load	LOAD
Argument	ARG	Logarithm	LOG

Conjugate	* or STAR	Maximum	MAX
Context	CTX	Modulus	MOD or NORM
Contract	CON	Multiply	
Cosine	COS	Predicate	PRED
Display	DISPLAY	Reflect	REFL
Divide	/	Repeat	REPT
Enlarge	ENL	Reset	RESET
Enter	ENTER	Right shift	RS
Evaluate	EVAL	Sine	SIN
Exponential	EXP	Square	SQ
Forward difference	DIFF	Square root	SQRT
Identity	ID	Store	STORE
Inverse	INV	Subtract	−
Kroenecker-Dirac	DEL	Substitute	SUB
Delta		Sum	SUM
Left shift	LS	Test	TEST

A.8   Description of Operators

Floating-point Arithmetic—Level I

General Description

On this level the data objects consist of single numbers represented with seven decimal digits and a decimal scale. You have storage for 26 such numbers under the 26 letters of the alphabet on the operand keyboard. To enter a number into the system press LOAD and type in the desired number using the operand numeric keys. The computer makes the following assumptions:

1. If no sign is used, the number is positive.

2. If no decimal point is used, the number is an integer.

3. If any key other than +, −, 0, 1, . . . , 9 is pressed, then you are through typing the number.

4. If a sequence of sign symbols occurs, then the last one is correct. If a sign symbol occurs after a digit, then the following integer moves the decimal point right or left depending on whether the sign was + or − respectively.

5. If more than seven digits are used, then all but the first seven are ignored. If less than seven are used the number is exactly represented.

Now suppose we press LOAD and type in a number. That number is held in temporary storage much in the same way the number 12 is held in temporary storage during the mental arithmetic operation $3 \times 4 + 7 = 19$. It is possible to combine a number in temporary storage with any of the other numbers previously stored under the alphabetic keys by using any of the elementary operations on Level I. It is also possible to save the number which is in temporary storage by pressing STORE and then the alphabetic key that you wish to store it under.

It is frequently useful to be able to read a number which has been stored under a particular alphabetic key. To do this merely press DISPLAY followed by the appropriate alphabetic key.

Example

On the operator keyboard press I, then press LOAD. Now type 30.7 and press STORE A DISPLAY A LOAD 4.72 + 1 STORE B DISPLAY B LOAD $A + B$ STORE C DISPLAY C. Your answer should be 36.42. Notice that we did not type L-O-A-D but rather depressed the button with the symbol LOAD on it. (The numbers 30.7 and 5.72 resulting from DISPLAY A and DISPLAY B will also appear on the scope.)

In the following definitions let a represent an arbitrary alphabetic operand and k represent a sequence of numeric keys interpreted as a number in the sense described above. Let t stand for temporary storage.

Operator Definitions for Level I

Operators Requiring an Operand

$+, -, ., /$	If followed by a or k, these compute the indicated combination with the number in t and leave the answer there.
LOAD	If followed by a or k, then the resulting number is placed in t.
STORE	If followed by a, then t is placed in the indicated permanent storage position. If followed by k, it is ignored.
DISPLAY	If followed by a, the numeric value of the number stored in a is displayed on the display scope.
	If followed by RETURN, the numeric value of t is displayed.
	If followed by SPACE, the scope is erased.
EVAL	If followed by a or k, the ath or kth component of the Y register (see Sec. A.8, Level II) is placed in t. If a or k is negative or zero, the binary scale of Y is placed in t. If a or k is nonintegral, the integral part of a or k is used.
SUB	If followed by a or k, t is placed into the ath or kth position of the Y register (see Sec. A.8, Level II) with the same conventions as in EVAL above. a and k are bounded by the currently defined vector length.

Direct-action Operators

SQ	Squares the number in t.
SQRT	Takes the square root of the number in t.
*	Negates the number in t.
INV	Takes the reciprocal of the number in t.
MOD	Takes the absolute value of the number in t.
SIN, COS, LOG, EXP, ATAN	Performs the indicated operation on the number in t.
ARG	If the number in t is positive, it is replaced by zero. If it is negative, it is replaced by 3.141593 (i.e., pi).

DEL   If the number in t is not zero, it is replaced by zero.   If it is zero,
            it is replaced by 1.

Real Function Operations and Curvilinear Display—Level II

General Description

The data objects used on Level II can be thought of as vectors or as lists of
real numbers.   We denote such vectors in a typical vector-coordinate manner
such as

$$Y = (Y_1, Y_2, \ldots, Y_n)$$

The number n of coordinates allowable in our present system is restricted to
be less than or equal to 124; the number m of such vectors allowable in an array
is likewise restricted to be less than or equal to 124.   The number of arrays is
restricted not only by the total amount of storage used, but, from the point of
view of names, is restricted to arrays A through Z.   These arrays may in turn
be either real or complex and for a description of how they are defined and
what is implied concerning subscripts and indices and component vectors, refer
to Sec. A.5 on Data Structures.   Throughout our description of Level II, we
will presume that the arrays needed have previously been defined and are available for our use.   To understand how to change reference from one array to
another, refer to CONTEXT in Sec. A.6 on Operations for Program Control.

The mathematical capability represented by Level II is a form of discrete
calculus, but for the sake of convenience one can frequently ignore the discrete-
ness and think of data vectors as values of functions defined on some real interval.
The selection of operations has been made in such a way to make a happy balance
between ease of formula construction in mathematical expressions and simplicity
of operator definition.   As a means of conveniently picturing what takes place
during application of these operations, we like to think of temporary storage as
consisting of two list registers, an X register and a Y register.   Now we also
must treat combinations of functions and for this purpose it is convenient to
think of auxiliary function registers U and V.   The direct-action operators are
defined on the Y register.   If the array presently referenced happens to be complex, then the X register will contain the X coordinates of the last complex
vector that has been loaded either by LOAD or DISPLAY.   The X coordinates
are left unchanged by most of the operations on this level, the exceptions being
SUB and EVAL, and for complex arrays LOAD.

The alphabetic keys on the operand keyboard provide a means for referencing
the set of functions presently available to the user.   Each set $A, B, \ldots, Z$ is
one bank of some data array, and depressing the SHIFT key followed by a number will change banks within this data array and thereby make some other 26
functions available.

In the following definitions let a represent an arbitrary alphabetic operand
and k represent a sequence of numeric keys interpreted as a number, as discussed in Sec. A.8, Level I.

Operator Definitions for Level II

Operators Requiring an Operand

LOAD   If followed by a, then the function under a is placed in Y (or in the
            case of a complex array in X and Y). If followed by k, then a con-
            stant function each of whose coordinate values is the number k is
            placed in the Y register.

STORE   If followed by a, then the function in the Y register is stored under a
            for real arrays; for complex arrays the arc in the X and Y registers
            is stored under a. If followed by k, it is ignored.

DISPLAY   If followed by RETURN, a curvilinear display of the function in
            the X and Y registers is shown on the display scope. Each compo-
            nent of Y is taken to be the ordinate with corresponding abscissa
            the corresponding component of X.

            If followed by a, then LOAD a is automatically performed and a
            curvilinear display of the function now in the X and Y registers is
            shown on the display scope. When displaying a function from a
            real array, care must be taken that the X register has the desired
            correspondence with the function.

            If followed by a period (on the operand keyboard) and then
            RETURN or a, a "small dot" display is generated instead of a
            curvilinear display.

            If followed by two periods and then RETURN or a, a "large dot"
            display is generated instead of a curvilinear display.

            If followed by k (followed by RETURN to signify that typing
            of k is finished), then the numerical value of the kth component of
            the Y register is displayed. If k is zero, then the binary scale of the
            Y register is displayed. If RETURN is pushed again, then the
            next component of the Y register is displayed. RETURN may be
            repeated as many times as desired.

            If followed by SPACE, the scope is erased.

$+, -, ., /$ If followed by a, the function stored under a is placed in V (or for
            complex arrays in the pair UV) and combined with Y as indicated
            by the operation. The resulting function is left in Y. If the
            denominator in a division has some of its coordinate values zero,
            then these same coordinate values will be zero after the division
            has been completed.

            If followed by k, then a constant function whose values are k
            is loaded into V and the indicated combination with the function in
            the Y register is formed and left in the Y register.

SUB   If followed by a then the Y coordinates of a are placed in the X
            register. If followed by k then the constant function determined
            by k is placed in the X register.

EVAL   If followed by a, then the function under a is placed in V (or for a
            complex array in UV). For each value $V(J)$ in V, the least upper
            bound and the greatest lower bound of the X register is obtained

relative to $V(J)$ and a linearly interpolated value is then computed from the function in the Y register.

$$Y(J) = \frac{(Y(K+1) - Y(K))(V(J) - X(K))}{X(K+1) - X(K)} + Y(K)$$

where K is such that $X(K) \leq V(J) \leq X(K+1)$. If the array is complex, then the U coordinates replace the X coordinates; if the array is real, the X coordinates are left unchanged.

If followed by k, then the interpolated value corresponding to k is placed in the Y register.

Direct-action Operators

SQ	Squares the function in the Y register.
SQRT	Takes the square root of the function in the Y register giving a zero result whenever the square root is undefined.
*	Negates the function in the Y register.
INV	Divides 1 by the function in the Y register.
DIFF	Forms the forward difference of the function values in the Y register and supplies the right-hand value by a second order extrapolation.
SUM	Is a running summation of the values in the Y register, i.e., the corresponding subtotal is stored in each Y coordinate.
LS	Places the $(j+1)$st coordinate of the Y register into the jth position, and places the first coordinate in the last coordinate position. If followed by $k > 0$, it performs this operation k times.
RS	Places the jth coordinate of the Y register into the $(j+1)$st coordinate position and the last coordinate in the first coordinate position. If followed by $k > 0$, it performs this operation k times.
REFL	Interchanges the order of the coordinates in the Y register.
ENL	Doubles the values of each Y coordinate and diminishes the binary scale by one. Can be used to change the appearance of a displayed function. If followed by $k > 0$, it performs this operation k times.
CON	Halves the value of each Y coordinate and adds one to the binary scale. Can be used to change the appearance of a displayed function. If followed by $k > 0$, it performs this operation k times.
MAX	Makes a constant function equal to the maximum value in the Y register.
MOD	Takes the absolute value of the function in the Y register.
SIN, COS, LOG, EXP, ATAN	Performs the indicated operation on the Y register leaving a zero whenever the operation is ill defined.
ARG	Replaces negative function values by 3.141593 (i.e., pi) and positive function values by zero.

DEL If the function in the Y register has a zero or if it can be interpolated to have such a zero, then the nearest coordinate value is replaced by one and all others are replaced by zero.

ID The Y register is loaded with a representation of the interval $[-1, 1]$ consisting of N equally spaced points.

Operations on Complex Arcs—Level III

General Description

There are two strong reasons for having easily available operations on complex arcs. One of these is the mathematical need for dealing with complex functions which is so necessary to go very far with classical mathematical analysis. The other, which is trivial beside this in importance but of considerable value to the person solving problems, is that operations on complex arcs provide the easiest means of mathematically specifying how to control display information. Putting these two requirements together, we are led to a simple generalization of Level II, which is a proper base for applications involving analytic functions and conformal mappings and also provides an easy means for geometric motions. The data objects on which Level III operations are defined consist of vectors whose coordinates are complex numbers. If these complex numbers are visualized as points in the complex plane which are joined by line segments, then our data objects are representation of polygonal arcs. It is equally possible to think of these data objects as consisting of two real vectors, each of which would be appropriate for use on Level II; that is, one of these providing the real part and one the imaginary part of the so-called complex arcs.

In order to fix our discussion, let us emphasize this relationship between Levels II and III. Suppose that a complex array has been defined and is available for our use (refer to Sec. A.5 on Data Structures). Let Z be a column of that array, then

$$Z = (Z_1, Z_2, \ldots, Z_n)$$
$$Z = (X_1 + iY_1, X_2 + iY_2, \ldots, X_n + iY_n)$$
$$Z = (X_1, X_2, \ldots, X_n) + i(Y_1, Y_2, \ldots, Y_n)$$
$$Z = X + iY$$

A comparison of the first and last of these expressions illustrates the different views described above. With the last of these in mind, we think of a complex arc as having its real part in the X register and its imaginary part in the Y register. Whereas the Level II operations primarily transform the information in the Y register, the Level III operations transform the data in both X and Y. U and V are auxiliary registers which provide temporary data storage for operations requiring an operand.

Most of the operations on Level III can be defined as extensions of the Level II operations based entirely on the relationship between the arithmetic of real numbers and the arithmetic of complex numbers; however, since we must deal with analytic functions defined on complex arcs, the mathematical definitions of such functions must be carefully provided in a manner consistent with the usual applications of the level. This means we must provide for branch cuts, multiplicities, etc. in such a way as to minimize the work that must be done by the user in adapting his problem to the operations we have selected. Our approach is based on the assumption that the data objects really are discrete samples of continuous arcs in the plane and therefore the image of such an arc under transformation by elementary functions should itself be continuous. To do this in a consistent fashion, we first define the argument function, ARG, by specifying that the first point of the function shall have an argument in the interval (0, 2pi), and that the argument of each subsequent point is determined by summing the changes in argument as one passes along the points of the curve. This choice makes it meaningful to use the ARG operation as a means for computing the winding number of the curve about the origin. The functions LOG, ATAN, and SQRT are then defined in terms of this argument function and these are the only ones on Level III that have branches or multiplicities.

In order to make an appropriate definition of EVALUATE, we need to provide facilities to define SUBSTITUTE on the complex level in such a way as to extend the relationship between SUB and EVAL on Level II. To do this we introduce a new register called the "Zeta" register which can hold a complex arc. SUBSTITUTE will then store data in the Zeta register analogous to Level II SUB storing data in the X register. With Z as the combination of the X and Y registers, we can then have a direct correspondence between Zeta and Z representing $Z = f(\text{Zeta})$ analogous to $Y = f(X)$ for the real function level.

It is possible to perform significant real operations on the Y coordinates of even a complex array on Level II. On Level III we consider a real array just to be the real part of a complex array, the imaginary part of which is zero. Consequently, for the one-place predicates (except for LOAD and SUB) operating with CTX set to a real array, we begin by filling the V register with zeros. In the usual case, then, with CTX set to a complex array, the incoming data is placed in U and V. In both instances the results of the operation are left in the X and Y registers.

In the following definitions let a represent an arbitrary alphabetic operand and k represent a sequence of numeric keys followed by a comma, and this followed by a sequence of numeric keys. That is, we enter a complex constant $k_1 + ik_2$ by typing k_1, k_2.

Operator Definitions for Level III

Operators Requiring an Operand

LOAD   If followed by a, then for a complex array the arc under a is placed in the X and Y registers (or for a real array, the real vector under a is placed in the Y register). If LOAD is followed by a constant k_1, then k_1 is placed in the X register; if k_1 is followed by a comma and a constant k_2, then k_2 is placed in the Y register. Thus the sequence for loading a complex constant $k_1 + k_2$ into Z is LOAD k_1, k_2.

STORE   If followed by a, then for a complex array, the arc lying in the X and Y registers is stored under a (or for a real array the vector lying in the Y register is stored under a). If followed by k, it is ignored.

DISPLAY   If followed by RETURN, then the X and Y registers are transformed so that they have the same scale and a curvilinear display of the arc in the X and Y registers is shown on the display scope.

    If followed by a, then LOAD a is automatically performed, the X and Y registers are transformed as above, and a curvilinear display of the function now in the X and Y registers is shown on the display scope.

    If followed by a period (on the operand keyboard) and then RETURN or a, a "small dot" display is generated instead of a curvilinear display.

    If followed by two periods and then RETURN or a, a "large dot" display is generated instead of a curvilinear display.

    If followed by k (followed by RETURN to signify that typing of k is finished), then the numerical values of the kth X and Y coordinates are shown on the display scope in decimal form. If k is zero, then the binary scale will be displayed. If RETURN is pushed again, then the next component of X and Y will be displayed, RETURN may be repeated as many times as desired.

    If followed by SPACE, the scope is erased.

$+, -, ., /$ If followed by a, then the arc stored under a is placed in U and V for complex arrays (or for real arrays the vector stored under a is stored in U and zero is placed in V). The indicated combination is taken with the arc in the X and Y registers; the result being left in the X and Y registers. If followed by k_1 then U and V are filled with constants (analogous to LOAD above) and the combinations with X and Y are taken as above.

SUB   If followed by a with CTX set to a complex array, then the arc under a is placed in a correspondent storage register, Zeta. We denote a typical correspondence by

$$Z = f(\text{Zeta})$$

regarding the Z register as the pair of X and Y registers.

    If followed by a with CTX set to a real array, then the vector under a is placed in the X register. If followed by k then the constant k is placed in the Zeta register.

EVAL   (1) If followed by a and CTX is set to a complex array, then an interpolated image of Zeta is placed in Z and the arc under a is placed in Zeta. This interpolation is obtained from a local extension of the mapping correspondence

$$Z = f(\text{Zeta})$$

to a region containing the arc Zeta.

    (2) If followed by a and CTX is set to a real array, then Zeta is used in place of the X and Y registers for a Level II EVAL. The resulting pair is then treated as an incoming a and (1) is carried out.

    (3) If followed by k, then after k is formed, either (1) or (2) is carried out according to whether k is real or complex.

Direct-action Operators

SQ	Squares the complex arc in the Z register.
SQRT	Takes the square root of the complex arc in the Z register such that the ARG of the answer is one-half the ARG of the original function.
*	Takes the conjugate of the complex arc in the Z register.
INV	Computes the complex reciprocal of the complex arc in the Z register.
DIFF	Forms the forward difference of the complex points in the Z register and supplies the right-hand end point by a second order extrapolation.
SUM	Computes the running sum of the complex values in the Z register, i.e., the corresponding subtotal of the X and Y coordinates is stored in each X and Y coordinate position.
LS	Places the $(j + 1)$st coordinate of the Z register into the jth coordinate position, and places the first coordinate in the last coordinate position. If followed by $k > 0$, it performs this operation k times.
RS	Places the jth coordinate of the Z register in the $(j + 1)$st coordinate position and the last coordinate in the first coordinate position. If followed by $k > 0$, it performs this operation k times.
REFL	Exchanges the data in the X and Y registers which is equivalent to reflecting the Z register about the 45-degree line.
ENL	Doubles the value of each Z coordinate and diminishes the binary scale by one. Can be used to change the appearance of a displayed arc. If followed by $k > 0$, it performs this operation k times.
CON	Halves the value of each Z coordinate and adds one to the binary scale. Can be used to change the appearance of a displayed arc. If followed by $k > 0$, it performs the operation k times.
MAX	Makes a complex constant equal to the maximum value of the X register for the real part and maximum value of the Y register for the imaginary part.
MOD	Takes the modulus of each of the points of the complex arc and stores these in the X register while placing zeros in the Y register; thus MOD of a complex arc is real.
SIN, COS, LOG, EXP, ATAN	Performs the indicated operations on the Z register and, when required, uses ARG as a suboperation to make the complex operation well defined.
ARG	Computes the argument of the first point in the Z register in the half-open interval $(0, 2pi)$, and computes the argument of the remaining points by summing the difference in arguments for adjacent points. The values are stored in the X register and zeros are placed in the Y register; thus ARG of a complex arc is real.

DEL   Consists of the product of the real DEL operation applied to the X register and to the Y register. Thus, if the complex arc passes through a small rectangle about the origin, then the nearest point will have the value 1 and other points outside this small rectangle will have the values zero.

ID   Loads both the X and Y registers with a representation of the interval $(-1, 1)$ consisting of N equally spaced points.

Miscellaneous—Level VIII

General Description

This level consists of a potpourri of operators.

Operator Definitions for Level VIII

SQRT Sorts the numbers in the Y register and leaves them in the Y register in ascending order.

LOG Replaces each component of the Y register with a random number (rectangularly distributed between 0 and 1) generated using a multiplicative congruential process applied to each component.

Typing and Definition

General Description

This level serves two basically different functions:

1. It allows you to compose, on the display scope, alphanumeric messages of any kind. Pushing DISPLAY converts the operand keyboard into an ordinary typewriter, save that the messages appear on the display scope and that the typewriter has four banks any of which may be selected by pushing SHIFT and then the number of the bank (the keyboard is initially set to bank 1). Bank 1 contains the standard character set. Banks 2–4 are available for the definition of special symbols by the user (see MOD in the Operator Definitions section). The carriage-return button, RETURN, the backspace button, BACK, and the SPACE bar perform as on an ordinary typewriter. When the right-hand margin is reached by typing a sequence of symbols and spaces, a carriage return is automatically executed so that the next symbol typed appears at the left-hand margin on the row.

When Level IX DISPLAY is first initiated, typing starts in the upper left-hand corner of the display scope. When Level IX DISPLAY is pushed subsequently, typing is resumed at the place where it left off. Typing can be restarted in the upper left-hand corner by pushing the RS key. The "carriage" can be moved up or down with CON and ENL, respectively.

2. The definition of a data array may be initiated by pushing CTX and then one of the alphabetic keys on the operand keyboard. This letter will become the "name" of the array. The computer will respond by asking you, via the display scope, to indicate the characteristics of the array. An array may be real or

complex and may contain at most 124 vectors each of which may contain at most 124 components.

If an array A has already been defined, pushing CTX A will cause the information in its definition to be displayed on the display scope.

If the user wishes to redefine a previously defined array, he pushes CTX A RETURN, where A is the name of the array. The computer will then ask the user for the new characteristics of the array.

If the user wishes to delete all presently defined arrays, he pushes CTX . (where . is the period on the operand keyboard). The computer will instruct him (via the display scope) on how to proceed.

In the following discussion, let a represent an arbitrary alphabetic operand.

Operator Definitions for Level IX

DISPLAY   Converts the operand keyboard into a typewriter where all "printing" is done on the display scope.

    Upon initialization of the OLC the current bank from which characters are displayed is Bank 1. Special characters stored on other banks can be displayed by SHIFTing to the appropriate bank and pressing the desired button.

    Pushing RS will restart the user in the upper left corner of the scope. Pushing CON will roll the carriage up one line, and pushing ENL will roll the carriage down one line.

    If followed by ID the scope is erased.

MOD   If followed by k where k is a two-digit number, the display process for symbol generation is initiated by displaying a point. The two digits are interpreted as cartesian coordinates in a grid as shown in Fig. A.2. After this initiation, the operand keys marked with the small vector symbols will respond by displaying that vector on the scope attached to the end of the last vector. Standard size letters are 8 units high and are centered in the grid (i.e., about the point $(5, 5)$).

    This symbol construction can be halted at any time, but if the symbol is to be stored for further use, then press SHIFT k (where k is the number of a bank (2 through 4)) STORE a. For each new user, the symbol table on Bank 1 is initially provided with uppercase letters, 25 per line and 18 lines per display scope. The remaining banks are open for your own definition.

ID   Causes the display scope to be erased.

CTX   If followed by a, a is taken to be the name of an array.

    If the array had been previously defined, the characteristics (real or complex, number of vectors, number of components per vector) are displayed on the display scope.

    If the array had not been previously defined, the computer interrogates the user via the display scope as to the desired characteristics of the array. The user must type only *after* the computer

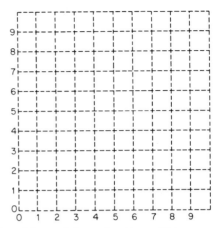

Fig. A.2 Reference grid used in symbol construction. This symbol construction can be halted at any time, but if the symbol is to be stored for further use, then press SHIFT k (where k is the number of a bank (2 through 4) STORE a. For each new user, the symbol table on Bank 1 is initially provided with uppercase letters, 25 per line and 18 lines per display scope. The remaining banks are open for your own definition.

presents each request. In response, the user pushes R for real or C for complex and pushes numeric keys to input the desired number of vectors, m, and the desired number of components per vector, n. Both m and n must be followed by RETURN as an indication to the computer that typing of the number has been completed.

If array a is to be redefined, push RETURN after pushing a. The computer will then go through the interrogation described above.

If followed by . (on the operand keyboard), the process for deletion of all arrays is initiated. The computer will instruct the user (via the display scope) on how to proceed.

A.9 Acknowledgment

This system has been made available for your use through an equipment donation by the Bunker-Ramo Corporation and through cooperation with Rome Air Development Center, USAF. The pilot program under which we developed software and showed feasibility of telephone driven curvilinear display consoles is supported by the Office of Naval Research. The program to develop a communication laboratory and associated classroom applications is supported by the Advanced Research Projects Agency. The dissemination of the system over national carriers is made possible via support by the National Science Foundation.

The Harvard University hookup has been arranged by Prof. Anthony G. Gettinger and is supported in part by the Advanced Research Projects Agency. The UCLA console is partially supported by the National Science Foundation.

This manual is edited and maintained by Kenneth Winiecki at the Harvard Computation Laboratory using the IBM TEXT90 program on an IBM 7094 computer.

REFERENCES

1. Culler, G. J., and B. D. Fried: *STL On-line Computer*, vol. 1, General Description, TRW Space Technology Laboratories, Redondo Beach, Calif., 1964.
2. Farrington, C., and D. Pope: *STL On-line Computer*, vol. 2, User's Manual, TRW Space Technology Laboratories, Redondo Beach, Calif., 1964.

NAME INDEX

A

Adler, M. J., 300, 302
Alexander, S. N., 16
Ambrosio, B. F., 16
Anderson, A., 289
Arden, B. W., 17

B

Baker, M., 177
Bauer, W. F., 74, 106
Beierle, J. D., 106
Bekesy, G. von, 115, 128
Benington, H. D., 16
Bennett, E., 262
Berkeley, E. C., 219

Berry, M. M., 288
Birkhoff, G., 288
Blackwell, F. W., 172, 178
Blumenthal, S. C., 106
Boilen, S., 17
Borrow, D. G., 219
Bourne, C. P., 289
Bullock, D. L., 177
Bunting, J. R., 298, 302
Burton, R. E., 289

C

Carnap, R., 289
Chasen, S. H., 181, 215, 219
Cheng, H., 177
Christy, R. W., 171

SUBJECT INDEX

A

ADP system (*see* OPCON ADP system)
AED, 180
ALGOL, 57
Alphanumeric printing capability, 193–194
Analysis and design of system, 21
   general time-sharing analysis, 22–36
   specific design, 6060 Control Data remote calculators, 37–55
   (*See also* Design; Design problems)
Animation in Sketchpad-type systems, 201–202
APT (Automatically Programmed Tools), 57, 67, 215, 217
Assembler, 7–8

B

Batch processing, economics of, compared with on-line, 77–82
   arguments pro and con, 78–80
   input and interrogation, 80–81
   operating and implementing experience, 81–82
   hardware costs, 96–101
   historical considerations, 2, 3
Bessel functions, 147–152

C

C.A.D. (computer-aided design) project, 215–217
CAL, 8